*European studies in social psychology*

# The social dimension
# Volume I

*European studies in social psychology*

The series is jointly published by the Cambridge University Press and the Editions de la Maison des Sciences de l'Homme, in close collaboration with the Laboratoire Européen de Psychologie Sociale of the Maison, as part of the joint publishing agreement established in 1977 between the Fondation de la Maison des Sciences de l'Homme and the Syndics of the Cambridge University Press.

It consists mainly of specially commissioned volumes on specific themes, particularly those linking work in social psychology with other disciplines. It will also include occasional volumes on 'Current issues'.

Cette collection est publiée en co-édition par Cambridge University Press et les Editions de la Maison des Sciences de l'Homme en collaboration étroite avec le Laboratoire Européen de Psychologie Sociale de la Maison. Elle s'intègre dans le programme de co-édition établi en 1977 par la Fondation de la Maison des Sciences de l'Homme et les Syndics de Cambridge University Press.

Elle comprend essentiellement des ouvrages sur des thèmes spécifiques permettant de mettre en rapport la psychologie sociale et d'autres disciplines, avec à l'occasion des volumes consacrés à des 'recherches en cours'.

*Already published*:

*The analysis of action: recent theoretical and empirical advances*, edited by Mario von Cranach and Rom Harré

*Current issues in European social psychology*, volume 1, edited by Willem Doise and Serge Moscovici

*Social interaction in individual development*, edited by Willem Doise and Augusto Palmonari

*Advances in the social psychology of language*, edited by Colin Fraser and Klaus R. Scherer

*Social representations*, edited by Serge Moscovici and Robert Farr

*Social markers in speech*, edited by Klaus R. Scherer and Howard Giles

*Social identity and intergroup relations*, edited by Henri Tajfel

# The social dimension

European developments in social psychology
Volume 1

*Edited by Henri Tajfel*

*preparation for publication completed by Colin Fraser and Joseph M. F. Jaspars*

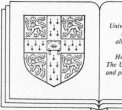

*The right of the University of Cambridge to print and sell all manner of books was granted by Henry VIII in 1534. The University has printed and published continuously since 1584.*

**Cambridge University Press**

*Cambridge*
*London   New York   New Rochelle*
*Melbourne   Sydney*

**Editions de la Maison des Sciences de l'Homme**
*Paris*

Published by the Press Syndicate of the University of Cambridge
The Pitt Building, Trumpington Street, Cambridge CB2 1RP
32 East 57th Street, New York, NY 10022, USA
296 Beaconsfield Parade, Middle Park, Melbourne 3206, Australia
and Editions de la Maison des Sciences de l'Homme
54 Boulevard Raspail, 75270 Paris Cedex 06

First published 1984

Printed in Great Britain by the
University Press, Cambridge

Library of Congress catalogue card number: 83–15060

*British Library Cataloguing in Publication Data*

The Social dimension – (European studies in social psychology)
Vol. 1
1. Social psychology
I. Tajfel, Henri II. Series
302    HM251

ISBN 0 521 23972 9 volume 1 hard covers
ISBN 0 521 28383 3 volume 1 paperback
ISBN 0 521 23978 8 volume 2 hard covers
ISBN 0 521 28387 6 volume 2 paperback
ISBN 2 7351 0068 5 volume 1 hard covers (France only)
ISBN 2 7351 0069 5 volume 1 paperback (France only)
ISBN 2 7351 0070 7 volume 2 hard covers (France only)
ISBN 2 7351 0071 5 volume 2 paperback (France only)
ISSN 00758 7554 (France only)

UP

# Foreword

Guiding these volumes through their final stages has been for us a minor labour of love and of admiration, and, at the same time, a task of great personal sorrow. For Henri Tajfel, the creator, editor, translator and inspiration of these volumes, died, at the age of 62, on 3 May 1982.

The idea for this work came to Henri less than eighteen months before his death. Serge Moscovici and Willem Doise had proposed the editing of a European handbook of social psychology. On reflection, Henri argued that such an enterprise might prove premature; a more informal, personal, 'state of the art' appraisal of European social psychology's distinctive contributions would be more practicable, and probably much more fun, to edit. They agreed to differ, and Henri proceeded very rapidly to implement his notion. In January 1981 he wrote to most of the eventual contributors to this book outlining his proposal. By April 1981, he had received so many positive replies, and synopses of chapters, that he was able to circulate a provisional, but very full, table of contents that overlapped to about 85 per cent with the table which follows this preface. Chapters arrived fast but, because of Henri's strict limit on length, not too thick. Henri proceeded to edit, request modifications, translate from several languages, and commission a few additional chapters, all with great enthusiasm and a strong conviction about the value of the project. By February 1982, when he fell ill, the work was near completion and Henri was confident that he would be able to send the entire manuscript to the press in early spring.

Our contributions, as editorial assistants, have been limited. We have been responsible for editing a handful of chapters, which Henri had commissioned and seen but to which he had not been able to give a final polish. In the light of those chapters, we have introduced minor modifications in structure and ordering. Otherwise, we are confident that the volumes are as Henri intended them to be, with one exception. We have taken the liberty of claiming joint authorship, with Henri, of the brief introductory chapter, written by us, in

v

Volume 1. Although the chapter's title is the one Henri proposed to use, this is not the more ambitious chapter that Henri intended to write once he had completed his editing of all the other contributions. We have contented ourselves with a modest statement of the rationale, aims and structure of the volumes. Wherever possible, however, we have made use of extracts, and modifications of extracts, from letters, memos and brief notes which Henri had written about the volumes. In this way, he has the first, as well as the last, words in his own book. We have added our names to the introduction in order to accept responsibility for omissions and infelicities.

In addition to those who appear in the list of contributors, three other people have played important parts in bringing this work to fruition. Alma Foster typed very much more of the manuscript than is normal for an editor's secretary. As Henri revised, translated and extracted messy drafts from authors who had not quite met deadlines, Alma, as always, typed rapidly and immaculately.

Jeremy Mynott, of Cambridge University Press, was much more a friend and academic adviser than business editor to Henri throughout the entire period Henri worked on this book, and also to us as we worried about the final minor details.

We would not presume to guess at the encouragement and suggestions that Anne Tajfel may have offered Henri as he conceived and edited this book, but we do wish to thank Anne for the interest and helpfulness that she has shown to us.

Not many people are able, or deserve to be able, to edit their own *festschrifts*. That, in a way, is what Henri, deservedly, has done in *The social dimension*. Of course, had everyone who would have wished to contribute to a more conventional *festschrift* been able to do so, this book would have run to many volumes. This work, however, is not only, or even primarily, a *festschrift*. They, too often, are well-intended excuses for the editing of bad books. Since we are not the editors of this one, we feel entitled to say that Henri Tajfel has edited a very good book indeed, which, we believe, will prove to be a major milestone in the journey of European social psychology. But, however valuable and important this work proves to be, it will never be more than the smallest of compensations for the absence of the man who was such a major, creative and energy-giving part of the social dimension of European social psychology.

Colin Fraser
Joseph M. F. Jaspars

*Cambridge and Oxford, 1983*

Henri Tajfel

# Contents

## VOLUME 1

# Contents

# Contributors

PETER BALL
  *Department of Psychology, University of Tasmania, Hobart*
MICHAEL BILLIG
  *Department of Psychology, University of Birmingham*
ROLV MIKKEL BLAKAR
  *Psykologisk Institutt, Universitatet i Oslo*
RUPERT J. BROWN
  *Social Psychology Research Unit, University of Kent at Canterbury*
JEAN BRUN
  *Faculté de Psychologie, Université de Genève*
FELICE CARUGATI
  *Istituto di Psicologia, Università di Urbino*
JEAN-PAUL CODOL
  *V.E.R. de Psychologie, Université de Provence, Aix-en-Provence*
JEAN-PIERRE DECONCHY
  *Laboratorie de Psychologie Sociale, Université Paris VII*
JEAN-CLAUDE DESCHAMPS
  *École des Sciences Sociales et Politiques, Université de Lausanne*
STEVE DUCK
  *Department of Psychology, University of Lancaster*
JUDY DUNN
  *M.R.C. Unit on the Development and Integration of Behaviour, University of Cambridge*
J. RICHARD EISER
  *Department of Psychology, University of Exeter*
DONALD FOSTER
  *Department of Psychology, University of Cape Town*
ADAM FRACZEK
  *Polska Akademia Nauk, Zaklad Psychologii, Warszawa*
COLIN FRASER
  *Social and Political Sciences Committee, University of Cambridge*
HOWARD GILES
  *Department of Psychology, University of Bristol*
ROM HARRÉ
  *Sub-faculty of Philosophy, University of Oxford*
MILES HEWSTONE
  *Laboratoire Européen de Psychologie Sociale, Maison des Sciences de l'Homme, Paris*

CARMEN HUICI
*Departamento de Psicologia, Universidad Nacional de Educación a Distancia, Madrid*

GUSTAV JAHODA
*Department of Psychology, University of Strathclyde, Glasgow*

JOSEPH M. F. JASPARS
*Department of Experimental Psychology, University of Oxford*

PETER KELVIN
*Department of Psychology, University College, London*

GÉRARD LEMAINE
*Groupe d'Etudes et de Recherches sur la Science, École des Hautes Etudes en Sciences Sociales, Paris*

JACQUES-PHILIPPE LEYENS
*Faculté de Psychologie, Université de Louvain*

DOROTHY MIELL
*Department of Psychology, University of Lancaster*

GEROLD MIKULA
*Institut für Psychologie, Karl-Franzens-Universität Graz*

DAVID MILNER
*School of the Social Sciences and Business Studies, Polytechnic of Central London*

GABRIEL MUGNY
*Faculté de Psychologie, Université de Genève*

SIK HUNG NG
*Department of Psychology, University of Otago, Dunedin*

AUGUSTO PALMONARI
*Istituto di Scienze dell'Educazione, Università di Bologna*

ANNE-NELLY PERRET-CLERMONT
*Séminaire de Psychologie, Université de Neuchâtel*

PIO ENRICO RICCI BITTI
*Istituto di Filosofia, Università di Bologna*

W. P. ROBINSON
*School of Education, University of Bristol*

EL HADI SAADA
*Faculté de Psychologie, Université de Genève*

GUIDO SARCHIELLI
*Dipartimento Studi e Ricerche sui Problemi del Lavoro, Università di Trento*

KLAUS R. SCHERER
*Fachbereich Psychologie, Universität Giessen*

MARIA-LUISA SCHUBAUER-LEONI
*Faculté de Psychologie, Université de Genève*

G. M. STEPHENSON
*Social Psychology Research Unit, University of Kent at Canterbury*

MARGARET S. STROEBE
*Psychologisches Institut, Universität Tübingen*

WOLFGANG STROEBE
*Psychologisches Institut, Universität Tübingen*

HENRI TAJFEL
*Department of Psychology, University of Bristol*

JOHN C. TURNER
*Department of Psychology, University of Bristol*

LADISLAV VALACH
   *Psychologisches Institut, Universität Bern*
JOOP VAN DER PLIGT
   *Department of Psychology, University of Exeter*
AD F. M. VAN KNIPPENBERG
   *Vakgroep Social Psychologie, Rijksuniversiteit te Groningen*
MARIO VON CRANACH
   *Psychologisches Institut, Universität Bern*

# 1. The social dimension in European social psychology

HENRI TAJFEL, JOSEPH M. F. JASPARS and COLIN FRASER

It is now nearly twenty years since theoretical and research work in social psychology in Europe took off in a number of new, diverse and independent directions. This has been reflected in an increase in the number of publications and in the slow but steady creation of a lively and interacting community of social psychologists in Europe. Many of the organizational and publishing activities of this community have been a direct consequence of the various academic developments, and these activities in turn have often acted as spurs towards new intellectual departures. The term 'community of scholars' is no empty abstraction. Its existence and vitality have been reflected in European summer schools, colloquia and conferences, visits from one country to another, joint cross-national publications, the *European Journal of Social Psychology*, the European Monographs in Social Psychology, the recently initiated series of European Studies in Social Psychology, as well as the continuing expansion of the European Association of Social Psychology.

The mark of these developments has been their diversity. There is no doubt that their continuing vitality depends upon the continuation of this diversity. And yet, amidst the variation, there seems to exist a very general common denominator: in a phrase, it can be referred to as *the social dimension* of European social psychology. This is simply described: in much of the work – whatever its background, interests, theoretical approach or research directions – there has been a constant stress on the social and interactive aspects of our subject. Social psychology in Europe is today much more *social* than it was twenty years ago.

The purpose of these two volumes is to take stock after these twenty years of development; to provide a reflection of what has been happening and a useful resource for the future. The diversity of European developments becomes clear when one realizes in how many different fields advances have been made. In developmental studies, for example, there has been ever increasing interest in the relationship between social interaction and concep-

I

tual development, in language, social development and early social interaction, in the development of social concepts and attitudes and in problems of
identity in children and adolescents. Communication processes have been
studied in their social context, especially as interpersonal linguistic accom-
modations, although non-linguistic aspects of communication processes have
continued to receive attention. The study of interpersonal behaviour has
widened its social focus and begun to pay attention to longer-term relationships.
Studies of friendship, attraction, interpersonal skills and aggression have all,
at least in part, been affected by this new perspective. Small group studies have
developed a concern for the position of groups in society. The effects of
minority groups on the majority have been extensively studied. Social
differentiation has received more attention than ever before. The relations
between groups have become a major field of research in European social
psychology. Group identity, legitimacy of group membership, status, power
and intergroup conflict have been studied intensively by researchers in a
number of countries. The study of attitudes and opinions of individuals has
begun to give way to research on social representations of social reality. It
has become more and more clear that such representations are not just
expressions of acquired behavioural dispositions, but are important reflections
of the social reality in which we live and have a shared and collective nature.
Political ideologies have begun to attract the attention of European social
psychologists. The social nature of causal and non-causal attributions is being
explored. The effects of social categorization are studied in a variety of ways.
Goal-based explanations of action and conceptions of behaviour as rule-
governed are some of the newest ideas that have affected the development
of social psychology in Europe.

Many of these trends are reflected in these two volumes. No doubt some
important topics have been neglected; in particular, there are no chapters
specifically concerned with applied social psychology. In the first place this
is due to practical considerations. The book already contains 33 chapters and
at some point, enough has to be enough. Secondly, several major volumes
on applied social psychology have either appeared recently or are in preparation
in Europe. Finally, although no chapters have been devoted explicitly to
'applied' topics, this has not prevented many of the contributors from making
clear the social relevance and applications of the ideas and research they have
presented.

We also regret that it has not proved possible to include contributions from
our colleagues from Eastern Europe other than the present co-authorship of
one chapter; again, the primary obstacles have been practical ones.

What we do offer in these two volumes is a large number of contributions in which the various authors present: (i) a statement of one or more of the problems mentioned above, very often accompanied by a description of the background against which the study of the problem was developed; (ii) their own theoretical positions or general standpoints; (iii) a critical review of selected literature, mainly from the author's point of view, and/or an overview of his or her own work; (iv) in many cases, a discussion of where to go from here. The two volumes, therefore, do *not* constitute a handbook of social psychology. There is, in most chapters, no systematic and exhaustive review of the literature and the two volumes do not pretend to cover the whole of social psychology. The strength of the enterprise, as we see it, lies in the diversity of the personal viewpoints and contributions presented, which share the common denominator of *the social dimension* characteristic of so much of the best work conducted in European social psychology during the last twenty years.

The perspective that the two volumes present can be simply outlined. It consists of the view that social psychology can and must include in its theoretical and research preoccupations a direct concern with the relationship between human psychological functioning and the large-scale social processes and events which shape this functioning and are shaped by it. This integration can take many forms and these two volumes testify to that fact.

The first volume deals very much with the individual in her or his interpersonal and social context. Part I is devoted to the processes of social development. Dunn discusses the relationship between early social interaction and the development of emotional understanding. Robinson presents a social psychological perspective on the development of communicative competence with language in young children. Perret-Clermont and her colleagues report studies on the effect of social interaction on cognitive development. Jahoda deals with the development of thinking about socio-economic systems, and Milner with the development of ethnic attitudes. Palmonari and his collaborators are concerned with problems of adolescent identity. Clearly, much of developmental psychology has taken on the patina of a social perspective. Many traditional topics of developmental psychology have been placed in their proper interpersonal contexts, and some studies have widened the scope of developmental enquiry even further by including in it the study of large-scale social groups and social systems.

In Part II, the emphasis shifts to interpersonal behaviour and communication. As a link to the previous part, it opens with a contribution by Blakar on communication in the family and its relation to psychopathology. This chapter is followed by Scherer's proposals of how best to enrich the study of nonverbal communication. In Chapter 10 Leyens and Fraczek take up the study of aggression from a social psychological perspective, which includes attention to the impact of such a major social phenomenon as television. In his discussion of justice and fairness in interpersonal relations, Mikula emphasizes the need for a social psychology of justice which can not only deal with interpersonal processes but is also capable of taking into account large-scale phenomena of social injustice. Duck and Miell reveal their dissatisfaction with the limited and unprovocative nature of much of the social psychological study of interpersonal attraction. Both their chapter and the one that follows by the Stroebes, on the relations between attraction and bereavement, show how far the study of interpersonal behaviour has moved away from easily manipulable laboratory effects towards the study of long-term relationships and the formation and dissolution of close emotional ties.

In the last part of the first volume, Part III, individual action is considered within its social context. Von Cranach and Valach emphasize the social dimension of goal-directed behaviour by arguing that goal-directed action is social in origin, has social consequences and constitutes the fabric of social life. For Harré, social rules and social rituals provide a powerful entry to certain kinds of social activity which until now have hardly attracted the attention of social psychologists. Codol and Lemaine, in the next two chapters, are both concerned with social differentiation: Codol at a very fundamental level of basic social and psychological processes, Lemaine at the level, again, of considering a large-scale social phenomenon such as the scientific community. As such, his chapter forms an apt transition to the second volume, which approaches the question of large-scale social phenomena in two different ways.

The first part of the second volume, Part IV, is mainly concerned with representations of social reality. The first chapter, by Eiser and van der Pligt, is, to some extent, more traditional than, and hence serves as an introduction to, the following chapters; it considers the classic concept of attitudes, but it places them in a social context. Hewstone and Jaspars also start from a traditional problem in social psychology, the study of attribution processes, and show how much, and in what ways, the social dimension has been neglected in previous attribution research. Billig, Deconchy and Kelvin are all concerned with the representation of large-scale social phenomena: political ideology, ideological and religious orthodoxy, and assumptions about the nature of unemployment. These two volumes may not appear to be about applied social psychology, but it is not difficult to see that these three chapters not only represent a contribution to our understanding of important social psychological phenomena but might well form the bases of sound applications relevant to major social problems.

The same can perhaps be said with even more emphasis of the last two parts of the second volume. In the first chapter of Part V, Fraser and Foster raise the discussion of laboratory groups, and the almost pure laboratory phenomenon of group polarization, to a much more ambitious social level. The study of minorities, on which Mugny reports, hardly needs commentary: if any area of research has challenged the classic individualistic perspective in social psychology it is this one. It has, almost literally, turned upside down the study of the experimental laboratory majority by viewing it from a social perspective as an active minority in society at large. In Turner's chapter we see a similar rejection of the classic group dynamics view of psychological groups in favour of a much more social conception of groups which emphasizes the sharing of a common social identification rather than cohesive interpersonal relationships, thus anticipating the final part of the second volume.

In Part VI we arrive at the consideration of relations between groups. Deschamps reviews much of the research which has been conducted by himself and others in Europe since the early 1970s. Van Knippenberg adds to this a critical analysis of differences in group perceptions, and Huici is especially concerned with sex role stereotypes. Brown studies the role of similarity in intergroup relations. Ng analyses social power. Stephenson reports on his studies of bargaining and negotiation in industry. Ball, Giles and Hewstone investigate second language acquisition from an intergroup perspective. The final chapter, by Tajfel, is devoted to social myths and social justice in social psychology, a theme which permits links to be drawn to many of the contributions to these volumes.

In all the chapters of Part VI we see an emphasis upon the individual both as a social agent and as a representative of large-scale social categories. In our judgments of other people, in forming stereotypes, in learning a second language, in our work relations, in our concern with justice, we do not act as isolated individuals but as social beings who derive an important part of our identity from the human groups and social categories we belong to; and we act in accordance with this awareness. Social psychology has, until recently, forgotten that this perspective is in fact one of the oldest viewpoints in the study of social behaviour. It is our hope that these two volumes will succeed in creating a renewed interest in this, more fully social, view of human actions.

# Part I
# Social development

# 2. Early social interaction and the development of emotional understanding

JUDY DUNN

In the course of the first two or three years of life, children change very dramatically indeed. From helpless infants they become people who understand and use language, who amuse, provoke and manipulate the members of their family, who enjoy rich, elaborate and varied relationships with the other people in their social world.

The dramatic nature and the astonishing speed of these developments in their powers of communication and social understanding are not a matter of dispute. But psychologists do disagree strongly on the question of what precisely is the nature and extent of a very young child's understanding of the other people in his world, his sensitivity to their emotions, intentions and perceptions. The classical Piagetian view that children under 5 years old are not sufficiently cognitively mature to take another's point of view has been the focus of a great deal of research, yet there is wide disagreement about the extent to which such young children do perceive others as different from themselves. On the one hand, some psychologists hold that the capacity of preschool children to make inferences about the experiences of others and to act appropriately towards them is very limited (Chandler & Greenspan 1972; Hoffman 1975, 1981; Shantz 1975). On the other hand, others argue that the design of many perspective-taking tasks or tests of empathy leads to a gross underestimation of the ability of children to perceive the intentions and perspective of others (Borke 1972; Donaldson 1978). And Bretherton and her colleagues (1981) have argued, on the basis of a systematic study of children's references to the 'inner states' of others, that very young children do have a 'fairly sophisticated model of themselves and of others as psychological beings' – beings who are distinct and separate. It is increasingly evident that to think of the development of 'perspective-taking' abilities, or the ability to 'empathize' as *single* developmental processes is a mistake (Hoffman 1981; Urberg & Docherty 1976).

At issue is a series of questions about children's responses to other people.

What kind of interest and curiosity do very young children show concerning other people? How do they respond to the emotional state of others with whom they have close relationships? Do they have difficulty in distinguishing the emotional reaction of others from their own responses? Do they respond to the emotional state of others only by projecting their own feelings? Are differences in social experiences related in any systematic way to children's interest in the feelings and intentions of others? In this chapter I want to consider these issues in the light of some recent work on children observed at home with their infant siblings and their mothers. The findings indicate that the capabilities of children to perceive the intentions, perspective and feelings of others have been seriously underestimated by studies which have relied on an experimental approach, testing children with relatively abstract tasks in formal settings. The results of the sibling study suggest, furthermore, that certain differences between families in the way in which the motives, feelings and intentions of others are discussed may well influence the development of the young child's sensitivity towards others.

The details of the study, the nature of the sample, the methodology and the findings are described fully in Dunn & Kendrick 1982b. In brief, 40 families (largely lower middle-class and working-class) were followed from a point when the mother was pregnant with her second child, through the infancy of the second child. They were visited at four time points: during the mother's pregnancy, in the first month after the birth, then eight months, and 14 months later. At each time point two hour-long observations and interviews with the mother were carried out in the home. The observations were unstructured: pre-coded categories of behaviour were recorded on a ten-second time base (a method based on that of Clarke-Stewart 1973). Only one observer was present. A tape-recording was made during the observations of the family conversation, and this was transcribed after the observation by the observer.

## 1. The children's comments on other people

Although there has been much interest among psycholinguists in the speech and conversations of children in the early stages of language acquisition, relatively little attention has been paid either to the question of what topics arouse children's interest in their earliest conversations, or to the nature of children's comments about other people. As David Wood comments in his study of the conversations which preschool children have at nursery school 'We do not have any insights into the nature and content of talk between parents and their preschoolaged children' (Wood, McMahon & Cranstoun

1980). His analysis showed that children in nursery schools never talked about what the absent members of their family might be doing while they themselves were at nursery, a finding which led him to speculate that a child aged 3 or 4 years may be 'unwilling or unable to conceptualise what those near and dear to him are about while he lives on in playgroup...whether such things are best left unsaid or are too difficult to think about we cannot say'.

His findings are very much at odds with what our transcripts of children talking to their mothers and siblings *at home* reveal. These show that reference to absent fathers, grandparents, friends and relatives were common even among the children who were not yet 2 years old. The children's comments were, without exception, either references to where the 'non-present' people were at the time and what they might be doing, or exchanges where child and mother recalled in narrative fashion events in which the other people and the child had been involved, as in this example of a 22-months-old girl talking with her mother:

*Susan S.*
C: Where's Ken gone? Where's Ken gone?
M: He's at work.
C: Work. On bike.
M: Yea. Gone on his bike.
C: Bus and on bike. Where's Grandad?
M: Oh he's at work as well.
C: Where's Uncle Liz?
M: *Aunty* Liz.
C: Aunty Liz?
M: She'll be at work as well.

The frequency of these references showed us how important the network of family members and friends can be, even for a child under 2 years, and they reflect the interest and enjoyment the young children felt in knowing where their family and friends were, and what they were doing.

While these references to absent people were relatively frequent, it was notable that the children very rarely made references to the feelings, wishes or intentions of these absent people. They did indeed comment on feelings and wishes, but such comments were references almost exclusively to the expression of feelings or intentions of someone who was *present*. For instance, during the observations made in the first month after the sibling was born, 97 per cent of the children's references to the feelings and wants of others concerned someone who was present – and 60 per cent of these concerned the sibling (table 1). As young as 20 months, then, our children were referring with interest to the actions and whereabouts of the familiar people in their world, and commenting on the feelings and needs of their new baby sibling.

Table 1. *Percentage of references to people's wants, feelings, intentions*

| | Child | Mother | Father | Sibling | Pretend character | Book character | Pet | Observer |
|---|---|---|---|---|---|---|---|---|
| Mother | 52 | 9 | 2* | 29 | 3 | 3 | 3 | 0 |
| Child | 47 | 1 | 3* | 32 | 8 | 6 | 0 | 3 |

Note: * Indicates reference to an absent person.

But crude indices of the frequency with which the children referred to others cannot, of course, help us to answer the questions raised initially on the beliefs of the children about the intentions and feelings of others, and on the extent to which the children recognized and distinguished the emotional states of others as different from their own. To consider these questions we used three different kinds of information: firstly, the comments made by the children to their mothers, or to us as observers, about the baby's wants, intentions, feelings or capabilities; secondly, the actions of the child when the baby was upset, excited or frustrated; and thirdly, the child's speech to the baby was analysed, to see how the child responded to the difficulties of communicating with a baby who was linguistically and cognitively so different from the other people in the child's world.

**1.1. Comments about the baby.** A majority of the children (64%) commented on the wants and intentions of the baby at the visits made when the baby was 14 months old, and these comments were as frequently made by the children who were under 3 years old as by the older children. Sometimes these remarks followed actions or expressions by the baby which the mother had not noticed or had ignored: 'He wants go out', 'Kenny wants bit meat' – often such comments were very accurate predictions of what the baby was about to do. Others were comments on particularly expressive behaviour of the baby: 'Ronnie's happy...He likes that – Isn't he funny!' And many of the firstborn children apparently took pleasure in 'explaining' the baby to the observer: 'She wants to come to you', 'He likes me', 'Jackie not like monkey' (after Jackie had thrown down toy monkey), 'Callum's crying 'cos he wants his food cold'.

Some of these remarks on the baby's wishes reflected what could be seen as 'wishful thinking' on the firstborn's part, rather than a sensitive interpretation of the baby's actions: 'Baby wants to crawl' said one 2-year-old when her father picked up the baby sibling to cuddle him. 'He doesn't *want* to sleep in my bunk' said a 3-year-old when his mother suggested putting the baby to sleep in the elder's bed. But there were also many incidents when the elder child commented on the baby's behaviour in a way that certainly did not reflect the firstborn's own interests in any direct way, but was finely tuned to the baby's range of wishes. The crucial point on the issue of perspective taking is that the comments by the firstborn certainly did not always represent a projection of their own feelings about their own situation. The differences between the perspective of the first child and the baby was often made quite explicit: one boy, watching his baby brother who was playing with a balloon, commented to the observer: 'It going pop in a minute. And he going cry. And he going be frightened of me too. I *like* the pop.' And the explanations offered when the baby was crying (sometimes given with delight) made it clear that the children were not simply projecting their own feelings: 'He crying 'cos Mummy's in garden. In't he silly? *I* don't cry for that.' These examples show clearly that the firstborn children were not confused about the situation of self and of other when the 'other' was their own sibling: they make clear too that the children did respond to the situation of the 'other' in a way which was certainly not always a simple projection of their own feelings.

Comments were also made about what the baby did or did not understand and remember, or on what he could or could not do. One 3-year-old girl, for instance, remarked to her baby sister 'You don't remember Judy. I do.', and a 2-year-old commented on her baby brother's wariness 'He doesn't know you'. New achievements by the baby were frequently remarked on. 'She called you Mum', 'He said Ta'.

Often the presence of the baby, and the discussions which the mother and child engaged in about the baby, led to comments by the first child about categorization and dimensions of *self* and baby. In many of these exchanges the firstborn *played* with the dimensions of age, gender, size, good/bad, older/younger, as applied to himself and to the baby. The certainty and the confidence with which the children played with these notions, shifting identity and 'pretending' to be the baby sibling, or to be themselves as babies, demonstrated that such categories were indeed well understood in relation to the baby.

These comments by the firstborn children reveal their perception of the baby as someone with likes, dislikes, intentions, feelings and capabilities which would develop. In these ways the baby was apparently seen to be 'like' the first child. In other ways the baby was regarded as 'unlike': his limited capabilities were frequently discussed, and it was clear that while the baby was seen as someone to whom social rules applied, there were many examples where the first child suggested that the rules which applied to the baby were different from the rules which applied to *him*. One extreme example: a little girl whose baby brother was trying to follow the mother into the street commented to the observer: 'He can't go out. No. 'Cos only people can go out.'

The evidence for the children's interest in the psychological state of the sibling parallels the findings of the study by Bretherton and her colleagues (1981) which showed that as early as 20 months children referred explicitly to the states of others and of themselves, commenting on the following states: happy, hungry, tired, mad, scared, cold.

It is clear too, that children of 2 and 3 years of age are not only interested in other people's psychological states, but are also interested in the *cause* of these states. In a study of the speech of 2- and 3-year-olds, Hood & Bloom (1979) found that the children did, in fact, make causal utterances five years earlier than Piaget (e.g. 1955, 1969, 1972) or Werner & Kaplan (1963) would have presumed possible, but that their discussion of causes was exclusively concerned with *psychological* rather than physical causality. Their causal statements were concerned with the intentions and motivation of people, not with causal events that occurred between physical objects. Hood & Bloom point out that experimental studies of the development of the concept of causality have always presented children with tests involving physical objects, and they suggest that the content of these tasks probably explains the comparatively poor performance of children under 7 years and the discrepancy between the ages at which children make causal utterances in their own spontaneous speech, and in the experimental studies. It is an argument which echoes that of Donaldson (1978) – one which is taken up later in this chapter. The evidence that children's first comments on causality occur in relation to people rather than objects fits well with a Vygotskyan view of the central importance of social interaction in developmental advance (Vygotsky 1977).

**1.2. Observations of empathetic and antipathetic actions.** The comments on the baby's state or feelings which we described above were by no means always *empathetic*, in the sense that they were associated with a practical attempt to help or comfort. But in 63 per cent of the families observed when the baby was 14 months old there were incidents from which we inferred that the elder child was concerned about, or understood well the other child's state, and took practical action to help or comfort him. These were often nonverbal actions, as when a distressed whimper from a 14-month-old boy was followed promptly by the firstborn running over to give him a bit of his biscuit. It is obviously important not to read too much into such incidents, and in categorizing them as showing concern at the other's state we were extremely conservative. Incidents were only included if one child helped the other with a toy when he or she was frustrated by it, offered toys or food when the other was crying, asked the other if he or she wanted a drink and fetched it, or showed concern that the other should be included in games. We have discussed elsewhere the problems involved in drawing inferences from such incidents and the theoretical issues raised by apparently 'egocentric' responses to the emotional states of others (Dunn & Kendrick 1982b). Here we wish to emphasize three general points that the observations raise, which bear on the issue of the limited ability of such young children to act in a 'decentred' way in response to the distress, pain or excitement of their siblings.

The first concerns the issue of projection. While the observations do not, of course, provide direct measures of the extent to which the children understood the baby's affective state, or a systematic exploration of their beliefs about the baby, they do show that before the age of 2 years firstborn children recognize some feelings and expressive behaviour shown by their baby siblings. They show moreover that the children's response to this behaviour indicates that their recognition does not simply involve the projection of their own feelings on to the baby. The children frequently responded to the distress or pleasure of the baby in a way that was *not* the way they would expect or wish to be treated themselves, but that was more appropriate for the baby's own state.

The second point concerns the baby sibling rather than the elder child. There were some incidents which strongly suggested that as early as 14–15 months some of the younger siblings were beginning to understand both how to provoke the firstborn, and how to comfort him. One example of the former:

Callum (second child, 14 months) repeatedly reaches for, and manipulates the magnetic letters with which Laura (37 months) is playing. Laura repeatedly says NO gently. Callum goes on trying to reach the letters. Finally Laura picks up the tray on which the letters are, and carries it to a high table which Callum cannot reach. Callum is furious. Starts to cry. Then Callum turns, and goes straight to the sofa where Laura's comfort objects, a rag doll and a dummy, are lying. He takes the doll and holds it tight, looking at Laura. Laura, for the first time very upset, starts crying and runs to take the doll.

Evidence that children of about a year old are indeed sensitive to the need states of others is provided by the study by Yarrow & Waxler (1975) of children observed by their mothers at home. The observations showed that the children were both quick to respond, but also discriminating in their responses, to the emotional state of others. They were, for instance, distressed at arguments between their parents; they also responded to demonstrations of affection between the parents, by trying either to join in or to separate the parents. Between the ages of $1\frac{1}{2}$ and 2 years their attempts to comfort became quite sophisticated. Burlingham & Freud (1944), in a study of children brought up together in residential care, also give some vivid examples of comforting and consoling behaviour by children under 2 years old.

The third point concerns the difference between the abilities attributed to children on the basis of experimental tasks and those shown by the children in our observations, or in the studies of Yarrow & Waxler or of Hood & Bloom. The discrepancy is important. It shows us that the capabilities which we attribute to children do depend crucially upon the particular social situation in which we choose to study them. In situations which have real emotional meaning for them, children demonstrate capabilities which are not apparent when they are tested in more formal settings. Observing children with their siblings, moreover, provides a particularly distinctive perspective on their abilities to 'understand' another person's feelings, if our criterion for 'understanding' is a practical, remedial one. Since the situations which cause the sibling fear, joy or excitement are situations which are highly familiar to the first child, he is in a very good position to generate theories about the life-world of the infant – far better placed than he is to judge what constitutes an adequate remedy for an adult in distress, or for the story-book characters so often used in tests of empathy. The demonstration that children do show empathy towards *familiar* adults and to those in familiar situations well before they show empathy towards *unfamiliar* others, has been taken as evidence that the empathy expressed towards those in familiar situations reflects self-projection, and 'may be no more than self description' (Shantz 1975). However it is hardly a convincing argument that because a child is unable to judge the emotions of an unfamiliar person in an experimental setting, his ability to infer the emotions of his sibling and to act appropriately towards the sibling is merely self-projection.

**1.3. The children's speech to the baby sibling.** The third source of information which we examined was the speech of the firstborn children to their siblings. It is known that children as young as 4 years do adjust their speech when addressing younger children, and indeed when talking to a doll designated to be a 'baby' (Sachs & Devin 1976; Shatz & Gelman 1973, 1977). Shatz & Gelman argued that both the simpler and the syntactically more complex utterances of the 4-year-olds addressing 2-year-olds reflected their selection of utterances which the younger children could be expected to understand in the particular social setting in which they were studied. How early does such a sensitivity to the comprehension of the listener develop? How do 2- or 3-year-olds respond, for instance, to the problems of communicating with a baby sibling, whose powers of expression and comprehension are so different from those of the other people in the children's world?

To answer this question, the speech of the 2-year-olds in the sample was compared as they talked to their mothers and to their siblings. Two features of 'baby talk' were examined: first, features characterized by Brown (1977) as 'clarification' features – shortened utterances, repetitions, and attention-getting devices (exhortations such as 'Now!' 'Hey!' 'Look!', the use of the addressee's name, and so on); and second, features of baby talk which are also found in the speech of people to pets, and to lovers – the use of endearments, diminutives and pet names – features termed 'affective-expressive' by Brown.

The analysis (reported in full in Dunn & Kendrick 1982a) showed that all the children did adjust their speech when addressing their siblings. When they spoke to the babies, the children shortened their utterances, repeated what they had said and effectively drew the babies' attention with their exclamations and emphasis. These 'clarification' features of the baby talk were in fact *more* marked in the speech of the 2- and 3-year-olds to the babies than in the speech of their mothers to the babies (table 2). A typical example was the attempt of a 31-month-old child to prevent his brother from licking a sweet which the younger one had picked up off the floor. In telling him that the dog, Scottie, will eat the sweet, and in urging him to go into the kitchen, he repeats and progressively shortens his utterances, and uses many attention-getting devices:

*Duncan K.*
No don't you eat it. Scottie will eat it. Scottie will eat it. No not you. Scottie will eat it. Not you. Scottie. Not you. Shall we go in door? Right. Come on. Come on. In door Robin. In door.

The ways in which these very young children adjusted their speech did not, however, parallel very closely the adjustments made by their mothers. The differences and the similarities in the baby talk of 2-year-olds and mother, and their pragmatic significance, are discussed in Dunn & Kendrick (1982a). Here we wish simply to emphasize that the children did, in the contexts in which they addressed their baby siblings (usually situations where they were attempting to prohibit the baby, or to direct him in play) modify their speech in a way which was appropriate, and usually effective. It was clear from these adjustments that they did differentiate their baby siblings from the adults to

Table 2. *Comparison of child's speech to mother and to 14-month-old sibling,
and mother's speech to sibling (Wilcoxon T test)*

|  | Child to sibling | Child to mother | Mother to sibling |
|---|---|---|---|
| Mean length of utterance (median) | 2.49 | 3.45* | 3.40* |
| Proportion of attentional utterances (median %) | 40.0 | 9.8* | 17.5* |
| Proportion of repetitions (median %) | 30.8 | 17.7* | 16.3* |

Note: * p < 0.01, compared with child to sibling.

whom they spoke. We should not, of course, find this differentiation and this
sensitivity to the cognitive and linguistic status of their hearers surprising,
given the explicit comments made by the children on the capabilities,
intentions, and feelings of the baby.

## 2. Individual differences: the influence of the mother

Very little is understood about the origins of individual differences in
children's sensitivity towards others. Throughout our observations individual
differences in the children's behaviour towards their siblings were marked.
There were striking differences in the frequency and the affective tone of their
interactions, and in the frequency with which the elder child made comments
on the baby's affective state, or acted in a concerned way towards the baby.
The analysis of the children's speech, for instance, showed that the *affectionate*
features of baby talk – the 'affective-expressive' features of endearments,
diminutives and the questioning style that is so striking in the speech of
mothers to their babies – were evident in the speech of some of the firstborn
children, and absent from the speech of others. These differences in speech
style were closely linked to the nonverbal expression of affectionate interest.
Those children who used endearments and questions in their speech were far
more frequently friendly in their behaviour to their siblings (table 3).

This range of differences in affectionate interest and in sensitivity to the
sibling's emotional state highlights the importance of understanding more
clearly the influences on the development of children's emotional responsiveness to others. One possible source of influence is the mother's behaviour
towards the two children, and her response to their interest in each other.
In the study we found that there were indeed systematic associations between

Table 3. *Association between use of diminutives, questions and playful repetitions in child's speech to the 14-month-old sibling, and observed positive social approaches*

| | Diminutives | | Questions | | Playful repetitions | |
|---|---|---|---|---|---|---|
| | Present | Absent | Present | Absent | Present | Absent |
| Positive social approaches (median per 1000 10-second units) | 24.1 | 17.8* | 26.6 | 17.0* | 29.8 | 17.0** |

*Note:* Mann Whitney U test: * $p < 0.05$; ** $p < 0.01$.

the quality of the mother's relationship with each of her children, and the behaviour of the children towards each other. In this chapter we want to consider one aspect of the mother's behaviour which appeared to be of particular significance in the development of the sibling relationship – the way in which the mother talked to the first child about the baby as a person with needs and feelings.

During the first week after the baby was born, there were striking differences between the families in the discussions which mothers held with the first child about the baby. Some of the mothers talked to the first child about the baby's feelings and wants. They drew the first child into discussion about what the baby might be feeling, and about the interpretation of his crying. These mothers were also more likely to include the first child in discussions about what should be done for the baby. In these families the decisions about whether to bath the baby, cuddle him, feed him or leave him alone appeared almost a matter of joint responsibility. The mothers also drew the first child's attention to the baby's interest in him, and to the baby's expressive behaviour: 'Do you reckon he's hungry or is he just waiting for his bath?', 'Is he tired do you think?', 'He likes his bath doesn't he?', 'Shall we feed him, or just let him cry?', 'What do you think he wants?', 'Look he's calling you', 'He's watching!'

In other families the mothers never commented on the feelings and interests of the baby in this way, and never consulted the first child about what course of action should be taken. In these families the firstborn were significantly less likely to comment on the baby as a person with wants and needs than the children in the families where the mothers did discuss the baby in this way. Fourteen months later there were dramatic differences in the friendliness of the children towards each other in the two groups. In families where the mother had talked about the baby as a person, and had drawn the first child,

Table 4. *Frequency of positive social approaches by first child and 14-month-old second child: comparison of families in which mother had referred to second child's wants and feelings in first three weeks after birth (Group A), and those in which she had not (Group B)*

|  | Group A | Group B | p level* |
|---|---|---|---|
| First child: positive social approach to second (median per 1000 10-second units) | 26.7 | 11.1 | 0.02 |
| Second child: positive social approach to first (median per 1000 10-second units) | 26.8 | 14.4 | 0.01 |

*Note:* * Mann Whitney U test.

as an equal, into discussions about his needs and his care, both first and second children were significantly more friendly towards one another than the children in families where no such discussion had taken place (table 4).

Were these differences in the early discussion of the baby associated with other differences in the quality of the mother's behaviour with her firstborn? We found no links between the mother's references to the baby as a person and the marked differences in the qualities of maternal playfulness and attentiveness, or restrictiveness and punitiveness, which had been found both before and after the sibling birth (Dunn & Kendrick 1980), nor (perhaps surprisingly) with the degree of disturbance the first child showed at the birth, nor with the mother's state of exhaustion or depression after the birth. There were also no links with the age or sex of the firstborn. But the differences in the discussion of the baby *were* associated with other features of the way in which the mothers talked to their children. The mothers who referred to the baby, during those first weeks, as a person with wants and needs were also more likely to discuss other people's motives and intentions; they gave more justification when attempting to control the first child; they more frequently used language for relatively complex cognitive purposes, using comparisons, conditionals, generalizations and definitions, pointing out logical inferences and so on (see Tizard *et al.* 1982). They were also more likely to join in verbal pretend games with their firstborn.

What was striking about this conversational style was that these mothers treated their children, at least in formal terms, more as *equals* in discussing social rules and control issues, or the interpretation of other people's motives, than the other mothers did; and their interest in joining in the children's pretend games reflected a close 'tuning-in' to the children's fantasies. It was a style of relating to their children which cut across the differences in playfulness, permissiveness or punitiveness which were so marked. Some of the mothers who talked to their firstborn in this way were relatively permissive and playful, others were far more controlling.

Their way of relating to their children reflected an *equality* between mother and child that perhaps parallels the 'symmetry' in the mother–child relationship that Light (1979) found to be linked to the development of 'role-taking skills in 4-year-olds. In drawing attention to the association between this style of relationship between mother and first child, and the later behaviour of the siblings towards one another, we are not, of course, arguing that there are simple links between any one single aspect of the mother's conversational style and the quality of the relationship that developed between the siblings over the next year. To suggest any such simple causal association on the basis of these data would clearly be absurd. However, there is one implication of the findings which deserves serious consideration. If the discussion of a person's wants, feelings and intentions by the mother is linked to how a child behaves towards, and presumably feels about, that person, this pattern suggests a far higher degree of reflection about other people in such very young children than would have been presumed likely by many psychologists. Since the children whose mothers talked in this way *themselves* were significantly likely to refer to the needs, wants and feelings of the baby, it is surely an implication to be taken seriously.

The differences in conversational style between the mothers were certainly not the only variables which we found to be associated with the marked individual differences in the sibling relationship. The sex constellation of the sibling pair was important: in same-sex pairs, both firstborn and secondborn made far more frequent friendly approaches to the other than the children in different-sex sibling pairs, a result paralleled by the findings reported by the Whitings (1975); see also Whiting & Edwards (1977) for children in very different cultures. The first child's reaction to the arrival of the sibling was also an important variable, as was the amount of time the mother spent with the baby, and for girls, other aspects of the first child's relationship with the mother (for a full description of these findings, see Dunn & Kendrick 1982b). However, the differences in the way in which the mothers talked about the baby as a person with feelings did, according to multiple regression analyses, make a separate, independent contribution to the variation in the sibling's behaviour 14 months later.

### 3. The development of responsiveness to the emotions and expressions of others

We have argued that children are, by the middle half of their second year, both interested in and responsive to the emotional state and intentions of familiar others, and that differences in the way in which people's intentions and emotions are discussed by their mothers may well influence in an important way the development of this responsiveness. What do we know about the development of this responsiveness to the emotions of others during the first 18 months of life?

The information available is scattered and scarcely systematic, but it is certainly intriguing. Emde and his colleagues (personal communication), for instance, have carried out some experiments in which 12-month-old babies were placed in a variety of situations which involved some uncertainty for them – for example, they were placed on a 'visual cliff', or in the presence of unfamiliar people. In these situations, the babies immediately *looked at their mothers' faces*. The mothers were trained to express a variety of emotions – fear, interest, anger, sadness and so on. When the babies examined their mothers' faces in the 'uncertain' situations, their behaviour then varied dramatically according to the emotions which their mothers were expressing. If a mother showed *interest* when her baby reached the edge of the 'deep' side of the visual cliff, the baby, after monitoring her face, crawled rapidly forward to her, while if she showed fear, the baby backed off from the edge of the 'cliff'. The sensitivity of 1-year-olds to the emotion of others has also been well documented in the very different studies of Waxler, Yarrow and their colleagues (Yarrow & Waxler 1975), carried out in the home. By 12 months, then, babies are comparatively sophisticated in recognizing, and responding to, a range of emotional expressions in other people with whom they are familiar. What about earlier?

There is now a great wealth of research on the interaction between child and mother during the early months of the first year. This research documents, on the one hand, the sensitivity with which mothers time, pattern and 'tune' their own behaviour to their babies' actions and, on the other, the interest and responsiveness which babies show towards other people (for a review, see Schaffer 1979). These studies have also shown that mothers impute communicative meaning to the gestures, grimaces and sounds which the very young baby makes. From birth, a mother interprets her baby's responses as indicating wishes, needs, feelings and intentions. This imputation of meaningful communication to the baby's actions is seen to be of great significance in the development of shared understanding between mother and baby, and in the beginning of intentional communicative acts on the baby's part (Newson 1974).

From 5 to 6 months onwards babies become increasingly interested in objects, and at around 8 to 10 months of age a change of great significance for the development of social behaviour takes place. Whereas, before this age, the baby tended to focus his attention and activity *either* on the mother *or* on objects, he now manages to co-ordinate his interest and attention to both. For babies growing up in many different societies it is reported that after 8 to 10 months of age, the baby begins to invoke adult help in dealing with objects, to take part in give-and-take games with objects; he also begins to begin to play appropriately with representational toys, to obey requests, to perform appropriate learned gestures such as waving 'bye bye', to imitate acts which he has seen others perform (Trevarthen & Hubley 1978), and so on. The crucially important point to stress about these developments is that they are all actions within *a shared system of reference*. It is suggested that it is through the joint games which he plays with his mother, and through his mother's response to his actions and expressions, that the baby begins to learn what his actions 'mean' for other people and thus begins to use them with intention in a social context. The mother's interest and empathy, which in earlier work on the mother–child relationship has been emphasized as essential for the child's *emotional* adjustment, are now seen as important in enabling her to monitor carefully the child's interests, to develop ways of making social contact which change as he develops, and thus to provide a framework within which he begins to understand the social meaning of his acts.

It is this achievement of cooperative action with the parent that Bruner (1977; Bruner & Sherwood 1976) sees to be of particular significance in the development of language, reflecting as it does a joint agreement about a communicative framework. He emphasizes that cooperative play between mother and child is of great importance here: peekaboo, give-and-take, games involving anticipation all provide opportunities for mastering rules and conventions, a shared frame of reference. In one study, Bruner (1977) traced the course of the development of give-and-take games, showing how the child learns to 'get things done jointly' and at the same time learns to use appropriate communicative signals to engage his partner in the process. From such studies it is clear that well before the child speaks he can make known his needs and wishes, can engage in joint communication within a shared frame of reference.

It has, then, been well argued, and widely accepted, that the mother's interpretation of the child's communicative intention plays a central role in the development of the child's understanding of the meaning his behaviour has for other people. One implication of this argument is that the child must be paying close attention to his mother's response to his acts. For the early months there are, indeed, careful studies describing the precision with which babies follow the direction of their mothers' gaze (Collis & Schaffer 1975; Scaife & Bruner 1975), the focus of their attention and the sensitivity with which they respond to changes in their mothers' mood. Trevarthen (1977: 267) noted in the 7–12-week-old babies he studied that 'very slight, temporary and subtle changes in the mother's actions, made experimentally over one minute, produced strong but entirely reversible changes in the infants' communication'. But for the second half of the first year, when cooperative and sharing behaviour develop most fully and when it seems likely that there are crucial developments in the baby's sensitivity to the behaviour of others, we have very little information. We know almost nothing about the changes in his responsiveness and sensitivity during this period, the changes which lead to the comparative sophistication of the 12-month-old documented by Yarrow & Waxler, and by Emde and his colleagues. It is worth reflecting for a moment on *why* we should be so ignorant of such a crucial stage in the child's development.

One contributing factor is that in the research on the development of communicative skills in babies of this age, the focus has been on the development of *verbal* communication. Psychologists have concentrated on the development of demanding and referential gesture, the linking of gesture to vocal signal and then to words. It is perhaps in part *because* their focus has been on the development of demand for, and reference to objects – 'protoimperative' and 'protodeclarative' in Bates' terms (Bates, Camaioni & Volterra 1975) – that little interest has been shown in the child's developing skills in monitoring and understanding the behaviour of other people. Of course the development of language is of immeasurable significance for a child's understanding of others and his social world. Yet this concentration on the development of language, and the use of a linguistic model to describe the behaviour of a baby with his family – a glance at the mother is a 'comment on a topic' (Bruner 1977) or 'referential' (Jones 1977) – in practice has meant ignoring the development of a whole range of human abilities, for example, the ability to interpret and anticipate the intentions and reactions of others, to empathize with and console, to annoy deliberately and manipulate others. Here, the observations of babies with their siblings provide a provocative contrast with the work on babies and their mothers. They show us, firstly, that by 14 months a baby can and does engage in a variety of elaborate, cooperative, *nonverbal* games with a child only a little older than himself, games which involve anticipating the actions and mood of the other, matching and signalling these moods and intentions, alluding to previous games between the siblings and reversing 'roles' within the games. Secondly, they make clear that, as early as 14 months old, babies already possess considerable skill at deliberately frustrating and provoking as well as at comforting the older sibling – again *non-verbally*. That no *language* is involved in such sibling exchanges draws attention to the significance of these interactions for the display (and perhaps also for the development) of a range of human abilities much broader than the acquisition of language.

## 4. Conclusion

In this chapter some findings from an observational study of siblings have been described, findings which suggest first that the extent of young children's understanding of other people has been much underestimated by many psychologists and second, that differences between mothers in the ways in which they discuss other people's motives and intentions may well contribute to differences in the development in children of this sensitivity to others. Two points seem worth underlining in conclusion. The first point is that it is clear that it is crucial to study very young children in situations of real emotional significance to them – that is, within their families – if we are not to misrepresent their abilities. When we do study them in such settings, it is apparent that well before 3 years children are interested in, and involved with, a world of significant others in which they understand and respond with considerable subtlety to the emotions and intentions of those others. They already share with the people of that world some notions of feelings, needs, intentions, and of social rules. By studying the sibling relationship – a relationship that is marked by its uninhibited emotional quality and by its intimacy and familiarity – we see with particular clarity the beginnings of this understanding. The second point is that there are important gaps in what we know of the development of children's sensitivity to other people's behaviour, particularly between 8 and 18 months of age. What do we know of the development of 'showing off', of blushing and embarrassment, of humour and teasing, of deceit, cruelty and guilt? Very little. A more flexible and imaginative approach to the study of children's responses to, and references to, other people should give us new insights into both their understanding of others and their developing consciousness of self.

## References

Bates, E., Camaioni, L. & Volterra, V. 1975. The acquisition of performatives prior to speech. *Merrill Palmer Quarterly, 21*, 205–26.

Borke, H. 1972. Interpersonal perception of young children: egocentrism or empathy? *Developmental Psychology, 7*, 107–9.

Bretherton, I., McNew, S. & Beeghly-Smith, M. 1981. Early person knowledge as expressed in gestural and verbal communication: when do infants acquire a 'theory of mind'? In M. E. Lamb & L. R. Sherrod (eds.) *Infant social cognition.* Hillsdale, NJ: Erlbaum.

Brown, R. 1977. Introduction. In C. E. Snow & C. A. Ferguson (eds.) *Talking to children.* Cambridge: Cambridge University Press.

Bruner, J. 1977. Early social interaction and language acquisition. In H. R. Schaffer (ed.) *Studies in mother–infant interaction.* London: Academic Press.

Bruner, J. & Sherwood, V. 1976. Peekaboo and learning of rule structures. In J. Bruner, A. Jolly & K. Sylva (eds.) *Play: its role in development and evolution.* Harmondsworth: Penguin.

Burlingham, D. & Freud, A. 1944. *Infants without families.* London: George Allen and Unwin.

Chandler, M. J. & Greenspan, S. 1972. Ersatz egocentrism: a reply to H. Borke. *Developmental Psychology, 7*, 104–6.

Clarke-Stewart, K. A. 1973. Interactions between mothers and their children: characteristics and consequences. *Monographs of the Society for Research in Child Development, 38.*

Collis, G. M. & Schaffer, H. R. 1975. Synchronization of visual attention in mother–infant pairs. *Journal of Child Psychology and Psychiatry, 4*, 315–20.

Donaldson, M. 1978. *Children's minds.* Glasgow: Fontana/Collins.

Dunn, J. & Kendrick, C. 1980. The arrival of a sibling: changes in patterns of interaction between mother and first-born child. *Journal of Child Psychology and Psychiatry, 21*, 119–32.

1982a. The speech of two- and three-year-olds to infant siblings: 'baby talk' and the context of communication. *Journal of Child Language, 9*, 579–95.

1982b. *Siblings: love, envy and understanding.* Oxford: Blackwells.

Hoffman, M. L. 1975. Developmental synthesis of affect and cognition and its implications for altruistic motivation. *Developmental Psychology, 11*, 607–22.

1981. Development of prosocial motivation: empathy and guilt. In N. Eisenberg-Berg (ed.) *Development of prosocial behaviour.* New York: Academic Press.

Hood, L. & Bloom, L. 1979. What, when and how about why?: a longitudinal study of early expressions of causality. *Monographs of the Society for Research in Child Development, 44* (6).

Jones, O. H. M. 1977. Mother–child communication with pre-linguistic Down's syndrome and normal infants. In H. R. Schaffer (ed.) *Studies in mother–infant interaction.*

Light, P. 1979. *The development of social sensitivity.* Cambridge: Cambridge University Press.

Newson, J. 1974. Towards a theory of infant understanding. *Bulletin of the British Psychological Society, 27*, 251–7.

Piaget, J. 1955. *The language and thought of the child.* New York: Meridian.

1969. *Judgement and reasoning in the child.* Totowa, NJ: Littlefield, Adams.

1972. *The child's concept of physical causality.* Totowa, NJ: Littlefield, Adams.

Sachs, J. & Devin, J. 1976. Young children's use of age-approach speech styles in social interaction and role-playing. *Journal of Child Language, 3,* 81–98.

Scaife, M. & Bruner, J. 1975. The capacity for joint visual attention in the infant. *Nature, 253,* 265–6.

Schaffer, H. R. 1979. Acquiring the concept of the dialogue. In M. H. Bornstein & W. Kessen (eds.) *Psychological development from infancy: image to intention.* Hillsdale. NJ: Erlbaum.

Shantz, C. V. 1975. The development of social cognition. In E. Maris Hetherington (ed.) *Review of child development research.* Chicago: University of Chicago Press.

Shatz, M. & Gelman, R. 1973. The development of communication skills: modifications in the speech of young children as a function of the listener. *Monographs of the Society for Research on Child Development, 38* (152).

1977. Beyond syntax: the influence of conversational constraints on speech modifications. In C. E. Snow & C. A. Ferguson (eds.) *Talking to children.*

Tizard, B., Hughes, M., Pinkerton, G. & Carmichael, H. 1982. Adults' cognitive demands at home and at nursery school. *Journal of Child Psychology and Psychiatry, 23* (2), 105–16.

Trevarthen, C. 1977. Descriptive analyses of infant communicative behaviour. In H. R. Schaffer (ed.) *Studies in mother–infant interaction.*

Trevarthen, C. & Hubley, P. 1978. Secondary intersubjectivity: confidence, confiding and acts of meaning in the first year. In A. Lock (ed.) *Action, gesture and symbol: the emergence of language.* London: Academic Press.

Urberg, K. A. & Docherty, E. M. 1976. Development of role-taking skills in young children. *Developmental Psychology, 12,* 198–203.

Vygotsky, L. S. 1977. *Mind and society.* Cambridge, Mass.: Harvard University Press.

Werner, H. & Kaplan, B. 1963. *Symbol formation.* New York: Wiley.

Whiting, B. B. & Edwards, C. P. (eds.) 1977. *The effects of age, sex and modernity on the behaviour of mothers and children.* Report to the Ford Foundation.

Whiting, B. B. & Whiting, J. 1975. *Children of six cultures: a psychocultural analysis.* Cambridge, Mass.: Harvard University Press.

Wood, D., McMahon, L. & Cranstoun, Y. 1980. *Working with under fives.* London: Grant McIntyre.

Yarrow, M. R. & Waxler, C. Z. 1975. The emergence and functions of prosocial behaviour in young children. Paper presented at the Society for Research in Child Development meeting, Denver, Colorado.

# 3. The development of communicative competence with language in young children: a social psychological perspective

W. P. ROBINSON

The eventual descriptions and explanations of the development of communicative competence with language in young children will not consist of a small number of sweeping generalizations posed at high levels of abstraction. There will be a large number of answers to a large number of relatively specific questions pursued with empirical persistence.

The questions themselves will need to be set within taxonomic frameworks. To date, linguists have been most successful in providing these for the phonological and lexico-grammatical components of language conceived as system rather than resource. Lexico-grammatical analyses have only recently been developed above the unit of 'sentence', but category systems for extended discourse (text) have begun to appear (Coulthard 1977; van Dijk 1972). The semantic component and the links between this and phonology and lexico-grammar exhibit patches of progress (Dean-Fodor 1977; Lyons 1977). How this system comes to be used in conversation is beginning to be tackled (Shields 1978; Wells 1981), while Searle's elaboration of speech act theory (1975) is beginning to realize hopes that sound taxonomies of how speech functions in behaviour would begin to emerge (Robinson 1972).

These components have not only to be articulated with each other, but also integrated into language in action in communication. The developing mastery of this whole will need to be set in adequate models of the developing child for the story to move towards completeness.

## 1. Conceptions of young children

How are we to conceive of children and their development? How are we to conceive of the human beings they become (Chapman & Jones 1980)? In child development, cognitive (intellectual) processes have been a major preoccupa-

28

tion, with Piaget's ideas acting as the major frame of reference. What are the capacities and limitations of the *fundamental* structures of the mind when put to tests of its competence, and what changes occur with age? Some interest has been shown in how or why changes occur. In a different arena, Chomsky's structuralist approach to language captivated the American imagination, again emphasizing the importance of discovering the fundamental regulatory principles of linguistic competence and what changes occur. In this approach, questions about reasons for and mechanisms of change were, to all intents and purposes, avoided. Both approaches have generally paid more attention to deep competence than to everyday competence, to cognitive factors than to motivational–emotional ones, much more attention to their operation in relation to the physical than to the social world, and more attention to what could happen than to what does happen. According to some of their critics, both Piaget and Chomsky offer structure without growth, whereas alternative stories of contiguity principles of learning (with or without reinforcement added) offer growth with no structure and foundation.

Fortunately, we are now learning to attend to the details of what actually takes place between real children, other people and their contexts of situation. There is still a tendency to escalate the generality of the inferences drawn from very small-scale studies and to dream of universality, orderliness, and efficiency in development to an extent that seriously underestimates the fumbling and bumbling of young children and their significant others and the disjunctive possibilities of variable routes for development. We are also a little too prone to overestimate the unity of the activities taking place within the confines of the baby's skin.

A conception of the developing child as a unified person has been challenged provocatively by Harré (1979, 1981). He argues that the single contrast of 'individual' and 'society' obscures important distinctions and he offers a four-fold analysis into collective vs. individual and public vs. private; 'public' is what is available for any individual to experience, 'private' refers to what happens within our skins; 'collective' refers to what concerns people, 'individual' relates to a single person. Harré wishes to argue that persons emerge as self-conscious individuals capable of reflection upon their past, present and future qualities and actions, and capable of wilfully influencing both their present and future only through their interactions with other human beings – and that talk is a major means by which this achievement is realized. What Vygotsky (1962) argued for speech, Harré wishes to extend. The capacity for internal dialogue characteristic of Vygotsky's 'inner speech' is a development from speech communication with others. This speech has been public. Vygotsky's 'socialized speech' has been about both the collective and the individual. Harré broadens this to assert that 'persons are made in the course of a wide variety of different language games'. Young children are told they are happy, sad, frightened or tired. They are told they are hungry and thirsty. They are told what they want. What may be discomforts of a global character become differentiated and identified through verbal labelling. Prophylactics and explanations are offered and co-ordinated with the verbal. Likewise, significant others direct and co-ordinate social activities, acting on and announcing what is happening and why, defining rules of proper and improper conduct behaviourally, verbally or both.

This is not to say there is no argument between child and others; it is to suggest that the emergent components of self are a constellation of dynamic resultants of the interplay between definitions of others and self-evaluated experiences, past and present. Individuality is a consequence of others treating the child as an individual accountable for his actions. The child comes to believe he has a mind because of the qualities of his contacts with other minds. Other minds help to provide him with beliefs about his own history; other minds assure him of his responsibility for his actions and his future development. Perceptions of possibilities of self-intervention arise from the judgments of others.

Harré's approach stresses the role of speech addressed to the child and speech heard by the child to an extent that may only reflect the socialization practices of particular cultures at particular times, but at least he serves to remind us of a general orientation that is inconsistent either with extreme individualism or with 'social determinism'. The child is offered interpretations about himself which may or may not be accurate in the particular circum- stances, but which at least present the kinds of categorization (and evaluations of these) which the caretaker uses to guide his or her actions in relation to the young child. Hence the child may be able to discover the kind of descriptive and evaluative constructions of personality and social behaviour used by caretakers in his subculture. Initially, at least, he is unlikely to realize that there are alternative ways of conceptualizing people and their social behaviour, but should his culture be one that encourages reflective analysis about such matters, he may come to see his cultural perspective on the nature of human beings as being but one of many possibilities. Much of the representation and conceptualization of these matters may be mediated via speech (and later, writing). It is in this sense that learning the language is to learn the culture. The categories and the relations between them, as provided in a language, do constitute an initial frame of reference for conceptualizing all those matters about which members of a culture talk. Weakened formulations of the Whorf–Sapir hypotheses are valid when they are applied to issues for which people do not have alternative symbolic formulations. The predilection of the English language for clear separations of nouns and verbs, adjectives and adverbs, its pressure towards the categorical and stable rather than the relational and fluid, renders it difficult to express some of the ideas some psychologists would like to promote. Elsewhere in this book we find reference to the vexing problem of when an individual acts in terms of personal identity and when in terms of social group membership. It is interesting that in our culture the question has usually been formulated with that orientation. How and when does individual identity become submerged in the social? Shona speakers might see the assertion of individual identity as the more problematic. Many of us may simply have failed to experience social activity except as individuals. Those of us who have, and who wish to communicate such experiences, find ourselves limited by a language that discourages the representation of such experience. In any case we can only communicate any such understanding with others who have had the prerequisite experience for the ideas to make sense!

My more limited unartificial intelligence persuades me that although Harré's exposition will fail, it will do so heroically, and its heroism emphasizes ideas about the development of young children that are closer to reality than the individualism and social determinism he criticizes.

## 2. Claims about development of mastery of language for communication

These considerations render it difficult to organize a systematic review of the social bases of language development. Many potentially relevant empirical studies have adopted a stance that presumes the child is an individual whose mental apparatus is relatively unified from birth. They have sought to describe sequences of development of language as a unitary system, particularly at the grammatical levels. They have not asked about the psychological processes involved. Where adult input has been examined, atheoretical correlational studies have predominated. Many important topics have not yet been examined.

The majority of the claims that follow are summarizing hypotheses about some of the major principles which appear to be guiding current research. They are selected to highlight the socio- rather than the psycho-linguistic, the social psychological rather than the sociological or anthropological. The bulk of the work reported concerns young children in the intermediate strata of the socio-economic status hierarchy of monolingual English-speaking families. The claims mentioned focus on the influence of proximal variables. More distal, locational variables of age, sex, socio-economic status or ethnicity are not included. Individual differences are given precedence over socially based differences as a vehicle for illustrating likely process–product relationships. Most of the work reported relates to children who have not yet entered formal education. Wells & Robinson (1982) have offered a wider review of studies of adult activities relevant to speech development in children. More broadly based collections of papers are also available (Ervin-Tripp & Mitchell-Kernan 1977; Garnica & King 1977; Lewis & Rosenblum 1977; Lock 1978; Snow & Ferguson 1977; Waterson & Snow 1978).

*Claim 1: The exploitation of language develops out of already established nonverbal means of communication.* From birth the child interacts with people as well as with his non-social environment; child and particularly caretakers act upon and react to each other. This reciprocal exchange of signals involves mutual learning as well as performance in relation to each other and the immediate environment. Some of this co-ordinated activity appears to be inherently pleasurable to both parties – states of phatic communion can be temporarily satisfying in and of themselves. Soft vocalization by baby and caretaker is included in mutual gaze contacts from the earliest days. Communicative motor activity is added to the direction of gaze as an indicator of interest and becomes differentiated within itself, e.g. pointing separates from reaching, and is potentially detachable from visual signalling. Vocalization of the participants exhibits contingently related properties including turn-taking, particularly during mutual gaze. Vocalization as a complement to pointing and reaching in turn eventually becomes detachable from gestures. The development of the nonverbal repertoire itself, and its extension and elaboration into proto-verbal communication, can now be described in some detail (see, for example, Bates, Camaioni & Volterra 1975; Bullowa 1977; Lock 1980; Ninio & Bruner 1978; Schaffer 1977; Trevarthen & Hubley 1978).

It would seem that in the first instance some of the extensions are involuntary accretions that only subsequently are subordinated to willed direction. This developing interchange of communicative acts through postures, gestures, facial expressions, and vocalizations, and the eventual addition and incorporation of verbal communicative acts, includes both instrumental and consummatory activities; the instrumental potential of the earlier acts for regulating the states and behaviour of others and self being perceived by babies only after they have observed the consequences of their enactment.

*Claim 2: Initial functions of language are social interactional.* If we distinguish between language uses which appear to emphasize a commitment to comment on beliefs about the nature of the world *per se*, e.g. making statements which are either true or false, and those which appear to be attempts to regulate the states or behaviour of self and others or to define role relationships (Robinson 1978), then in Halliday's child, Nigel, the former only began to appear over nine months after the first socially relevant language units had emerged. Halliday (1975) found that instrumental (getting things for self), regulatory (making others do things), interactional (encounter-regulation), and personal (reactions to events or states) units were the first to appear. Among these were nǎ (give me that), bø (give me my bird), ɔ̃ (do that again), dø (nice to see you), nñ (that tastes nice). This child began to 'talk', it seems, because verbal interaction with others was pleasurable; it was not because he was hungry or in pain. The design of the baby appears to include an impetus to interact with people, an impetus to interact with other features of the environment, and an impetus to develop the schemes of interaction. If one wishes to say that the reasons babies begin to talk are biological, then they are socio-biological – joint action and interaction with caretakers.

As Halliday illustrates, Nigel later expanded his functional range to include heuristic (finding out) and imaginative (let's pretend) functions, and increased the number of communicative acts associated with each of these until by the age of $1\frac{1}{2}$ years he had over 50 in his repertoire. About this time Nigel ceased to rely solely upon inventing his own units (mainly un-English in form and actually heavily reliant on tone), and two other important changes occurred.

First, Nigel interpolated a third level of linguistic structure, the *lexico-grammatical*, between soundings and meanings. Individual sounds ceased to be expressive of individual meanings. Combinations of sounds were used to form 'words', words and tones were sequenced to create 'meanings'. Thus the *tristratal* essence of language became established. (At some later point in time the child has also to learn to distinguish between the semantic and pragmatic levels; different forms can serve the same *general* functions, the same grammatical form can serve different functions, the appropriate choice requiring information about particular cultural conventions.) Second, the functions appear to coalesce into pragmatic (doing things with wordings) and mathetic (finding out about language) cores.

To describe these developments is not to explain them. The description offers no reasons for the emergence or the development of these activities. That they enhance the pleasures of the participants may be true. That both would become bored by repetition of a static repertoire may also be true. For the present we seem to be left with the observation that the design characteristics of the child include an impetus to develop such interactive capacities as well as one to interact *per se*.

*Claim 2a: Prosodic features of early (and later) communicative acts are an integral component of those acts.* Garnica (1977) has illustrated how a number of prosodic features in mothers' speech discriminate between their interactions with 2- and 5-year-olds, 2-year-olds being addressed with higher fundamental pitch, a greater pitch range, rising final pitch terminals, greater duration for words, more multiple primary stress in sentences and more whispering. Menyuk & Bernholtz (1967) claimed that at the 'one-word stage' the child they were studying discriminated three functions of uttering 'door' through duration and pitch contour to convey 'That's a door' (Statement), 'Is that a door?' (Question), 'Shut the door!' (Command).

Brazil (1978) suggests that English utilizes five pitch changes (tone): low rises (neutral), fall-rise (refer), rise (intensified refer), fall (proclaim), rise-fall (intensified proclaim), in which the refer–proclaim opposition marks the contrast between what is assumed to be shared, already negotiated, common ground and what is new.

I would draw attention here to two points about this line of argument. First, Brazil is offering a prosodic means of dividing topic from comment, what is old and presumed to be shared, from what is new and offered for sharing or discussion. Second, the tone group prescribes the general pragmatic significance of the utterances. Is the hearer expected to perform some nonverbal action? Is the hearer required to offer a verbal answer? Is the hearer invited to acknowledge the assertion, accepting or rejecting it as the case may be? In what manner is the utterance to be interpreted?

These questions are of crucial significance for pragmatics, and if they are integral to the meanings of messages, they must presumably be included in studies.

*Claim 2b: Contextual features of early (and later) communicative acts are an integral component for the transmission of meanings.* We have already seen in Claims 1 and 2 how speech can be used to promote action. Gestures combine with speech to form integrated structures from which the speech itself can only subsequently become separated. Even then this separation will not, and never can be, complete, in that listeners must be able to locate the meanings of utterances in relation to the nonverbal meanings of a speaker. Beliefs about language use becoming more and more context-free can be misleading, if all this means is that the assumptions of mature interactants which can be taken for granted as shared are very numerous.

The studies of language development that have counted deictic markers – those units that necessarily rely on extra-linguistic or linguistic contextual information for the identification of their reference (e.g. demonstrative and personal pronouns, articles, spatial and temporal adjuncts such as *here, there*) – reveal the high frequency of their occurrence in early interaction (e.g. Wells 1980). Concern with the here-and-now presumably remains a significant reason for face-to-face interaction throughout childhood and beyond, potentially depriving any second-hand observer, confined to listening, of the rationale of what is taking place.

*Claim 3: The young child makes deliberate efforts to learn language (and about language).* With the emergence of the tristratal character of his language system and the move into Phase II, Halliday suggested that Nigel combined instrumental, regulatory and interactional functions into a general *pragmatic* one, and interactional, personal and heuristic into a *mathetic* one – this latter serving to find out about the world, including language and its relationships to the world – rising tone meaning 'undecided' and falling tone 'decided' (complete). Mathetically intoned utterances required verbal replies relevant to the uncertainty expressed. This is not to claim that the sole function, or even the primary functions, of apparently heuristic utterances are what they appear to be. Sometimes they may be ways of sustaining interaction and commanding the attention of others. Anyone who has been the victim of 'What's that?' games is likely to have been suspicious of the child's thirst for names on some occasions, but not so on others. At present we do not have evidence to show that the labels learned and remembered actually differ as a function of the child's motivation, however. Neither do we know how deliberate efforts relate to the learning of communicative competence with language, but we can take account of the early emergence of a self-directing learner.

*Claim 4: Units (and structures) are accumulated piecemeal.* An extreme position might be taken in which it is maintained that units and structures are mastered one at a time, for example, see Ruder & Bunce (1973), and some of their evidence is interestingly consistent with such an idea. If this is so then it must be remembered that this mastery is not *in vacuo*; it involves assimilation to existing schemes. Neither is a unit mastered as a single level item. For example, children learn a word as a sounding/meaning combination in relation to the use of that sounding. Children do not learn unattached soundings *per se* (Nelson & Bonvillian 1978). (This is not to say they cannot learn nonsense syllables assimilable to soundings already available, nor that they cannot learn to imitate such soundings.) Units learned may be forgotten.

By 'unit' is meant any feature of the language at any level, e.g. phonemes (individual sounds), tonic stresses, pitches, intonation patterns, morphemes, words, groups, clauses, sentences, utterances, rules of explicitness, rules of politeness, rules of differential social status. (It should be remembered that a unit at one level can be a structure at another, e.g. a sequence of particular pitches can form an intonation pattern, but this pattern serves as a unit if it serves to form an interrogative; a principle or rule can become a unit when treated as such.)

A new unit will be more likely to enter and remain in the child's repertoire if he is intellectually capable of grasping some aspect of its approximate meaning or significance. Capability is not the only factor; a unit is more likely to be mastered if its meaning and significance are relevant to something the child wishes to communicate or comprehend. A unit will only become stabilized in use if it is encouraged to be so by others (see Claim 7).

*Claim 5: The new is often first learned in terms of the old.* A classical Greek paradox points to the impossibility of change, and this principle is sometimes invoked as a reason why children cannot learn language! If understanding a word must precede the learning of that word, how can it be learned? If learning must precede understanding how can the child come to understand something that has no meaning? And yet children clearly do learn. One of several lines of escape from the paradox is to argue that the child can express new meanings 'badly' with personally invented units or with old, already available units, and that caretakers can reformulate the child's meaning with the new units and structures which the child may then be able to assimilate to the meaning intended (Bloom 1970). Evidence is consistent with the idea that the child learning to associate the various kinds of negation in English with the appropriate adult lexical and syntactic structures, relies for its development upon adults continuing to supply the new forms upon occasions of the child using those already in its repertoire (Bloom 1970).

*Claim 6: Caretakers control the probability of new features being learned and remaining in the child's repertoire.* In numerous studies of what has been identified as a special register of 'baby talk' (Ferguson 1964), investigators have drawn attention to its differences from speech addressed to older children and other adults (see Wells & Robinson 1982, for a summary). This speech is slower and more clearly articulated, uses a wider pitch range especially towards the higher frequencies. Utterances are shorter and grammatically simpler. The lexis has special 'baby' words. Semantically, topics focus on the immediately observable environment. The semantic relations realized accord with those the child expresses. It is repetitious. That such speech is intended to regulate the behaviour and both regulate and ascertain affective states of the child, is implied by the relatively high incidence of imperative and interrogative forms (Sachs, Brown & Salerno 1976). It can also be used to inform the child about language and the world.

These adaptations of adult to child are not surprising; it would be very strange if they were not made, given that the adult wishes to communicate to and with the child. One would expect most adults to expect to have to accommodate to the child, and if serious in intent and regularly in contact, a monitoring of feedback should serve to render the requisite information for generally, but not wholly, successful adaptation. Such overestimation as occurs, and deliberate instruction if any, should provide data about language and its workings for children to enhance their repertoire. The clarity of discrimination and contiguities afforded, especially if extended into opportunities for rehearsal and practice, should, on associationist principles of learning, render such new linguistic features as are within the contemporary competence of the child more readily assimilable – given that the child is an active learner. Rates of progress will hence be a joint function of the motivation and current capacity of the child to learn, the availability of learnable features in adult speech, and the suitability of the conditions for learning practice and retention.

Two studies can be quoted to illustrate the power of caretakers to influence the rate of mastery at the relatively early period of language development, when the child's utterances are on average between 1.5 and 3 MLU (Mean Length of Utterance – at this stage of development the number of morphemes is closely related to the number of words).

Ellis & Wells (1980) contrasted the maternal interaction characteristics of slow and fast language developers. At the outset the latter mothers talked more during routine household activities, issued more instructions and commands, were more likely to acknowledge their child's utterances, and more likely to repeat or correct these. By the time the children had reached 3.5 MLU, maternal differences were still present, but they were different in type, the early fast children's mothers using more statements and questions, particularly teaching-type questions to which the mother already knew the answers. Cross (1978) obtained comparable results in a contrast between faster and slower developers, and also found that different maternal speech variables discriminated at different ages. The implications of these two studies are several. Optimal facilitation of development may require the employment of different *tactics* at different points in development (language and personal), and may even require the application of different *strategies*. But more basic general principles are also relevant. Mothers whose speech is less intelligible, in that it is mumbled and incoherent with no clear breaks and stresses at customary points, are likely to have children whose speech is developing more slowly (see Newport, Gleitman & Gleitman 1977). We would expect to discover other principles that hold true regardless of space or time.

In a study of the mother–child interaction among 6-year-olds (see W. P. Robinson 1981) that was geared to higher levels of communicative activity via language, it was found that children who asked more questions, more complex questions, and revealed more verbally mediated knowledge about an assortment of objects, games and toys, had mothers who were more likely to: (1) set any remark in a previously shared context; (2) answer any question with a relevant, accurate reply that extended somewhat beyond the question posed; (3) confirm children's utterances which were true and well-formed and to point out or correct errors; (4) maintain themes over several utterances. The findings need qualification and supplementation, but the strategies are similar in content and spirit to those already mentioned.

If two words were to be used to sum up the contrast in these studies they would be 'push' vs. 'pull'. Pushing does not work, mild pulling does: adults can set up the contexts of situation in which activity takes place, but beyond that the child decides what he is interested in. Adults can set the scene, offer suggestions, and tempt the child, but the child directs the form and content of the script. The 'push' is already there; it seems to be a design characteristic of human children. By rigging the environment and by their reactive behaviour adults can encourage and develop both this intrinsic motivation and the learning which results from its activity. They may also be able to treat it in ways which may slow down, check, deflect, distort, prevent or otherwise impede, development.

Providing, tempting, modelling and utilizable correction appear to be the main activities caretakers can offer to facilitate language (and general) development in its early stages. How far the success of these actions depends upon the caretaker's genuine concern with the child and his behaviour remains unknown. One would have to suggest that caring in action, entering both intellectually and emotionally into the spirit and perspective of the child's orientation to his world, ought to make the processes easier to achieve.

*Claim 7: Coming to 'believe that' reorganizes the possibilities of developing procedural competence.* As Shatz & Gelman (1973) have shown, some children aged 4 can state that there are rules governing how things are to be said and can say something about the qualities of these rules – they display metalinguistic capacities. We have asked how children come to realize that speech can be ambiguous, that a speaker may send messages too vague for correct comprehension and appropriate action and what differences such a development makes (E. J. Robinson 1981). At an early stage children do not realize a message should refer uniquely to its referents if it is to be acted upon appropriately. In a situation where speaker and listener have identical sets of cards, each set depicting stick-men holding flowers differing in size and colour, they will pick up a card in response to 'A man with a flower' without necessarily asking for more information. If their choice turns out to be wrong they will state that the speaker had said enough (told properly) and that it was their fault that the mismatch had occurred (Phase 1, below). When older, they will be more likely to demand more information by asking questions, and if a mismatch still occurs they can blame the inadequacy of the message and the speaker for the failure. They 'believe that' messages can be inadequate. They can reflect upon and analyse the efficiency and precision of their own speech and that of others (Phase 2, below).

At present we can only speculate about the general significance of this work, but the possible implications are considerable and can be represented roughly in a three-phase model that could apply to many aspects of the development of communicative competence. Let X be a belief, principle or fact about language and/or its use.

*Phase 1.* The child is mainly a victim of X. His capacity for being an agent with control over X is limited by his ignorance of the character of X and how it functions in language in communication. However, he achieves a measure of mastery of X in use (know-how) partly as a result of associative learning both in its classical and instrumental conditioning guises; he may also learn about X in use through observation. He is additionally an agent however and *can* purposefully use X, relying on corrective or explanatory feedback from others for the development of context-bound rules of use. These various processes acting separately and in combination may lead to the child using X successfully much of the time. However, limitations of intellectual capacity and an absence of opportunities, and/or capacities for *reflecting* upon the workings of X, will be manifested when his rules for using X fail. He will not be able to diagnose the reasons for failure and will not be able to formulate a diagnosis and act effectively upon it.

*Phase 2.* Either through his own reflective efforts or as a result of a competent other teaching and telling him about the workings of X, or as a result of socio-cognitive conflicts with others, he will come to realize how (and perhaps why) X works as it does. As a result of contemporary reflective analysis in particular new situations or through a consideration of past events, or through imaginative rehearsing of situations involving X (or by attending courses about X), he will consciously develop and organize his understanding about X. We might expect an associated period of learning practice in which the use of X is tried out frequently with care and awareness. The child (or adult) has become a reflecting agent in respect of X, organizing his 'believing that' – and perhaps temporarily less efficient in his 'know-how'. His/her competence has been raised to a higher level of understanding (programming) with greatly enhanced potential for efficient use of X.

*Phase 3.* Once the principles relating to X have been understood, the use of X will probably become reduced to an automated skill, except for situations where for various reasons it might be important not to make mistakes with X, and for situations where trouble in using X occurs. In the face of anticipated or present trouble the problem can be raised to a conscious reflective analysis, diagnoses made, and corrective action taken – other things being equal. The 'know-how' is greater than at the transition from Phase 1 to Phase 2 and is in a potential dialectic relation to a 'believing that' of understanding.

We are currently thinking in this fashion only about the child's control of ambiguity in verbal referential communication, but see a range of possible application to a whole variety of behaviours within the orbit of language in communication: learning the meanings of words, rules of spelling in the written language, rules of pronunciation in the oral, rules of grammar, rules for varying forcefulness and politeness of requests, rules of etiquette more generally, rules for taking the listener into account, rules for telling jokes well, rules for persuading an audience.

Perhaps one important set of reasons why children have difficulty in learning to use language more competently is that we ourselves cannot or do not formulate the rules for them. Instead we leave them to continue to operate at a particular and concrete level, learning many instances rather than fewer principles and rules. Even when we can formulate the rules and principles we do not necessarily set up conditions of learning and practice that carry the child's competence through to the phase of out-of-awareness efficient use, with reflective facilities for analysis available when trouble occurs or is anticipated. It is worth comparing the ease of learning a game, like chess or tennis, with and without the help of information about rules. To learn how to play will require observation, practice, and correction, but acquaintance with the rules renders these easier.

*Claim 8: The ultimate frame of reference for studies of the development of communicative competence with language has to extend to all functions of language, paying due attention to particular functional/structural linkages.* The final claim is not a summarizing hypothesis. The other seven claims have not referred to functional specificity, except for the proto-language of one child in which the function/unit linkages were alleged to be separable. The subsequent complex merging of functions and structures should not, however, be seen as symptomatic of the construction of a monolithic system. The repertoire of normal adults is composed of variations in the phonological, lexico-grammatical, semantic and pragmatic characteristics of their speech and writing, listening and reading. Whatever commonality of organization is achieved is combined with selection procedures that confine the occurrence or incidence of certain linguistic features to certain contexts. Functional specificity acts as one of the selectional constraints, and learning which features are to be used for which functions is one of the child's learning problems.

At this point in time derivations from Searle's speech act theory (1969, 1975) are likely to be a major point of departure for studies of functionally specific communicative features, although they suffer from two limitations. First, they relate only to single acts and not to sequences of acts, that is, the child has to learn what can and ought to follow what if his more general purposes are to be achieved. Clarke's (1983) analysis of episode structures in terms of speech acts offers one approach to this extended treatment of conversational discourse. Second, they do not deal with several of the functions of relevance in social psychology (Robinson 1972).

The beginnings and subsequent development of these culturally prescribed and individually preferred communicative competences have hardly been touched on as yet. Since what Searle calls 'directives' have so far attracted most of the attention, these are chosen for brief presentation.

## 3. Directives

In terms of Searle's main criteria of discrimination the 'direction of fit' is from world to words (to make the state of the world correspond to the words uttered) and the 'sincerity condition' is the speaker's wanting, the 'propositional content' is that the hearer performs some future action A.

Examining adult usage of such speech acts, Ervin-Tripp (1976) classified her observations into six categories: Personal need or desire statements (I need a match), Imperatives (Give me a match), Imbedded imperatives (Could you give me a match?), Permission directives (May I have a match?), Question directives (Have you got a match?) and Hints (The matches are all gone). To relate linguistic form to behavioural function Sinclair & Coulthard (1975:

32–3) argue that rules of interpretation need to be applied and propose that, for example:

> Any declarative or interrogative is to be interpreted as a command to stop if it refers to an action or activity which is proscribed at the time of utterance...(but) as a command to do if it refers to an action or activity which teachers and pupil(s) know ought to have been performed or completed and hasn't been.

Ervin-Tripp (1977: 169) adds an elaboration:

> Those utterances will be interpreted as directives which break topic continuity in discourse, and which refer to acts prohibited to or obligatory for addressees, mention referents central to such acts, or give exemplars of the core arguments of understood social rules.

In her adult study Ervin-Tripp was able to specify some of the social-contextual parameters that appeared to guide the selection of particular forms. The parameters she lists are status relations in terms of both differential rank and familiarity, expectation of compliance and type of task.

A number of the questions which might be posed about children's movement towards adult usage can be given partial answers (Ervin-Tripp 1977). Carter (1978) listed eight gestural means of regulating the behaviour of adults, which later became linked to particular sounds. The gestures later became optional and the soundings began to approximate to conventionally acceptable linguistic forms (see Claim 1). Initially, words seemed to be used to name desired objects without specifying what was to be done with them; only later did the child's bases of directives appear. Before the age of 2 years, Bates' (1976) children had command of seven telegraphic verbal directive types: (1) vocatives with situational specification of desire; (2) rising intonation; (3) desire statements (more); (4) goal objects (more juice); (5) possessives (that mine); (6) imperatives (book read); (7) problem statements (Carol hungry). Failing directives tended to be repeated with rising pitch. Other studies help to chart the emergence of other forms and movements towards adult forms, and Garvey (1975) notes that by age 4 years children would try a variety of tactics and plan several utterances ahead to achieve their goals. Ervin-Tripp (1977) reports a study by Lawson claiming that a 2-year-old used predominantly simple imperatives to peers but desire statements, permission requests and questions to adults. At school she issued no imperatives to a 4-year-old, but to a 3-year-old she issued imperatives moderated with 'please' or 'OK?'. At home father received more repetition and politeness modifiers than mother. Other studies cited indicate that children through the ages 3, 4 and 5 are varying their directives as a function of hearer (age status, familiarity, kind of task problem). Stalder (in press) has shown children change forms within a continuing interaction.

Clearly there is no shortage of empirical or theoretical problems in this area. Even the basic forms show early differentiation, and their uses are linked to contextual variables. Moderation of forms by adding lexical markers of 'please', and no doubt nonverbal variability are also present. Very quickly the exposed systematic variation can challenge us to chart and explain its growth, but it also presents us with the question as to when we stop collecting data.

Ervin-Tripp cites evidence from Turkish, Hungarian, and Italian as well as American children. Do we need to study all other languages in all other cultures? Do we need to study all subcultural differences within any society? Do we need to study individual differences within subcultures? Clearly, for real children the specific details of the systems they are to experience are the most important ones. For developmental social psychologists such particulars are only of interest if they have to be explained in ways other than those currently extant.

## 4. Epilogue

Entrepreneurial social psychologists are free to peg mining rights over many of the areas discussed in this chapter, but they are advised to remember that, for some of these, other disciplines have already done much more than conduct exploratory surveys. A plea must be made for anticipating the dangers of naive presumptions of the ignorance of others. At least we can mitigate our errors by asking colleagues in other disciplines what we should read and experience before we start digging.

That said, we can see some achievements, some potential achievements and some large gaps in the field. Perhaps the most obvious gap in what has been discussed is our ignorance about children's progress in their mastery of conversation: which rules and principles they learn, in what order and how. Clearly the pre-linguistic interactions of caretaker–child–environment already display such characteristics as attention gaining, turn-taking, topic maintenance and topic switching, and the realization of these in speech may be mainly an orderly extension of already mastered actions. We shall have to be on our guard against endowing the child with skills that are apparent or artifactual rather than real. The coherence of conversation can be created mainly by the expertise of one of the participants. However, such modelling and controlling could of course provide useful data for children learning to move into more equal partnership. Regretfully, I observed nothing noteworthy in my own children's conversational development. Topics revolved around their worlds rather than mine, but initiation, tactical maintenance, and dissolution of conversations seemed not to have presented special observable learning problems for them. With the exception of taking too much for granted as shared knowledge, Gricean maxims of propriety also seemed to be observed by both children *ab initio*. (Perhaps the actions of these children only mark their subscription to a higher order maxim of not helping with parents' research work.)

Conversation also involves more specific proprieties, such as not butting-in, and some of these are perhaps likely to be announced by caretakers as rules to be followed. Harré (1979: 54) cites Clarke as finding that people can not only order, and achieve significant agreement in their ordering of, actual utterances, they can do likewise if supplied with just the names of acts of speech, e.g. Question–Answer; Compliment–Acknowledgement. As Harré points out, such people have coded social orderliness at the conversational level in a manner in which they probably could not code grammatical orderliness: they are behaviourally competent at both levels, they can articulate and label activities only at the level of discourse. This opens up numerous questions about the learning of the proprieties of conversation, indeed speech making in all its forms. At the present time we know nothing about the efficacy of the variety of approaches to teaching children how to be polite in conversation, for example. While there may be universal principles in politeness phenomena, the particular realizations in cultures are conventional inventions. A child can only discover the rules and the realizations in social activity; other people have to be the source of the information. Brown & Levinson (1978) offer a useful frame of reference for such developmental studies. We know nothing about the consequences of having a two-level representation of orderliness in conversation, or when and how it arises. Certainly it offers the possibility of dialectical relationships between surface realizations and the actions being undertaken. Children should be able to operate in Phase 2 of the model mentioned in Claim 8 earlier than they would if orderliness were not labelled.

Very early mother–child interaction has yielded much. The work has been marked by very painstaking and detailed analyses on the one hand and bold theorizing on the other, a healthy combination of alternately immersing oneself in the data hoping for inspiration, and prior conviction that certain relations will be there in the data if only one looks hard enough. Both natural and experimentally derived data are being exploited.

The conception of the mother as a conductor/player in a duet where the music is being generated by both players, and the score for future performances is being written as and after it is played, seems to capture much of the reality. Notes become arranged into phrases, phrases into melodies, the separate parts becoming articulated into music; but the analogy has to be with a jazz duo rather than with Mozart. The notion of movements that occur becoming actions becoming subsequently wilfully controlled acts is one crucial component of the thinking about development. The particular procedures and materials that would need to be chosen to facilitate these changes must be a joint function of individual learner and particular learning task. It follows that the more homogeneous the individuals in respect of entry characteristics, the more homogeneous the learning tasks, and the more heterogeneous the procedures used by 'teachers', the greater the probability that procedure–product relations can be discovered in correlational studies, and it is perhaps no accident that the sub-sampling techniques used by Ellis & Wells (1980), Cross (1978) and similar studies whose results were not described (e.g. Furrow, Nelson & Benedict 1979) yield the more readily interpretable results. It is perhaps also no surprise that the maternal strategies and tactics that emerge as being conducive to faster rates of development of language mastery in general, or to particular sub-systems within language, look to be consistent with those despised associative and/or modelling principles of learning, operated in combination with the erstwhile equally despised qualitative feedback principles. What may be different about the role of these principles in my attempt to make sense of what is happening, is that I do not locate these principles as S–R mechanisms inside the child's head but rather as environmentally situated contiguities that render the *data* to be programmed more clearly discriminable and manipulable by the information-processing capacities of the child. The child itself I see as a Piagetian child upgraded in terms of the Artificial Intelligence capacities mentioned by Boden (1979), fleshed out with feelings and motivation, and at the same time a socially being-constructed constellation.

Vygotsky (1962) suggested that 'what the child can do today in co-operation, tomorrow he will be able to do on his own'. This idea is apposite. It implies that some movements (including soundings) which occur in the flux of activity are selected for learning and development, most frequently perhaps on the initiative of the mother; they are transformed into actions that have utility and meaning. Essentially, they arise as joint products from the social nexus. Their development consists of their eventually becoming wilfully controlled acts. This complex notion of socially (publicly) situated movements that occur becoming privately and individually controllable acts seems to me to be a crucial advance on earlier thinking about mother–child interaction, and it invites comparison with the three-phase model for the development of understanding about ambiguity mentioned under Claim 8. (There are differences as well as similarities.)

Another important advance in this area is the notion of initial accretion and co-ordination within and across modalities being followed by subsequent dissociation. It should be noted that in these developments, A is not simply a template for reproducing more As; it serves as a temporary host for an initially parasitic B that then becomes symbiotic and may finally achieve independence, itself available as a potential host for further developments. Speech appears to exploit gesture in this manner. What is perhaps of especial interest to social psychologists is that A and B need not be actions of the same person. B can be a reaction of other to an A from ego arising out of coactive or cooperative activity.

While such ideas are based mainly on the studies of pre- and peri-linguistic children's interactions with their mothers, they have great potential for application to later developments. They are dramatically social to a degree that would have seemed strange only a few years ago.

Such ideas are consistent with the shift in views about language development emanating from linguistics. While in no way wishing to diminish the contributions of others, I think we can be grateful that a linguist with Halliday's interests and sympathies had a son when he did. *Learning how to mean* (1975) is embedded in sociology and anthropology to an extent that other descriptions of early language development are not. Alas that the social psychology perspective is not more prominent. Confined as it is to very early language development, his analysis is necessarily confined to public speech and hence does not extend to intra-individual dialogues and their relations to the development of communicative competence. Focused as it is on the child, it neglects both the activities of Hasan and Halliday senior, and the conversational competence of Nigel. What it does achieve is an elevation of the importance both of functions of speech and function–structure relations, and again the social origins and relevance of speech gain precedence over the non-social.

Once this kind of orientation is linked with developments of Searle's classification we are enabled to see the study of directives, commissives, expressives, and declaratives (as acts not forms) as being as necessary and desirable as the study of the development of the linguistic realizations of representatives. At least directives are being pursued, and no doubt the other three types are already the targets of some postgraduate research.

By comparison, the correlational approach to general linkages between maternal speech and child speech seems to be rather unexciting. Some of the studies convey an atmosphere of 'let's hope the computer outputs will make sense of the data', when the ways in which these might make sense have not been adequately thought through in advance and formulated as examinable hypotheses based on theories of development and learning. Theories of learning and instruction extant would all emphasize the character of the relationships between present level of belief and understanding of the individual learner and what is to be learned, as crucial to the probabilities of learning. By definition, learning is a process; it is dynamic. In a training study that examined children's realization that representational statements could be ambiguous, we found that reacting to ambiguous utterances from pre-understanding children with 'I don't know which one you mean. There are $n$ like that. You have not told me the $x$ or the $y$' led, in most cases, both to advances in understanding and to improvements in performance (Robinson & Robinson 1981). We would not pretend, however, that this somewhat cosy portrayal of learning is the whole story. It emphasizes assimilation rather than accommodation, the child processing and mastering readily assimilable data. Under what conditions do children accommodate and begin to engage in substantial reorganization of existing schemas?

We have yet to examine that problem in relation to message ambiguity, but in a succession of studies people in Geneva have taken up Piaget's idea of quarrelling among peers as a context for learning (see Doise & Mugny 1979; Perret-Clermont & Schubauer-Leoni 1981). They have shown that experimental arrangements that provoke socio-cognitive conflict enable *some* children to learn to achieve conservation of spatial relations and amount. Heber (1981) offers a consistent exemplification with seriation, which emphasizes the power of verbally-based dialectical confrontation as an impetus to learning. Valiant, Glachan & Emler (1982) found, in a replication of Genevan experiments, that only pairs which actually registered disagreement (in their case nonverbal) progress. While there must be limits as to which children can learn what exposed to what kind of confrontation, the principles seem to be clear. To parody Vygotsky, intra-mental conflicts arise out of inter-mental conflicts.

Perret-Clermont (1980) points out that models can be construed as offering views or behaviour that conflict with the child's views or behaviour, and hence can be assimilated by their socio-cognitive framework. This approach opens up a field to social psychology that has not been seen as within its provenance. Piaget's (1970) own predilection was for ideas of contradiction or disagreement to arise within the child from his individual interactions with the physical world. His model of equilibration through accommodation/assimilation requires the child to discover inconsistencies and to invent and test superordinate resolutions of these. That this can occur is true, but in real life it is perhaps more likely that the conflicts will arise from clashes between the child and other people.

Three main points can be made. First, socio-cognitive conflicts may often be verbally anchored. Second, what they are about may well concern how language works. Third, they are likely to promote understanding and not just modifications of or additions to behaviour.

There are good reasons why these ideas were not mentioned under the claims *per se*. One is that their relevance to the development of communicative competence with language has not been examined. Another is that the particular kinds of conflicts cited are predicated upon various presumptions, e.g. the child has already learned the idea that logical contradiction is unacceptable – a view from which very young children are spared. Hence their relevance to learning may come later rather than earlier. It remains to be seen what power the ideas have, but they are complementary to the Vygotsky claim about cooperation – what emerges in social conflict today, the child may be able to do on his own tomorrow.

Throughout the years focused upon here the child has been communicatively parasitic. It is older people, especially parents, who have made the effort. They have made the adjustments as both speakers and listeners. Their adjustments have meant that by the age of 5 or 6 years the child can have achieved considerable communicative competence with language, especially if reared by adults whose theories of language and child development approximate to reality and whose values encourage growth. Parents may reduce their willingness to make such adjustments, while younger children, peers and strangers will not be so 'accommodating' from the start, and as these people figure more saliently, so socio-cognitive conflicts and their resolution, as well as their cooperative complements, have a role to play in the later learning.

At this point in time it is impossible to assess which aspects of the development of communicative competence with language require substantial reorganizations of information-processing structures and which may involve simpler accretions of new units for enhancing the range of meanings that can be expressed and understood; this latter process involving steps of initial purchase, improving use refined through monitored feedback, and finally semi-automated use. In so far as much of the learning task involves no more and no less than the accumulation and integration of a very large number of units of nonverbal and verbal behaviour over an extended time period, we may not need to invoke more than modified and qualified associative principles of learning to explain their accumulation. However, we also need an understanding and active agent to process the data.

## References

Bates, E. 1976. *Language and context: the acquisition of pragmatics.* London: Academic Press.

Bates, E., Camaioni, L. & Volterra, V. 1975. The acquisition of performatives prior to speech. *Merrill Palmer Quarterly, 21*, 205–26.

Bloom, L. 1970. *Language development.* Cambridge, Mass.: MIT Press.

Boden, M. A. 1979. *Piaget.* Glasgow: Fontana.

Brazil, D. C. 1978. Discourse intonation 1. In R. M. Coulthard, J. McH. Sinclair & D. C. Brazil. Supplement to Final SSRC Report: *An investigation of discourse intonation.* London.

Brown, P. & Levinson, S. 1978. Universals in language usage: politeness phenomena. In E. N. Goody (ed.) *Questions and politeness.* Cambridge: Cambridge University Press.

Bullowa, M. (ed.) 1977. *Before speech: the beginnings of human communication.* Cambridge: Cambridge University Press.

Carter, A. L. 1978. The development of systematic vocalisations prior to words: a case study. In N. Waterson & C. Snow (eds.) (1978).

Chapman, A. J. & Jones, D. M. 1980. *Models of man.* Leicester: British Psychological Society.

Clarke, D. D. 1983. *The structural analysis of verbal interaction.* Oxford: Pergamon.

Coulthard, C. M. 1977. *Discourse analysis.* London: Longman.

Cross, T. G. 1978. Mothers' speech and its association with rate of linguistic development in young children. In N. Waterson & C. Snow (eds.) (1978).

Dean-Fodor, J. 1977. *Semantics.* Hassocks: Harvester Press.

Doise, W. & Mugny, G. 1979. Individual and collective conflicts of centration in cognitive development. *European Journal of Social Psychology, 9*, 105–8.

Ellis, R. & Wells, C. G. 1980. Enabling factors in adult–child discourse. *First Language, 1*, 46–62.

Ervin-Tripp, S. M. 1976. Is Sybil there? The structure of some American English directives. *Language in Society, 5*, 25–66.

1977. Wait for me, roller skate. In S. M. Ervin-Tripp & C. Mitchell-Kernan (1977).

Ervin-Tripp, S. M. & Mitchell-Kernan, C. 1977. *Child discourse.* New York: Academic Press.

Ferguson, C. A. 1964. Baby talk in six languages. *American Anthropologist, 66*, 103–14.

Furrow, D., Nelson, K. & Benedict, H. 1979. Mothers' speech to children and syntactic development. *Journal of Child Language, 6*, 423–42.

Garnica, O. K. 1977. Some prosodic and paralinguistic features of speech to young children. In C. E. Snow & C. A. Ferguson (eds.) (1977).

Garnica, O. K. & King, M. L. 1977. *Language, children and society.* Oxford: Pergamon Press.

Garvey, C. 1975. Request and responses in children's speech. *Journal of Child Language, 2*, 41–63.

Halliday, M. A. K. 1975. *Learning how to mean.* London: Arnold.

Harré, R. 1979. *Social being.* Oxford: Blackwell.

1981. *Social cognition.* Unpublished MS, Oxford.

Heber, M. 1981. Instruction versus conversation as opportunities for learning. In W. P. Robinson (ed.) *Communication in development.* London: Academic Press.

Lewis, M. & Rosenblum, L. A. (eds.) 1977. *Interaction, conversation and the development of language.* Chichester: Wiley.

Lock, A. (ed.) 1978. *Action, gesture and symbol: the emergence of language*. London: Academic Press.

1980. *The guided reinvention of language*. London: Academic Press.

Lyons, J. 1977. *Semantics*, vols I and II. Cambridge: Cambridge University Press.

Menyuk, P. & Bernholtz, N. 1967. Prosodic features and children's language production. *Quarterly Progress Report*, 93, MIT Research Laboratory of Electronics.

Nelson, K. E. & Bonvillian, J. O. 1978. Early language development: conceptual growth and related processes between 2 and 4½ years of age. In K. E. Nelson (ed.) *Children's language*, vol. 1. New York: Gardner Press.

Newport, E. L., Gleitman, H. & Gleitman, L. R. 1977. Mother, I'd rather do it myself. In C. E. Snow & C. A. Ferguson (eds.) (1977).

Ninio, A. & Bruner, J. S. 1978. Achievements and antecedents of labelling. *Journal of Child Language*, 5, 1–16.

Perret-Clermont, A.-N. 1980. *Social interaction and cognitive development in children*. London: Academic Press.

Perret-Clermont, A.-N. & Schubauer-Leoni, M.-L. 1981. Conflict and cooperation as opportunities for learning. In W. P. Robinson (ed.) *Communication in development*.

Piaget, J. 1970. Piaget's theory. In P. H. Mussen (ed.) *Carmichael's manual of child psychology*, 3rd edn. New York: Wiley.

Robinson, E. J. 1981. Conversational tactics and the advancement of the child's understanding about referential communication. In W. P. Robinson (ed.) *Communication in development*.

Robinson, E. J. & Robinson, W. P. 1981. Ways of reacting to communication failure in relation to the development of the child's understanding about verbal communication. *European Journal of Social Psychology*, 11, 189–208.

Robinson, W. P. 1972. *Language and social behaviour*. Harmondsworth: Penguin.

1978. *Language management in education: the Australian context*. Sydney: Allen and Unwin.

1981. Mothers' answers to children's questions: from socio-economic status to individual differences. In W. P. Robinson (ed.) *Communication in development*.

Ruder, K. & Bunce, B. 1973. Training suprasegmental features of speech: effects of memory load. Unpublished Working Paper, Bureau of Child Research Laboratories. Lawrence: University of Kansas.

Sachs, J. G., Brown, R. & Salerno, R. 1976. Adults' speech to children. In W. von Raffler-Engel & Y. Lebrun (eds.) *Baby talk and infant speech*. Lisse, The Netherlands: Swets and Zeitlinger.

Schaffer, H. R. 1977. *Studies in mother–infant interaction*. London: Academic Press.

Searle, J. 1969. *Speech acts: an essay in the philosophy of language*. Cambridge: Cambridge University Press.

1975. A classification of illocutionary acts. *Language in Society*, 5, 1–23.

Shatz, M. & Gelman, R. 1973. The development of communication skills. *Monographs of the Society for Research in Child Development*, 38, (152).

Shields, M. 1978. Some communicational skills of young children – a study of dialogue in the nursery school. In R. N. Campbell & P. T. Smith (eds.) *Recent advances in the psychology of language*. New York: Plenum Press.

Sinclair, J. Mc. & Coulthard, C. M. 1975. *Towards an analysis of discourse*. Oxford: Oxford University Press.

Snow, C. E. & Ferguson, C. A. (eds.) 1977. *Talking to children*. Cambridge: Cambridge University Press.

Stalder, J. in press. Effects of knowledge about the addressee on children's request behaviour.

Trevarthen, C. & Hubley, P. 1978. Secondary intersubjectivity: confidence, confiding, and acts of meaning in the first year. In A. Lock (ed.) (1978).

Valiant, G., Glachan, M. & Emler, N. 1982. The stimulation of cognitive development through cooperative task performance. *British Journal of Educational Psychology*, 52, 281–8.

Van Dijk, T. A. 1972. *Some aspects of text grammars*. The Hague: Mouton.

Vygotsky, L. A. 1962. *Thought and language*. New York: Wiley.

Waterson, N. & Snow, C. (eds.) 1978. *The development of communication*. Chichester: Wiley.

Wells, C. G. 1980. Adjustments in adult child conversations: some effects of interaction. In H. Giles, P. M. Smith & W. P. Robinson (eds.) *Language: social psychological perspectives*. Oxford: Pergamon.

1981. *Learning through interaction: the study of language development*. Cambridge: Cambridge University Press.

Wells, C. G. & Robinson, W. P. 1982. The role of adult speech in language development. In C. Fraser & K. Scherer (eds.) *Advances in the social psychology of language*. Cambridge: Cambridge University Press.

# 4. Learning: a social actualization and reconstruction of knowledge[1]

ANNE-NELLY PERRET-CLERMONT, JEAN BRUN, EL HADI SAADA

AND MARIA-LUISA SCHUBAUER-LEONI

## 1. Cognitive and psychosociological processes: difficulties in relating them

In psychological debates, the field is often divided by a border between what is deemed 'internal' and what 'external'. This division risks simplifying certain questions of research by placing researchers who have demonstrated the existence of individual processes (considered as 'unique to the subject') against those who have found evidence for social processes (so-called 'external determinants'). In order to situate the gist of this debate, as well as our object of study, we shall outline this dilemma.

For some, the individual is the primary object of study. He[2] is considered as having his proper identity, abstracted from its social context. He is the source of all his elaborations (especially cognitive), and the determinants of his behaviours are to be found in their biological origins and the individual's own experience. While allowing that social factors may have an influence, this perspective imbues them *only with the status of supplementary variables*, liable to affect individual behaviours yet not constitutive.

For others, the individual is but an element of a larger phenomenon: the social group. It is the group which gives meaning to the individual behaviour of its members by its collective representations, norms, roles and the structurations it imposes. While admitting inter-individual differences, the adherents to this perspective tend to consider them to be only the result of *statistical fluctuations* or part of the variance which remains to be explained by other social processes. The individual is the actor of 'external' determinants.

This sketch is perhaps something of a caricature but rarely is the individual considered *simultaneously* as being engaged in a psychological activity of

---

1 This chapter was written with the collaboration of Nancy Bell, François Conne and Michèle Grossen, and was translated from French by Nancy Bell.
2 For the sake of simplicity, we will consider the pronoun 'he' as generic.

construction of meanings *and* as a member of a social group which conveys models of comprehension.

In the domain of cognitive psychology, the subject's behaviour is most often examined in individual terms, despite the fact that the experimental paradigms used always stage[3] particular *social* situations with predetermined social agents. These elements are not considered as such in most of the theoretical conceptualizations referred to in cognitive psychology; however, several studies *have* shown the importance of these relational contexts. For example, Katz (1970, 1973) and Labov (1972) have both demonstrated that social characteristics of the interlocutor play an important role in the determination of the modalities and quality of the subject's performance. Rose & Blank (1974), and McGarrigle & Donaldson (1974) have demonstrated differences in the performances of the subjects, varying in function according to what could be interpreted as differences in the experimental 'scenarios'. Light, Buckingham & Robbins (1979) have also presented data illustrating similar context dependency of performances. These studies all show that evaluation of a subject's competences is dependent on, or affected by, the characteristics of the testing situation itself.

Examining the effect of adult counter-suggestions made to children during Piagetian clinical interviews, several experiments have shown that the simple fact of presenting an opposing point of view to the child is capable of inducing progress on operational tests (Lévy 1981; Mugny, Doise & Perret-Clermont 1975–6; Mugny, Lévy & Doise 1978). Researches concentrating on clinical descriptions of cognitive processes have sometimes incidentally described analogous phenomena (see, for example, Comiti *et al.* 1980). Similarly, Schaffer (1979), in his studies of mother–infant relations, has shown the extreme interdependence between the child's first interest in objects and the reactions of his mother in a given situation (see also this book, Chapter 2).

We have chosen these examples to call attention to the impossibility of describing and evaluating the cognitive competences of a subject without considering the social context which elicits their actualization. The failure to consider the social and the micro-social context of data collection leads to the construction of a *social abstraction of the individual* which attributes perceived differences in behaviours to individual characteristics, and which consequently neglects their social significance.

For those who are interested in education, in all of its complexity, it is useful to keep in mind that cognitive behaviours cannot be reduced to individual autonomous psychological processes. The individual is nourished by a culture

3 In using this term we are referring to Goffman's approach (1959) to the presentation of self.

and an education conveyed to him by the various social groups with which he identifies and must remain in communication. The subject is constantly solicited in his cognitive and emotional life by particular social demands inherent in the coexistence with others: conversations, interactions, exchanges, negotiations, etc. However it does not suffice simply to state that the individual is inserted in a field of social relations. The mechanisms and processes of these subject–environment exchanges must be specified. Studies whose methodology has been inspired by ethnology have evidenced the interplay between the structuration of the subject and the specific social and cultural demands of the context.

The observation of cognitive exchanges between dyads has shown that the development of communication and thinking obeys certain cultural rules which structure conversation (Cook-Gumperz & Gumperz 1982). Only by grasping the presiding cultural rules of these exchanges can the researcher understand their meaning.

Ervin-Tripp (1982) has observed, in her studies of the evolution of strategies of comprehension of others, that the implicit or declared intentions of others do not play a large role in the child's comprehension of the situation. His comprehension can only be explained by reference to the social experience that the child has acquired in his specific environment.

When psychology establishes developmental scales, or hierarchies of stages, for subjects of different social and cultural backgrounds without taking into account these rules which regulate social relations (including tester–testee relations) it inevitably unconsciously biases the evaluation of the behaviours of others.[4] One could well wonder if these biases are not always sociocentric, that is to say, biased in favour of the researcher or his own membership group.

We now know that it is impossible to render a test 'culture-free'. But the testing *situation* is itself also socially marked. The performances of the partners in this situation can not be understood independently of their social significance (Donaldson 1978). It is likewise evident that an analysis formulated uniquely in terms of social marking is not sufficient for an exhaustive explanation of individual performances. It is the interplay of these social processes with psychological ones which interests us.

We will therefore examine the contributions of recent studies which permit an articulation between these different levels of psychological and sociological

4 The existence of close correlations between cognitive performances and social or cultural origin has often been reported (see, for example, Bruner *et al.* 1966; Coll, Coll & Miras 1974; Dasen & Heron 1981; Doise & Mugny 1981a; Haroche & Pêcheux 1972; Perret-Clermont 1980; Perret-Clermont & Schubauer-Leoni 1981). But some such studies also report that the cognitive hierarchies observed are liable to change noticeably when the characteristics of the testing and/or educative situations change.

analysis. We will first centre our attention on the social conditions of the subject's elaboration of a particular type of competence, namely operatory notions (as Piaget defines them). We will then turn to educative situations: can the psychosocial processes described in explaining the acquisition of operational competence in laboratory-type settings aid the understanding of the socio-cognitive dynamic of the school-teaching setting, i.e. the conditions in which culturally constructed knowledge, mathematics for example, can be successfully transmitted to the individual?

To comprehend the dynamics of situations which elicit cognitive development of the participating subjects necessitates theoretical references besides those of the psychology of intelligence. We wish to link the necessary description of the processes of thinking to the relational processes which elicit them. This requires, beyond cognitive psychology, contributions from other disciplines, including social psychology, ethnology, sociology. It is therefore a question of finding the theoretical and experimental means to integrate the study of the 'internal' cognitive dynamic of the individual with that of the 'external' factors, such as social environment, task, etc., which affect it, remembering that the attribution-making individual always interprets these external factors, giving them particular meaning according to the context.

Our object of study is learning. But we postulate that learning does not take place in a social vacuum, nor does it happen in a cultural desert where all has to be re-invented by each individual. The context of cognitive development is marked institutionally, culturally, historically.

We are interested in learning as a *signifying* activity, not only for the researcher or teacher observing the pupil, but also for the learner himself in his search for mastery or comprehension. The different partners of the experimental or didactic situations may tend to attribute different meanings to these situations: the study of these 'misunderstandings' is an intrinsic part of our study. Rather than considering them as artifacts, we will examine by what 'art' shared social meanings are constructed.

## 2. The learning of operatory responses

**2.1. Learning to construct a response.** For many subjects, taking an operatory test is probably already, in itself, an occasion for learning. In the course of the experimenter's questioning the individual finds himself confronted with the need to understand the situation, to produce a behaviour and to formulate a response.

How are psychological and social processes articulated in learning phenomena which can be considered as the adoption or the elaboration by the subject of meanings and responses? We have described elsewhere (Perret-Clermont & Schubauer-Leoni 1981; Perret-Clermont *et al.* 1982) how such experiments, whose purpose was not to induce learning but to test subjects' competence levels, have nevertheless induced learning because of the psycho-social dynamic of the testing interaction. We would expect to find the same type of processes in experiments expressly designed to elicit learning or to observe development.

**2.2. Testing and learning situations.** In a given learning situation an individual constructs a response. In so far as this response is new, one can say that he 'learns' it. This learning was observed even when such was not the intention of the tester. It seems useful, however, to make a distinction between *testing situations* which are designed as such by the researcher (psychologist or teacher), who wishes to assess the subject's level of behaviour at a given moment, and *learning situations*, which are constructed in such a way as to give the subject temporal and relational space in which to explore reality, gather information and try out his behaviours and responses with the aim of attaining a superior state of knowledge.

Testing situations are marked by evaluative finality and the subject's responses are elaborated toward this end. We suggest that nearly all learning situations are likewise marked. In so far as all behaviour is, to a certain extent, a 'response', i.e. the result of an interaction with the social environment, it is clear that didactic situations can be considered as essentially analogous on many levels to testing situations. However, the social interactions which accompany didactic situations differ in significance and explicitness and vary in their relative importance.[5]

The tester guides the situation and expects acceptable responses in a relatively brief period of time. The eventual long-term learning consequences for the subject of the testing itself are neither investigated nor even considered by those desiring to establish a diagnosis. Yet with regard to research on learning, it is precisely these long-term effects which are expected and which will be evaluated, though sometimes without the subject being explicitly informed of the nature of these expected effects! This can be considered as another way of neglecting the role of the subject's activity in the construction of meanings.

Elsewhere we have discussed these distinctions in referring to individual situations (Perret-Clermont *et al.* 1982). Here we will consider the study of

---

5 It would be desirable to examine how subjects perceive testing and learning situations as a function of their past history, social interactions and experience: do they make such a distinction between the two contexts?

collective performances in order to illustrate these questions. Moscovici & Paicheler (1973), in their review of literature on the subject, have already shown that it is not possible to establish a superiority (or an inferiority) of collective performances *per se* with regard to individual performances. In fact, the quality of collective performances depends upon a number of processes, e.g. the relation of the communication network to the structure of the task, the existence of an isomorphism between social relations and exchange network, etc., which cannot always be optimized for greater group performance.

Studies of children's cognitive behaviours have shown that, according to the circumstances, collective performances can be more advanced, in the sense of being more logically structured, or can be equal or inferior to individual performances (often in the same experiment), depending on the experimental, psychological and sociological conditions of subject groups studied (see, e.g. Bearison 1981; Doise 1973; Doise, Mugny & Perret-Clermont 1975; Mugny & Doise 1979).

In two studies, Russell (1981a, b) has observed that performances of child dyads are not always superior to individual performance and that 'when dyadic superiority did result in these studies it was by virtue of the influence of one child's correct judgement'. Russell explains this by 'the notion that incorrectly judging children tend to adopt a correct partner's answer, rather than by the notion of socio-cognitive conflict' (Russell 1981b: 160). But how does the subject come to recognize the partner's answer as correct and to accept it? We suggest that 'conflict' should be taken in a larger sense than Russell's so as to include the simple confrontation of two distinct opinions.

Above all, these researches point to important questions: how do subjects function intellectually when they 'realize' their responses are incorrect, and how do they *validate* their intuitions? To speak of a 'correct' or 'incorrect' response presumes the existence of a norm of correctness: what are its criteria? How does the subject appropriate them? What material, cognitive or relational aspects of the situation does the subject take into account in order to respond 'logically' to the problem, i.e. 'logically' in the eyes of the psychologist?

Although Russell has not done so in the two experiments cited, it would be interesting to examine the important differences that can be said to exist between various situations of socio-cognitive conflict by studying their long-term cognitive *consequences* for the participants. What effect would a confrontation with a differing response have on another situation at a later time? For a number of epistemological and methodological reasons, it is neither pertinent nor possible to resolve the general question of the possible superiority of individual or collective situations with regard to the cognitive performances of participating subjects. On the contrary, an examination of the long-term effects of collective situations could prove to be particularly illuminating for the understanding of the dynamic of the cognitive processes which produce these observed performances. This is what we will now discuss.

**2.3. In what circumstances do collective situations have long-term consequences?** Simple co-presence or any form of work in small groups, e.g. dyads or trios, or large groups, e.g. teams or classes, represent, at least potentially, an occasion for social interaction. The possible modalities of collective work are numerous; one could even include in the definition of 'collective situations' those in which the presence of another is simply invoked. Yet, the precise cognitive repercussions of these collective situations on their participants have rarely been studied and they are likely to vary considerably. Here we will centre our attention on several experiments with children which have examined the possible effects of social interaction between two or three individuals on participants' performances on operatory tests.

Several of these studies have an explicit didactic purpose of eliciting learning, while others aim to observe a development. But they are all characterized by the fact that they are concerned with 'closed' problems, i.e. problems to which the experimenter holds the 'correct' solution (in terms of logical norms), and not 'open-ended' problems (such as those investigated by scientific researchers and described by Latour & Woolgar 1979).

These studies have diverse theoretical references as well as differing experimental procedures; some are concerned with group work, others consider more limited examples of social interaction, such as a simple confrontation with a model. The results of several of these studies are interpreted by their authors in terms of social learning theories (Bandura 1971; Rosenthal & Zimmerman 1978). Extending the hypotheses advanced by Smedslund (1966) and others about the social origin of decentration, other authors (Doise & Mugny 1981a; Doise, Mugny & Perret-Clermont 1975; Perret-Clermont 1980; Perret-Clermont & Schubauer-Leoni 1981), in dealing with analogous experimental situations, claim that they observe more general processes: not mere imitation and transmission of behaviour models, but the social construction or reconstruction of meaning.

In experiments using a three-step paradigm (i.e. a collective situation with an individual pre- and post-test) it has been repeatedly observed that situations where individuals must co-ordinate their actions with one another lead them to produce new cognitive co-ordinations of higher competence.

Subsequent individual performances demonstrate that these collectively attained competences are consequently interiorized by the actors.

Analogous results have been attained using different tasks: a judgment of conservation of quantity, spatial representation, inter-dependent motor activity, replication of geometric designs (Doise & Mugny 1981a; Perret-Clermont 1980) and mathematical formulations (Schubauer-Leoni & Perret-Clermont 1980). Other authors present similar results regarding these same operatory skills (Mackie 1980; Rijsman *et al.* 1980) or in regard to other mental operations, such as the evolution of the representation of distance (Frésard 1980), the structure of moral argumentation in adolescents (Bourquin 1981), the 'Hanoi Tower' game (Glachan & Light 1981) and exercises of cross-classification (Valiant, Glachan & Emler 1982).

Most of these experiments report some generalization of learning: the subjects exhibit newly acquired behaviours on tasks other than the specific learning one, and in some cases they produce arguments which can be considered as evidence of a deep understanding, going beyond simple memorization or habit.

In one of the experiments cited above (Perret-Clermont & Schubauer-Leoni 1981), we tried to consider not only the generalization of learning to other *tasks* but also to other *social settings* or experimental scenarios. Two types of social interaction between children of socially disadvantaged backgrounds were examined. In one experimental condition, the non-conserving child was instructed to divide the juice equally between himself and a conserving peer. In the other condition, the non-conserving child was confronted by a conserving adult model whose behaviour was matched to the conserving child in the first condition except that he was presented as a model. These confrontations resulted in learning for both groups of subjects. However, the children performed on a more advanced cognitive level on the pre-test if they were in a situation of sharing with an adult, rather than in an analogous one using dolls. On the post-test, these differences disappeared for those subjects in the experimental peer condition but not for those of the modelling condition. Thus it seems that the learning situation invoked by peer confrontation is more liable than a modelling situation to produce behaviours which can be generalized to different socially marked situations. Is this difference between peer interaction and modelling a general one, i.e., is the explanation to be found in the nature of the subject's social relations with the model or the peer? This is, in any event, what was observed for this operatory activity, at this specific developmental level, in these circumstances with subjects from socially disadvantaged backgrounds.

Situations which are identical in the eyes of the experimenter can, in fact, have different consequences for participants. These consequences can be, at least partially, predicted by variables such as age, previous operatory level, socio-professional category of parents, sex (Doise & Mugny 1981a; Perret-Clermont 1980), place of habitation (Frésard 1980). But the causes of the influence of such variables remain to be explained. It should be noted that 'previous experience' of the subject refers not only to what he has experienced and elaborated outside the experimental situation but also to the experience accumulated during the experiment itself.

As reported above, it makes a difference whether the subject is confronted by an adult model to imitate rather than by a peer with whom he must actively seek an agreement. We have also observed that the latter experience permits children from socially disadvantaged backgrounds to bridge the gap between their operatory performances and those of peers from advantaged backgrounds. The social experience offered by the experiment leads them to perform as well as the others. Heber (1977, 1981), in her studies of conversational interactions, has suggested that 'perhaps talking to another person produces interactive influences which have less to do with semantics and grammar of the utterances than with learning to appreciate a problem from the standpoint of another' (1981: 185). She likewise finds that adequate learning conditions can eradicate observed differences between children of differing social backgrounds.

The antecedent experience of the subject, as well as that accumulated during experimental social interactions, are thus likely to play a major role in the subject's elaboration of his cognitive behaviour. These experiences could be said to shape the manner in which the subject interprets the situation, evaluates the social relations in which he is involved, and engages himself in abstract cognitive activity. In several studies we have therefore varied the experimental conditions with regard to the social regulation of the relations between partners in order to observe their specific learning consequences.

Perret-Clermont (1980) found it necessary to constitute groups of subjects which were homogeneous with regard to school grade, so that children would consider themselves equals and therefore would not escape from conversing with their partners by using 'excuses' such as '...he's too young, he cannot understand!' Finn (1975), cited by Doise et al. (1981), who replicated and confirmed Finn's results, obtained superior operatory performances when subjects had to share lemonade after invoking the right to equal recompense for equal work. Doise & Mugny (1981b) have conducted several experiments in which they explore further the influence of group work on learning.

But here again it is not possible to define 'objectively' the social characteristics of situations. They are always marked by the subjectivity of the individual who perceives and interprets them. Another field of investigation, therefore, would be to identify under which conditions, cognitive, social, material and historical, characteristics of a situation are perceived as demanding a resolution. Pertaining to our study, we can ask ourselves in which circumstances and by what procedures can an individual be led to believe that a conflict has just such a 'rational' solution.

Lévy (1981) has studied the effect of adult questioning on the reasoning of the child. She has shown that the simple questioning of the subject's responses, even if it does not confer any explanatory or correct information, can trigger a re-structuration of his thinking in the direction of greater precision. However, this questioning loses its effect if, for social reasons, the adult seems aberrant to the child. It would be interesting to extend this experiment, using other conflicting tasks with a number of possible outcomes other than 'rational' elaboration. We know that all social interactions do not necessarily produce more rationality. Yet it would be illuminating to be able to specify in what circumstances so-called 'logical' reasoning is elaborated. This could be done by varying different types of tasks and scenarios as well as the relational and sociological positions of partners.

These experimental studies on operational thinking, although admittedly limited to occidental children in school situations, can clarify certain aspects of the dynamic of cognitive activity, at least in a Western cultural environment. It seems evident now that it is not sufficient to separate the cognitive and social origins of these behaviours. They are interdependent, and we have attempted to illustrate that an interactionist and constructivist approach can be appropriate to the understanding of the observed facts.

If we now consider the field of education, we can ask what can be ascertained from the processes that we have observed and described above, regarding the chances of realizing *didactic intentions* in this same socio-cultural context?

## 3. Mathematics in didactic situations[6]

**3.1 Mathematics and operatory notions.** In the preceding part of this chapter, we tried to show how, in every test or learning situation, the subject's responses depend upon his interpretation of others' expectations of him. It is identical for pedagogical situations, where learning can only occur if the pupil has understood what he is supposed to do or know. The pupil's attempts

6 The research on didactic situations which is presented here was supported by project no. 1.706.078 from the Fonds National Suisse pour la Recherche Scientifique.

to understand the questions posed by the experimenter or teacher are often undertaken in an active and conscious manner: one can observe him trying out his responses, modifying and validating them. But sometimes the interpretation of a situation imposes itself initially without a conscious effort on the part of the subject. This would imply a simple transfer, using salient analogies between the new situation and others that the subject has previously experienced. This generalization of behaviours can be facilitating at times and at others the source of error. It is always the subject's representation of the learning situation constructed in the framework of the 'intersubjectivity' established between participants which is the base upon which the dialogue and performances are elaborated (Rommetveit 1976, 1978).

The question which therefore interests us, and seems to be particularly appropriate for opening up a wide field of specifically pedagogical inquiry, is the following: how could one explicitly create 'didactic' situations (Brun 1981), constructed in such a way that when the child seeks to understand and to respond to what is expected of him he will already be led *by this very activity* to elaborate cognitions we want him to acquire?

We have seen that the subject's capacity to actualize a competence is not independent of the social and cultural situation in which he must perform. Although these competences assuredly have a certain generality, it would be unrealistic to consider them as abstractions independent of the contexts in which they function. For example, examining the existence of *décalage* (pertaining to the notional content, the task, the relational context, the circumstances, etc.) illustrates the limits of such an abstraction.

Most of the studies that we have reported up to this point have been concerned with *operatory notions* in a Piagetian sense. If we now turn to more complex and more culturally marked notions, such as those found in primary school mathematics, we would expect to find that mathematical learning is also (and perhaps even more) dependent upon the situations and circumstances in which it is engendered.

On a paper-and-pencil test presented in class, most of the 7-year-old pupils tested showed a mastery of mathematical skill previously taught, i.e. the solving (filling) of lacunary equations (for example: $5 + \ldots = 8$). They seemed accustomed to this kind of task. However, when asked outside the class to write similar additive problems in another context (using bouquets of flowers, or trays of sweets) almost all the children failed to demonstrate any transfer of this previously acquired knowledge (Schubauer-Leoni & Perret-Clermont 1980).

In order to construct social situations where pupils are led to develop mathematical competences generalizable to other important contexts, it is thus necessary to understand the dynamic of thought, and its cognitive and social complexity, in the particularity of tasks, relationships and circumstances. The simple apprehension of the subject's operatory structures is not sufficient for the inference of his mathematical competences. It is necessary to distinguish the teacher's, or mathematician's, interpretation of the task from the interpretation developed by the learner through his attempts to respond.

We have examined these points in more detail elsewhere (Perret-Clermont *et al.* 1981, 1982). Mathematical knowledge and the operatory structure of logical thinking are not directly interdependent as the existence of *'décalage'* suggests (Brun 1975; Brun & Conne 1979; Schubauer-Leoni & Perret-Clermont 1980; Vergnaud 1981). An adequate curriculum cannot be 'inferred' from stages of cognitive development. Neither mathematical operations, nor the writing of mathematical operations, should be confused with operatory notions: they are distinct skills and competences. They cannot easily be hierarchized on the same developmental scale (Brun & Schubauer-Leoni 1981).

**3.2. Didactic situations.** A didactic situation can be characterized as an encounter in a particular school setting between a learner and a teacher who carries a message or intention concerning the learner. This modality of social interaction, with its cognitive, social and material characteristics, is in turn inscribed in a larger institutional context – i.e. the school – by which society constructs, reproduces and transforms itself.

However, the activity which the subject displays in the learning situation is not necessarily a direct reflection of the properties of this situation. It is therefore interesting to describe the progressive evolution of the strategies and procedures adopted by the subject within the constraints of the task. The teacher can vary these constraints and attempt to relate them to the representations of the situation actively formulated by the subject. In doing so, he also has the means to observe repercussions of his own interventions and of the task's constraints. The teacher is always engaging in social interaction with the pupil. Under which circumstances is this interaction the source of progress for the child? The causality is never direct. It depends on the child's previous learning and experience, his interpretation of the situation and its demands, his abilities to draw correct analogies between previously acquired mathematical knowledge and the requirements of the present task, and his awareness of the success or failure of the problem-solving strategies and generalizations that he develops. But all these activities are themselves likely to be markedly affected by social circumstances in ways that remain to be studied.

On this subject see, for example, Brousseau (1978a, b) who examines how circumstances create opportunities for the subject to reconstruct pre-existing knowledge or to transform his understanding of a notion. Balacheff (1981) has observed how peer group interactions between secondary school pupils on mathematical problems, affect their production of proofs. It might be noted that a mathematical procedure is not always immediately adopted by the child and is likely to appear only much later in his responses. It seems as though the meaning of this procedure is only slowly reconstructed by the pupil via a multiplicity of experiences. The question remains as to the circumstances in which pupils perceive a problem as belonging to the field of mathematics, and hence as deserving a 'mathematical solution', rather than as being, for instance, a social issue (Cavicchi-Broquet & Florimond 1981).

The didactic situations presented to pupils are culturally marked and will be understood by them as a function of their previous school and social experience. Mathematics has particularly powerful social connotations, especially in the school context; it holds an important place in education today, as indicated by the amount and duration of instruction given. Moreover, it often plays a primary role in the processes of school selection.

## 4. Conclusion

We have tried to show, firstly that social interactions and their cultural contexts play an essential role in the elaboration of thinking and, secondly, that the subject himself is actively implicated in the acquisition of his instruments of comprehension. The child's activity is essential to his cognitive development; however, this activity is in constant interplay with the activity of others. The individual is, as it were, the 'co-author' of the development of his intelligence. His partners are the persons, adults or children, with whom he interacts. He also inherits pre-constructed systems of meaning (symbolic systems, structured by social norms, elements of established or informal knowledge, etc.) which he must appropriate, i.e. reconstruct, in order to be able to use them.

From the studies examined here, it is evident that the learner cannot be considered as a simple receiver of the knowledge that one seeks to transmit to him. He appears to be actively engaged in an activity which is neither a total creation nor a simple assimilation, but rather an appropriation of knowledge, in a dynamic which can be described in terms of construction and interaction. This knowledge is either the result of a cultural production historically antecedent to the psychological development of the individual in question, or the *hic et nunc* fruit of a continuous collective elaboration in which he takes part.

We think it important to go beyond the simple observation of *signs* of a competence, e.g. operatory competence, to re-situate them in the context of their elaboration in order to determine their dynamic.

When these signs are considered *in abstracto*, i.e. abstracted from the situational conditions in which they appear, they can only be interpreted as fundamental characteristics of the individual. In fact they are the fruit of a social, psychological and cultural dynamic. The individual manifestation of competences (operatory levels, strategies of problem resolution, reasoning) can be understood as active *responses* of an individual who, with others, interprets the demands of the situation and attributes meaning to his behaviour (not always consciously, of course) as a function of his personal history and the specific circumstances in which he finds himself. It is certain that the individual is not always actively involved in generating meaning. However, we have limited our present investigation to what could be called the 'creative side' of thinking. The 'orthodox side' remains to be explored. This could be done using the theory elaborated by Deconchy (1980) on the social regulation of thinking (see also Chapter 21).

Since our preoccupation is with the relevance of these studies for pedagogical practice, we do not seek a 'total' explanation. Reality is always more complex than experimental schemas. We see our experiments rather as a means of analysing our own representations of learning processes in order to test them, that is, to elaborate, validate or refute them according to the particularity of the context studied. In some ways, our research process is analogous to the processes we have observed during subjects' activity of learning.

### References

Balacheff, N. 1981. Étude de l'élaboration d'explications par des élèves de Troisième à propos d'un problème combinatoire. Report on research to Laboratoire d'Informatique et de Mathématiques Appliquées, University of Grenoble, April.

Bandura, A. 1971. *Social learning theory.* New York: General Learning Press.

Bearison, D. J. 1981. New directions in studies of social interaction and cognitive growth. In F. Serafica (ed.) *Social cognition, context and social behavior: a developmental perspective.* New York: Guilford Press.

Bourquin, J. F. 1981. Le rôle de la télévision dans le processus de la socialisation. Unpublished doctoral thesis. École des Hautes Études en Sciences Sociales, Paris.

Brousseau, G. 1978a. L'observation des activités didactiques. *Enseignement élémentaire des mathématiques.* IREM de Bordeaux, *18*, 22–43.

1978b. Les obstacles épistémologiques et les problèmes mathématiques. *Cahier de l'IREM de Bordeaux, 18.*

Brun, J. 1975. Education mathématique et développement intellectual. Unpublished doctoral thesis. University of Lyon II.

1981. A propos de la didactique des mathématiques. *Math-école, 100/101.*

Brun, J. & Conne, F. 1979. Approches en psychopédagogie des mathématiques. *Cahiers de la Section des Sciences de l'Education, Université de Genève, 12.*

Brun, J. & Schubauer-Leoni, M.-L. 1981. Recherches sur l'activité de codage d'opérations additives en situations d'interaction sociale et de communication. IMAG, University of Grenoble, March.

Bruner, J. S., Olver, R. R., Greenfield, P. M., *et al.* 1966. *Studies in cognitive growth.* New York: Wiley.

Cavicchi-Broquet, I. & Florimond, M. 1981. Étude empirique du rôle des représentations sociale qu'évoque un problème sur le raisonnement logico-mathématique d'adolescents. In A.-N. Perret-Clermont (ed.) Objectivité et subjectivité dans les processus pédagogiques. *Cahiers de la section des sciences de l'éducation, Université de Genève,* 22, 93–113.

Coll Salvador, C., Coll Ventura, C. & Miras Mestres, M. 1974. Genesis de la clasificación y medio socio economico. Genesis de la seriacion y medios socio economicos. *Anuario de Psicologia.* Department of Psychology, University of Barcelona, 10, 53–99.

Comiti, C., Bessot, A., Pariselle, C. *et al.* 1980. Appropriation de la notion de nombre naturel. IMAG, University of Grenoble.

Cook-Gumperz, J. & Gumperz, J. 1982. Communicative competence in educational perspective. In L. C. Wilkinson (ed.) *Communication in the classroom.* New York: Academic Press.

Dasen, P. & Heron, A. 1981. Cross-cultural tests of Piaget's theory. In C. Triandis & A. Heron (eds.) *Handbook of cross-cultural psychology,* vol. 4. Boston: Allyn and Bacon.

Deconchy, J. P. 1980. (*Religious*) *orthodoxy, rationality and scientific knowledge.* The Hague: Mouton.

Doise, W. 1973. La structuration cognitive des décisions intellectuelles et collectives d'adultes et d'enfants. *Revue de Psychologie et des Sciences de l'éducation,* 8, 133–48.

Doise, W. & Mugny, G. 1981a. *Le développement social de l'intelligence.* Paris: Interéditions.

1981b. Le marquage social dans le développement cognitif. Paper presented to the conference 'Représentations sociales et champ éducatif', Laboratoire Européen de Psychologie Sociale, Aix-en-Provence, November–December.

Doise, W., Mugny, G. & Perret-Clermont, A-N. 1975. Social interaction and the development of cognitive operations. *European Journal of Social Psychology,* 5, 367–83.

Doise, W., Rijsman, J. B. Van Meel, J., Bressers, I. & Pinxten, L. 1981. Sociale markering en cognitieve ontwikkeling. *Pedagogisch Studien,* 58, 241–8.

Donaldson, M. 1978. *Children's minds.* Glasgow: Fontana/Collins.

Ervin-Tripp, S. 1982. Structures of control. In L. C. Wilkinson (ed.) *Communication in the classroom.*

Finn, G. 1975. The child's conservation of liquid quantity and its embedding in the social world. Unpublished MS, Department of Psychology, Jordanhill College of Education, Glasgow.

Frésard, M. D. 1980. La représentation de l'éloignement dans des dessins individuels et collectifs d'enfants de neuf à douze ans. Unpublished doctoral thesis, University of Geneva.

Glachan, M. & Light, P. 1981. Peer interaction and learning: can two wrongs make a right? In G. E. Butterworth & P. Light (eds.) *Social cognition: studies in the development of understanding.* Hassocks: Harvester Press.

Goffman, E. 1959/76. *The presentation of self in everyday life.* New York: Doubleday Anchor, 1959; Harmondsworth: Penguin, 1976 edn.

Haroche, C. & Pêcheux, M. 1972. Facteurs socio-économiques et résolution de problèmes. *Bulletin du CERP*, 21, 101–11.

Heber, M. 1977. The influence of language training on seriation of 5–6-year-old children initially at different levels of descriptive competence. *British Journal of Psychology*, 68, 85–95.

1981. Instruction versus conversation as opportunities for learning. In W. P. Robinson (ed.) *Communication in development*. London: Academic Press.

Katz, I. 1970. Experiments on Negro performance in bi-racial situations. In M. W. Miles & W. W. Charters (eds.) *Learning in social settings*. Boston: Allyn and Bacon.

1973. Negro performance in interracial situations. In P. Watson (ed.) *Psychology and race*. Harmondsworth: Penguin.

Labov, W. 1972. The study of language in its social context. In P. P. Giglioli (ed.) *Language and social context*. Harmondsworth: Penguin.

Latour, B. & Woolgar, S. 1979. *Laboratory life: the social construction of scientific facts*. London: Sage.

Lévy, M. 1981. La nécessité sociale de dépasser une situation conflictuelle générée par la présentation d'un modèle de solution de problème et par le questionnement d'un agent social. Unpublished doctoral thesis, University of Geneva.

Light, P. H., Buckingham, N. & Robbins, A. H. 1979. The conversation task as an interactional setting. *British Journal of Educational Psychology*, 49, 304–10.

Mackie, D. 1980. A cross-cultural study of intra-individual and inter-individual conflicts of centration, *European Journal of Social Psychology*, 10, 313–18.

McGarrigle, J. & Donaldson, M. 1974. Conservation accidents. *Cognition*, 3, 341–50.

Moscovici, S. & Paicheler, G. 1973. Travail, individu et groupe. In S. Moscovici (ed.) *Introduction à la psychologie sociale*, Vol. II. Paris: Larousse.

Mugny, G. & Doise, W. 1979. Factores sociologicos y psicosociologicos en el desarrollo cognitiva: una nueva ilustración experimental. *Anuario de Psicologia*, 21, 5–25.

Mugny, G., Doise, W. & Perret-Clermont, A.-N. 1975–6. Conflit de centrations et progrès cognitif. *Bulletin de Psychologie*, 29, 199–204.

Mugny, G., Lévy, M. & Doise, W. 1978. Conflit socio-cognitif et développement cognitif. *Revue suisse de psychologie pure et appliquée*, 37, 22–43.

Perret-Clermont, A.-N. 1980. *Social interaction and cognitive development in children*. London: Academic Press.

Perret-Clermont, A.-N. & Schubauer-Leoni, M.-L. 1981. Conflict and cooperation as opportunities for learning. In W. P. Robinson (ed.) *Communication in development*.

Perret-Clermont, A.-N., Brun, J., Conne, F. & Schubauer-Leoni, M.-L. 1981. Décontextualisation et recontextualisation du savoir dans l'enseignement des mathématiques à des jeunes élèves. Paper presented to the Colloque du Laboratoire Européen du Psychologie Sociale 'Représentations sociales et champ éducatif'. Aix-en-Provence, November–December.

Perret-Clermont, A.-N., Brun, J., Saada, E. H. & Schubauer-Leoni, M.-L. 1982. Processus psychosociologiques, niveau operatoire et appropriations de connaissances. *Interactions Didactiques*, 2, University of Geneva and University of Neuchâtel.

Rijsman, J.-B., Zoetebier, J.-H. Th., Ginther, A. Jf. & Doise, W. 1980. Sociocognitief conflict en cognitieve ontwikkeling. *Pedagogische Studiën*, 57, 125–33.

Rommetveit, R. 1976. On the architecture of intersubjectivity. In L. Strickland *et al.* (eds.) *Social psychology in transition*. New York: Plenum Press.

68   A.-N. Perret-Clermont, J. Brun, El H. Saada & M.-L. Schubauer-Leoni

1978. On piagetian cognitive operations, semantic competence, and message structure in adult–child communication. In I. Markowa (ed.) *The social context of language*. London: Wiley.

Rose, S. A. & Blank, M. 1974. The potency of context in children's cognition: an illustration from conservation. *Child Development, 45,* 499–502.

Rosenthal, T. & Zimmerman, B. 1978. *Social learning and cognition*. New York: Academic Press.

Russell, J. 1981a. Dyadic interaction in a logical reasoning problem requiring inclusion ability. *Child Development, 52.*

1981b. Why socio-cognitive conflict may be impossible: the status of egocentric errors in the dyadic performance of a special task. *Educational Psychology, 1, 2.*

Schaffer, H. R. 1979. Acquiring the concept of the dialogue. In M. Bornstein & W. Kessen (eds.) *Psychological growth from infancy*. New York: Erlbaum.

Schubauer-Leoni, M.-L. & Perret-Clermont, A.-N. 1980. Interactions sociales et représentations symboliques dans le cadre de problèmes additifs. *Recherches en didactique des mathématiques, 1,* (3), 297–343.

Smedslund, J. 1966. Les origines sociales de la décentration. In F. Bresson & M. de Montmollin (eds.) *Psychologie et épistémologie génétique. Thèmes Piagétiens.* Paris: Dunod.

Valiant, G., Glachan, N. & Emler, N. 1982. The stimulation of cognitive development through cooperative task performance. *British Journal of Educational Psychology, 52,* 281–8.

Vergnaud, G. 1981. *L'enfant, la mathématique et la réalité.* Collection Exploration, Berne: P. Lang.

# 5. The development of thinking about socio-economic systems

GUSTAV JAHODA

Mais, quand il s'agit de faire la dame âgée et respectable, préposée a la caisse, je me trouvai soudain embarrassé. En cette conjecture, je sortis du magasin et allai demander à ma chère maman un éclaircissement sur le point qui restait obscur pour moi. J'avais bien vu la dame âgée ouvrir son tiroir et remuer des pièces d'or et d'argent; mais je ne me faisais pas une idée suffisament exacte des opérations qu'elle effectuait. Agenouillé aux pieds de ma chère maman qui, dans sa bergère brodait un mouchoir, je lui demandai: – Maman, dans les magasins, est-ce celui qui vend ou celui qui achète, qui donne de l'argent? (Anatole France, *Le petit Pierre*)

What has come to be known as 'social cognition' is a broad and somewhat ill-defined field which may be regarded as having originated in its modern form with the publication in 1932 of Piaget's book on *The moral judgement of the child*. What was new about Piaget's approach was not the topic, on which there have been numerous descriptive studies before and since, but his attempt to establish certain principles underlying the development of children's ideas about moral behaviour. In the most direct line of descent from this tradition is the work of Kohlberg (e.g. 1976), which has recently been subjected to a penetrating critical scrutiny on this side of the Atlantic (Eckensberger & Silbereisen 1980). Generally, the problem of moral development is probably the most intensively researched aspect of social cognition, and has also been studied cross-culturally (Edwards 1981).

A somewhat different aspect of social cognition that has become an important focus of interest during the 1970s and 1980s concerns the growth of children's understanding of personal relationships, the rules governing these, and the acquisition of active skills, such as role-taking, that require insight into the needs of 'the other' (Damon 1977, 1978; Flavell & Ross 1981; Glick & Clarke-Stewart 1978; Youniss 1980). Since children interact from birth onwards with other people of varying ages, the development of moral ideas, of social conventions and such-like may be regarded as being closely tied to, and largely arising from, first-hand experience (see Chapter 2).

The situation is not the same as far as the development of concepts relating to the wider society are concerned. The child only has peripheral contact with it, and is therefore dependent on bits of initially unconnected information filtering through such sources as adult conversation and the media. Curiously enough, there appears to be very little formal teaching about society at large, either at home or in school. The reason is probably that adults, and also older children, take certain things so much for granted that they cannot imagine anybody being ignorant of them. Hence, in such spheres children are mostly dependent on their own intellectual resources and have to construct for themselves progressive approximations to a working model of the wider society.

The aspect of society that has been most frequently studied in relation to children's thinking, more often by political scientists than psychologists, is government; accordingly, it is frequently known as 'political socialization' (Stacey 1978). The development of ideas about the functioning of economic institutions, which is the theme of the present chapter, has received rather less attention. There have been a number of studies concerned with economic relationships, and especially money (Danziger 1958; Strauss 1952; Sutton 1962); these have on the whole been not merely confined to descriptions, but have left out of account the systems character of economic institutions. An important new departure was the work of Furth (Furth 1980; Furth, Bauer & Smith 1976), who operates within a modified Piagetian theoretical framework, which will be considered in due course. Furth collected his material by giving children free rein to talk about social institutions, merely interspersing appropriate questions to ascertain the level of thinking. For example, one general question was 'What things, jobs, people are important in a town?' (1980: 17). This yielded a rich and varied set of materials that are delightful to read. The drawback, however, is that such data are difficult to analyse and the lack of uniformity in the context of the responses means that comparisons across either subjects or topics are often hazardous. In order to avoid these problems, my own methods were more narrowly focused and structured. Nonetheless, insofar as they overlap, the findings were broadly similar to those obtained by Furth.

The two economic institutions to be discussed here are the shop and the bank, though brief reference will be made to other issues and some of the theoretical implications examined.

## 1. The shop

If one stops to think about it, or better still attempts a systematic representation of the kind shown in figure 1, it will become evident that the apparent simplicity of the shop as an economic system is delusive. It should be noted

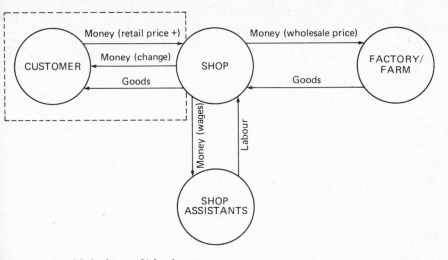

Figure 1. Simplified schema of 'shop' system

that a number of things have been omitted from the figure, for example, overhead costs such as rent, the existence of middlemen, the relationship between the shop and the bank, and so on. Even with these omissions, the overall shop system represented in figure 1 can be seen as consisting of three distinct sub-systems, namely (a) customer–shop (retail sale); (b) shop–supplier (wholesale purchase); and (c) shop–sales staff (wage system). Now it is important to realize that only the first of these sub-systems contained within the dotted rectangle in figure 1 becomes wholly visible to a child who goes to a shop. Moreover, for a young child whose grasp of monetary values is still shaky, even this seemingly elementary transaction contains an ambiguity. This arises from the fact that change is frequently given, which confused Pierre in the epigraph at the head of this chapter; and he was in this respect typical. There is also the fact that money as a generalized medium of exchange is a sophisticated notion – after all, the mysteries and paradoxes of money have puzzled wise men from Aristotle onwards, and in some of its aspects still puzzle contemporary economists and politicians? It should therefore be clear that there are several reasons why children initially find it hard to understand what happens in a shop. The broad sequence of development, based on studies with Scottish children,[1] will now be outlined. Children's modes of thinking will be illustrated by extracts from the interview material, though it should be mentioned that this was not the only source of data.

1 The original report (Jahoda 1979), which also contains details of methods, was based on research done with working-class children; subsequent studies with Scottish middle-class, and Dutch children of varying socio-economic status yielded essentially the same patterns (Jahoda & Woerdenbagch 1982).

Many of the youngest children, aged about 6 years, lack, like Pierre, any conception of the fact that the transactions taking place in the shop form part of a system. They seem to be viewed as game-like ritual actions serving no purpose beyond themselves. Here is an example from a 6-year-old:

I:  What do you do when you buy something?
S:  Give the shoplady the money.
I:  What does she do with it?
S:  Gives the money back.
I:  Is it the same money?
S:  Yes.
I:  Can you tell more about this?
S:  The people pays her, she pays the people.
I:  Where does the milk in the shop come from?
S:  Cows – the man brings it.
I:  Does the lady have to pay for the milk?
S:  The lady pays the man and the man pays the lady because he gives her milk.

This child was somewhat unusual among the younger ones in thinking that money changed hands when goods came into the shop. Most commonly the idea was that goods are simply given to the shop when asked for. Moreover, many of the youngest children did not regard selling as a job, so that the question as to how shop assistants could be paid did not even arise. This does not imply that young children are completely unaware of the link between doing a job and getting money. It is an issue on which most children are likely to overhear adult conversation, and it is thus not surprising that such knowledge appears to be acquired rather early (Berti & Bombi 1979); however, at first it appears to be a kind of general formula that may or may not be applied to specific cases, depending on whether a particular activity is viewed as a job.

The first substantial advance to take place is the abandonment of the 'empty ritual' notion that gives way to a realization that an exchange of money and goods takes place such that the shop is left with fewer goods but more money at the end of the transaction. But when it comes to the question as to what happens to the money acquired by the shop, ideas are still nebulous: the children hazarded such guesses as that it is given to charity, or deposited somewhere and goes out of circulation. The basic customer–shop sub-system has thus become clarified, but everything outside it remains largely obscure.

Around the ages of about 7 or 8 years, i.e. at the period of the passage to concrete operations within the logico-mathematical sphere, two fresh insights tend to be added. One is that the people doing the selling have a job, for which they get paid; thus the second sub-system is fully grasped, though as yet in isolation. The second is the realization that shops also have to pay for the goods they receive for re-sale. When it comes to the question of how much, comparatively, shops have to pay, the most common idea is that the price to the shop is *the same* as that charged by the shop to the retail customer. As long as this belief persists, there is no possibility of understanding the nature of the relationships between the sub-systems. This emerges very clearly from the answers to the question as to where the money comes from for paying the sales staff – the children have to fall back on some external source such as the bank, with a fair sprinkling of rather quaint ideas, as in the case of this 8-year-old:

I: Is the lady doing a job?
S: Yes.
I: Who do you think pays her?
S: The owner of the shop.
I: Where does he get the money from?
S: The mint.

There were a few children who struggled unsuccessfully to resolve the problem from within the constraints in which they remained trapped. One 10-year-old boy, for instance, ingeniously suggested (without actually using the term) that bank interest could be used; a girl of the same age put forward the idea of a cheaper price, whereby more people would buy from the shop and this would produce surplus cash!

From age 10 onwards there was an increasing awareness of the difference between the buying and selling prices, which is a prerequisite for discovering how the several systems intermesh. Some children thought, first of all, that the price-difference applied only to certain commodities. In the following protocol, a 10-year-old girl was challenged to say what she would do if she had to pay the wages:

S: (Pauses and thinks) Oh, I'd take the money from the till. I'd get extra money from selling the fruit. I'd buy better fruit and put the price up. I would charge 2p more than I paid for it. This only happens with some things, like fruit.

Finally a clear picture emerges, but even in this example from a 10-year-old, the somewhat tentative tone of the replies should be noted:

I: What happens to the money at the end of the day?
S: I think it gets counted out. I don't think they give it out till the end of the week.
I: Who do they give it out to?
S: They pay the people who've been serving.
I: Do they give it all out?
S: They keep some to buy more stuff for the shop.
I: Does the shop pay the same for the things?
S: I think they get them cheaper. If they got them at the same price they wouldn't be making anything.

The general progression towards mastery, which is usually attained around the age of about 11, will now be briefly summarized. First, the nature and function of money has to be basically understood, including an appreciation of a quantitative continuum, so that the giving of change can make sense within the context of an exchange of money and goods. Second, not merely a general abstract notion of the relationship between jobs and wages is required, but some concrete knowledge of occupational roles, so that 'selling', for instance, is correctly perceived as a job for which one is paid. Lastly, the child must come to realize that the price charged to a customer is higher than that paid to the supplier; in other words, the concept of 'profit' must be attained. As will appear later in the discussion, there are some resistances to be overcome before this final step is taken.

It is worth mentioning in passing that occupational roles whose function is not directly apparent are hard to understand by children – and perhaps also some adults! They may be familiar with the appropriate term without attaching much actual meaning to it, as in the case of the 10-year-old below who referred spontaneously to the 'manager':

I:  . Who pays the shoplady?
S:  The manager.
I:  Where does he get the money from?
S:  Off some of the money out of the till.
I:  Is the manager doing a job?
S:  No.
I:  Where does he get the money for his food?
S:  He might have another job.

Thus the child did not define the manager's function in terms of a job, and several of the older children regarded the manager as being only partly within the shop system. For instance, one thought that he would be appointed by a local councillor and paid from people's tax money, thereby confusing two quite distinct systems. This illustrates the problem children have (and probably also adults, albeit at a different level) in sorting out the complex nexus of institutional functioning in society.

One thing that emerged quite clearly from the interviews was that a large majority of the children were not just repeating something they had learnt at school or had been told at home. They were faced with questions that were usually quite new to them, and they actively tried to fit together whatever information was at their disposal in order to produce answers. This is the justification for employing the term 'construction' to characterize their efforts. In their responses there were frequently long pauses while they considered before venturing an answer. Here are two examples, from a 10- and 8-year-old, respectively:

I:   Does the shoplady have to pay for the bread?
S:   No.
I:   So the bread is just given to the shops?
S:   (Pauses, then laughs) No – they'll pay for it.

I:   Who pays the shoplady?
S:   The owner of the shop.
I:   Where does he get the money to pay her?
S:   (Pause and illumination) From the till!

This last boy was the only one among those aged 8 who went on to state correctly that the selling price would be higher than the cost to the shopkeeper, and he obviously thought the problem through all the way and reached the right conclusions. The mistakes made are also enlightening, reflecting as they did some salient features of the milieu in which they lived. Thus it is a fact that the social services are the major source of money for many families in the area, and it is therefore not unreasonable for them to assume that this also applies to the retail sale system. Hence many of the errors were by no means errors of logic, but had an informational origin. On the other hand logical errors were also encountered, as when certain valid principles came to be misapplied. For instance, while it is true that lowering the price of goods is likely to result in an increase in sales, this is irrelevant when the shop's buying price is believed to be the same as, or higher than, the selling price. There is one issue that needs to be considered in this context: is it possible that some children believed that even the re-sale at the same price somehow yields a surplus? The answer must be in the negative, for it was evident that when the interviewer confronted them with the problem of where the money to pay the shop assistants came from, they invariably acknowledged the existence of a problem and attempted to cope with it. This was also confirmed by the data from a role-playing study, when children were asked how the shopkeeper gets his living: those who did not yet understand profit always seemed puzzled and came up with answers suggesting extraneous sources of income. The error therefore appears to be one of failing to recognize the applicability of an otherwise valid principle in the given hypothetical circumstances.

One aspect of this set of studies, conducted with children between the ages of 6 and 12, has so far not been touched upon: a number of children mentioned the bank as a place where money from the shop was being deposited, or, less frequently, as a place from which shops could get money. While the issue was obviously a peripheral one in relation to the work focusing on the shop, some of the ideas spontaneously voiced seemed of considerable interest. It was therefore decided to embark upon further research concerned specifically with exploring the developing of ideas about the bank as an economic institution.

## 2. The bank

Although many primary school children appeared to be familiar with the *word* 'bank', this institution is obviously far more remote from their direct experience than the shop. Moreover, unless the concept of 'profit' has already been mastered (which occurs generally around the age of 11 years), the functioning of a bank as an economic institution cannot be understood. Hence only children and adolescents between the ages of 11 and 16 were studied. The 96 subjects were Scots, evenly distributed by sexes and into working- and middle-class. While some relatively minor social class variations were found, only overall patterns of results will be considered here.

The first task was to establish whether or not the child understood the notion of 'profit', and for this purpose a simplified version of the 'shop' task was employed. Children were told that a butcher sells a chicken for £2 and were then asked: 'Now when the butcher himself buys the chicken, does he pay *more, less,* or *the same?*' Whatever the response, the subject was requested to explain it. The outcome was a straightforward dichotomy between those answering 'less' *and* offering a correct justification – who were credited with an understanding of 'profit' – and the remainder. The results for each class (N = 32) are summarized by giving the number of correct answers below (approximate mean ages in brackets):

Primary 7 ($11\frac{1}{2}$) – 19
Secondary 2 (14) – 27
Secondary 4 (16) – 31

It is noteworthy that a minority of secondary school pupils had not yet attained the concept!

The procedure for the 'bank' task was rather elaborate, the product of extensive pre-testing, so that only the critical features will be singled out here. Further details may be obtained from the full report (Jahoda 1981). After an initial open-ended question about the functions of a bank, subjects were asked to suppose that a person deposits £100 into a bank, withdrawing it after one year: would he get back more, less, or the same? The identical question was also asked regarding the repaying of a *loan* of the same amount over the same period. Any response had to be explained, and children were also asked about the source of a bank's financial resources (though of course not in these words). Next, children were requested to estimate the actual amounts repaid by and to the bank, respectively. The set of responses was jointly used to allocate subjects to six levels of understanding, which were as follows:

A. *No knowledge of interest.* These subjects stated that you always get back, or pay back, exactly the same amount.

B. *Interest on deposit only.* It was believed that you get back more, but pay back the same.

C. *Interest on both, but more on deposit.* Here it was recognized that there is always interest (i.e. answer 'more' to both questions), but the estimated figure for deposit interest is *higher* than that for loan interest.

D. *Interest same on deposits and loans.* Again the answer was 'more' to both questions, but the estimates for both were identical.

E[1]. *Interest higher for loans – no initial evidence for understanding.* Children in this category said that you get 'more' back for deposits. On being questioned as to how the bank obtains the money for paying interest, they were unable to give an adequate explanation. However, following this they not merely responded 'more' in connection with loans, but correctly estimated higher interest for these than for deposits. The category is thus a transitional one reflecting in most cases, as will be shown later, the impact of the study itself. Without it, these children would have 'naturally' belonged to either Category C or D.

E[2]. *Interest more for loans – correctly understood.* The criterion here was that the subject either spontaneously volunteered the correct explanation, or gave it no later than in response to the question as to how the bank gets its money.

In response to the open-ended question about the functions of a bank, virtually all said in effect that 'it keeps your money'. About one-third knew nothing else, another quarter also made mention of 'interest' and the remainder talked about 'borrowing' as well. The dominant idea produced spontaneously was clearly that the bank is a place that keeps your money.

Three subjects already at that stage gave detailed accounts of a bank as a system: one of these accounts is cited below:

A person puts money in and the bank loans that money out; and when the person gets that money back, there is interest on it. If someone gets a loan they have to pay interest, which is higher than the interest the bank pays you.

They were of course quite exceptional, and the overall patterning of responses to the detailed questions is set out in table 1. As indicated by the table title, the table shows the state of affairs before the final testing of the limits, to be described in more detail later. It may thus be regarded as

Table 1. *Levels achieved before impact of study: numbers of subjects in each response category by age groups*

| Category | Age groups | | | Total | Numbers in collapsed categories |
|---|---|---|---|---|---|
| | P7 | S2 | S4 | | |
| A | 10 | — | — | 10 ⎫ | |
| B | 13 | 3 | 1 | 17 ⎭ | 27 |
| C | 5 | 5 | 1 | 11 ⎫ | |
| D | — | 11 | 12 | 23 ⎬ | 51 |
| E₁ | 2 | 5 | 10 | 17 ⎭ | |
| E₂ | 2 | 8 | 8 | 18 | 18 |
| | 32 | 32 | 32 | 96 | |

representing the 'natural' development of thinking according to age. In order to present a clearer picture of trends, the categories have been collapsed into A and B, constituting a rather primitive level; C, D, and $E_1$ are intermediate, the last in fact being a transitional state. Finally, $E_2$ denotes full understanding of the kind illustrated above. If one tests the collapsed categories with chi-squared (df = 4), the outcome is highly significant (p > 0.001), which is hardly surprising. More interesting is the fact that the greatest contribution comes from the comparison of P7 (mean age $11\frac{1}{2}$) and S2 (mean age 14), there being little change thereafter.

What does all this mean? It can only be understood by a consideration of the qualitative aspects of children's thinking, which will now be surveyed.

Those in Category A (who had no knowledge of interest) viewed the bank as a storage place for money. Some conceived that in a literal sense, believing that it is put into a safe and you get the very same money back. From such a perspective, interest is simply inconceivable:

I: Please explain why you would get the same back.
S: They couldn't give you more because that would be taking from other people's money.

Others said that a bank would not be so generous as to give people extra, and such personalization was common, especially with regard to loans: 'It would not be fair on a person if, when you borrow £100, the bank asks for more back.'

Thus the bank was not conceived of as an economic institution, but as a kind of public service, and with regard to its functioning the children employed as their implicit model the rules of reciprocity familiar from borrowing from each other. Consequently, when asked about the sources of funds for running a bank, their notions were pure fantasy produced *ad hoc*, like 'from the money factory' or 'from the people the manager works for'.

A majority of the children in Category B (interest on deposit only), had not really advanced noticeably beyond the thinking of Category A. The main differences were their knowledge of the word 'interest' and/or the fact that you get more back if you leave your money in the bank for some time. When it came to the question of where the bank gets the money to pay interest, they were also baffled. Mention should be made, however, of a minority who displayed some awareness that the bank not just stores money, but *uses* it. At the same time a sharp disjunction persisted, interest being due *from* but not *to* the bank; in the latter relationship the interpersonal model continued to hold sway.

Most of the children in category C (interest on both, but more on deposit) exhibited some grasp of the link between interest and the use of the money made by the bank. The double standard began to break down with the recognition that the same principle that applies to the bank is also relevant for the bank customer. Yet such an admission appeared to be reluctantly conceded as exemplified by the following comments by two children:

You'd have to pay something for keeping their money.
A wee bit more, I think; it would be like you giving them interest for keeping their money.

There was also a sharp decline in arbitrary and fantasy answers to the question as to how a bank gets its necessary money. While the answers were still not correct, it began to be recognized as a problem and various attempts were made to cope with it.

In the case of Category D subjects (interest same on deposits and loans) two major advances may be noted. The first is a growing realization that a bank somehow has to make profit; the second is a resolution of the imbalance between personal and institutional relationships characterizing Category C. However, it cannot be said that personal norms have been altogether abandoned, since the strict reciprocity that is now applied probably also has its roots in interpersonal relationships. In fact, this may well be the obstacle preventing them from recognizing the possibility of getting a profit from loans, which led them to struggle in search for other sources such as investments or operating as a building society. Several subjects came close to making the final step towards differential interest charges, and they had certainly begun to treat the bank as an economic institution and thereby achieved at least partial understanding.

Table 2. *Levels reached after impact of study itself: numbers of subjects in each response category, by age groups*

| Category | Age groups | | | Total | Numbers in collapsed categories |
|---|---|---|---|---|---|
| | P7 | S2 | S4 | | |
| A | 10 | — | — | 10 ⎫ | |
| B | 10 | 3 | 1 | 14 ⎭ | 24 |
| C | 5 | 3 | 1 | 9 ⎫ | |
| D | 1 | 7 | 9 | 17 ⎬ | 28 |
| $E_1$ | — | 2 | — | 2 ⎭ | |
| $E_2$ | 6 | 17 | 21 | 44 | 44 |
| | 32 | 32 | 32 | 96 | |

As has been explained earlier, $E_1$ is a special transitional category characterized by the fact that subjects correctly estimated interest rates on loans higher than those on deposits after having been unable to say how a bank obtains its money. They were thus on the brink of full understanding, though as yet unable fully to articulate the connections of the system.

Lastly, there were those in Category $E_2$ who had mastered the issue. For example, asked how a bank gets money, such a subject answered simply, 'It charges more money for the use of loans.'

Let me now turn to an assessment of the impact of the study itself on levels of thinking of the subjects. Following the question as to how a bank gets its money, there were two opportunities for restructuring one's ideas. The first came with the issue of interest on loans, which could be related back to the interest on deposits; but this was not very obvious, and only three children saw the light at that point. The second opportunity was deliberately created to present a challenge and test the limits: it will be recalled that subjects had to estimate actual amounts of money paid by and to the bank, followed by a repeat of the question about the bank's source of money. The bulk of the changes took place during that final confrontation, and the nature of the responses was quite unmistakable: worried frowns giving way to broad smiles and triumphant exclamations – typical 'aha!' experiences.

The resulting redistribution into categories is shown in table 2. With one exception (a move from B to D), all the changes, irrespective of starting point, were to $E_2$, which means complete understanding. The pattern of changes was consistent with the assumption that the categories form a regular progression, numbers of those to $E_2$ being as follows: A = 0; B = 2; C = 2; D = 7; $E_1$ = 15. The overall trends can be seen by comparing the marginal frequencies on the right of tables 1 and 2; very few of those in the lowest two categories moved up, but more than half of those in the intermediate categories did.

On scanning the response patterns of those who gained new understanding in the course of the interview, it became apparent that two preconditions are involved. The first is, of course, that the child must have realized that the bank makes some use of the money deposited and does not just keep it locked up. The second condition is less obviously apparent and, often being subtle in its manifestations, is hard to pin down quantitatively. Broadly, it is that the child should experience a degree of uncertainty in response to the question as to how the bank gets money to pay interest and/or pay its staff. In other words, the children do not just volunteer some absurd (e.g. 'people who die leave their money to the bank') or glib (e.g. 'the government') answer and seem perfectly content with that. Rather they hesitate and search, treating it as a problem to which they have to find a solution, rehearsing possibilities overtly or in their mind and dismissing them as not feasible, perhaps ending up with 'don't know'. This is of course to some extent speculative, but the hesitation phenomena are real and readily observable. One can, as it were, see the equilibration process at work as Furth (1980: 91) described its manifestations:

They express discontent about their own opinions and correct themselves or hesitate in an otherwise fluent conversation; they expressly volunteer their gap in understanding and subsequently get excited as they discover a new insight.

There were a number of cases where the successive steps in thinking were very clear, and an example will be cited:

I: How does a bank get its money?
S: (Ruminates for a while, then says) The bank has to make a profit somehow, but I've no idea how.
I: What does one have to pay back after borrowing?
S: (Triumphant exclamation) That's how the bank makes its profits.

Most of those who subsequently changed in this manner had arrived at the point where they realized that the bank has to make a profit, but they attributed this to extraneous business transactions of some kind. A major obstacle to full understanding was the previously mentioned persistence of interpersonal norms of equality and reciprocity; imposing extra interest on government or private firms may be regarded as justified, but apart from the minority who had a clear grasp at the outset, it was seldom spontaneously considered in the context of loans to individual persons. It was mainly when the juxtaposition of the figures powerfully suggested extra interest as a solution for what was felt to be a problem that the resistance was overcome.

### 3. On the nature of 'social' thinking

Some empirical data having been presented, their theoretical implications will now be considered. Attention will be focused especially on two questions: (a) what are the factors governing the development of 'social' thinking; and (b) to what extent does it seem to be related to the development of logico-mathematical thinking?

If one examines the requirements for the growth of understanding of socio-economic systems, it would appear that two main elements are involved. These consist, first, of what I shall call general information about the social world, such as the fact that there are factories producing goods that eventually end up in a shop, or the fact that there is a difference between an activity performed for its own sake (like a game) or an activity done for a reward (when it becomes a 'job'). The second requirement is a knowledge of the rules and norms regulating relationships within the socio-economic sphere. Insofar as there is any explicit teaching, the evidence strongly suggests that it tends to be confined to the informational aspects. As mentioned in the introduction, much of the information is probably picked up in an unsystematic manner from adult conversations and the media, especially television. It is much more difficult for the child to get to know rules and norms, since these are usually implicit and seldom fully articulated except in situations of conflict (see Chapter 3). The child is therefore dependent on such models as are within his or her experience.

Let us look at developments with these considerations in mind. The child aged 6 will have to rely mainly on home, and to some extent on school. Neither setting offers much opportunity for observing the norms of economic exchanges. Moreover, the child may as yet be unable to conserve number – in which case monetary transactions simply cannot make any sense. It is thus not surprising that a young child is apt to regard the monetary aspect of what happens in a shop as a game-like, peripheral feature of the main purpose of the shop, namely, as a place where one gets things. At that stage it probably never occurs to the child to enquire how the goods are obtained by the shop. If questioned on the matter, as was done in the present study, they fall back naturally on their experience within the home, where people simply give each other things; hence, the idea that the shop also merely has to call for what it needs in order to get it.

One of the earliest facts the child learns, it would seem, is that you get money for doing a job. However, when first acquired this is probably little more than an empty formula. This is not merely because a clear understanding of the function of money is lacking, for the reasons indicated, but also because the concept of 'a job' is an abstraction which the child is apt to attribute to more or less mysterious goings-on beyond the immediate horizon. While most fathers, unless they are unemployed, are known to be in a job, the average child never sees what this actually entails – hence the frequency with which children fail to appreciate the fact that the people serving in shops are doing a paid job.

When children discover the generalized exchange function of money, they also find out that everything has a price. However, when first becoming acquainted with the concept of price, they tend to think in absolute terms. In other words, everything has an intrinsic value in monetary terms that cannot, or at least should not, be changed. This came out very clearly in another study where the understanding of the concept of 'price' was explored with 10-year-old children at the top of the primary school. The most common conception was that every commodity somehow has a certain price attached to it, though how this comes about remained obscure. When questioned about changes in prices, many responses were along the lines of 'If they don't stay the same it would be cheating people.'

If prices stand for intrinsic values which it would be dishonest to alter, then one can see why the children who knew that a shopkeeper has himself to pay for any goods believed that the price paid would be the same as that charged to the customer. Note that the normative framework underlying these ideas is modelled on that found within family and school: if brothers or sisters, or school fellows, enter into an exchange relationship, the presumption is usually that the objects are of the same value – otherwise, it would be 'cheating'; such exchanges are governed by the principle of (in theory) strict reciprocity. At that stage children have also learnt, presumably from ambient information in their environment, that people who serve in shops are doing a paid job. While they know about each of three systems (customer–shopkeeper, shopkeeper–supplier, shopkeeper–shop assistant), these are still thought of in isolation from each other.

It is only when some external influence (such as an investigator requesting them to perform a task or asking questions) leads them to focus on the relationships, that co-ordination of the separate systems is brought about. The fact that such insight typically does not come about spontaneously until the age of about 11 indicates that the grasp of the concept of 'profit' is a far from insignificant intellectual achievement. It involves not merely an increase in factual knowledge, but the passage from what Furth (1980) called 'personal' to 'societal' norms.

The difficulty entailed in such a transition is also apparent from the fact that the new insights gained are not just automatically transferred to the thinking about a formally equivalent system, that of the bank. It has been shown that while an adequate concept of profit is necessary for understanding how a bank works, it is not sufficient. Admittedly the reasons for this are complex, one important one being that the bank often is not viewed as an economic institution but as a kind of public service. However, even where there was no such misconception, the existing knowledge about profit was not often readily applied. One problem that had to be overcome here was that of transcending the link between money and goods so as to be able to envisage the payment of money for the *use* of money, a second-order relationship. Yet this particular stumbling block was itself considerably aggravated by a reluctance to abandon personal norms. The principles governing the operation of a bank tended to be conceived as akin to those underlying the transactions between siblings or friends: if you borrow something you return the same, no more and no less – anything else would not be 'fair'. When this norm came to be relaxed, it was first in relation to non-persons: the bank is entitled to exact interest from businesses or government, but not individuals. Finally there came a – sometimes reluctant – acceptance of societal norms as *sui generis*, which cleared the path to complete understanding.

This discussion of the development of certain salient aspects of social thinking has been very different from those commonly encountered in Piagetian studies of the development of logico-mathematical operations. Are these, then, to be regarded as entirely different spheres with distinct courses of development? This is a hard question that cannot be readily answered by a 'yes' or a 'no'; the answer depends to some extent upon what one considers to be the essential features of Piagetian theory.

The original formulation of the theory postulated a fixed sequence of developmental stages whereby structures are built up through direct interaction with the environment. If one adheres to this criterion, then the development of social thinking must be viewed as outside the scope of Piagetian theory. However, such a narrow conception of theory is now outdated. In the first instance it has never been true; nor was it claimed by Piaget that development takes place independently. of socially transmitted information. If this were strictly true, and given the fact that the physical environment has the same fundamental characteristics everywhere, development would follow precisely the same line in all cultures. But empirical study has shown that this is not the case (Dasen 1977). Piaget argued only against the view of the child as a passive recipient of information, not that such information is irrelevant:

the development of the child takes place through continual interactions, and it is much too simplistic to see this as the simple response to the educative activity of parents or teachers. Here, as everywhere, there is a dialectical relationship, and the child only assimilates social nourishment to the extent that it is active and engaged in real interactions, not passive or purely receptive. (1966: 249)

It can, in fact, be shown that even some of Piaget's own experiments concerned with the growth of children's understanding of physical systems also frequently presume the availability of socially provided information. This might be illustrated by taking the case of the roulette wheel, which was deliberately biased by the introduction of a magnet (Piaget & Inhelder 1951). Here the cause of the regularity of the behaviour of the roulette wheel was not directly observable by the child, the nature of the system having to be inferred by the child on the basis of such information as was at his disposal. It could be argued that this is essentially what is involved in the understanding of a social system. In their responses to this situation one can also find a parallel with those to the shop problems. The youngest children displayed a naive acceptance of the givens, and on being pressed for explanations merely confabulated; for example, younger children would say the wheel stopped there because it was tired. Then there came an appreciation that there is something to be explained and the children attempted to make sense of it on the basis of available knowledge, but failed to reach a correct conclusion; the oldest ones were able to construct the system by inferring the presence of a magnet. Evidently, for subjects who have never heard of a magnet such a phenomenon would remain inexplicable, and to that extent relevant information is essential in the physical as well as the social sphere.

There is at least one study of social thinking that was deliberately designed to assess the extent to which adolescents are able to handle socio-economic information provided in a manner corresponding to the expectations based on Piagetian theory. Jurd (1978) devised historical problems, administered in the form of a group test, that were structurally analogous to the logico-mathematical tasks usually employed in studying formal operations. In order to be able to achieve this, pseudo-historical material was supplied and the task of the subjects was that of drawing appropriate inferences. On the basis of the findings, Jurd claimed that they substantially conformed to Piagetian stages.

The studies discussed here differ from that of Jurd inasmuch as no information was fed to the subjects, who had to rely on such resources as they already had at their disposal. There was evidence (not included here) that the information stored was partly dependent upon the social background of the subjects. Moreover, it is likely that available information will also vary as a function of specific spheres, e.g. economic as compared to political systems. For these and other reasons more fully discussed by Furth (1980), there seems little prospect of being able to establish 'stages' of social thinking parallel to the stages of concrete and formal operations in the physical world.

This does not mean, however, that social thinking follows an entirely different course of development. In a study comparing various aspects of social and logico-mathematical thinking, no evidence was found of any sharp disjunction (Jahoda 1984). The correlations obtained between levels of social and logico-mathematical thinking were of the same order of magnitude as most of those reported for inter-relationships among different kinds of logico-mathematical and physical tasks.

Another, more important, consideration is that the concept of fixed 'stages' has been, if not entirely abandoned, yet relegated in recent years to a far less prominent position within the Piagetian theory itself. What has moved into the foreground is the process of equilibration (Piaget 1977). This is, of course, not the place to explicate such a complex theoretical issue, but one of its salient implications has elsewhere been stated concisely by Piaget himself, namely, 'that the most productive factors in acquisition [are] the disturbances brought about by conflict...' (Piaget 1975: 25). The elements of such a conflict may be crudely characterized as being, on the one hand, the structured content of a child's mind, and on the other hand, external reality. While the child is securely ensconced at a particular level of functioning, these elements remain in a state of somewhat precarious balance. In situations of cognitive conflict, normally generated externally, this balance is upset, and the process of equilibration leads to a restructuring and the re-establishment of balance at a higher level. It must be added that the occurrence of a cognitive conflict depends, of course, on prior development of the relevant structures to the necessary level, otherwise any fresh input that is incompatible is powerless to affect the balance and is therefore not even experienced as a conflict.

Now on this crucial issue the findings discussed above are fully in accord with what might be called neo-Piagetian theory. Time and again it was striking to observe how some children remained blissfully unaware of inconsistencies and contradictions; and when these were drawn to their attention, they either shrugged them off or sought refuge in fantasy. Others, by contrast, perceived them as problems with which one had to come to terms, even if they did not succeed in resolving them.

Before concluding, it will be useful to return briefly to the question of the extent to which thinking in relation to such economic institutions as the shop or the bank may be dependent upon information. It is worth noting that Piaget's own views regarding this issue changed. While he had originally assumed that all necessary information is available to everyone within their environments, Piaget later (1972) conceded that at least as far as formal operations are concerned, the achievement of that level will be dependent upon educational and occupational background. This means that individuals are likely to function at the formal operational level in certain spheres familiar to them, but not necessarily in others.

In the case of the young children faced with the task of making sense of the transactions in a shop, information about such things as the role of suppliers and the range of paid jobs is undoubtedly necessary; and insofar as they lacked it, they had no means of understanding the systems involved. However, the situation is somewhat different as far as the bank is concerned. A large majority of the older primary school children and practically all the adolescents knew about it, from conversations at home or teaching at school. It is worth noting that there was no indication that school experience as such helped with the understanding of the system: it was ascertained that some of the children had been told about interest in their lessons during the weeks prior to the testing; but they did not perform any better than other children without that advantage. A majority of subjects thus had at their disposal the necessary bricks for constructing a model of the system. If they failed, it seems to have been due largely to their inability to free themselves from the norms governing interpersonal relations which they misapplied to the economic sphere. It may well be that this constitutes the fundamental difference between thinking in the socio-economic and logico-mathematical sphere. The former, but not the latter, entails a shift from a personal to a societal orientation.

## References

Berti, A. E. & Bombi, A. S. 1979. Where does the money come from? Queries of links between money and work in children. *Archivio di Psicologia Neurologia e Psichiatria*, 40, 53–77.

Damon, W. 1977. *The social world of the child*. San Francisco: Jossey-Bass.
(ed.) 1978. *Social cognition*. San Francisco: Jossey-Bass.

Danziger, K. 1958. Children's earliest conceptions of economic relationships. *Journal of Social Psychology*, 47, 231–40.

Dasen, P. 1977. Are cognitive processes universal? In N. Warren (ed.) *Studies in cross-cultural psychology*, vol. 1. London: Academic Press.

Eckensberger, L. H. & Silbereisen, R. K. (eds.) 1980. *Entwicklung sozialer Kognitionen*. Stuttgart: Klett-Cotta.

Edwards, C. P. 1981. The comparative study of the development of moral judgement and reasoning. In R. H. Munroe, R. L. Munroe & B. B. Whiting *Handbook of cross-cultural human development*. New York: Garland Press.

Flavell, J. & Ross, L. (eds.) 1981. *Developmental social cognition: frontiers and possible futures*. New York: Cambridge University Press.

Furth, H. G. 1980. *The world of grown-ups*. New York: Elsevier.

Furth, H. G., Bauer, M. & Smith, J. E. 1976. Children's conceptions of social institutions: a Piagetian framework. *Human Development*, 19, 341–7.

Glick, J. & Clarke-Stewart, K. A. (eds.) 1978. *The development of social understanding*. New York: Gardner Press.

Jahoda, G. 1979. The construction of economic reality by some Glaswegian children. *European Journal of Social Psychology*, 9, 115–27.

　　1981. The development of thinking about economic institutions: the bank. *Cahiers de psychologie cognitive*, 1, 55–73.

　　1984. Levels of social and logico-mathematical thinking: their nature and inter-relations. In W. Doise & A. Palmonari (eds.) *Social interaction in individual development*. Cambridge: Cambridge University Press.

Jahoda, G. & Woerdenbagch, A. 1982. The development of ideas about an economic institution: a cross-national replication. *British Journal of Social Psychology*, 21, 337–8.

Jurd, M. F. 1978. An empirical study of operational thinking in history-type material. In J. A. Keats, F. K. Collis & G. S. Halford (eds.) *Cognitive development*. Chichester: Wiley.

Kohlberg, L. 1976. Moral stages and moralization: the cognitive-developmental approach. In T. Likona (ed.) *Moral development and behavior*. New York: Holt.

Piaget, J. 1932. *The moral judgement of the child*. London: Routledge.

　　1966. La psychologie, les relations interdisciplinaires et le système des sciences. *Bulletin de Psychologie*, 254, 242–54.

　　1972. Intellectual evolution from adolescence to adulthood. *Human Development*, 15, 1–12.

　　1975. L'équilibration des structures cognitives. *Études d'Epistémologie génétique*, vol. XXXII. Paris: Presses Universitaires de France.

　　1977. *The development of thought: equilibration of cognitive structures*. New York: Viking.

Piaget, J. & Inhelder, B. 1951. *La genèse de l'idée du hasard chez l'enfant*. Paris: Presses Universitaires de France.

Stacey, B. 1978. *Political socialization in western society*. New York: St. Martin's Press.

Strauss, A. L. 1952. The development and transformation of monetary meanings in the child. *American Sociological Review*, 17, 275–86.

Sutton, R. S. 1962. Behavior in the attainment of economic concepts. *Journal of Psychology*, 53, 37–46.

Youniss, J. 1980. *My friends, my parents and me: a Sullivan–Piaget perspective*. Chicago: Chicago University Press.

# 6. The development of ethnic attitudes[1]

DAVID MILNER

As recently as twenty years ago students of ethnic attitude development could confine their attention within the boundaries of the United States. Theory and research in this field were almost exclusively American and for the most part pertained to black–white relations in that country. For obvious reasons this concern with race-related research reached its zenith in the 1960s; now, not only has the interest value of racism (in the United States) been surpassed by that of sexism, ageism and handicappism, in successive waves of fashion through the 1970s, but the American monopoly of racial attitude research has also been set aside. Other unsuspecting nations have found the race issue thrust towards the centre of their socio-political life through substantial black immigration; not far behind the immigrants have come social psychologists intent on painting, by numbers, the unfolding picture of majority–minority relations. This chapter deals only with a portion of that research, though an important one: the development of ethnic/racial attitudes in children. Naturally, Britain's recent history of immigration and settlement has ensured that these issues have presented themselves more forcibly here than in other European countries; that imbalance is reflected in research and therefore in this chapter.

The theoretical perspectives which form the backdrop to this body of research have not been distinctively European, though this may be changing as we shall see later. Prejudiced racial attitudes[1] have *not* been seen, primarily, as the consequence of displaced, frustration-induced aggression, nor authoritarian personality tendencies; rather as a consequence of social influence via the socialization of children within societies where a hostile climate of attitudes towards particular ethnic minorities prevails. Within that context, it allows that 'externalising personality variables' (Pettigrew 1958) may still

[1] 'Racial', 'ethnic' and 'intergroup' have been used virtually synonymously in the literature; similarly, the frequent use of 'prejudiced' simply reflects the frequency with which these attitudes have been found to be negative, allowing this convenient, if pejorative, shorthand.

operate, and may indeed account for individual differences and for the extreme manifestations of prejudice; or that local or wider variations in that climate may be accounted for by particular socio-political circumstances, including various social 'frustrations' that may lead to the displacement of aggression and/or prejudice against minorities (given the wherewithal of ideology and social organization, which extremist groups seem anxious to provide). Nevertheless, the over-riding assumption (and one grounded in persuasive evidence) in the majority of these studies has been that hostile attitudes towards black minorities are widespread amongst adult members of the majority group. The task has then been to examine the ways in which the next generation come to apprehend this social reality and to construct their own. That this developmental process begins in the preschool years suggests that parents have a central role in transmitting attitudes; however, the influence of elder siblings, peers, teachers and other socializing agents such as literature and the mass media has also been recognized – though not systematically studied, as they are, for practical purposes, virtually inseparable.

## 1. A background to 'race' research: national attitudes in children

While inter-racial tensions are a relatively recent European concern, at least on the home front, international tensions are the very stuff of which the continent's history is made. It is not surprising, then, to find that research into the development of national attitudes in children anticipated our present concern by some years; in several important ways it also gave a foretaste of later findings. The earliest studies tended to focus on children's cognitive abilities: their capacity to handle the rather complex concepts of nations, countries and so on, and their evolving ability to grasp the logical relationships between the entities these concepts denoted. Thus, in his earliest study of this kind, Piaget (1928) looked at children's understanding of part–whole relationships, and their attainment of the concept of inclusion, whereby they came to realize that it is possible to be, say, Parisian and French simultaneously, having previously seen the categories as mutually exclusive. This kind of study laid the foundation for later work directed more specifically at children's national *attitudes*. It was entirely in keeping with prevailing conceptions of attitude formation that investigations should begin with the cognitive aspects; there must, after all, be factual or informational elements on which the affective or evaluative aspects are based – 'facts' which give rise to 'feelings'. Piaget & Weil (1951) understood the development of a notion of nationality, and the subsequent development of attitudes towards other nations, to involve a dual process of cognitive and affective development, the two elements being isomorphous, or in parallel. Later research, however, questioned this simple relationship and buried the notion that factual information about nations (of a geographic or demographic kind) was a prerequisite for the child to develop evaluations of those nations. Tajfel & Jahoda (1966) looked at children's preferences for various countries and their factual knowledge about them. They found that:

at the ages of six and seven children in Britain agree rather more about which countries they like and dislike than about practically anything else concerning those countries...[they] agree rather more that they prefer America and France to Germany and Russia than that *both* America and Russia are larger in size than *both* France and Germany. *There is no theoretical difference between the learning of these two kinds of 'facts', and if anything the knowledge of facts about preferences crystallises rather earlier than the corresponding knowledge of facts about size.* [italics added]

So it seems that, far from children basing their feelings about different countries on facts of the kind found in geography books, they rather arrive at their preferences on the basis of learning various social facts like 'Britons don't like Germans'. This of course requires a considerably lower level of cognitive development in order for simple national attitude statements to be made by the child than was implied by earlier, more cognitive views. It was an important finding, for our purposes, in that it demonstrated children's sensitivity to the evaluative nuances of adult attitudes, even when they concern such abstract notions and distant entities as foreign nations.

Implicit in this developing system of international preferences is, of course, a marked identification with, and preference for, the child's own country. When asked to assign photographs to boxes labelled, for example, 'English' and 'not English', and on a separate occasion asked to place the same photographs in boxes indicating degrees of liking–disliking, young English children show a clear preference for those photographs which they also categorize as 'English', as indeed do the majority of children from other national groups presented with a similar task (Tajfel *et al.* 1970). Later this relationship weakens somewhat, perhaps as the child moves from using essentially the same criterion (liking) for both judgment tasks, to a more differentiated response in which the nationality assignment is made on the basis of some simple physical stereotype, thus reducing the association with the judgments made on the basis of liking *per se*. Nevertheless, the child's disposition to evaluate favourably his/her own national group (and thus implicitly to disfavour others) is clearly demonstrated, cross-nationally, in England, Belgium, Austria, Italy and Holland. This consistency of orientation is interesting, but what is more interesting for the purposes of our later discussion of minority group orientations is the single inconsistent result of this study. Scottish children did not always prefer the photographs they identified as 'Scottish'. The study was conducted before the upsurge of Scottish nationalism of the early 1970s, and the results were thought to reflect the relatively less favourable evaluation of 'Scottish' as compared with 'English' in Britain. This interpretation was borne out in a subsequent study which employed the same tests with English, Scottish and Israeli children (Tajfel *et al.* 1972). The English children discriminated in favour of their own group, as before. The Scottish children did not discriminate in favour of 'Scottish' when choosing between 'Scottish' and 'not Scottish' and discriminated against their own group when subsequently choosing between 'Scottish' and 'English'. It seems, then, that these children had absorbed sufficient information which devalued their own national group for this to outweigh the 'natural' ingroup identification of other European children. This analysis of status considerations is taken a step further by the Israeli children's responses to the tests. They – not surprisingly – evidenced strong preference for the photographs they classed as Israeli, amongst the strongest ingroup national identification of any group. But in *ethnic* terms both the subjects and the stimulus materials were made up equally of 'European' and 'Oriental' Jews. *Both* groups of subjects more frequently assigned the 'European' photographs to the 'Israeli' category. Taken together with both groups' marked preference for the photographs placed in the 'Israeli' category, this suggests that a pronounced national ingroup preference co-exists with a pronounced ethnic ingroup devaluation in these 'Oriental' Israeli children.

Taken together these studies suggest that there is a great deal of highly evaluative information about national and ethnic groups 'in the air', in a form which is readily accessible to young children. Some of the national alliances and enmities that the children's attitudes reflect are now nearly 40 years old; as we can surmise that the war with Germany is no longer a regular topic of breakfast-time conversation, we have to look beyond parental influence alone for an adequate explanation. For example, Johnson (1966) has shown how boys' preferences for the 'Allied' nations and disfavour for the 'Enemy' nations was related to the extent of their readership of war comics. In the case of ethnic or racial attitudes there is undoubtedly far more immediate and tangible information in the child's environment to be absorbed than is the case with national attitudes. It is not my purpose here to rehearse the theory and research which have developed from the Tajfel *et al.* (1971) 'minimal group' experiments (see, for example, Tajfel 1978a, 1980; and Chapters 26 and 27 of this book), but this work nevertheless provides an important theoretical baseline for our present concerns. At the simplest level, if children's social categorization and social comparison processes do indeed foment intergroup discrimination where there are no important differences between the groups involved, no individual benefit from discrimination and no pre-existing hostility between the groups or individuals concerned, then real-life discrimination

between social groups distinguished by definite physical and cultural characteristics, with a history of competitive relations and accompanying intergroup ideologies, and tangible economic, social or political reasons for continuing conflict, is, to say the least 'over-determined' and almost inevitable. Race prejudice is a case which includes all these ingredients. (Milner 1981)

While it represents an immensely important theoretical development, Tajfel & Turner's (1979) theory is both necessary and insufficient to account for children's racial attitude development. The theory provides us with a persuasive description of some fundamental social psychological processes which may have the effect of encouraging negative dispositions towards outgroups. The knowledge that such dispositions exist – indeed may be intrinsic to intergroup behaviour – provides us with a context within which we can consider the further 'real-life' determinants of attitudes already indicated, the cultural circulation of information about the groups concerned which will build upon these dispositions,[2] and the actual developmental sequence of the child's synthesis of these influences. This recent theoretical departure represents a distinct advance over the theoretical underpinning of most American research in this area, which has scarcely taken account of the influence of inter- and intra-group processes *per se*, with the exception of Sherif's seminal studies of intergroup competition and cooperation (see, for example, Sherif & Sherif 1953; Sherif *et al.* 1961; see also Billig 1976, for a critical discussion of these studies).

## 2. Children and race: the research

In contrast to this theoretical innovation there has been very little methodological development, either in Europe or the United States. Essentially the same methods are currently employed as were originally introduced by Clark & Clark (1947): what Teplin (1974) has called 'projectively-based methods', which involve the presentation to the child of figures (dolls or pictures) representing the racial groups in the vicinity, from which the child must choose in response to various questions concerning identification, preference, friendship choice, social aspirations, etc. These methods have not escaped

---

[2] For an account of the socialization of race attitudes in children via significant others and cultural media, see Milner (1983).

criticism (for a review, see Milner 1981) but they have escaped substantial modification; their longevity suggests a genuinely intractable problem of finding alternative methods which would cater adequately to the abilities and limitations of, for example, preschool children, rather than lassitude on the part of researchers.

Pushkin (1967) conducted the first study of this kind in Britain in the early 1960s, and his results provide a chronological anchor point with which to compare later studies. In a period when the British racial climate was arguably somewhat less pervasively hostile than it was later to become, the study nevertheless showed an early awareness of race amongst London children (and developing racial preferences) comparable with the results that had consistently emerged from American studies over the previous two decades (see, for example, Goodman 1952; Morland 1962). Using 'tea-party' and 'see-saw' tests in which children had to choose companions to invite home and play with from a selection of black and white dolls, Pushkin found that 22 per cent of the white 3-year-old children interviewed were consistently unfavourable towards the black figures. This proportion increased to 65 per cent at age 6, apparently the peak of hostility. This was one of the few studies that attempted to go beyond the test situation to investigate the origins of these embryonic attitudes, through interviews with the children's mothers. However, no association was found between the children's ethnic attitudes and their mothers' attitudes towards child care and control (thus giving no support to an authoritarian personality-type explanation); and while there was no overall association between mothers' ethnic attitudes and those of their children, there was evidence that where there was greater hostility towards black people expressed by the mother, there was a significantly greater chance of the child being consistently unfavourable. The racial climate prevalent in the locality also exerted an influence on the child's attitudes.

No further studies of British children's race attitudes *per se* were conducted for a number of years, during which time there were many significant developments in British race relations, not least the contributions of politicians who both articulated and legitimized a growing hostility towards black British citizens. This is surely reflected in Milner's (1971, 1973) studies which, while portraying a broadly similar picture to Pushkin's study, nevertheless indicated a significant deterioration in racial attitudes, as evidenced by the children's responses. As with most studies in this area, variations in materials and methods preclude exact comparisons, as of course do differences in subject populations. However, 70 per cent of the 5–8-year-olds in Milner's studies were consistently favourable towards the white figures with which they were presented, and the same proportion attributed the majority of negative characteristics to the dark figures they were shown, a clear increase over the 30–65 per cent of Pushkin's subjects of this age range who were consistently unfavourable towards blacks. Milner used both dolls and pictures as stimuli; his study suggested greater uniformity of attitudes across areas of high and low black concentration than had the earlier study, and it did not indicate any diminution of hostility after age 6, as Pushkin had found. This last finding received some confirmation in a contemporaneous study by Brown & Johnson (1971). Using materials which were perhaps less obviously realistic representations of black and white people – namely white and 'shaded grey' line drawings – the authors nevertheless found that 64 per cent of children aged between 3 and 4 attributed negative characteristics to the shaded figures, rising to 75 per cent of the children in their ninth year. Richardson & Green (1971) also looked at older primary school children, and added a novel, if macabre dimension, to their study by pitting the effects of race on children's preferences against the effects of obvious physical handicap. Their 10–11-year-old subjects were asked to rank order their preference for figures representing a non-handicapped white child, a similar black child, and a variety of white children who were physically stigmatized in some way, from obesity, through facial disfigurement, to amputation of limbs. For white girls, the black children were chosen in preference to any of the stigmatized children (though, 'naturally', after the unstigmatized white child). In the case of the white boys, however, the facially disfigured white child was preferred to the black child, a choice which, given children's usual distaste for abnormality of this kind, seems a rather chilling index of hostility towards blacks. During the same period, Jahoda, Thomson & Bhatt's (1972) study of 6–10-year-old Scottish and Pakistani immigrant children's ethnic attitudes provided partial support for the picture described so far. Where they used materials comparable with other studies, they found that white children predominantly attributed good characteristics to light figures and negative qualities to dark ones, and that this bias was reduced when the tests were administered by an Asian interviewer.[3] However, the authors noted that there was little overt expression of hostility towards 'immigrants' of the type that Pushkin and Milner had both found to a marked degree. Similarly Laishley (1971) and Marsh (1970), studying young children principally in areas outside London with small or non-existent immigrant concentrations, also found evidence of lower salience of race and little hostility.

Since this flurry of research activity there has been relatively little empirical work which has addressed itself directly to this issue; nevertheless, the few

[3] For a review of studies of racial experimenter effects, see Sattler (1973); see also Thomas (1978).

studies that have been conducted demonstrate both continuities and contrasts with the earlier work. As part of a wider research project in the mid-1970s, Milner (1979) repeated tests from his earlier studies on a comparable sample of children, thus potentially providing some indication of changes in the climate of children's attitudes over the intervening four to five years. In the event, some 42 per cent still consistently chose white figures as companions and attributed negative characteristics to the dark figures at every opportunity. That this apparent reduction in hostility is not necessarily grounds for optimism is suggested by the fact that a further 33 per cent of the children made only one choice (out of a possible seven) that could be construed as favourable towards black people. In the most recent study in the field, Davey & Norburn (1980) came up with a similarly equivocal picture, five years further on. Again, test differences severely limit comparability with other investigators' work, but some points of comparison exist. On a 'stereotypes' test the 7–10-year-old white children involved were more prepared than were other groups to assign favourable attributes to their own group and derogatory attributes to Asian and West Indian figures. In a 'paired comparison' test, each child was shown a pack of 12 photographs representing both sexes of the three ethnic groups (English, West Indian, Asian), well-dressed and poorly-dressed. The photographs were presented in pairs in a predetermined way so that every card was compared with every other card, and a rank position between 1 and 12 was obtained for each photograph. On this test the white children put their own-race photographs in the top four positions (with the well-dressed figures above the poorly dressed) and then the West Indian and Asian photographs in descending order. On a further 'sweet-sharing' test the white children were once again the most ethnocentric (the equivalent results for the minority children in the study will be discussed later). Davey & Norburn were also interested in discovering how high a profile race assumes in the children's social landscape; in other words, how salient was the race cue as a basis for choice, as compared with other cues, in this case sex, dress and age? When the children were asked to sort 24 photographs (equally divisible by sex, dress, age and race) into two piles, and then sort the remainder into two boxes when one pile has been removed (the procedure being repeated until the rank-order of cues was established), 'the most significant finding was the overwhelming importance which all the children accorded to the "race" cue' (Davey & Norburn 1980: 57). However it seems that the saliency of this cue may be reduced by context and purpose. When the children were required to sort other cards (embodying the same grouping cues) into pairs of children playing on a roundabout in a park, then the sex cue became the most salient feature, followed by race and dress. This undoubtedly reflects social reality; it is a matter of common observation, if not of empirical research, that the politics of the playground proscribe cross-sex play far more vehemently than inter-racial contact. The tension between the two kinds of cue saliency test results is nevertheless interesting and we shall return to it in due course in discussing the relation between racial attitudes and behaviour in childhood.

Finally, setting the chronological narrative aside, we should mention the very few studies of older children's attitudes. There is something of a vacuum in the literature here, a vacuum which has arisen because the projectively-based methods described are no longer appropriate with children above 9 or 10 years, while it is not until late adolescence that adult attitude scales have been deemed to be applicable. Nevertheless Pushkin & Norburn (1973) attempted to adapt some of the former methods for use with an older sample in order to follow up the attitudinal development of the subjects from Pushkin's earlier study. This longitudinal perspective is unique among British studies, and unusual in any context, but its value is obvious and it creates a precedent which should be followed. Eight years on, Pushkin's subjects had re-distributed themselves somewhat on a scale of favourability–hostility towards black people: the proportion of children expressing 'extremely unfavourable' and 'very unfavourable' attitudes had declined somewhat, but the 'moderately unfavourable' category had increased by 67 per cent. This was partly due to a movement from the favourable categories, too, so that the overall picture was one of retreat from the extremes, and concentration around moderate disfavour towards blacks. Dove (1974), in a study of later adolescents, also found a relatively low level of hostility, some 25 per cent of the students making overtly hostile comments about pictures of inter-racial situations, a further 25 per cent making positive comments, while the majority could only be classified as neutral. The author points out, however, how 'surprising was the extent to which the context of the enquiry inhibited the expression of attitudes on such matters' (Dove 1974: 260). It was clearly felt that a norm of 'tolerance' in the school where the research was conducted may well have depressed the outward expression of prejudice below its true level. This alerts us to the context-dependence of this kind of research (as indeed Madge 1976 found with younger children), which is probably an influence which increases with age as the subjects become more aware of normative pressures, whether from 'authority', political or peer groups. No research has been conducted with this age group since the Young National Front became active in British schools (and the Anti Nazi League in opposition to them), and it would be instructive to discover the extent of their influence over current racial attitudes in adolescence.

## 3. Black attitudes

We have so far studiously avoided the other principal dimension to this issue: minority children's attitudes. These clearly have (at least) two aspects – their attitudes towards other groups and towards their own group – and neither develops in isolation from the influence of the majority group's attitudes towards the minorities. When we consider the research in this area and attendant problems of interpretation, it soon transpires that it is a vexed issue, one which has reflected considerable social and ideological change, and one which therefore requires a chronological account.

Milner (1971, 1973) replicated aspects of the classic American studies of black children (e.g. Clark & Clark 1947) at a time when, it now seems, hostile racial attitudes were at their zenith, insofar as they were reflected in white children's attitudes at that time. With hindsight it seems unsurprising that, accordingly, the minority children studied alongside them showed the most pronounced reactions to the current racial climate evidenced in any study in this country. Nearly half the 5–8-year-old West Indian children and nearly a quarter of the Asian children interviewed maintained that the *white* figure, rather than their own-race figure, looked like them, despite clear indications on other tests that they were well aware which figures represented which ethnic groups. As Goodman wrote, of black American children who responded in the same way, 'the relative inaccuracy of (their) identification reflects not simple ignorance of self, but unwillingness or psychological inability to identify with the brown doll because the child wants to look like a white doll' (Goodman 1946: 626). While the issue may not be as clear-cut as this interpretation suggests, the fact that 82 per cent of the West Indian children and 65 per cent of the Asian children maintained they would 'rather be' the white doll than their own-race doll undoubtedly gives it some credence. The same degree of outgroup orientation has not been found in all research contexts. Marsh (1970) found little evidence of outgroup identification amongst his minority-group subjects, albeit fostered West African children in East Sussex, an area not noted for its racial tension. Similarly, Jahoda *et al.* (1972) in their study mentioned earlier, using a considerably more elaborate identification task requiring the children to construct their own likeness by superimposing transparent sheets with different facial features printed on them, found mis-identification to be negligible among their young Asian subjects in Glasgow. It seems likely that the protracted nature of this more intricate task would make the fiction of mis-identification more difficult for the child to sustain. In fact the level of mis-identification (25 per cent of subjects tested by a white experimenter, 32 per cent of those tested by an Asian experimenter[4]) is comparable with the Asian subjects' responses of this kind in Milner's (1971) study, where 24 per cent of the 5–8-year-old Asians mis-identified. The difference lies in the fact that the Asian subjects of Jahoda *et al.* did not differ significantly from their Scottish counterparts, whereas none of the white majority children in Milner's study mis-identified.

In these early studies there was a marked contrast in the degree of outgroup orientation shown by the Asian and West Indian subjects. It was suggested that the lower level of mis-identification amongst the former was a reflection of the more detached and autonomous relationship to the white majority that the Asian communities had maintained, but more importantly a consequence of the more positive sense of identity fashioned from the resources of a separate and valued language, religion, dress, diet and culture. The cultural backgrounds of the West Indian settlers, on the other hand, were far more firmly underpinned by British influences and values, including racial values. The racial ordering of, for example, Jamaican society as they knew it, explicitly valued white over black, and this context, together with the immigrants' early and earnest desire to integrate with white society in Britain may account for their children's initial mis-identification, as much as the racism which frustrated these hopes.

Through the 1970s, however, this picture radically changed – and from both directions. Inevitably the Asian cultures began to be diluted (or, as Asian parents regarded it, polluted) by contact with urban British youth culture. Intergenerational conflict diminished both parental control and, perhaps, the appeal for the children of distant homelands and the cultures of their parents. At the same time the West Indian community also transformed itself, particularly its younger members. Born and brought up within British society, they had experienced pervasive prejudice and discrimination throughout their lives and it was perhaps inevitable that they should turn away from the ideals of their parents, which they had seen disappointed. Alternative cultural identities were fostered which owed nothing to white society and little to their parents or their backgrounds. A black British youth culture evolved from many separate influences: reggae, with its roots in the experiences of the urban dispossessed in Jamaica, Rastafarianism, black politics from America and emergent Africa.

While these developments visibly affected black adolescents and young

---

[4] It is interesting to note that other tests in this study gave evidence of a racial experimenter effect, an Asian (E) unwittingly producing responses more favourable to her own group; on the identification test, however, the reverse appears to be true, though the difference does not attain statistical significance.

adults, it seems that they did not escape the notice of their younger siblings either. By the mid-1970s studies of children's racial attitudes were yielding substantially different results from the previous generation of findings already described. As part of a larger study conducted in 1974, Milner (1979) repeated the identification tests from his earlier studies and found significant changes in both the West Indian and Asian children's responses. On identification tests ('Which one looks most like you?') 27 per cent of the West Indian children (compared with 48 per cent five years previously) and 30 per cent of the Asian children (compared with the earlier figure of 24 per cent) identified with the white figures. In the case of the West Indian children it is difficult to interpret this change in any other way than as a reflection of the changes in community consciousness, and the changing connotations of 'blackness' in a local, national and international context. This interpretation would be supported by the data from the United States in the early 1970s in which the responses of young black children to tests like these showed the same changes, albeit, appropriately, a few years earlier (e.g. Fox & Jordan 1973; Hraba & Grant 1970). Clearly, in that period there was an immense transformation in the social and psychological situation of black people which was surely reflected in more positive attitudes towards black people among those children. Although, in the British context, there was less black social advancement, we have already referred to some socio-psychological advances in terms of cultural identity development which contributed, it seems, to the new findings. It would be tempting to conclude, therefore, that black movements had been entirely successful in the United States, and to a large extent in Britain, in fostering black pride and identity. However, the situation is not quite as simple as that. About 80 per cent of both the West Indian and Asian children in Milner's (1973) study still maintained, despite identifying themselves correctly, that they would *rather be* white if they could. A contemporaneous study, using a rather different method of investigation, pointed in the same direction (Bagley & Coard 1975). They asked East London children of between 5 and 10 years of age a series of questions about how they would like to be if they could be 'born again' (i.e. physically rather than spiritually). The questions were asked as part of a longer series of questions, and the race of the tester was varied with no significant effect on the children's responses. It transpired that while 88 per cent of the white subjects did not want to change their skin-colour, 57 per cent of the black children did. Sixty per cent of the black children wanted to change their skin-colour, their hair-colour or texture, their eye-colour or all three. When these children were also questioned about their knowledge of Africa and the Caribbean, their responses 'frequently reflected the cultural stereotypes of colonialism:

'They're diseased. They don't live good lives…the people don't wear clothes, they live in the jungle…sometimes they have to be servants…The people are coloured, and they dance about…I don't like it. People will think that all coloured people are like that"' (Bagley & Coard 1975: 155–6). Taken together then, these studies suggest that black identity, as reproduced by children, had moved – though not far – from the negative pole.

Returning to the Davey & Norburn (1980) study, described earlier in connection with white children's attitudes, we find a continuation of the same trends. Mis-identification among the children of West Indian and Asian immigrants had declined to 8 per cent and 15 per cent respectively (though it is noteworthy that, as in the mid-1970s, the Asian figure is the larger); together, these percentages are not significantly different from the English children incorrectly identifying themselves. On a further 'ideal' identity question we see a further continuity with the earlier studies: in answer to the question, 'If you could choose, which one would you most like to be?', 51 per cent of the West Indians and 55 per cent of the Asians indicated the white figure. In other words, despite mis-identification having disappeared, there nevertheless remained a high level of outgroup preference, though once again significantly lower than the previous set of data. The studies through the 1970s, then, show a fairly consistent development. The influence of black consciousness on identification responses is unmistakeable, though apparently not yet so profound as to eradicate the children's expressed desire to be white if given the choice. Perhaps, as Davey & Norburn suggest, this latter response is no more than a recognition of 'who has the favoured place in the social pecking-order' (1980: 54). In any event, it suggests that young children are only too keenly aware of the results of racism, and that black identity development has not yet transcended such considerations.

It has always been assumed (and rather less often demonstrated) that outgroup orientation of the type described would have serious consequences for the individual black child. In other words, that mis-identifying, or preferring the majority group involved a devaluation of the ingroup and, by implication, the self. Thus the minority child was conventionally viewed as more likely than the white child to suffer identity conflict, lowered self-esteem or more serious psychological disturbance. This view came under increasing fire in the United States through the 1970s, as accumulating evidence to the effect that black children no longer mis-identified and had equal self-esteem with white children caused some investigators to return to earlier findings and question their validity (e.g. Banks 1976). The question was asked as to whether these findings of white orientation amongst blacks could really sustain the superstructure of interpretation (low self-esteem, psychological disturbance etc.) that had been placed upon them. It is certainly true that lowered self-esteem in blacks *was* more a matter of intuition and interpretation than hard empirical data, though it may be equally mistaken to fly to the other extreme and maintain that mis-identification has *no* individual psychological consequences or correlates. The issue is hotly debated elsewhere (see, e.g. Adam 1978; Milner 1981; Simmons 1978), but its implications are worth considering here for their relevance to British studies.

Bagley & Coard's (1975) study did provide some British data congruent with the conventional view, in that they found rejection of identity (as evidenced by a desire to change their physical characteristics) to be quite common among their black subjects. That this reaction may have wider behavioural concomitants is suggested by the correlations they found with classroom behaviour (or misbehaviour). Thus there is no direct measure of self-esteem in this study, but in later studies this was rectified by self-esteem measurement both in young children (Young & Bagley 1979) and adolescents (Bagley 1979). With children from infant school classes in London and in rural Jamaica, Young & Bagley showed that there was a significant correlation between ethnic identification and self-esteem. The children who were most strongly identified with their own group were also higher in self-esteem (on the Ziller self-esteem measure). In Bagley's (1979) study of 15–17-year-olds he included 145 West Indians whose self-esteem was measured, though not their ethnic identification. The results indicated that the West Indian boys had significantly lower self-esteem than West Indian girls and white European boys, and were at a level close to that of white European girls. (The cross-sex comparisons here are interesting on two counts: the difference between the West Indian boys and girls corresponds rather well with Driver's (1980) findings concerning sex differences in school achievement, and the sex differences in white self-esteem offer further evidence, feminists would argue, of the psychological consequences of inferiorization – though now disputed in the racial context, as previously outlined.)

British studies of self-esteem and/or ethnic identification in black adolescents do not present a coherent picture *in toto*, for while Dove's (1974) West Indian adolescents showed more identity confusion than their peers, in line with the general thrust of Bagley's findings, Hill (1970) found that West Indian adolescents did not tend to devalue themselves (compared with their English peers) and Lomax (1977) found that West Indian girls had higher levels of self-esteem than their white peers. Louden (1978) gives perhaps the most convincing account of the contemporary picture, though a familiar one from the American studies. In his own study he found that there were no overall differences in self-esteem between English, West Indian and Asian adolescents.

though there were considerable sex differences, the boys scoring higher than the girls in each ethnic group. Louden maintains that although

the assumption that the low social status of a group will generate low self-esteem appears reasonable…the matter is not so simple, *for it fails to take account of the specific environment of the adolescent and of the range of his possible responses to the outside world's definition*. People do not passively and inertly accept and internalise threatening communications about themselves. They react. In so far as the social environment offers them the option, they selectively perceive, selectively remember, selectively interpret these communications to fend off the threat to their self-esteem (Louden 1978: 228; emphasis as in original).

There is, here, the implication of a long-term process involved in identity and self-esteem development, which is a more helpful perspective than simply posing the rather blunt question, 'Do blacks have lower self-esteem?' For the answer to that question would, one suspects, be different at different times, in different contexts and with different-aged children. It would be more constructive to look at the issue longitudinally, both in terms of the individual's development and the developing social context.

Clearly, low self-esteem is not an automatic consequence of being black in a racist environment. As both Louden and Simmons (1978) point out, black children are initially socialized within a black environment, insulated from some of the inferiorizing messages of racism and enjoying the same confirmation, emotional support and fostering of self-esteem as other children. Later, moving out from this environment into the harsher reality of the school, the playground and beyond, they will encounter the full force of racist ideas, attitudes and behaviours. *Some* children will have greater exposure to these forces or be more vulnerable to them; they may well internalize them to a degree, and feel equivocally about their group and themselves (at least in inter-racial contexts which bring these issues and inter-racial comparisons into focus), and may perhaps give indications of lowered self-esteem. Increasingly in the last few years, though, these pressures will have been confronted by opposing pressures from within the peer group and the community, re-defining blackness positively and properly externalizing blame for blacks' low status on to whites. This, together with the ultimate disappointment and futility of a pro-white ethnic identification, is likely to inspire an aggressive identification with the ingroup, acceptance of its positive image of black people, and thus bolster self-esteem. Nevertheless, to the extent that this process is not complete, and in any case has to be re-traced by each individual, we may still find lowered self-esteem in some instances. Thus, overall self-esteem may be satisfactory, but tested in inter-racial contexts in which blacks are believed to be low achievers, for example in educational institutions, inter-racial comparisons of self-esteem may disfavour blacks. In this way, much of the disparity between different research findings can be reconciled, in particular, differences between earlier and later studies (reflecting social change in the interim), and between older and younger children, reflecting both social change and individual identity development.

Louden's (1978) account of black identity and self-esteem is a considerable advance over the conventional view, in that it does not *assume* psychological damage to result from racism and describes alternative ways in which individuals can avoid the imposition of a derogatory identity upon themselves. However, he gives rather less emphasis to *active, social* strategies than observation suggests is required. To be sure, there are individual coping strategies in response to racism (including a relatively passive avoidance strategy) but the larger picture of black identity development is one in which *creative, collective* actions have assumed the highest profile. This brings us back to Tajfel & Turner's (1979) theory of intergroup relations, which predicts the latter social strategies to develop as a result of the former, individual strategies. As Tajfel wrote:

for the black Americans...the expectation or the hope that there is a chance to integrate *as individuals* and on the basis of individual actions alone has more or less vanished. The remaining alternative, both for changing the present 'objective' social situation of the group and for preserving or regaining its self-respect, is in acting in certain directions not as individuals but as members of a separate and distinct group...In addition to obtaining some forms of parity, efforts must also be made to delete, modify or reverse the traditional negative value connotations of the minority's special characteristics. In social competition for parity, the attempt is to shift the position of the *group* on certain value dimensions which are generally accepted by the society at large...In the simultaneous attempts to achieve an honourable and acceptable form of separateness or differentiation, the problem is not to shift the group's position within a system of values which is already accepted, but to change the *values* themselves. (Tajfel 1978b: 16)

This analysis accords well with not only the black American experience but also, as we have seen, developments in black British identity. It proceeds from the same theoretical foundation as the theory's account of majority group strategies, in which 'individuals strive to achieve or maintain a positive social identity...(which) is based to a large extent on favourable comparisons that can be made between the in-group and some relevant out-groups' (Tajfel & Turner 1979: 40). It is precisely this need for positive social identity which was expressed in the early identification experiments with young black children; identification with the ingroup could not, for many children, provide this and therefore an individual 'fantasy' alliance with the outgroup was made. However this not only contradicted objective reality, it ran counter to the developing pro-black ethos among the child's significant others and peers in the community. There was, then, a tension set up by outgroup orientation/ingroup devaluation, which itself became part of the emotional dynamic behind black identity development – and helped to foment the transition from the individual to the group strategy.

## 4. Attitudes in action

One further aspect of children's racial attitudes remains to be discussed, namely the extent to which they find expression in day-to-day behaviour. It is an issue on which little direct evidence can be offered, since time and resource considerations invariably deter investigators from the minute observation and analysis of playground or out-of-school behaviour. Instead we have a compromise solution, which is the collection of sociometric data on friendship choices. Although Teplin (1974) champions sociometric techniques as more valid measures of racial orientation than projectively based methods, others would argue that there are inherent problems in the interpretation of choices on these tests. Any one child who may or may not be chosen as a 'best friend' (or whatever the relevant criterion) embodies many different attributes: personality, age, class, race, sex, and so on. It is seldom unambiguously clear as to which attribute or combination of attributes is made the basis for the child's selection or rejection by other children, let alone whether the choice actually does correspond with the reality outside the testing situation. Young children's 'best friends' often vary by the week, and may often lie outside the school population being sampled.

Despite a very early finding by Silberman & Spice (1950) that there was no cleavage between ethnic groups in friendship choices (a study carried out well before the bulk of black immigration and attendant prejudice), the majority of British sociometric studies have pointed in the opposite direction. Studies by Durojaiye (1970) in junior schools, Saint (1963) in secondary schools, and by Kawwa (1968) and Rowley (1968) at both age levels, have all indicated basically own-group orientated patterns of preferences, often more pronounced among the English than the children of immigrants. These choices have not always been accompanied by outright rejection of the other groups, though Kawwa did find some overt hostility at the secondary level. Age trends have varied from study to study, there being some evidence of an improvement in inter-racial choices during the course of the junior school years, though often followed by a deterioration on transition to the secondary school. This is not surprising, given that this development can often mean the breakdown of established neighbourhood friendship groups as the children are dispersed more widely to different secondary schools, where new friendship groups may form, at least initially, along racial lines.

The most recent data comes from the Davey & Norburn (1980) study, which is particularly interesting in that it gives information on responses to projectively-based tests *and* sociometric tests, allowing comparison between the two. We have already described the results of the former tests, in which ingroup preference amongst white children had declined somewhat since earlier studies, while outgroup orientation amongst black children had decreased more markedly. The sociometric tests reveal a comparable picture:

In schools where the ethnic mix is such as to allow children a more or less equal opportunity of choosing own-race friends or other-race friends, only a minority wish to confine their friendships exclusively to members of their own group. From a total of 238 children, 66.5% preferred to have some other-group friends. This sentiment was most pronounced among the West Indians (78.5%) and least often expressed by the Asians (55.5%) with the white children falling between the two (63.6%). (Davey & Norburn 1980: 56)

The children who had named no other-race friends were more likely to have preferred own-race figures on the picture tests. There is, then, a statistically reliable relationship between the choices on the two kinds of test, though not a strong one. As Davey & Norburn comment, 'It would be disturbing if it were...(for it) would imply that the children's stereotypes were already so inflexible that the children were no longer amenable to the discovery of characteristics which conflicted with their ethnic expectations' (p. 56).

The degree of relationship between 'attitudes' (as measured by projectively-based tests) and 'behaviour' (as observed, or measured by sociometric techniques) is an important practical as well as theoretical issue. For the discrepancy that has often been found between apparently friendly inter-racial behaviour in the playground and apparently hostile inter-racial attitudes in the testing situation has persuaded many teachers, for example, to prefer the evidence of their eyes and refute the validity of the test findings – and with them the need actively to foster more positive racial attitudes in their pupils. The tension between these observations may be largely resolved if we consider the two, virtually separate, kinds of learning involved. One concerns individual, personalized learning *about* individuals who are real, concrete and immediate facets of the child's world, and whose ethnic membership may pale into insignificance by comparison with their proficiency at kicking a ball, making jokes in the classroom or simply providing good friendship. The other kind of learning is altogether more abstract, generalized *categorical* learning, a growing awareness of *group* attitudes towards other *groups*, entailing concepts which are not very meaningful to the young child. As category descriptions that are compatible with a low level of cognitive development, they are necessarily stereotyped, shorthand accounts of group characteristics; it is these kinds of images which will be elicited from the child in the doll and picture tests, while the playground reality determines his or her answers to sociometric questions. Where there is no reason for another child to be seen as a member of an ethnic group *and nothing else*, there is no reason for the stereotypes about that group to be applied. But where a particular social reality is structured in racial terms, or when a child is confronted by an *unknown* person of another group, then their group membership is elevated in importance and the child is more likely to fall back on his/her learning about that group: individual considerations give way to categorical implications. The effect is more pronounced when a person is confronted with several members of another group whose perceived common group membership (and therefore common characteristics) is highlighted. In this light, the child's transition from school to school, and school to work become rather crucial turning-points as individual inter-racial encounters decrease and therefore do not mitigate (through individual experience of known other-group members) the effects of apprehending others in category terms, bringing to the surface the more stereotyped, categorical learning. Clearly, individual inter-racial contact of long standing will help to immunize the child against this development, but given the device of differentiating the 'exceptional' individual from the group 'rule', it would be a mistake to assume that this immunity will necessarily persist in the face of contrary social pressures. If there is an optimistic aspect to the research surveyed here, it is that since the mid-1960s there appears to have been some improvement in children's racial attitudes *and* behaviour. This may reflect the revision of stereotypes through individual experience, changes in adult attitudes or educational initiatives to circumvent negative attitude development. In any event, the research has given us insights, in addition to the American experience, into racial attitude and identity development and has provided an empirical basis for social and educational policy recommendations where only bromides existed before.

## References

Adam, B. 1978. Inferiorisation and 'self-esteem'. *Social Psychology*, 41, 47–53.

Bagley, C. 1979. Self-esteem as a pivotal concept in race and ethnic relations. In C. B. Marrett & C. Leggon (eds.) *Research in race and ethnic relations*, vol. 1. Greenwich, Conn.: JAI Press.

Bagley, C. & Coard, B. 1975. Cultural knowledge and rejection of ethnic identity in West Indian children in London. In G. K. Verma & C. Bagley (eds.) *Race and education across cultures*. London: Heinemann.

Banks, W. C. 1976. White preference in blacks: a paradigm in search of a phenomenon. *Psychological Bulletin, 83*, 1179–86.

Billig, M. 1976. *Social psychology and inter-group relations.* London: Academic Press.

Brown, G. & Johnson, S. P. 1971. The attribution of behavioural connotations to shaded and white figures by Caucasian children. *British Journal of Social and Clinical Psychology, 10*, 306–12.

Clark, K. & Clark, M. 1947. Racial identification and preference in Negro children. In T. M. Newcomb & E. L. Hartley (eds.) *Readings in social psychology.* New York: Holt.

Davey, A. G. & Norburn, M. V. 1980. Ethnic awareness and ethnic differentiation among primary school children. *New Community, 8*, 51–60.

Dove, L. A. 1974. Racial awareness among adolescents in London comprehensive schools. *New Community, 3*, 255–61.

Driver, G. 1980. *Beyond under-achievement: case studies of English, West Indian and Asian school-leavers at 16 plus.* London: Commission for Racial Equality.

Durojaiye, M. O. 1970. Patterns of friendship choices in an ethnically mixed junior school. *Race, 12*, 189–200.

Fox, D. J. & Jordan, V. B. 1973. Racial preference and identification of black, American Chinese and white children. *Genetic Psychology Monographs, 88*, 229–86.

Goodman, M. E. 1946. Evidence concerning the genesis of inter-racial attitudes. *American Anthropologist, 48*, 624–30.

    1952. *Race awareness in young children.* Cambridge, Mass.: Addison-Wesley.

Hill, D. 1970. The attitudes of West Indian and English adolescents in Britain. *Race, 11*, 313–21.

Hraba, J. & Grant, G. 1970. Black is beautiful: a re-examination of racial identification and preference. *Journal of Personality and Social Psychology, 16*, 398–402.

Jahoda, G., Thomson, S. S. & Bhatt, S. 1972. Ethnic identity and preferences among Asian immigrant children in Glasgow: a replicated study. *European Journal of Social Psychology, 2*, 19–32.

Johnson, N. B. 1966. What do children learn from war comics? *New Society,* 7 July.

Kawwa, T. 1968. Three sociometric studies of ethnic relations in London schools. *Race, 10*, 173–80.

Laishley, J. 1971. Skin-colour awareness and preference in London nursery-school children. *Race, 13*, 47–64.

Lomax, P. 1977. The self-concept of girls in the context of a disadvantaging environment. *Educational Review, 29*, 107–19.

Louden, D. 1978. Self-esteem and locus of control: some findings on immigrant adolescents in Britain. *New Community, 6*, 218–34.

Madge, N. 1976. Context and the expressed ethnic preferences of infant school children. *Journal of Child Psychology and Psychiatry, 17*, 337–44.

Marsh, A. 1970. Awareness of racial differences in West African and British children. *Race, 11*, 289–302.

Milner, D. 1971. Prejudice and the immigrant child. *New Society,* 23 Sept., 556–9.

    1973. Racial identification and preference in black British children. *European Journal of Social Psychology, 3*, 281–95.

    1979. Does multi-racial education work? *Issues in Race and Education, 23*, 2–3.

    1981. Racial prejudice and social psychology. In J. Turner & H. Giles (eds.) *Intergroup behaviour.* Oxford: Blackwell.

    1983. *Children and race: 10 years on.* London: Ward Lock Educational.

Morland, J. K. 1962. Racial acceptance and preference among nursery school children in a southern city. *Merrill-Palmer Quarterly, 8,* 271–80.

Pettigrew, T. F. 1958. Personality and socio-cultural factors in intergroup attitudes: a cross-national comparison. *Journal of Conflict Resolution, 2,* 29–42.

Piaget, J. 1928. *Judgement and reasoning in the child.* London: Routledge.

Piaget, J. & Weil, A. 1951. The development in children of the idea of the homeland and of relations with other countries. *International Social Science Bulletin, 3,* 561–78.

Pushkin, I. 1967. A study of ethnic choice in the play of young children in three London districts. Unpublished Ph.D. thesis, University of London.

Pushkin, I. & Norburn, M. V. 1973. Ethnic awareness in young children: a follow-up study into early adolescence. Mimeo, Institute of Education, University of London.

Richardson, S. A. & Green, A. 1971. When is black beautiful? Coloured and white children's reactions to skin-colour. *British Journal of Educational Psychology, 41,* 62–9.

Rowley, K. G. 1968. Social relations between British and immigrant children. *Educational Research, 10,* 145–8.

Saint, C. K. 1963. Scholastic and sociological adjustment problems of the Punjabi-speaking children in Smethwick. Unpublished M.Ed. dissertation, University of Birmingham.

Sattler, J. M. 1973. Racial experimenter effects. In K. S. Miller & R. S. Dreger (eds.) *Comparative studies of blacks and whites in the U.S.* New York: Seminar Press.

Sherif, M. & Sherif, C. 1953. *Groups in harmony and in tension.* New York: Harper.

Sherif, M., Harvey, O. J., White, B. J., Hood, W. R. & Sherif, C. 1961. *Intergroup conflict and co-operation: the robber's cave experiment.* Norman, Oklahoma: University of Oklahoma Press.

Silberman, L. & Spice, B. 1950. *Colour and class in six Liverpool schools.* Liverpool: Liverpool University Press.

Simmons, R. 1978. Blacks and high self-esteem: a puzzle. *Social Psychology, 41,* 54–7.

Tajfel, H. (ed.) 1978a. *Differentiation between social groups.* London: Academic Press.
  1978b. *The social psychology of minorities.* London: Minority Rights Group.
  1980. Experimental studies of intergroup behaviour. In M. Jeeves (ed.) *Psychology Survey, 3,* London: Allen and Unwin.

Tajfel, H. & Jahoda, G. 1966. Development in children of concepts and attitudes about their own and other nations: a cross-national study. *Proceedings of XVIIIth International Congress in Psychology,* Moscow, Symposium 36, 17–33.

Tajfel, H. & Turner, J. 1979. An integrative theory of intergroup conflict. In W. G. Austin & S. Worchel (eds.) *The social psychology of intergroup relations.* Monterey, Calif.: Brooks Cole.

Tajfel, H., Flament, C., Billig, M. & Bundy, R. 1971. Social categorisation and intergroup behaviour. *European Journal of Social Psychology, 1,* 149–78.

Tajfel, H., Jahoda, G., Nemeth, C., Rim, Y. & Johnson, N. B. 1972. The devaluation by children of their own national and ethnic group: two case studies. *British Journal of Social and Clinical Psychology, 11,* 88–96.

Tajfel, H., Nemeth, C., Jahoda, G., Campbell, J. D. & Johnson, N. B. 1970. The development of children's preference for their own country: a cross-national study. *International Journal of Psychology, 5,* 245–53.

Teplin, L. A. 1974. Misconceptualisation as artifact? A multitrait-multimethod analysis of interracial choice and interaction methodologies utilised in studying children.

Paper presented to the annual meeting of the Society for the Study of Social Problems in Montreal.

Thomas, K. C. 1978. Colour of tester effects on children's expressed attitudes. *British Educational Research Journal*, 4, 83–90.

Young, L. & Bagley, C. 1979. Identity, self-esteem and evaluation of colour and ethnicity in young children in Jamaica and London. *New Community*, 7, 154–68.

# 7. Imperfect identities: a socio-psychological perspective for the study of the problems of adolescence[1]

AUGUSTO PALMONARI, FELICE CARUGATI,

PIO ENRICO RICCI BITTI AND GUIDO SARCHIELLI

## 1. Adolescence as an object of study for the social sciences

This chapter is presented as a social psychological contribution to the study of adolescence. The basic ideas contained in it are not particularly new; Lewin wrote a long time ago:

the problem of adolescence...shows clearly that a way must be found to treat bodily changes, shifts of ideology and group-belongingness within one realm of scientific language in a single realm of discourse or concepts. (1951: 133)

But he added immediately: 'How can this be done?' (*Ibid.*).

Lewin did not really give to this question an answer which outlined a method for the study of the adolescent period. It was not useful, he maintained, to argue to what extent adolescence emerges as a result of factors which are biological, psychological or social, nor to try and decide on a statistical basis in what measure it is a phenomenon of a biological or a psychological nature. It would be more useful instead to engage in a study of situations and instances 'which show the so-called typical difficulties of adolescent behaviour' (Lewin 1951: 135), so as to identify the conditions in which these symptoms become more or less pronounced.

The period of adolescence is best considered as a period of transition and it can be viewed from a variety of perspectives. Thus, it can be seen as a change in group affiliations, a transition from being a member of the group of children to being a member of the group of adults, with all the behavioural and emotional consequences that this entails. These consequences become more salient in social contexts in which the separation between the worlds of children and adults is particularly clear-cut.

This passing from childhood to adulthood can also be considered as a

[1] The research reported in this chapter was supported by research grant C.N.R. CT80.02770.10. This chapter was translated from the Italian by Henri Tajfel and Nicholas Brown.

situation unfamiliar to the participants, representing for them a region of experience for which they have not had an opportunity to build up adequate cognitive structures. It is easy to foresee that the uncertainty of behaviour in such a situation will be directly related to the extent to which an individual has previously been kept outside the adult world. The variety of upheavals caused to the individual by sexual maturation needs also to be taken into account. The bodily changes which occur at that time create strangeness and unfamiliarity in an area of experience which is close and important for the individual. It is not only that new motives emerge which are due to the uncertainties associated with finding oneself in this new area, but also the individual's confidence in the stability of his social terrain, which supported him previously in his surrounding world, is now shaken. All this is related to an increase in conflict and aggressiveness which is characteristic of some adolescent reactions.

There are also the effects of the widening of spatial, temporal and social interests; the first relates to happenings in faraway places which cannot be directly observed; the second to longer future perspectives including expectations, fears and hopes; and the last to new interests in social groups, ideologies, organizations and social conflicts. Because of all this, the adolescent broadens his knowledge, multiplies his social contacts, is pushed to project his own future in relation to social objects which become important to him, and comes to realize the unavoidable incompatibility of various points of view.

The simultaneous discoveries of ideal aims and of conflicts and contradictions sometimes create in the adolescent new enthusiasms, but sometimes they drive him to doubt and, at the limit, to positions of complete distrust. The poor articulation of his cognitive field gives rise to sudden changes and 'extremes' of beliefs concerning groups and ideologies. As Lewin subsequently wrote: 'in all these areas of experience the adolescent occupies a position, intermediate between those of the child and the adult, which is similar in its marginality to that of a member of an underprivileged minority group'. Lewin's conceptual scheme has not been used in practice. Educationalists continued to stress above all the discontinuity, and the break implied in the individual's transition to a stable adult world, as the presumed most characteristic aspect of adolescence (e.g. Debesse 1936, 1943). Psychologists mainly paid attention to the recapitulation in adolescence of infantile sexuality and the consequent conflicts between instinctual impulses and internalized ethical norms, pointing to the risk of loss of autonomy associated with such upheavals. Anna Freud (1936), in particular, saw in the defence mechanisms the principal means employed by adolescents in dealing with these conflicts. Sociologists stressed the fact that the period of adolescence as we know it is manifested only in he context of industrial societies, which have at their disposal the resources hat can be used for the lengthening of the stage of formal instruction required by these societies in their modes of organization (for details, see Keniston 1971). Starting from these arguments, attempts have been made to show that adolescence must be considered as a dependent variable of social functioning, in as much as it amounts to a period of an individual's life in which '...society ceases to regard [the adolescent] – whether male or female – as a child but does not accord to him full adult status, roles and functions' Hollingshead 1949/75: 6–7).

Some of these various orientations contributed to our knowledge about adolescence, although they tended to remain circumscribed within their own conceptions and were not able to do more than provide provisional answers to one question at a time. Thus, they helped to clarify the issue of differences amongst societies in the social behaviour of adolescents (Mead 1928) and of differences between social classes within one society (Hollingshead 1949/75). They also drew attention to the fact that groups of the same age are as important in the process of socialization as is the family, and that this is particularly the case in Western industrialized and urban societies in which the family has now lost its ability to transmit to the young some of the more complex social rules (Eisenstadt 1956); that 'deviant' groups of adolescents are by no means without their own rules of conduct, and that these rules follow a code which is clearly defined, subtle and complex (White 1943). The very large amounts of time that adolescents spend together enables them to develop modes of internal communication which are easy, unhampered and specific to their groups. This led some authors to argue, not perhaps entirely convincingly, that there exists a separate subculture of youth (Coleman 1961; Friedenberg 1963); one example of this subculture was taken to be the students of American colleges.

In the 1970s, some sociological studies focused their attention on the fact that the school education of the mass of adolescents functions as a means of 'reproduction' of the existing social order which is assumed by the school system in the advanced capitalist societies (Althusser 1970; Bourdieu & Passeron 1970); at the same time, these studies cast serious doubts upon the effectiveness of the educational system in functioning as a widespread support for upwards social mobility.

The most relevant psychological contributions concerned issues of adolescent identity. In his well-known studies, Erikson (1950, 1959) considered the way in which the recapitulation of libidinal infantile processes, which constitute for the psychoanalysts the core of the adolescent 'crisis', influences the adolescents' definition of their own identity. He did not maintain that the problems of identity are universally posed in individual development *solely* during the period of adolescence, but considered instead that the adolescent phase is 'critical' for the definition of identity. The adolescent is preoccupied by his physical and sexual development not only because he has no clear understanding of the urges he experiences and does not know what to expect of his own body, but also because he has no more than a vague idea about how he is perceived and assessed by others. The integration which he seeks concerns the capacity of the 'I' to combine infantile identifications with new requirements, with aptitudes newly developed on the basis of innate capacities, with new possibilities offered by social roles. To acquire a new identity of his own means, for the adolescent, to be able to feel 'the same' despite the upheavals of the changes through which he goes; to accept the physical transformations and the new sexual urges associated with genital maturation; to be aware of the requirements arising from being considered and assessed at a new level of physical appearance and social evaluation. Erikson (1950: 253) stressed that for the adolescent: 'The sense of ego identity...is the accrued confidence...[in]...the inner sameness and continuity of one's meaning for others, as evidenced in the tangible promise of a "career".'

The probability of failure is high. Erikson discussed 'ego-diffusion', that is, successive and temporary identifications with reference models, often uncritically adopted, whose choice is not based on the autonomous requirements of the 'I'.

In the period of the academic success of structuralist-functionalist sociology, Erikson's scheme was accepted as capable of explaining the varying success of adolescent socialization in terms of social integration (such as embracing a career) understood as an index of achieved identity. It is true that amongst Erikson's many publications there are some which seem to confirm such an interpretation of his views; but a careful reading of his major texts leaves no doubt that he understood the acquisition of identity in terms of an individuation of the self and a self-recognition set against the background of a wide and complex representation of the social and the physical world.

Keniston (1968) returned to the concept of identity in his efforts to provide an explanation for the radical political positions taken by a group of leaders of the students' protest movement (the Vietnam Summer) in the United States. They had a powerful commitment to remaining loyal to values which they held to be impossible to renounce and which they considered as being often outraged by the adult world (including their families) from which they had learned them. These loyalty requirements led them as far as actively refusing a 'good' career which would, in their view, stand in contradiction to these values. Thus, according to Keniston's observations, identity is a process mediating important and responsible choices rather than serving as a mechanical tool for adapting to the existing realities of the *status quo*.

All these various considerations about adolescence do not, however, amount to the comprehensive framework that Lewin was seeking in order to construct a theory of adolescence understood as a period of transition and change. The sociological contributions (Hollingshead, Eisenstadt, Coleman, etc.) certainly focused upon some of the phenomena emerging during the period of adolescence; they did not, however, succeed in accounting for the processes responsible for the production of these phenomena. In general, the available empirical data were not sufficient to sustain the various interpretations (see, for example, the critiques of Jahoda & Warren 1965; Capecchi 1972). Moreover, theories were developed which claimed a general validity for all adolescents of industrial societies, while they were based on data mainly from subjects who were male, white and students. The problems of young workers, girls and adolescents from underprivileged ethnic minorities were only considered relevant as far as they concerned certain aspects of 'deviance'.

Above all, however, there has been a neglect in this work of the articulation between the phenomena it considered and the processes of social interaction, in which the psychological functioning of individuals and groups is explicitly taken into account. Because of this, little attention was paid to the active participation and social creativity of individuals, singly or in groups; the models presented were both mechanistic and reified (Sherif 1980). At the same time, the psychological contributions were not able to co-ordinate the intra-psychic processes, identified through clinical experience, with the social contexts in which these processes materialize. As a result, these processes were often assumed to reflect 'universal' phenomena rather than being considered as activated in certain social conditions at certain historical periods.

It might seem strange that a criticism of this kind can be made of the work of someone like Erikson, since it is generally acknowledged that 'although a psychoanalyst, he is able to take account of social and cultural circumstances...' (Coleman 1980: 51). But it seems difficult to locate the concept of identity, as it is defined by Erikson, within the framework of the social relationships and the social climate in which the subject lives. The numerous and suggestive examples provided by Erikson tend to do no more than illustrate these individual–social interactions in a *post hoc* manner. In other words, a concept was first defined within a psychoanalytic logic, then it was said to explain a paradigmatic 'case' from a historical period or a given culture, and the facts were so interpreted that they confirmed the model.

The clearest support for this objection came from some of the detailed discussions by Erikson of the concept of identity. The concept, as used by the structuralist-functionalist sociologists, mainly acquired its significance in the positive fulfilment of the 'adaptive' criteria of socialization (understood in the functional mode as historically given social and professional situations). Erikson (1963) accepted at times an interpretation of this kind. The same concept was later used by Keniston (1968) in a radically different way when he maintained that the achievement of ego-identity is an essential condition for the ability to take *autonomous* decisions which may be courageous and crucial in one's life.

The authors who took up the conceptual and methodological ideas about adolescence outlined by Lewin are Muzafer & Carolyn Sherif (1953, 1964, 1965). They focused their interest on the functioning of groups of adolescents, and on their aspirations and projects, while at the same time paying attention to the physical, social and cultural environment in which the adolescents lived. They did not confine themselves to a 'simple' attempt at observation and description. All the data gathered in their numerous studies on 'natural' groups of adolescents derived from a conjunction of participant observation and laboratory experiments, and they were guided by a central idea from which various theoretical intuitions were then developed.

The research methods developed by the Sherifs combined the study of the psychological with the social factors operating in concrete situations which the adolescents experienced and in which they planned their future actions. This enabled the Sherifs to confirm certain 'universal' generalizations concerning the adolescent period: namely, that the rapid physical development together with the modifications in responsibilities, activities and modes of conduct have direct repercussions upon the organization of the self-system of each individual.

These modifications of the self are at the origin of certain attitudes which initiate a process of personal change and of change in social relations. This process very rapidly takes a concrete form through the formation of adolescent groups. The groups are constituted on the basis of reciprocal interactions which enable the adolescents to engage in a variety of activities, learned to various extents from adults. All the elements of this complex scenario influence each other; what become particularly evident are the reciprocal influences of the psychological factors (the self-system), the social factors (the family, the gender relationships, the ambiance of daily life, the insertion into school and work, etc.) and social behaviour.

The term 'self-system' as used by the Sherifs (Sherif 1976; Sherif & Cantril 1947; Sherif & Sherif 1969) can be conceived as a system or a constellation of 'categorical structures' (Sherif 1980: 15) formed through interactions with the physical and the social environments which establish the relations between, on the one hand, 'me', 'I' and 'mine', and, on the other, the most significant objects present in the experiential field of an individual. The categorical structures of the self-system are specific, as some of them are of particularly direct concern to the person and are therefore endowed with affiliative connotations. These categories are co-ordinated according to their rank (superior–inferior) and direction of affectivity (such as positive–negative, acceptable–unacceptable, friendly–hostile). Some of these categories may at times become particularly relevant within the priorities of the self-system because they contribute at the time to the definition of the self or because the situation brings them into the focus of attention. In such cases, the involvement of a particular category in the psychological processes provides a point of anchorage for the perception and the evaluation by the individual of the events associated with it.

The discontinuities, ambiguities and uncertainties of the adolescent period disturb the stability of the relationships previously established within the self-system, and motivate the individual to engage in an active search for new rules or guidelines of stable relations with others and for new ways of discovering how to leave behind present uncertainties. It is at these various critical points that the organization based on age, at school and in other communities, which is typical of contemporary society, becomes decisive. An adolescent stops writing diaries about his solitude when he sees that other adolescents are in the same boat. Instead, relations with his contemporaries become more frequent, intense and significant. The impulse or attraction towards people of the same age signifies a general displacement inside the self-system, a displacement away from the authority of adults – at least in those activities and areas of life which cease to be dominated by the adults. The coevals become more and more the persons of reference (Grecas 1972; Rosenberg 1967).

## 2. A social psychological perspective

The importance attached by the Sherifs to the transformations occurring in the self-system during the period of adolescence can be attributed to the fact that contemporaries play a determining role in these transformations as the privileged reference group which, at the same time, allows itself to engage in autonomous forms of social conduct. It seems, however, that the model articulating the psychological and social factors proposed by the Sherifs still maintains a rigid separation between the 'psychological' (changes in the self-system) and the 'social' (the environment in which the groups of adolescents are formed and active).

It seems to us that the articulation between the 'psychological' and the 'social' is involved in the process of the organization and transformation of the self during adolescence. To clarify this view: the aspects of the cognitive field and the experience of an adolescent which appear as constantly problematic include social consensus in interpreting the information received from the social environment, the social values concerning morality, the relations between individuals and between groups, the aims which should be pursued and the behavioural means by which these aims should be achieved. For example, one of the values which typically appears problematic for some adolescents is the importance that they attribute to being students, with the attending possible consequences relating to upwards social mobility. This issue has become even more relevant since it has been shown (Backman & Secord 1968; Palmonari *et al.* 1979) that families evaluate differentially the socially promotive function of the school, depending upon their own social status.

Thus, the adolescent learns for a number of reasons to activate a process of categorization so as to clarify the relations which obtain between the self and other highly significant objects (see various chapters in Part VI of this book). This process of categorization is based on a variety of perceptual activities including selectivity, through which special attention is paid to certain qualities and components of the environment, awareness of similarities and differences applying to certain selected categories, and decisions as to which characteristics should be considered as typical and distinctive of each category in relation to other categories. These very complex activities involve the principal factors operating in the general processes of categorization (Tajfel 1972, 1981). In paraphrasing Neisser (1976), one could say that the cognitive activity of each individual and the process of categorization in which he is engaged may produce different effects depending upon the nature of the anticipatory schemata which are activated in the diverse situations in which the individual is required to provide descriptions of various social objects. As Neisser put it, the information concerning the self, just like all other information, can also be gathered by an individual only through the activation of the appropriate anticipatory schemata which are available to him.

In these general considerations, account must also be taken of the conception of the self introduced by Mead (1934). The mental activity of the adolescent (relating to the components of the self to which Mead referred as the 'I') focuses upon distinct aspects of the self (more specifically, the components characterized by Mead as the 'me') according to anticipatory schemata which are activated by the adolescent with regard to some special relations between the self and others. These may concern individuals, groups or social categories. We shall use the term 'representation of self' to refer to those aspects of the self brought to light through the appropriate anticipatory schemata used by the adolescent in order to establish relationships between himself and other social objects.

In cases in which the requirement must be met to clarify the representations of social objects such as 'males', 'females', 'the young', 'adults' and their reciprocal relations, we shall note, following Tajfel (1981), that the representations display the properties of 'social stereotypes' which are widely shared within a social context, and are derived and structured through the nature of the relations between large-scale social groups. Moreover, the reciprocal relations between these representations, their functioning and the use made of them by the adolescents, are closely connected with the functions that they fulfil in adaptation to the social environment. Ultimately, these representations not only perform the role of systematizing information and simplifying the cognitive field, but must also be considered as points of reference which help the adolescent to defend or reorganize his system of values, and also to create or preserve differentiations amongst a variety of social groups.

In these activities, concerned with organizing information around significant social objects, the adolescent tends to use the representation of the self as an essential point of reference which he strives to preserve as autonomous in relation to all other social objects. One can therefore assume that social factors will critically influence the definition of the relations between the self and all these other entities.

Therefore, using appropriate research tools for gathering data about relations between the self and others, it should be possible to show not only that different aspects of these relations are strongly affected by social factors, but also that the organization and evolution of the self-system are determined by synthesis emerging from a reciprocal influence of psychological and social factors. It should be possible to show that the representation of self functions as a cognitive anchorage in the representations that the adolescent achieves of the various social categories which are significant in his experience.

We attempted in our research to deal with this network of problems. In our studies of the cognitive field of the adolescent, we assumed, on the basis of the theoretical considerations previously outlined, that the most relevant categories relating to the self would be those of males, females, young people, adults, students and workers. This is in accordance with the general conclusions reached in those studies on adolescence which always stressed the importance of variables such as sex (Clausen 1975), generations (Bengston 1970; Mannheim 1928) and social class (Jencks *et al.* 1975: Rutter *et al.* 1979) for the differentiations in social behaviour and social perception. As far as educational-professional status is concerned, relevant background was found in the studies of Bianka Zazzo (1966) and our own previous work on perception of self, motivation and temporal perspectives in adolescents who were apprentices and students (Casadio & Palmonari 1969). In these studies, several differences between these two groups (aged between 15 and 18) were shown to exist. What emerged in particular was that the students retained opportunities of defining their own position in relation to social realities and of equipping themselves with the appropriate cultural and critical tools, whilst the weight of the immediate requirements of their everyday life confronting the apprentices was so restricting that it was impossible for them to engage in personal reflections about their relations with the outside world.

### 3. Research on the self-system of adolescents

**3.1 Hypotheses.** Our principal research interest, therefore, was in the ways in which adolescents organize relations between their representations of the self and other significant social categories, rather than in the possible influence of major social factors such as social class and educational and professional status. The subjects were requested to attribute a certain number of behavioural and personality characteristics to the following categories: male adults, female adults, male young students, female young students, male young workers, female young workers – as well as to themselves as individuals.

Thus, the subjects confronted a situation which implied a complex interplay of affiliations. It is important to note that their representations were organized with more consensus on the basis of the male–female dichotomy than the dichotomy of young students vs. young workers. This fits in with the general evidence from studies on stereotypes, which shows that traits attributed to sex and generation categories are more widespread and stable than are those relative to educational and professional status (see also Chapter 28).

(i) We predicted that the contra-distinctions between masculine and feminine categories, and those between the young and adults would emerge first of all. This prediction was related to our view that the self is conceived as being relatively more distinct from all the other categories and that therefore it would be less identified with any of the other target categories, even those which clearly designated the subjects' ingroup.

(ii) We also expected a marked similarity between all the representations of the self elicited from the various groups of adolescents. This was so because all the adolescents who participated in the study lived in a cultural area which was strongly homogeneous, and the conditions of the study were not so designed as to emphasize in the representations of the self, different shades of meaning deriving from variations in class and status.

(iii) On the other hand, those variables were bound to play some role in the representations of the relations between the self, the ingroup and the outgroup. While we expected that, in each of the groups, the distance between the self and the ingroup would be smaller in terms of representations than between the self and the outgroup, it was also likely that some differences in that respect would be found which were associated with the variables of social class and educational and professional status. More specifically, we assumed that the distance between the self and the ingroup would be smaller in the case of students of working-class origin than in the case of students from higher social status backgrounds, or of apprentices from the working class. This expectation was based on some of the considerations previously outlined. Students of middle-class origin have less need to identify with their ingroup, which is not seen by them as an effective instrument of social mobility. The same is true for the working-class apprentices, for whom their ingroup does not provide any salient contribution to their social identification. But the students of working-class origin are likely to identify intensely with their status as students, which is seen by them as an effective instrument of social mobility.

**3.2. Method.** The subjects were 124 male adolescents between the ages of 15 and 18, all resident in the city of Bologna for at least five years. They were selected from a wider sample on the basis of two sociological characteristics: social class (middle vs. working), and educational-professional status: students in secondary schools vs. students in technical schools vs. apprentices.

In fact, we were able to obtain only four groups instead of the six which would have been necessary in order to obtain the interaction of the two sociological variables. This was because we were not able to find a sufficient number of middle-class adolescents either in the technical schools or in the courses for apprentices. The remaining four groups, with their designations in the description of the results, were as follows:

Middle-class students in secondary schools (*studenti liceali*): $G_1$
Working-class students in secondary schools (*studenti liceali*): $G_2$
Working-class students in technical schools (*studenti tecnico-professionali*): $G_3$
Working-class worker-apprentices (*lavoratori apprendisti*): $G_4$

For the study of representations of self and of significant social categories, we used a partly modified version of a questionnaire constructed by Zazzo (1966). This consisted of 33 items which referred to personality traits and to the behaviour that each subject was requested to attribute to the following categories:

young male students (SM) young male workers (LM) young female students (SF) young female workers (LF) male adults (AM) female adults (AF)

Table 1. *Profiles of categories*

|  | | | | | |
|---|---|---|---|---|---|
| $G_1$ | $S_1$ | $SM_1$ | $LM_1$ | $AM_1$ |
|  |  | $SF_1$ | $LF_1$ | $AF_1$ |
| $G_2$ | $S_2$ | $SM_2$ | $LM_2$ | $AM_2$ |
|  |  | $SF_2$ | $LF_2$ | $AF_2$ |
| $G_3$ | $S_3$ | $SM_3$ | $LM_3$ | $AM_3$ |
|  |  | $SF_3$ | $LF_3$ | $AF_3$ |
| $G_4$ | $S_4$ | $SM_4$ | $LM_4$ | $AM_4$ |
|  |  | $SF_4$ | $LF_4$ | $AF_4$ |

*Note:* The numerical subscripts are used to identify the four groups which were studied.

Each subject was also requested to state whether each of the items also applied to himself. The procedure for the completion of the questionnaire ensured that each subject had available in front of him, simultaneously, all the categories, and was able to attribute to each of them only those items which he considered to be typical 'above all, of this category'. The subjects were allowed to attribute the same item to more than one category, but were asked not to attribute any of the items to all the categories. Both verbal and written instructions were used.

In this way, the subjects were requested to express judgments consisting of attribution of traits in conditions which implied explicit comparisons between the various categories, and also between these categories and the self. The items which were used can thus be conceived of as schematic and simplified definitions of behaviour and attitudes expressed in the dichotomous form of attribution–non-attribution. Table 1 presents a summary of the descriptive profiles produced by the four groups of subjects on the basis of attribution of the 33 items.

For each of the adolescent groups in the study we thus had at our disposal the representation of seven target categories, and for each of the categories a profile produced by the attribution to it of a certain number of items. It was therefore necessary to use a method of statistical analysis which would allow for a simultaneous assessment of the profiles produced by the subjects and the ensemble of the questionnaire items. It appeared that the analysis of correspondences (henceforth AFC; Benzécri *et al.* 1976; Giovanni & Lorenzi-Cioldi 1983), which is a form of multivariate analysis allowing for a transition from nominal to interval measures, would serve this purpose. With this method it is possible to obtain a reclassification (*codage*) of the items and the profiles, attributing to each variable a numerical value which allows for a maximization of the coefficient of correlation between the two sets of data;

it then becomes possible to extract the factorial axes which define the
dimensions along which are disposed the items and the profiles. To each of
the dimensions extracted in this way there is then assigned a value (*lambda*)
indicating the proportion of the total variance which is common to the two
sets of data (items and profiles of the target category) with respect to that
dimension. The AFC also allows us to examine the order, the distance which
separates the items and also the profiles from each other, and the proximity
between an item and a profile. The simultaneous spatial representation locates
an item and a target category and the nearer to each other they are, the higher
is the probability that the individuals belonging to a given group use more
frequently a particular item for the description of the target category.

Another possibility offered by the AFC is that of distinguishing, within each
ensemble of items and target categories, between the principal and the supplementary elements. The principal elements are directly involved in the
definition of the factorial axes and thence of the extracted dimensions. The
supplementary elements do not contribute to this definition, as they are
projected on to the factorial space only after the extraction of these
dimensions, and only in relation to their similarity to the profile. According
to the specific aims of the study, it is therefore possible to include categories
or items as supplementary elements without disturbing the general pattern
of the results, but employing these elements, whenever this is useful, to
indicate, through comparisons, their similarity to the profile.

In interpreting the results, the following points need to be taken into
account: (i) the values (*lambda*) of each of the extracted dimensions and
the coefficient of inertia (*taux d'inértie*) which express in percentages the
proportion of the total variance explained by each of the dimensions; (ii) the
graphic representation of the factorial axes, and thence of the extracted
dimensions on to which are projected the ensembles of the items, and of the
profiles of target categories – in particular, attention must be paid to the
distances (and proximity) of the items and the profiles; (iii) the contribution
in absolute terms (CTR) of each item and each target category. Each CTR is
an indispensable datum for the interpretation of the axes. The CTR expresses
the proportion of the variance for the items and the target categories
explained by each factor; in other words, it indicates the contribution of an
item or a target category to the meaning of a factor. Thus, the interpretation
of an axis is based upon a limited number of items or target categories – those
that yield a high CTR.

The description of our results will be based on these three indices of
interpretation. For reasons of space we shall present for each of the factors

only the respective coefficient of inertia and the value of the factor, and not the complete CTR tables. But all the data have been carefully taken into account in the interpretation.[2]

**3.3 Results.** The contingency table containing the 27 profiles of target categories and the 33 items of the questionnaire was analysed using the AFC program. The first two factorial axes amounted to 70.2 per cent of the coefficient of inertia (*taux d'inértie*) corresponding to a *lambda* of 0.1034 for the first axis and a *lambda* of 0.0693 for the second. Along the first axis were organized the target categories and the items contrasting males to females, while the second axis placed against each other the young and the adults. Items associated with the masculine extreme expressed socio-political interests, requirements of rationality in behaviour and various aspects of the routine of everyday life. At the feminine extreme were reflected the search for originality and the salience of emotional experience.

At the extreme corresponding to youth were reflected items stressing a general disposition towards individual commitment, but there was little definition of the objects of this commitment; there was also a stress upon the need for positive interpersonal relationships. The adult extreme was characterized by a requirement of self-assertion and personal autonomy associated with a recognition of the importance of family relationships.

A noteworthy result (see figure 1) was the central position, as compared with all other target categories, of the profile of the self (with which are associated items which refer to rationality of behaviour, independence and autonomy; special attention is also paid to social judgments about the self). In the factorial space identified by the first and second axes can also be observed dispersion patterns of profiles concentrated around target categories which are distributed in a circular form with the self at the centre. The various clusters are concentrated in a decreasing manner in the following sequence: AF, AM, SM, SF, LM, LF.

A third factorial axis (coefficient of inertia = 6.7 per cent, corresponding to a *lambda* of 0.0166) contrasts the self of all the groups with the young workers; in other words, it signifies the opposition between the self and the group which is an outgroup for the students. Associated with the self are the items referring to the importance attributed to family life, requirements of rationality in behaviour, and also the importance of physical appearance in the presentation of self to others; associated with young workers are items

2 The use of the AFC and the analysis of data was made possible thanks to the collaboration offered to us by Fabio Lorenzi-Cioldi of the Faculty of Psychology and Sciences of Education and the Faculty of Sociology of the University of Geneva.

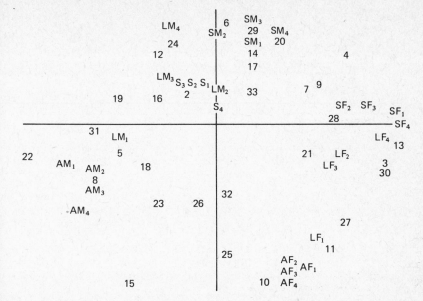

Figure 1. Distribution of profiles and items in factorial space: males–females and youths–adults

referring to the importance attributed to money, to politics and to personal security.

In view of the fact that the first factorial axis extracted an important general dimension, it seemed useful to conduct a second analysis from which were eliminated the effects, operating as supplementary elements, of the female target categories (AF, SF, LF). The first factorial axis of this second analysis (coefficient of inertia = 53.5 per cent; *lambda* = 0.0863) expresses a dimension which contrasts the young and the adults. The items associated with the youth extreme are concerned with the search for originality, emotional salience of the self, opening up towards new experiences and other people. The adult extreme is characterized by social and political interests and importance of family relationships, and also the requirements of self-assertion and of personal autonomy.

The second factorial axis (coefficient of inertia = 13.1 per cent; *lambda* = 0.0211) distinguished between the self and the respective outgroup. With the extreme corresponding to the self were associated the importance of physical appearance in the presentation of self, a certain romantic vision of relations with the other sex, interest in family life and in various aspects of the routines of daily life. The outgroups were associated with items referring to the assertion of self, autonomy and professional success.

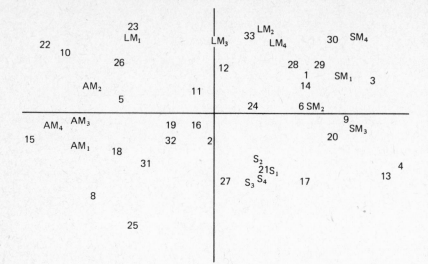

Figure 2. Distribution of profiles and items in factorial space: youths–adults and self–outgroup (with female profiles excluded)

The third factorial axis (coefficient of inertia = 9.5 per cent; *lambda* = 0.0153) opposes ingroups to outgroups ($LM_4$ vs. $SM_4$; $LM_3$ vs. $SM_3$; $LM_2$ vs. $SM_2$; $LM_1$ vs. $SM_1$). The outgroup extreme is characterized by the assertion of self and professional success; the ingroup is characterized by search for originality, freedom, autonomy, and also the wish for positive interpersonal relations and the rationality of one's own behaviour. It can be seen in figure 2 that the clusters of the target categories can assume a circular shape and that, in this case, the self constitutes an extreme of the factorial axis.

Figure 3 represents the locations on the second factorial axis of the profiles of the selves and the profiles of each ingroup and outgroup for the four groups of subjects which took part in the study.

It can be seen that the distance between self and the respective ingroups is smaller for all groups of subjects than the distance between self and the respective outgroups. The distance between self and the ingroups for the groups $G_2$ and $G_4$ is smaller than that for groups $G_1$ and $G_4$. The distance between the ingroup and the outgroup is smaller in the case of the apprentices ($G_4$) than for all other groups.

3.4. **Discussion.** The adolescents requested to produce a representation of significant social categories systematize the characteristics attributed to these categories according to very general criteria which discriminate between males and females, and between young people and adults. We have found

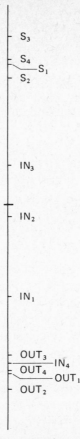

Figure 3. Distribution of self, ingroup and outgroup along self–outgroup axis

a very clear pattern in these representations, shared by all the adolescent groups in the study, which does not seem to have been influenced by social class membership or by educational and professional status. In line with our previous discussion, we can consider these results as originating from active social stereotypes (Tajfel 1981).

It also appears entirely clear that, in the case of our subjects, the characteristics they selected are strongly endowed with value connotations. Males are defined as interested in politics and the solution of social problems and as rational in their behaviour; females are characterized as attracted by the search for originality and a positive evaluation of feelings; the young are defined as ready to be committed to ideals and to friendship, and inclined to take decisions which are risky and audacious; adults emerge as intransigent, liking solitude, bound to family life.

In this scheme of the categories most significant for adolescent experience, the self occupies a central position for all the groups of subjects, is very similar in all of them and is clearly differentiated from all other categories. Thus, the representations of the self are not influenced by social affiliations and not identified with any of the categories, not even with the respective ingroups. The significance of these findings seems to us to derive from their support for the hypothesis of the central importance of the self in the cognitive field of the adolescent. It can be maintained that our subjects organize the social categories which have been elicited by anchoring them to the self. In fact, the self constitutes for the subjects the point of reference which serves as a basis of comparison for all the objects which form the field of their social perception.

As far as the definitions of the categories 'young male workers' and 'young female workers' are concerned, there is evidence in the data that for adolescent students, sons of professional people, these categories become assimilated to male adults and female adults, respectively, while for the adolescent apprentices, their contemporaries who work are assimilated to male and female students. In other words, the groups of subjects which differ in their social class and educational-professional status, differentiate very clearly the categories of young people on the basis of the criteria students vs. workers; but this is done with opposite results by the different groups. For middle-class students, the young people who work are defined as very similar to adults; whilst it seems that in the case of the apprentices, the principal characteristic of youth is the fact of being a student.

The effects of the differentiation between students and workers appear even clearer when the relations between the self, the ingroup and the outgroup are considered. Even though, in our results, the selves of all the groups of adolescents are very close to each other, maintain a position distinct from all other categories, and do not appear to be influenced by sociological factors, these factors do affect the distance between the self and the ingroup. In the findings there is clear support for the assumption, previously discussed, that the groups of students of working-class origin identify more strongly with their ingroup than do either the sons of professional people or the apprentices.

These results support the view that a reference to the characteristics of the position of being a student is crucial for all adolescents who live in a social context in which adolescence is predominantly defined as 'the age of the students'. However, whilst for the students originating from the middle class to be students can be assumed to reflect the 'obvious', for students from the working class, for whom being a student is considered as a means of social mobility, this becomes an aspect of their lives which has high cognitive salience. As far as the apprentices are concerned, the definition they adopt of their own membership category, involving as it does many of the characteristics which they also attribute to the students, may be considered as a sort of filling-in, or completing of, an image of themselves which otherwise has little social distinctiveness. Indeed, three of the four groups in the study, homogeneous in their educational-professional status, defined the category of the apprentices in terms of characteristics reserved for adults. In contrast, the apprentices defined their own group in terms very similar to those they used for defining students. None of the four groups attribute to the apprentices characteristics which would make them clearly distinguishable from students.

Thus, the category of apprentices is hardly 'visible' to its own members. This seems a finding which needs stressing, since it can be interpreted in terms of marginality. The relevant question is whether social conditions enable the apprentices to define themselves in an autonomous fashion inside the world of the young; the data we gathered appear to exclude the possibility that their social location provides them with sufficient resources to engage in such an undertaking. It seems that defining themselves as quasi-students is the only means the apprentices have of becoming 'visible' to themselves and to other social groups.

## 4. Towards a social psychological re-definition of adolescence

In our discussions about adolescence we were strongly influenced by the theoretical views of Muzafer & Carolyn Sherif; there are, however, some focal questions which, in our view, are not sufficiently clarified by their work.

We have been able to show that the organization of the self-system of adolescents is due to an articulated interaction of psychological and social factors. The joint influence of the social and the psychological is active in the process of the organization of the self and, in particular, in definitions of similarities and differences in relations between the representation of the self and of other significant social objects. The processes of social comparison, of differentiation and identification, which are set in motion by this organization can be considered as essential for the constitution of groups with which the subjects identify. In other words, the groups of coevals could be the first result of these processes rather than being the condition of their inception. The point which we have reached, starting from Lewin's suggestions and from the systematic work of the Sherifs, provides for the present no more than a clue about how far an appropriate social psychological perspective may enable us to extend further our knowledge about adolescence in the various social contexts of our lives.

The bulk of the work remains to be done. We shall now attempt to identify the directions of research which appear the most urgent. The first point to clarify concerns the general validity of the scheme proposed here for the assumed characteristics of the self-system in adolescence. The principal point made was that the self constitutes the anchorage of the organization given by the individual to his own cognitive field. Is this valid in relation to all the aspects of significant objects which are operationally relevant? Or is this validity confined to the stereotypic situations such as those which were constructed in our research? This point needs some further clarification. Would one replicate the relational organization of the cognitive field of the students found in the present study if contents of items which were presented had been replaced by other items concerned with, for example, social, manual or sexual competence, or systems of values characteristic of subjects in other social groups? Questions of this kind would have to be answered in relation to the modifications in the self-system of female adolescents, particularly with respect to their changing in social status. In addition, on what basis can it be asserted that the organization of the cognitive field enclosed in the self is generally valid for the adolescent period?

On the basis of the available data, all that can be said is that the organization of the self-system is characterized by the centrality of the representation of the self, and that this may take the form of various articulations as a function of the sociological variables which were considered. But this would have to be compared with the organization of the self-system of children (9- to 10-year-olds) and adults (beyond the age of 20) so as to develop a more solid foundation for the ideas about the specificity of the adolescent period. Further, these ideas would have to be generalized to other periods of an individual's life in which biological and institutional transitions also occur.

Even if these points were clarified, a wider question would have to be confronted. If, in fact, on the basis of the results which have been obtained, it were possible to maintain that the self-system of adolescents can be defined starting from processes of comparison and differentiation between the self, ingroups and outgroups, there exists another perspective, perhaps more fundamental, for the study of the formation of adolescent groups.

In their famous research of 1953, conducted in summer camps, the Sherifs studied the inter- and intra-group relations starting from the formation of various groups of coevals. But in these cases the groups were formed in the early stages of the camp, and this represented a particular social situation in which the boys were receptive to certain operative prescriptions produced by the adults who were in charge. It can be pointed out, without denying the heuristic value of this research, that the groups were not formed as a result of a spontaneous initiative of the boys, and that the processes of differentiation which followed were described and explained by the Sherifs as a consequence of the existence of these groups.

From the perspective proposed here, it would be possible to assume that groups of contemporaries are formed starting from a foundation of the activities of comparison, differentiation and identification in which adolescents engage in all social situations. The formation of adolescent groups could then be explained on the basis of what Turner (1981) calls the 'model of identification', explicitly abandoning at the same time the 'model of social cohesion' which, as he points out, is not able to account for the origins of some groups (see this book, Chapter 25).

In referring to the re-definition of the concept of social group proposed by Turner (1981: 94), it could be said that groups of contemporaries are formed when the adolescents, who are in the process of transforming their self-system, begin to perceive themselves as members of a particular social category; this implies the perception that they are different from other categories, not only those containing adults but also those including other adolescents.

There remains, however, a fundamental difference between the views discussed here and the model proposed by Turner. From our point of view, the social object which is the self can never be entirely replaced by the social object of membership group (or reference group). The individual (in more formal language, the 'I' of Mead) uses the social object, the self (the 'me' of Mead), as a point of reference for the organization of his perceptual field. But this is not the place to open a discussion of the work of Turner, which would entail a diversion from the purpose of this chapter and a re-definition of the key concepts.

To be able to use (although with a radical difference) Turner's model in order to provide an account of the formation of adolescent groups, an opportunity is needed to study the relations amongst such groups employing the fundamental concepts of the theory of intergroup relations proposed by Tajfel. It is possible to envisage that in the near future we may reach the stage of conducting studies on the age of adolescence using as fundamental concepts not only those of class, generation and social mobility, but also the concepts of categorization, differentiation, identification, social comparison, and self and social identity.

132    A. Palmonari, F. Carugati, P. E. Ricci Bitti & G. Sarchielli

References

Althusser, L. 1970. Idéologie et appareils idéologiques d'Etat. *La Pensée*, *151*, 3–38.
Backman, C. W. & Secord, P. F. 1968. *A social psychological view of education*. New York: Harcourt.
Bengston, V. L. 1970. The generation gap. *Youth and Society*, *2*, 7–32.
Benzécri, J. P. *et al.* 1976. *L'analyse des données*. 2 vols. Paris: Dunod.
Bourdieu, P. & Passeron, J. P. 1970. *La réproduction*. Paris: Éditions de Minuit.
Capecchi, V. 1972. Struttura e tecniche della ricerca. In P. Rossi (ed.) *Ricerca sociologica e ruolo del sociologo*. Bologna: il Mulino.
Casadio, G. & Palmonari, A. 1969. La motivazione e la prospettiva temporale nella percezione sociale di adolescenti studenti e apprendisti. *Rivista di Psicologia Sociale*, *2/3*, 175–245.
Clausen, J. A. 1975. Social meaning of differential physical and sexual maturation. In S. Dragastin & G. Elder (eds.) *Adolescence in the life cycle*. New York: Wiley.
Coleman, J. C. 1980. *The nature of adolescence*. London: Methuen.
Coleman, J. S. 1961. *The adolescent society*. Glencoe, Ill.: Free Press.
Debesse, M. 1936. *La crise d'originalité juvénile*. Paris: Alcan.
    1943. *L'adolescence*. Paris: Presses Universitaires de France.
Eisenstadt, S. N. 1956. *From generation to generation*. Glencoe, Ill.: Free Press.
Erikson, E. H. 1950. *Childhood and society*. New York: Norton and Co.
    1959. *Identity and life cycle: selected papers*. New York: International Universities Press.
    (ed.) 1963. *Youth: change and challenge*. New York: Basic Books.
Freud, A. 1936. *Das Ich und Abwehrmechanismen*. Vienna: Internationaler Psycho-analytischer Verlag.
    1958. Adolescence. *Psychoanalytic Study of the Child*, *13*, 255–78.
Friedenberg, E. Z. 1963. *Coming of age in America: growth and acquiescence*. New York: Random House.
Giovannini, D. & Lorenzi-Cioldi, F. 1983. L'analisi delle corrispondenze in psicologia sociale: un'applicazione allo studio dell'identità nell'adolescenza. *Giornale Italiano di Psicologia*, *2*, 289–312.
Grecas, V. 1972. Parental behavior and contextual variations in adolescent self-esteem. *Sociometry*, *35*, 332–45.
Hollingshead, A. 1949/75. *Elmtown's youth*, 2nd edn, New York: Wiley.
Jahoda, M. & Warren, N. 1965. The myths of youth. *Sociology of Education*, *38*, 138–49.
Jencks, C., Smith, M., Acland, H., Baue, M. J., Cohen, D., Gintis, H., Heyns, B. & Michelson, S. 1975. *Inequality: a reassessment of the effect of family and schooling in America*. London: Peregrine.
Keniston, K. 1968. *Young radicals: notes on committed youth*. New York: Harcourt Brace.
    1971. *Youth and dissent*. New York: Harcourt Brace.
Lewin, K. 1951. *Field theory in social science*. New York: Harper.
Mannheim, K. 1928. Das Problem der Generationen. *Kölner Vierteljahrshefte für Soziologie*, 157–85; 309–30.
Mead, G. H. 1934. *Mind, self and society: from the standpoint of a social behaviorist*. Chicago: University of Chicago Press.
Mead, M. 1928. *Coming of age in Samoa*. New York: William Morrow.
Neisser, U. 1976. *Cognition and reality*. San Francisco: W. H. Freeman.
Palmonari, A., Carugati, F., Ricci-Bitti, P. E. & Sarchielli, G. 1979. *Identità imperfette*. Bologna: il Mulino.

Rosenberg, M. 1967. *The dissonant context and the adolescent self-concept.* In S. E. Dragastin & G. H. Elder (eds.) *Adolescence in the life cycle.*

Rutter, M., Maurham, B., Mortimore, P. & Ouston, J. 1979. *Fifteen thousand hours: secondary schools and their effects on children.* London: Open Books.

Sherif, C. W. 1976. *Orientation in social psychology.* New York: Harper and Row.

1980. Coordination of the sociological and psychological in adolescent interaction. Unpublished MS.

Sherif, M. & Cantril, H. 1947. The psychology of ego-involvements: social attitudes and identification. New York: Wiley.

Sherif, M. & Sherif, C. W. 1953. *Groups in harmony and tension.* New York: Harper and Row.

1964. *Reference groups: exploration into conformity and deviation of adolescents.* New York: Harper and Row.

1965. *Problems of youth: transition to adulthood in a changing world.* Chicago: Aldine.

1969. Adolescent attitudes and behavior in their reference groups. In J. P. Hill (ed.) *Minnesota symposia on child psychology,* vol. 3. Minneapolis: University of Minnesota Press.

Tajfel, H. 1972. La catégorisation sociale. In S. Moscovici (ed.) *Introduction à la psychologie sociale.* Paris: Larousse.

1981. *Human groups and social categories.* Cambridge: Cambridge University Press.

Turner, J. C. 1981. Towards a cognitive redefinition of the social group. *Cahiers de psychologie cognitive,* 1, x, 93–118.

White, W. F. 1943. *Street corner society.* Chicago: University of Chicago Press.

Zazzo, B. 1966. *Psychologie différentielle de l'adolescence.* Paris: Presses Universitaires de France.

# Part II
# Interpersonal behaviour and communication

# 8. Communication in the family and psychopathology: a social-developmental approach to deviant behaviour

ROLV MIKKEL BLAKAR

The fundamental questions underlying and guiding our research can be formulated on two levels, the one more general than the other. The more general question is: under what conditions, broadly speaking, will an individual (for instance, a child) develop into a healthy person, and under what conditions will a person manage to maintain his or her healthy state of well-being? To clinically oriented psychologists the counterpart of this general enquiry would be: under what conditions, broadly speaking, will an individual (for instance, a child) develop deviant behaviour and/or psycho-pathology, and under what conditions will a person not manage to cope in maintaining his or her healthy state of well-being? Obviously, these questions are too general as a guide to more specific conceptual and methodological issues; but they are helpful in tracing the outlines of the theoretical framework within which our actual research has been conducted.

We adopted a communication perspective in dealing with these general problems. As a result, on the more specific level, the basic questions guiding and integrating our research and theory construction were as follows: what are the prerequisites for (successful) communication, i.e. under what conditions will somebody succeed (to a reasonable degree) in making something known to somebody else? To clinically oriented psychologists the counterpart of this enquiry would be: which of the preconditions have not been satisfied when communication fails? An important aim of our research, with obvious theoretical as well as practical implications, was hence an identification and systematic description of the various prerequisites for (successful) commun-ication. Such a research programme needs to encompass individual and situational as well as social variables (Blakar 1974).

The fact that each of the two basic questions underlying our research has been formulated with its 'counterpart' was deliberate. This was meant to express our view that clinically oriented research (the 'counterpart' enquiries) has to be conducted as an integral aspect of general psychology. For a full exposition of such a general programme, see Blakar (in press b).

137

## 1. Conceptual framework: a brief outline

A conceptual framework which can reasonably be labelled 'the ecology of (human) development' is needed as a general framework in the family/communication oriented research on psychopathology and deviant behaviour. Second, there is the need for a theoretical framework and corresponding models to conceive of the process of communication. Whereas the first should constitute the general framework for identifying essential problems for research, for integrating our studies and findings with the theories and research of others, etc., the latter should support the more specific conceptual framework for devising methods, designing studies, developing adequate concepts for analysis, and so on.

With regard to a conceptual framework and corresponding models of 'an ecology of development', we have freely borrowed from, and extensively built on, the theoretical analyses and empirical studies conducted by the Norwegian psychologist Hilde Nafstad and her collaborators (Nafstad, 1971a, 1976, 1978). In view of space limitations, it would not be possible to provide here a coherent presentation of her conceptual framework, let alone to review the empirical studies on which her theoretical work is grounded. However, three major characteristics that made her conceptual framework most relevant to the family/communication research on psychopathology and deviant behaviour will be briefly mentioned. First, she conceives of the individual's/child's development in terms of a 'box-within-box' model, where the child/individual in focus is understood within his or her family/household; the family is in turn understood as embedded in, and interplaying with, the surrounding local society, which in turn is understood as an integral part of the particular culture and society at large (Nafstad 1971b, c, 1973). The family operates as a crucial mediating agent or linkage between the child/individual and the surrounding society. In this respect Nafstad's theoretical framework is basically similar to the currently very popular model proposed by Bronfenbrenner (1977, 1979).

Second, Nafstad conceives of the interplay between the individual and the surrounding society in terms of welfare theory. This concerns the extent to which the actual living conditions of the individual satisfy his or her (basic) needs and wishes (Nafstad 1975, 1976, 1980). Welfare theory, previously applied exclusively to adults, and mainly within the disciplines of sociology and economics, has been re-formulated by Nafstad into a psychological theory with particular reference to the developing child/individual (Nafstad & Gaarder 1979). Third, and this follows in part from the above, there is the deliberate openness in her framework, which allows an understanding of an individual's behaviour and suffering not only in terms of his or her disease or handicap (be it asthma, deafness, or whatever), but in terms of the surrounding (local) society's reactions to the ability or lack of ability to cope adequately with the special demands posed by the particular disease or handicap (Nafstad 1977, 1978). For instance, a paralyzed person's social isolation may be more adequately understood in terms of a lack of access for the wheelchair to places where people meet (due to steep staircases, narrow doors, etc.), than to his or her paralysis. This is an obvious example, but the framework also allows for an analysis of the more subtle interplay between the individual and the surrounding (local) society in cases of psychopathology and deviant behaviour in general. A comprehensive exposition of the theoretical framework can be found in Nafstad & Gaarder (1979). An exposition which contains an explicit consideration of the family/communication oriented study of psychopathology and deviant behaviour is provided by Blakar & Nafstad (1981).

With regard to theory of communication, the conceptual framework of social-cognitive psychology of language and communication, as developed by Rommetveit & Blakar (Rommetveit 1968, 1972a, b, 1974; Blakar 1970, 1973, 1981a; Rommetveit & Blakar 1979) has been adopted. We have argued elsewhere (Blakar 1980b) that a major difficulty hindering progress in the field of family/interaction research is the application of a concept of communication which is too vague and extensive in its definitions (if 'communication' is defined at all). We shall therefore briefly illustrate here how communication is defined within the present framework.

In defining communication, the main problem is to capture the essential aspects of this common and universal human activity, while *at the same time* distinguishing 'communication' from processes and activities bearing basic resemblances to communication. The most essential characteristic of communication is that something is being made known to somebody. It follows from this that an act of communication is *social* and *directional* (*from* a sender *to* a receiver). A crucial characteristic distinguishing communication from the general flow of information is that the sender has an *intention* to make something known to the (particular) receiver. (The intentionality in acts of communication is reflected, for example, in the equifinality of different means.) When communication is defined as a (sender's) intentional act to make something (the message) known to others (the receivers), then the behavioural as well as the informational aspects become integrated, *at the same time* as we manage to distinguish communication from behaviour and information-processing in general. For elaborations of this communication theoretical framework in connection with this particular research programme, see Blakar (1980a, 1981a, in press a, b).

In the actual research projects, the conceptual frameworks are integrated as follows: the functions and structures of the familial unit of the first framework are investigated and conceived in terms of patterns of communication. Before we present the actual studies, two more characteristics bearing on both levels of our conceptual framework should be mentioned. First, it has been our aim to capture the *experiential perspective* of the involved family members (the communicating individuals) as well as their *observable behaviour*. It is only such double anchoring of concepts that can entail adequate understanding of the subtle processes taking place when a family interacts in actual situations (cf. Blakar 1980a). It is this intention to include the behavioural as well as the experiential components that forces us to employ the cumbersome double expression 'deviant behaviour and/or psychopathology'. Second, the analysis has to consider individual, situational and social/cultural variables as well as the interplay between these variables (Blakar 1974). To underline the social (communicational) and developmental dimensions as well as the extensive interplay between these dimensions, we have labelled our approach 'social-developmental'.

## 2. Our method: a standardized communication conflict situation

In an effort to identify and describe some of the prerequisites for communication, we developed a particular experimental method (Blakar 1973). The method was directly derived from our general conceptual framework, and it was further inspired by various studies of communication breakdowns, especially those typical for children (for example, Piagetian studies on egocentrism), and also by analyses of everyday misunderstandings and how they occur.

The general idea of the method was very simple, but in practice it proved very difficult to realize. The problem was how to devise a communication situation where one of the preconditions for (successful) communication was *not* satisfied. It can be hypothesized that the most basic precondition for successful communication to take place at all is that the participants have established '*a shared social reality*', a common 'here-and-now' within which exchange of messages can take place (Blakar & Rommetveit 1975; Rommetveit 1974). An ideal experimental situation would thus be one where two (or more) participants communicate with each other *in the belief* that they are 'in the same situation' (i.e. have a common definition of the situation's 'here' and 'now'), but where they are in fact in different situations. In other words, we tried to create a situation where each participant speaks and understands what is said on the basis of his or her own particular interpretation of the situation and falsely believes that the other (others) speaks and understands on the basis of that same interpretation (as is often the case in everyday quarrels and misunderstandings).

The problems encountered in developing an experimental situation that 'worked', i.e. a situation where the subjects would communicate for a reasonable period of time *without* suspecting anything awry, cannot be dealt with here (see Blakar 1973). The final design, however, was simple and seemed quite natural. Two persons, A and B, are each given a map of a relatively complicated network of roads and streets in a town centre. On A's map two routes are marked with arrows, one short and straightforward (the practice route), and another longer and more complicated (the experimental route). On B's map no route is marked. A's task is to explain to B the two routes, first the simple one, then the longer and more complicated one. B will then, with the help of A's explanations, try to find the way through town to the predetermined end-point. B may ask questions: for example, ask A to repeat the explanations, or to explain in other ways, and so on. The experimental manipulation is simply that the two maps are not identical. An extra street is added on B's map/a street is lacking on A's map. So, no matter how adequately A explains, no matter how carefully B carries out A's instructions, B is bound to go wrong. The difference between the two maps has implication only for the complicated route, however; the practice route is straightforward for both.

A study where students served as subjects convinced us that the experimental manipulation was successful (Blakar 1973). The most relevant findings in this connection were:

1. It took an average of 18 minutes from the start on the experimental route *before* any doubt concerning the credibility of the maps was expressed. During this time the subjects communicated under the false assumption that they were sharing the *same* situation (the same 'here').
2. Moreover, the situation proved successful in demonstrating how the subjects 'diagnosed' their communication difficulties, and what kinds of 'tools' they had at their disposal in order to remedy and improve their communication. The experimental situation seemed to make great demands on the subjects' powers of flexibility and ability to modify their communication patterns, and also on their capacity to decentre and see things from the other's perspective. (Blakar 1981b: 200).

The latter finding involves, actually, a tentative specification of such prerequisites for (successful) communication.

### 3. Schizophrenia and family communication: a social-developmental approach

A brief juxtaposition of the communicative behaviour shown in this particula situation and Haley's (1972) summary of findings within family researcl immediately reveals how promising this method seemed in the task of dealing with the theoretical and methodological problems in this field. Haley (p. 35 summarized family research as follows:

Abnormal families appear to have more conflict, to have different coalition patterns and to show more inflexibility in repeating patterns, and behaviour. *The most soun findings would seem to be in the outcome area: when faced with a task on which they mus cooperate, abnormal family members seem to communicate their preferences less successfull require more activity and take longer to get the task done.* (My italics)

In the first exploratory study (Sølvberg & Blakar 1975) we chose, both fo theoretical and for practical reasons, to concentrate on the parent dyad Obviously, this is the core dyad in the milieu into which the child is born an within which she/he later matures into a healthy or pathological person Moreover, we did not want to include the patient him(her) self in this ver first study, in which the method and conceptual framework itself were to b tried out. Inasmuch as the communication task given to each couple is ir principle unsolvable, it was determined on the basis of pre-tests that if the couple had not unravelled the induced communication conflict (i.e. discovere the difference between the maps) within 40 minutes, the communication tasl would be brought to an end. The subjects would be shown the discrepancy and told that the task was actually unsolvable. (For details concerning the termination criteria, see Blakar 1980a.) The distribution of the maps among the spouses had to be standardized. To counteract culturally determined mal dominance, we gave the map with the routes drawn in to the wives, so tha the husbands had to follow the directives and explanations of their wives.

An important issue was to establish two comparable groups, one consisting of parents *with* schizophrenic offspring (Group S) and one matched contro group *without* (Group N). During this early phase, we chose to limit ourselve to small, but strictly controlled and matched, groups. (For selection criteri and matching, see Blakar 1980a; Sølvberg & Blakar 1975.)

The major findings can be summarized as follows. As regards the simpl situation, where no conflict was induced, and hence no critical evaluation an readjustment of communication strategy were required, Group S parent performed as well as Group N parents, and similarly to highly educated studen dyads. However, *when a discrepancy with respect to premises* was induced, fou out of five of Group S parents failed, while the Group N couples managed

Detailed analysis of the patterns of communication in the simple and conflict-free situation, moreover, indicated subtle qualitative differences. These differences did not influence communication efficiency in the plain and simple situation, but they proved critical in the more demanding communication conflict situation. (For detailed presentation and discussion of results, see Blakar 1980a; Sølvberg & Blakar 1975.)

A tenable conclusion seems to be that a standardized conflict situation which was really *sensitive* with respect to the participants' abilities/inabilities to unravel underlying conflicts, had been established. From the perspective of social psychology in general and communication theory in particular, this should come as no surprise. In the method, fundamental preconditions for (successful) communication are systematically manipulated (see above), so that *if* there is any reality to the idea that families containing schizophrenic members demonstrate deviant communication, this should indeed be revealed under these conditions. Moreover, the relevant conceptual framework (see above) allows for specification of situational conditions *under which* the differences will be salient.

## 4. Towards an integrative social-developmental programme of research

The success of the above study did not imply that all conceptual and methodological problems in communication research on schizophrenia were settled. On the contrary, as we wrote elsewhere (Blakar 1980b), in retrospect this study 'may be conceived of as a lucky shot', and it raised more questions than it settled. Maybe the most significant contribution at this stage was that by this particular method the various couples' special patterns of communication were exposed to a degree that rendered possible the formulation of an array of theoretically grounded and researchable hypotheses. Traditionally, hypotheses in this field, if formulated at all, have been *ad hoc* (and atheoretical). A quotation from our 1975 paper should illustrate the kind of theoretically significant questions that emerged:

1.  Do Group S couples have a more egocentric and less decentrated form of communication? In other words, are Group S spouses less able and/or willing to take the perspective of, and speak on the premises of, the other? For instance, utterances such as '...and then you go up *there*', '...and from *here* you take a right', when 'here' and 'there' could obviously not be known to the other, were frequently observed in communication of the Group S couples.
2.  Are Group S couples less able and/or willing to endorse (and adhere to) contracts that regulate and monitor the various aspects of their communication (for example, role distribution, perspective, strategy of explanation)? Only a few contractual proposals were found (regarding, for example, categorization and explanation strategy).

Furthermore, many cases were observed in which implicitly or explicitly endorsed contracts were broken or ignored.

3.   Do Group S couples show less ability and/or willingness to attribute (adequately or inadequately) their communication difficulties to any potential causes? The Group S couples could apparently return to the starting point again and again without any (overt, explicit) attempt to attribute their communication difficulties to anything. (Sølvberg & Blakar 1975: 531)

Ever since 1974 we have been pursuing these and similar hypotheses through a variety of studies designed according to the above paradigm. (For review, see Blakar 1980a, in press b). Although the above study constituted a substantial step towards conducting family studies grounded in explicit communication theory (and social psychology in general), this exploratory study nevertheless fell short of various ideal theoretical-methodological requirements for studies designed to elucidate the condition of schizophrenia. (For a statement of such requirements, see Blakar & Nafstad 1981.) Through analysis of the shortcomings of the above study, we developed a research programme to amend these various flaws, a programme that has been implemented ever since (see Blakar 1980a, 1981b).

A satisfactory solution to the problems of schizophrenia would necessarily involve integration of knowledge obtained within different disciplines from studying the subject matter from differing perspectives – psychology, genetics, biochemistry, pharmacology, anthropology, etc. (cf. Blakar 1981a; Blakar & Nafstad 1981). In the following analysis, however, we will restrict ourselves to desirable and/or necessary continuations of the present project conceptualized *within* the present framework of social-developmental theory. Integration with other disciplines and perspectives belongs to the future. Furthermore, our theoretical and methodological considerations were at this stage also determined by the fact that we did not want to make any changes regarding the communication conflict situation itself. Given the promising results achieved in the first exploratory study, this seemed a reasonable choice (cf. Blakar 1980a; Sølvberg & Blakar 1975).

In analysing theoretical-methodological shortcomings in the Sølvberg & Blakar (1975) study, we identified six different issues or aspects on which further work had to be conducted to render conclusions possible (cf. Blakar 1980a, b). The classification is primarily of a formal-logical character. In practice, work along any one of these six lines will be mutually supportive, and follow-up studies should be planned and designed to address two or more of these theoretical-methodological shortcomings. It should be emphasized that whereas some of the controls (see (2) below) are indeed needed to render *any* conclusion of the Sølvberg & Blakar study possible, other of the follow-up studies can be conceived more as an attempt to outline a general research programme. Moreover, the order of presentation below does not reflect a hierarchy of importance.

(1) *Replications and expansions of the samples.* First and foremost, the two samples had to be enlarged, or the study replicated. But merely to increase sample size *without* improving the conceptual framework (see (6), below) and developing methods of analysis (see (5), below) would be nonsensical.

(2) *Different demand characteristics.* A vital requirement, in fact a *sine qua non* for studies designed to obtain conclusive evidence with respect to differences and similarities in the behaviour of different categories of subjects (families), is that their behaviour is observed under *identical* or *comparable* conditions. In particular, when it comes to social behaviour (for example communication), it is very difficult indeed to establish identical or comparable conditions (social situations) for different categories of social actors. Social behaviour is a product of subtle person(s)–situation interactions (Bem & Allen 1974; Bowers 1973; Rommetveit 1979; Stokstad, Lagerløv & Blakar 1979). Moreover, the meaning of a situation may vary from person to person, and from time to time for the same person. And the subjects do not act upon the situation as defined by the experimenter: they act upon the situation as defined and experienced by themselves. Hence the experimenter has to take great care to control *how* the various categories of subjects (families) experience and define the actual situation. Only in terms of their (the subjects') definition of the situation, is it possible to reach adequate understanding of their (social) behaviour (Blakar 1981a).

At first glance, the treatment of the participating couples in the Sølvberg & Blakar study may seem to be identical. However, closer examination of the two different categories of couples reveals that highly different expectations may be held towards the study as such. (For an analysis of differences with regard to situational demand characteristics, see Blakar 1980a, 1981b.) More urgent than enlarging the samples (see (1) above), therefore, is the need to 'test' the parents of children with diagnoses *other* than schizophrenia in this particular communication conflict situation. With respect to criteria for selecting adequate control groups, see Blakar (1980a).

(3) *Parent–child interactions.* Even though the present design does not address the issue of causality directly (cf. Blakar 1980a, 1981b; Blakar & Nafstad 1981), it would be intriguing to investigate the communication between the parents and the child (schizophrenic vs. control) in this conflict situation.

(4) *General variables in communication.* In critical analysis of this field of research (see above, and Blakar 1980a, b) we pointed out that various of the theoretical and methodological weaknesses could be ascribed to a lack of

contact with *general theory*. The fact that the present method was explicitly derived from general communication theory (Blakar 1973, 1981a) constituted an obvious improvement, but nevertheless there is an obligation to examine further our findings concerning schizophrenia (deviant behaviour and psychopathology), in terms of general theory, and to relate our findings to general social, personality and developmental variables.

(a) Anthropological and sociological studies have shown how people from different cultural and social (class) backgrounds employ differing patterns of communication and language use (cf. Bernstein 1971; Hall 1959; Labov *et al.* 1968). Moreover, it is known that the occurrence and distribution of various forms of psychopathology vary in different cultures and classes. In other words, communication characteristics that prove to be specific to, and 'normal' in, certain subcultures (e.g. a social class) could easily be interpreted as deviant characteristics in the familial communication of the schizophrenic. Hence it is desirable to obtain knowledge on how general social variables such as socio-economic status, urban as opposed to rural background, etc., are reflected in communication in such situations.

(b) In spite of the fact that the concept of personality remains problematic and controversial (cf. Bem & Allen 1974; Mischel 1968, 1973), there is, nevertheless, no doubt that the kind of variables that have traditionally been conceived of as 'personality traits' will be salient in communication. General variables such as anxiety, aggression, degree of confidence (in oneself and others), rigidity as opposed to flexibility, etc. will obviously affect the communication process. To assess the implications of the (deviant) communication found in the family of the schizophrenic, it will thus be of vital importance to know *how* the communication of rigid persons deviates from that of more flexible persons *within* the so-called normal range. In addition to indicating whether the communication of rigid (or flexible) persons have common characteristics with the pattern found in the familial environment of the schizophrenic, this type of study would, it is hoped, entail conceptual clarification with respect to variable labels which have been used as both individual and social variables (cf. Blakar 1974).

(c) Various concepts we employed in describing the familial communication, above, involve developmental aspects and are based on developmental theory. For example, the communication of the Group S couples was characterized as egocentric (lacking the capacity to decentre and take the other's perspective) (Sølvberg & Blakar 1975). In the literature (Glucksberg *et al.* 1966; Nafstad & Gaarder 1979; Piaget 1926; Strøno

1978) it is demonstrated how capacity to decentre develops from the child's nearly total egocentrism to the adult's (periodical?) decentration. Analogous to (a) and (b) above, knowledge about communication in conflict situations demonstrated by children at various stages of development, i.e. with differing capacity regarding decentration, could elucidate the 'deviations' found in the family of the schizophrenic.

(5) *Methods of analysis.* The exploratory Sølvberg & Blakar study revealed that we, like others in this field, were practically without systematic methods for analysing and describing *the qualitative aspects* of the communication exposed in this situation. A blind scorer, basing his predictions on clinical judgment only, correctly identified four of the five Group S couples by listening to the tape-recordings from this conflict situation (Sølvberg & Blakar 1975). This indicated that our conceptual apparatus was not yet sufficiently explicit and refined (see (6) below). Although we did have some relevant concepts (such as egocentrism), we lacked corresponding methods (with the exception of descriptive case reports) by which systematic scoring could be conducted.

(6) *Conceptual framework.* The outcome of this exploratory study constituted a great challenge towards further development of our theoretical framework and conceptual apparatus, to enable us to capture and understand the various patterns of communication which were so vividly exposed in that situation.

A few comments have to be made concerning the above list of points. First and foremost, we have discussed the various potential studies either as follow-ups or just as controls in connection with the study of schizophrenia and familial communication. This is, of course, too narrow a perspective to take towards the potential studies suggested under points (2), (3) and (4), let alone points (5) and (6).

Secondly, in the above analysis we have concentrated on purely methodological issues. Nevertheless, there is every reason to emphasize that the examples we have chosen as illustrations may prove to be substantially interesting in their own right. This is shown when the various examples given above are compared with the descriptions the blind scorer in the Sølvberg & Blakar study gave of the communication of the Group S couples:

the Group S couples (as compared to the Group N couples) were characterized by (a) more rigidity (in explanation strategy, in role distribution, etc.); (b) less ability and/or willingness to listen to, and take into account what the other said; (c) a more unprecise and diffuse language (unprecise definitions, concepts, etc.); and (d) more 'pleasing' and/or pseudo-agreement in situations in which the erroneous maps had made them lose each other. (Sølvberg & Blakar 1975: 527–8)

## 5. Implementation of the research programme

This section contains a brief review of what has been done until now within the research programme outlined above. In the presentation we will adhere to the order followed in the above list of theoretical-methodological issues. Each study will hence be presented and commented upon only from the perspective of theoretical-methodological issues outlined in the previous section.

(1)  *Replications and expansions of the samples.* Two accurate replications of the Sølvberg & Blakar study were conducted, first by Paulsen (1977) and then by Valdimarsdottir (1980). In this connection the widely acknowledged lack of replications of studies in this field should be noted (cf. Riskin & Faunce 1972). Whereas great care was taken to replicate the original study in all respects, one crucial variable was deliberately manipulated, in that the replicative studies were conducted in socio-cultural contexts other than the original study. Whereas the Sølvberg & Blakar study was conducted in Oslo, the first replication was carried out in a typical rural area of Norway and the latter in Iceland. In both these studies the findings of the original Sølvberg & Blakar study bearing upon *differences in patterns of communication* of parents having and not having a schizophrenic offspring were in all essential respects reproduced (Blakar, Paulsen & Sølvberg 1978; Blakar & Valdimarsdottir 1981). However, these studies also testified to the subtlety of social/cultural/ ecological factors, in that the differences between the so-called 'normal' control couples in the three studies proved considerable. This series of replicative studies thus questioned the notion of 'normal family communi- cation' implicitly underlying most interaction research (cf. Blakar & Valdi- marsdottir 1981). Taken together, the original study and the two replications yield a complex $3 \times 2 \times 2$ design, in that we get parental couples from three different socio-cultural backgrounds, with and without a schizo- phrenic offspring interacting in two different communication situations (one being simple and straightforward whereas in the other a conflict is induced). This design allowed for detailed analyses of normal as well as deviant patterns of family communication across varying situational and differing social/ cultural/ecological backgrounds (Blakar & Valdimarsdottir 1981; Valdimars- dottir 1980).

(2)  *Different demand characteristics.* With regard to the important metho- dological issue concerning the situational demand characteristics, several independent and substantially interesting studies have been conducted (Alve & Hultberg 1974; Andersson & Pilblad 1977; Fætten & Østvold 1975; Knutsen 1979; Kristiansen 1976; Rotbæk 1976; Wikran 1974; for a review, see Blakar 1980a, 1981b).

However, the substantial findings of all these studies would be of minor interest here. To examine the *theoretical-methodological problems* in focus, the one study of parental couples with a borderline offspring (Group B) will be chosen. The outcome of this study is particularly critical to the Sølvberg & Blakar study. First and foremost, borderline represents a 'non-schizophrenic control' to use Bannister's (1968) terminology. Second, the distinction between the diagnostic categories 'schizophrenia' and 'borderline' is subtle, and it is *not* likely to be known by the parents. Hence the two categories are likely to enter the situation with identical or comparable expectations, viz. that they are participating *because* they are the parents of a psychiatric patient/a 'mad person'. Moreover, parental couples having a child with a serious heart disease (Group H) represent a crucial control. Similar to parents having a schizophrenic offspring, they are the parents of a seriously ill person. The illness of their child will also strongly influence family life, although very differently from a schizophrenic member. And like the Group S parents, they will know that they participate because they are parents of a seriously ill child. But contrary to schizophrenia (and borderline), there is no reason to assume that the illness can be understood in terms of familial communication.

Given these four categories of parental couples, Group N, Group S, Group B, and Group H, a variety of possible combinations with regard to *differences* and *similarities* in patterns of communication can be imagined. The combination of outcomes has been most supportive with respect to further elaborations of the conceptual and methodological issues in the field, while at the same time providing intriguing substantive evidence. First, parents of seriously ill children (heart disease) *did not* deviate in their communication from Group N. Furthermore, *both* Group S *and* Group B demonstrated patterns of communication *different* from Group N, and moreover, they demonstrated patterns distinctively *different from each other*. And most intriguing of all, on various measures the communication of Group S and Group B deviated in *opposite directions* from Group N. (For detailed descriptions of communication of Group S, Group B and Group N, see Andersson & Pilblad 1977; Hultberg, Alve & Blakar 1978/80; Knutsen 1979.)

(3) *Parent–child interaction.* In these studies the mother and father together are asked to explain the two routes to their daughter or son. Jacobsen & Pettersen (1974) analysed communication between the parents and their schizophrenic or 'normal' daughter. Differences in communication between Group S and Group N families were revealed just as clearly in this three-person setting as in the Sølvberg & Blakar study (Mossige, Pettersen & Blakar 1979). Haarstad's (1976) investigation of parent–daughter communication of families in which the daughter was given the diagnosis of *anorexia nervosa* settled the issue with regard to demand characteristics, in that families of this category

revealed a communication pattern which was differentiated from *both* Group S *and* Group N families in essential respects. (In a series of other studies adopting this three-person design the above findings have been corroborated, cf. Antonsen 1980; Aspen 1981; Glennsjø 1977; Olsen 1981; Vassend 1979; Valstad 1980; for a review, see Blakar 1980a.)

(4) *General variables in communication.* As we have shown elsewhere (Blakar 1981a, 1981b), clinically oriented research in this field has not been properly integrated with more general research on communication (cf. also Helmersen 1981; Riskin & Faunce 1972). It follows from the programme we have outlined that it is necessary to conduct clinically oriented studies as an integral part of a general study of the process of communication. Only within the frame of general communication theory will it be possible to contribute to the understanding of psychopathology from a communication perspective. Concentrating exclusively on investigating patterns of communication in families with and without psychopathological members obviously involves the risk of labelling as 'deviant' or 'pathological' patterns of communication which would prove to be within the 'normal range' if one took care to explore systematically the variation of 'normal' communication.

As an illustration of how (a) personality variables are reflected in the process of communication, Lagerløv & Stokstad (1974) analysed the communication of persons with varying levels of anxiety. They compared the communication of students with high vs. low level of anxiety (as measured by Taylor's Manifest Anxiety Scale). It should be emphasized that we are not referring to extreme or 'pathological' anxiety, but to levels of anxiety found amongst normally functioning university students. In the simple situation there was no difference in efficiency of communication. In the conflict situation, however, there was a marked difference in that whereas all the low level anxiety dyads solved the induced conflict, more than half of the high level anxiety dyads failed. This study thus testified to subtle *person–situation interactions* in communication (Stokstad, Lagerløv & Blakar 1979).

With respect to (b), social (anthropological) variables, Dahle (1977) analysed the communication of couples with differing social backgrounds (urban vs. rural, and working-class vs. middle class couples). And Pedersen (1979a, b) studied how the communication is structured and defined by sex roles. Dahle demonstrated that the variations in style and efficiency in communication within the range of so-called 'normal' couples, i.e. in couples who do not have an offspring who is given some sort of psychiatric diagnosis, are indeed considerable, and covary systematically with social background. Again the interaction with type of communication situation should be noted in that, whereas no differences in communication efficiency were found in the simple situation, clear-cut differences emerged in the conflict situation. Moreover, Pedersen (1979a) revealed highly different patterns of communication depending on how the sexes of explainer and follower were combined. The four combinations: (1) man→man, (2) woman→woman, (3) man→ woman, (4) woman→man, yielded very different patterns of communication. One of the findings which may be briefly mentioned is that – in accordance with the commonsense 'knowledge' about sex roles – male→female dyads revealed the most efficient communication, and female→male the most inefficient. However, this was true of the simple situation only. The pattern was totally *reversed* in the conflict situation, in that male→female dyads were the most inefficient in solving the induced conflict (cf. Blakar & Pedersen 1980). Dahle's and Pedersen's studies yield interesting contributions to an understanding of social control and communication in general (Blakar 1981a, in press b).

Finally, with respect to (c), Strøno (1978) analysed the communication in this situation within the framework of general developmental psychology. She investigated the communication of children of various ages (6–16 years) and found, as would be expected, an increasing capacity to decentre and take the perspective of the other (Mead 1934; Piaget 1926). The communication became more adequate and efficient with increasing age. The categorization system developed by Strøno to identify and describe the various manifestations of egocentrism in communication has provided a general framework within which the communication of different categories of families can be assessed (cf. Blakar & Nafstad 1981).

The above review is not intended as an exhaustive analysis of how general social, developmental and personality variables are reflected in the process of communication. These studies are reviewed only to demonstrate that systematic studies along these lines are necessary to warrant any conclusions from studies conducted on the relation between communication and (development of) psychopathology (e.g. schizophrenia). First, only through this type of systematic study can we learn the normal variations. Without a thorough knowledge of normal variations in communication according to social class and cultural and ecological background variables, it would not be possible to assess and describe properly deviant or pathological communication. Studies of the kind that Dahle (1977) conducted are particularly crucial because the underlying (often implicit) model of 'normal communication' from which pathological communication deviates is seriously subject to question. We have argued elsewhere (Blakar & Valdimarsdottir 1981) that a special kind of experimenter ethnocentrism has been displayed by students of psychopathology and familial communication, in that the 'norm' for 'adequate communication' has been implicitly defined as the communication of the normal middle-class family living in cities.

Secondly, knowledge about how such general variables affect the process of communication may contribute to the identification of *what* (if anything) is failing in the communication of families containing members who have been ascribed psychiatric diagnoses (for example, schizophrenia). Conclusions concerning causality cannot be drawn from such covariation studies, but systematic comparisons of the communication of people having, for instance, a high level of anxiety, with families containing, for instance, a schizophrenic member, could give valuable clues for future research.

(5) *Methods of analysis*. We have argued elsewhere (Blakar & Nafstad 1981), and this follows almost by necessity from our general, integrative framework outlined above, that methods and concepts of analysis in family/ communication research should ideally have a three-fold anchoring, in that they should be anchored (a) in theory of communication, (b) in developmental theory, as well as (c) capture essential characteristics of the specific category of psychopathology in focus. With regard to the study of schizophrenia, we have demonstrated how, for instance, the concept of egocentrism-decentration satisfies these criteria (Blakar & Nafstad 1981).

In particular, when it comes to qualitative analysis of communication in families, most researchers seem to have given up, or forgotten all about, general communication theory. Overwhelmed by the richness of the material and its variations, they have resorted to mere clinical-casuistic descriptions, freely employing everyday language and *ad hoc* terms. (For critical reviews of this conceptual and terminological chaos, see Blakar 1980b; Helmersen 1981; Riskin & Faunce 1972.) Riskin & Faunce point out that 'interdisciplinary isolation' is striking. But if one turns, for example, to social-developmental psychology, a whole set of relevant and theoretically grounded concepts is available.

To illustrate, a few examples will be given. A basic precondition for successful communication is the participants' ability to take the perspective of the other (Mead 1934); and egocentrism (lack of decentration) (Piaget 1926) may strongly hinder communication. Related to this is Rommetveit's (1968) notion that 'encoding involves *anticipatory decoding*'. Another essential prerequisite for successful communication is that the participants have to endorse *contracts* (contracts concerning categorization, topic, perspective, etc.) by which the act of communication is being monitored (Blakar 1981a, in press b; Rommetveit 1972b, 1974). And when communication runs into more or less serious trouble, it is essential, in order to re-establish commonality, that the difficulties be adequately attributed by the participants. Even superficial familiarity with communication in relation to psychopathology makes one see that these concepts from social-developmental theory may be of direct relevance in the analysis of familial communication.

To investigate these concepts we have developed a set of methods of analysis and scoring procedures to assess the theoretically relevant qualitative aspects of the process of communication. A few such methods of analysis will be briefly mentioned. (For a more detailed and integrative presentation, see Blakar 1980a, 1981a, in press b.)

Hultberg, Alve & Blakar (1978, republished in Blakar 1980a) took as their point of departure the concept of attribution, and developed a procedure to describe the process of communication in terms of the couples' patterns of attribution of communication difficulties (*who* attributes *how* to *what*, and *how* does the other(s) react to the attribution). Already in the first exploratory study the concept of egocentrism (vs. decentration) proved useful in capturing qualitative differences in the patterns of communication of parental couples with and without a schizophrenic offspring. In his analysis of utterance level, Kristiansen (1976) managed to assess degree of, and development over time of egocentrism during the process of communication, as well as types of reaction to the egocentric utterances (e.g. Kristiansen, Faleide & Blakar 1977). Recently, Antonsen (1980) has pursued this analysis to assess the potential interplay between degree of egocentrism shown by individual family members and to what degree the family exposes a closed or open family system (cf. Mossige, Pettersen & Blakar 1979).

From a methodological point of view, an advantage of the present design is that we get excerpts of the communication process in two apparently similar, but actually highly different, situations. The one is simple and straightforward, whereas in the other a conflict is induced. In a sense we thus have a 'before–after' design. The difference between the two situations, moreover, is conceptualized within the framework of a general theory of communication (cf. Blakar 1973, 1980a, 1981a; Blakar & Pedersen 1980). The fact that in a study where 24 student dyads participated, a rank-order correlation of −0.19 was found between efficiency (time used) of communication in the two situations (Blakar & Pedersen 1980) indicates that we really have managed to establish two apparently similar, but in reality highly different, communication situations.

In principle, this methodological advantage may be exploited in many ways to gain insight into and obtain knowledge about the process of communication. So far we have mainly used various prediction or blind-scoring procedures. The general procedure may be described as follows: the scorer is only allowed to listen to the recording from the simple situation. On the basis of his or her analysis of the pattern of communication in the simple situation, the scorer is asked to predict – and give the reasons for the predictions – how these particular participants (family/couple/dyad) will manage to cope with the induced conflict. In this manner we can, to a certain extent, put our insights and the different methods of analysis to a test. A study by Teigre (1976) will serve as an illustrative example. He assessed the degree of confidence (in oneself and the other) in the simple situation for 30 married couples, and, on the basis of the type and degree of mutual confidence, the outcome in the communication conflict situation was predicted.

(6) *The conceptual framework.* As a transition to point (6), we will consider an issue which was originally encountered as an irritating methodological problem, but which proved to involve intriguing, basic theoretical issues. *When* is a problem in an act of communication unravelled? *When* is a communication conflict solved? The trivial problem of analysis which originally compelled us to undertake the study of these issues in general, was that we soon ran into trouble in distinguishing between those who managed (solvers) and those who did not manage (non-solvers) to unravel the induced conflict (cf. Blakar 1981a; Hultberg, Alve & Blakar 1978; Mossige, Pettersen & Blakar 1979; Wikran, Faleide & Blakar 1978). First, in some cases only one of the participants recognized the deception in the maps, while the other(s) would show great surprise when the error was afterwards uncovered by a direct comparison of the two maps. This type of solution, which we have classified as an individual solution, is very different from cases in which both (all) are firmly convinced about the existence of the error (a social solution). If the experimenter too readily accepted an individual solution, we would lose the chance to study how the member with insight convinces or fails to convince the other(s). Actually, this phase could be very revealing as to factors such as power and control.

Furthermore, various combinations of degrees of cognitive insight and social convictions *vis-à-vis* the experimenter have been observed. On the one extreme, we have the couples or families in which one (or all) members claim with conviction that something is wrong, and that consequently there is no reason in continuing, but without their having identified and localized the error on the maps. At the other extreme, we have the couples or families who have obviously achieved a certain insight about the deceptive maps (the degree of insight may vary from vague doubt to full understanding), but who are unsure of their own judgment and therefore hesitate to reveal their suspicions to the experimenter. The issue to be demonstrated here, however, is how the analysis of these methodological problems entailed an explication of general theory concerning social conflicts and their solution. To develop adequate criteria for terminating the experimental session, and accepting the induced communication conflict as being unravelled, an explicit model or theory of conflict solution had to be outlined (Blakar 1981a; Endresen 1977).

The above clinical studies have all contributed to theoretical and conceptual clarification. The development of scoring procedures in connection with some of the key concepts of social-developmental theory has in fact been one of the major purposes in several of these studies. However, as is always the case in clinical research, these studies were all devoted more or less exclusively to the study of one particular type of psychopathology (schizophrenia, *anorexia nervosa*, borderline syndrome, etc.). We have elsewhere (Blakar 1980b) pointed out various methodological pitfalls in the predominant strategy, according to which the study of familial communication and psychopathology is conducted exclusively within 'a clinical context' with little or no contact with general theory. Hence, if the conceptual framework was elaborated in connection with clinically oriented studies of the above types only, we would be guilty of ignoring our own criticism. To avoid these pitfalls, we have continuously conducted research on language, and communication in general, within the very same conceptual framework, and by employing the very same experimental paradigm. (For integrative presentations of this theoretical-empirical work, see Blakar 1981a, in press b; Rommetveit & Blakar 1979.)

## 6. Concluding remarks

Although the present chapter has reported on the yield of the joint efforts of many people over some years, the findings presented and the conclusions reached should be interpreted as highly explorative. This does not imply a modest down-grading of our work and its potential contribution. It reflects, however, an acknowledgement of the complexities and subtleties of the fundamental human problems that we have addressed.

The most honest conclusion at the present stage is thus that almost every study conducted within the above research programme so far has posed as many new questions and issues as it has settled. Communication-oriented research on psychopathology – the present research programme included – constitutes, therefore, a very intriguing challenge. However, the studies conducted so far have strongly convinced us that systematic investigation of the pattern of familial communication constitutes at least *one* promising way to gain insight into the complex processes leading to an individual developing or maintaining deviant or psychopathological behaviour. The above projects have fully demonstrated that the hurdles of such research are many and difficult, but also that an exhaustive exploitation of the conceptual framework

156     Rolv Mikkel Blakar

of social-developmental theory will represent an important supplement to the understanding of the various forms of deviant behaviour and psychopathology in general, and of schizophrenia in particular. For a more general discussion of such an implementation of social psychological perspectives in clinical psychological issues, see Blakar (in press b).

References

Alve, S. & Hultberg, M. 1974. Kommunikasjonssvikt hos foreldre til borderline pasienter. Unpublished dissertation, University of Oslo.

Andersson, R. & Pilblad, B. 1977. En metodologisk studie av samhandling i föräldra-dyader. Unpublished dissertation, University of Oslo.

Antonsen, L. 1980. Schizofreni og egosentrisme: Integrasjon av system- og individ orientert forståelse. Unpublished dissertation, University of Oslo.

Aspen, E. 1981. Identitetssvikt ved schizofreni og bekreftelse i familiens kommunikasjon. Unpublished dissertation, University of Oslo.

Bannister, D. 1968. Logical requirements of research into schizophrenia. *British Journal of Psychiatry*, *114*, 181–8.

Bem, D. J. & Allen, A. 1974. On predicting some of the people some of the time: the cross-situational consistence in behaviour. *Psychological Review*, *81*, 506–20.

Bernstein, B. 1971. *Class, code and control*. London: Routledge and Kegan Paul.

Blakar, R. M. 1970. Konteksteffektar i språkleg kommunikasjon. Unpublished dissertation, University of Oslo.

1973. An experimental method for inquiring into communication. *European Journal of Social Psychology*, *3*, 415–25.

1974. Distinguishing social and individual psychology. *Scandinavian Journal of Psychology*, *15*, 241–3.

(ed.) 1980a. *Studies of familial communication and psychopathology: a social-developmental approach to deviant behaviour*. Oslo: Universitetsforlaget; distributed in USA by Columbia University Press.

1980b. Psychopathology and familial communication. In M. Brenner (ed.) *The structure of action*. Oxford: Blackwell.

1981a. Communication: theory and research from a social-developmental perspective. *Informasjonsbulletin*, *17*, 1–75.

1981b. The social sensitivity of theory and method. In M. Brenner (ed.) *Social method and social life*. London: Academic Press.

in press a. Towards a theory of communication in terms of preconditions. In H. Giles & R. St.Clair (eds.) *The social psychological significance of communication*. Hillsdale, NJ: Erlbaum.

in press b. *Communication: a social perspective on clinical issues*. Oslo: Universitetsforlaget. Distributed in USA by Columbia University Press, and in UK by Global Books Resources.

Blakar, R. M. & Nafstad, H. E. 1981. The family as unit in the study of psychopathology and deviant behaviour: conceptual and methodological issues. Paper presented at the Conference on Discovery Strategies in the Psychology of Action, Bad Homburg, January.

Blakar, R. M. & Pedersen, T. B. 1980. Control and self-confidence as reflected in sex-bound patterns in communication: an experimental approach. *Acta Sociologica*, *23*, 33–53.

Blakar, R. M. & Rommetveit, R. 1975. Utterances in vacuo and in contexts: an experimental and theoretical exploration of some interrelationships between what is heard and what is seen or imagined. *International Journal of Psycholinguistics*, 4, 5–32; and *Linguistics*, 153, 5–32.

Blakar, R. M. & Valdimarsdottir, A. 1981. Schizophrenia and communication efficiency: a series of studies taking ecological variation into consideration. *Psychiatry and Social Science*, 1, 43–52.

Blakar, R. M., Paulsen, O. G. & Sølvberg, H. A. 1978. Schizophrenia and communication efficiency: a modified replication taking ecological variations into consideration. *Acta Psychiatrica Scandinavia*, 58, 315–26.

Bowers, K. S. 1973. Situationism in psychology: an analysis and a critique. *Psychological Review*, 80, 307–36.

Bronfenbrenner, U. 1977. Towards an experimental ecology of human development. *American Psychologist*, 32, 513–31.

1979. *The ecology of human development*. Cambridge, Mass.: Harvard University Press.

Dahle, M. 1977. Sosial bakgrunn og språklig kommunikasjon. Unpublished dissertation, University of Oslo.

Endresen, A. 1977. Modell för lösning av kommunikasjonskonflikt. Unpublished dissertation, University of Oslo.

Fætten, A. & Ostvold, M. 1975. Hysteri og kommunikasjon. Unpublished dissertation, University of Oslo.

Glennsjø, K. B. 1977. Marital schism og marital skew – en kommunikasjonsteoretisk tilnærming. Unpublished dissertation, University of Oslo.

Glucksberg, S., Krauss, R. M. & Weissberg, R. 1966. Referential communication in nursery school: method and some preliminary findings. *Journal of Experimental Child Psychology*, 3, 333–42.

Haarstad, B. E. 1976. Anoreksia nervosa: en eksperimentell studie av familiens kommunikasjon. Unpublished dissertation, University of Oslo.

Haley, J. 1972. Critical overview of present status of family interaction research. In J. L. Framo (ed.) *A dialogue between family researchers and family therapists*. New York: Springer.

Hall, E. T. 1959. *The silent language*. Greenwich, Conn.: Fawett.

Helmersen, P. 1981. Family interaction and communicational approaches to psychopathology and deviance: a critical evaluation. Unpublished dissertation, University of Oslo. To appear as a volume in the series European Monographs in Social Psychology, London: Academic Press.

Hultberg, M., Alve, S. & Blakar, R. M. 1978/80. Patterns of attribution of communicative difficulties in couples having a 'schizophrenic', a 'borderline' or a 'normal' offspring. *Informasjonsbulletin frå Psykopatologi og Kommunikasjonsprosjektet*, 6, 4–63. Reprinted in R. M. Blakar (ed.) 1980a.

Jacobsen, S. M. & Pettersen, R. B. 1974. Kommunikasjon og samarbeide i den schizofrenes familie. Unpublished dissertation, University of Oslo.

Knutsen, A. 1979. Kontroll i kommunikasjonen til foreldre til borderline-pasienter. Unpublished dissertation, University of Oslo.

Kristiansen, T. S. 1976. Kommunikasjon hos foreldre til barn med psykosomatiske lidelser. Unpublished dissertation, University of Oslo.

Kristiansen, T. S., Faleide, A. & Blakar, R. M. 1977. Kommunikasjon hos foreldre til barn med psykosomatiske lidelser: en eksperimentell tilnærming. *Tidsskrift for Norsk Psykologforening*, 14, 2–24.

Labov, W., Cohen, P., Robins, C. & Lewis, J. 1968. *A study of the non-standard English of negro and Puerto Rican speakers in New York City*. Final report, US Office of

158     Rolv Mikkel Blakar

Education, Cooperative Research Project No. 3288. New York: Columbia University.

Lagerløv, T. & Stokstad, S. J. 1974. Angst og kommunikasjon. Unpublished dissertation University of Oslo.

Mead, G. H. 1934. *Mind, self and society*. Chicago: University of Chicago Press.

Mischel, W. 1968. *Personality and assessment*. New York: Wiley.

1973. On the empirical dilemma of psychodynamic approaches: issues and alternatives. *Journal of Abnormal Psychology*, *82*, 335–44.

Mossige, S., Pettersen, R. B. & Blakar, R. M. 1979. Egocentrism and inefficiency in the communication of families containing schizophrenic members. *Family Process* *18*, 405–25.

Nafstad, H. E. 1971a. Enslige mødres barn i barnehage. *INAS-rapport*, *4* (2), 1–100.

1971b. Piker fra en- og to-foreldre familier i barnehagen. Unpublished thesis University of Oslo.

1971c. Different functions of the day care centre in relation to children from different home environments: an interactionistic model. Paper presented at the Conference on Preschool Children and the Preschool, Copenhagen, September.

1973. Barnehagens funksjoner for barn fra ulike hjemmemiljøer. *Norsk Pedagogis Tidsskrift*, *57*, 15–27.

1975. Velferdsforskning: noen refleksjoner. *Tidsskrift for samfunnsforskning*, *16* 350–5.

1976. *Barnehagen som oppvekstmiljø og arbeidsplass*. Oslo: Tiden.

1977. Barnehagen i støpeskjeen: Skisse til en alternativ integrert modell. In Norwegian Ministry of Familial and Consumer Affairs (ed.) *Forskning og utvik lingsarbeid på barnehageområdet*. Oslo.

1978. *Barnehagens innhold og funksjoner*. Oslo: Universitetsforlaget.

1980. The child's development environment: the nursery school as a welfar component. *International Journal of Early Childhood*, *12*, 17–22.

Nafstad, H. E. & Gaarder, S. 1979. *Barn: utvikling og miljø*. Oslo: Tiden.

Olsen, F. 1981. Anorexia nervosa betraktet utfra et systemteoretisk perspektiv Unpublished dissertation, University of Oslo.

Paulsen, O. G. 1977. Schizofreni og kommunikasjon: en replikasjonsstudie. Unpub lished Ph.D. dissertation, University of Oslo.

Pedersen, T. B. 1979a. Kjønn og kommunikasjon: en eksperimentell tilnærming Unpublished dissertation, University of Oslo.

1979b. Sex and communication: a brief presentation of an experimental approach Paper presented at the International Conference of Social Psychology an Language, Bristol, July.

Piaget, J. 1926. *The language and thought of the child*. New York: Harcourt, Brace.

Riskin, J. & Faunce, E. E. 1972. An evaluative review of family interaction research *Family Process*, *11*, 365–455.

Rommetveit, R. 1968. *Words, meanings and messages*. New York: Academic Press; Oslo Universitetsforlaget.

1972a. *Språk, tanke og kommunikasjon*. Oslo: Universitetsforlaget.

1972b. Deep structure of sentences versus message structure: some critical remark on current paradigms and suggestions for an alternative approach. *Norwegia Journal of Linguistics*, *26*, 3–22.

1974. *On message structure*. Chichester: Wiley.

1979. On 'meanings' of situations and social control of such meaning in huma communication. Paper presented at the Symposium on the Situation in Psycho logical Theory and Research, Stockholm, June.

Rommetveit, R. & Blakar, R. M. (eds.) 1979. *Studies of language, thought and verbal communication.* London: Academic Press.

Rotbæk, K. L. S. 1976. Enurese: en oversikt over de begreper og teorier som finnes i psykologisk/psykiatrisk litteratur, og en eksplorerende undersøkelse på kommunikasjonsteoretisk grunnlag. Unpublished dissertation, University of Oslo.

Sølvberg, H. A. & Blakar, R. M. 1975. Communication efficiency in couples *with* and *without* a schizophrenic offspring. *Family Process, 14,* 515–34.

Stokstad, S. J., Lagerløv, T. & Blakar, R. M. 1979. Anxiety, rigidity and communication: an experimental approach. In R. Rommetveit & R. M. Blakar (eds.) (1979).

Strøno, I. 1978. Egosentrisme og desentrering i verbal kommunikasjon hos barn og ungdom. Unpublished dissertation, University of Oslo.

Teigre, H. O. 1976. Tillit som forutsetning for kommunikasjon. Unpublished dissertation, University of Oslo.

Valdimarsdottir, A. 1980. Schizophrenia and communication efficiency: a modified replication taking ecological variation into consideration. Unpublished dissertation, University of Oslo.

Valstad, S. J. 1980. Barn med astma: foreldre-barn samhandling i en konfliktsituasjon. Unpublished dissertation, University of Oslo.

Vassend, O. 1979. Barn med astma: kommunikasjon og samhandlingsklima i familien i konfliktsituasjonar. Unpublished dissertation, University of Oslo.

Wikran, R. J. 1974. Kommunikasjon og samarbeide mellom astmabarnets foreldre. Unpublished dissertation, University of Oslo.

Wikran, R. J., Faleide, A. & Blakar, R. M. 1978. Communication in the family of the asthmatic child: an experimental approach. *Acta Psychiatrica Scandinavia, 57,* 11–26.

# 9. The nonverbal dimension: a fad, a field, or a behavioural modality?[1]

KLAUS R. SCHERER

The intellectual history of the scientific study of human behaviour seems to move in cycles, just like many other social phenomena. The history and sociology of knowledge show quite convincingly that periods dominated by a rational view of human nature have alternated with periods dominated by an irrational or emotional view of human nature. At present, we seem to be emerging from a period of extremely rationalistic models of man, characterized by the 'cognitive revolution' and an excessively verbal approach to human behaviour, and destined to move into a period of scientific endeavour characterized by greater concern with human emotionality (see Scherer 1981; Zajonc 1980). The remarkable success of the 'nonverbal movement' is not surprising then, since it is clearly in line with the *Zeitgeist*. After decades of concern with various kinds of human cognitive abilities as manifested in – sometimes rather narrow – types of verbal behaviour, the study of eyes, faces and voices in action and interaction is capturing the interest of an increasingly large number of social and behavioural scientists (in spite of the ugly head of vulgar 'body language' looming at close quarters). Thus, the relative success and increasing visibility of nonverbal communication research has many sources: over-satiation with highly abstract cognitive-verbal studies, growing realization that emotional and affective phenomena, many of which are closely related to nonverbal behaviour, have been neglected for too long, influence from biological and ethological research, a re-awakening of interest in the observation of actual behaviour, and last, but not least, the novelty and exoticism of the nonverbal communication literature, which should not be underestimated in a fashion-conscious industry.

This is not the place for a detailed sociology of science analysis of the

1 The research reported herein represents a long-term collaborative effort of all the members of the Research Group on Interaction and Communication at the University of Giessen. I specifically thank Jens Asendorpf, Ursula Scherer and Harald Wallbott for a critical reading of the manuscript.

growing popularity of nonverbal communication research in many disciplines of the social and behavioural sciences, particularly in social psychology. Even though there might be disagreement about the degree of popularity – it is true that there are some who consider this to be a rather seedy and unsavoury object of study – there can be little dispute about the explosion of research activity in this area, as shown in the ever-growing number of publications carrying the term 'nonverbal' in their title. It is also fairly evident that there are all the signs of a proper field or sub-discipline called 'nonverbal communication' in the making. There are textbooks (Harper, Wiens & Matarazzo 1978; Knapp 1972), books of readings (Weitz 1974, 2nd edn 1979; Scherer & Wallbott 1979), conferences, symposia, institutes, and even a special journal, the *Journal of Nonverbal Behavior*. Apart from these tangible signs of 'fieldship' there are many telling signs of a psychological reality, such as the existence of an abbreviation (NVC), routine ways of identification ('I'm in nonverbal') and quite a bit of ingroup–outgroup feeling. The latter is not surprising, particularly at a time when psychology is still dominated by an almost exclusively cognitive approach. We all have a natural tendency to search for reference groups in which others value what we are doing.

I believe that this development, understandable as it is, is very detrimental to the social and behavioural sciences, social psychology in particular, as well as to the study of nonverbal behaviour. Treating 'nonverbal communication' as a new and fashionable field has encouraged visions of a virgin territory devoid of history and uncontaminated by pre-existing conceptual or theoretical structures. The promise of quick pickings in such virgin territories tends to attract many of those who shun the drudgery of working the cultivated land. To continue the analogy, rather than toiling in a large plantation with modest prospects of eventually reaping the fruit, the explorers of new territories rely more on quick predatory forays to bring plentiful bounty home. I believe that this predatory stance characterizes a lot of present nonverbal communication research, although there are of course many notable exceptions. On the whole, however, much of the work that is published consists of one-shot studies with little conceptual sophistication and less theoretical integration. The result of more than a decade of rather intensive research, again with some exceptions, is rather dismal: there is no theory of nonverbal communication, nor are there many partial or middle-range theories, there is little accumulation of research findings, there is little cross-referencing except for the most obviously relevant prior work – although that seems to be a universal tendency these days – and most importantly, there is often no attempt to link the object of study to established, long-standing theories or paradigms in other areas of the social and behavioural sciences. The only unity there is to this area, is that everybody who is in it studies nonverbal behaviour, although there is not even much agreement as to what should be included under this heading.

This atheoretical approach has been aggravated by the fact that most researchers have concentrated on behaviours in a particular channel or modality such as bodily, facial or vocal behaviour. While there are a number of reasons for this development, including the tremendous complexity and difficulty involved in developing a rigorous methodology for the study of nonverbal behaviour (cf. Scherer & Ekman 1982), the effect has been rather unfortunate, in that it has led away from the functions of integrated behaviour patterns as they would be studied from the vantage point of many disciplines. It is rather telling that the only system that has been developed in this area to organize the research findings centres around channels or modalities (Harper, Wiens & Matarazzo 1978; Knapp 1972; Weitz 1974, 2nd edn 1979). In a book of readings in which I felt compelled to use the same system, finding it hard to organize the contributions in any other reasonable way, I compared this to a guidebook for hobby gardeners which was organized according to work to be done with the eyes, with the hands and with the feet (Scherer & Wallbott 1979: 11). The present state of the nonverbal garden looks very much like the result of such a guidebook.

One of the reasons for this unhappy state of affairs is that there is no *field* of nonverbal communication, and there will probably never be one, either, for the same reasons that all attempts to establish a field of verbal behaviour have failed. Similar to linguistics as the science of 'language as a communication system', one could conceive of a field that studies semiotic aspects of human nonverbal signalling as a communication system, presumably avoiding the term 'non-linguistics' for such a field. The pragmatic uses of these communication systems, however, have to be studied, as most other behaviour, in the context of particular phenomena such as person perception, social influence, social interaction and the like. Despite some attempts, so far there is no theory of verbal communication. I find it equally difficult to imagine a theory of nonverbal communication. Thus, unless one considers it sufficient for an area to 'own' a type or modality of behaviour as a necessary and sufficient criterion for 'fieldship', we must either develop a theory of nonverbal communication or at least middle-range theories of sub-aspects of nonverbal communication, or give up the claim that this is a proper 'field of investigation'.

Since I believe that all those approaches in nonverbal communication research that can boast of something approaching a theoretical framework (e.g. structural interaction analysis, the expression of emotion research) have imported that theoretical framework from another area or discipline of the social and behavioural sciences, I am in favour of the second alternative. Maybe some nonverbal imperialism was a necessary antidote to verbal imperialism and an important stimulant to interest in nonverbal behaviour. However, this having been achieved, it is now time to dissolve the incipient structure of nonverbal communication as a field and to establish the rigorous empirical study of nonverbal behaviour as an important part of research in virtually all approaches to the study of human behaviour, no matter what theories or paradigms underlie the research. I believe that this is where students of nonverbal behaviour can make the greatest and most lasting contribution. There are some hopeful signs. The psychology of emotion, as one would expect, has been greatly advanced by an increasing concern with the methodologically rigorous study of nonverbal behaviour, particularly facial expression (Ekman 1982; Izard 1971; Tomkins 1962, 1963). Another example is person perception, an area that for many years looked more like applied semantics than a proper part of social psychology, but where one has started to take note of the importance of nonverbal cues in impression formation (see particularly, Schneider, Hastorf & Ellsworth 1979).

This chapter is a plea to start treating nonverbal behaviour as a dependent or independent *variable*, to treat the measurement of nonverbal behaviour as one *method* among others of studying behaviour – albeit a highly neglected method – and to integrate the study of these behaviour patterns into theories and paradigms in psychology that have been shown to be conceptually promising. Rather than having an exclusive concern with isolated nonverbal behaviours in a particular channel, the study of nonverbal behaviour *in the context of* important psychological issues will contribute to the growth of knowledge in our field, possibly to the settling of some disputes and certainly to an accumulation of findings. In the remainder of the chapter, I will provide examples to illustrate this suggestion, drawing mostly from my own work and the work of my collaborators and students. These examples will demonstrate the importance of nonverbal behaviour for three social psychological phenomena: coping with stress and emotion, the influence of attitudes and personality on behaviour, and person perception and interpersonal attribution.

## 1. Coping with stress and emotion

During the heyday of the 'cognitive revolution', social psychologists have seriously neglected the role of emotion in social interaction and the actor's attempt to manage or cope with stress and emotion on the intra-personal and social-interactional level. There is, of course, a major tradition of studying stress and coping in psychology (Haan 1977; Lazarus 1966, 1980), but researchers in this area have mostly focused on individual differences, psychodynamic processes or psychophysiological reactivity. Owing to the theoretical approaches and the research paradigms used in this tradition there has been very little concern with social factors. Furthermore, studies in this area have been almost exclusively concerned with the verbal questionnaire report of feeling states and with the physiological measurement of autonomic arousal. The vocal/verbal and nonverbal behaviours associated with coping attempts in interactive settings have almost never been studied.

This is all the more unfortunate, since it is highly likely that these behaviours play an important role in coping with emotion – coping rarely occurs in a social vacuum. Stress and emotion are often produced by the behaviour of others in a social interaction. It is to be expected that verbal and nonverbal behaviour are important aspects of the total response to affective arousal. These behaviours may actually occupy the centre of attention during coping attempts because of the need to control various aspects of these behaviours, a need motivated both by strategic concerns and social norms in social interaction and by the importance of self-attribution processes. As usual, Aristotle had something pertinent to say about this: in his *Nicomachean Ethics* he emphasized that we have to show *appropriate* affect in an *appropriate* manner in *appropriate* situations if we don't want to be taken as fools (Aristotle, ed. McKeon 1941: 966).

The study of social factors in coping with stress and emotion, and particularly the control of verbal and nonverbal behaviour, is important not only in its own right but also because it may provide a more adequate paradigm for the empirical study of coping processes. It may allow us to disentangle the many different explanations proposed to account for the outcomes of coping processes. As the following example will show, it is often the case that many types of explanations for differential responses to emotional arousal are possible. In 1972 I joined Paul Ekman and his co-workers to study the vocal response to a stressful deception situation (see Ekman & Friesen 1974). Using digital speech analysis, I extracted the fundamental frequency ($F_0$, the acoustic basis for perceived pitch) of the subjects' voices in responding to an interviewer's questions on a pleasant film, which provided a baseline, and on a stress film. The results showed a significant increase in $F_0$ of about 9 Hz on the average (N = 31, p = 0.003) from the baseline to the stress situation. This result was in line with hypotheses that had been mentioned in the literature (cf. Scherer 1979a). Furthermore, Streeter *et al.* (1977), in a study modelled closely after the approach of Ekman, Friesen &

Scherer (1976), replicated the finding that average $F_0$ for a group of speakers increases under stress.

However, I had been puzzled all along by the large individual differences in $F_0$-responses to stress. It turned out that $F_0$-response correlates with some of the personality traits that had been assessed with the California Personality Inventory, specifically with Achievement via Independence. The overall picture that emerges for the subjects whose $F_0$ rises strongly under stress is one of a non-conforming, independent, active, dominant, demanding and flexible person (Scherer 1979a). There are a number of possible explanations for this result in terms of underlying differences in coping processes.

(1) $F_0$-increasers may be more aroused by the stressful film or by a strong desire to succeed in deceiving the interviewer, or by the requirement to lie to the interviewer.

(2) The physiological substratum of arousal may be different for $F_0$-increasers, i.e. the musculature involved in phonation might be more affected.

(3) $F_0$-increasers may not have mastered efficient self-presentation strategies to control vocalization parameters under stress since, unlike more conformist persons, they may not normally suppress their arousal in interacting with other people.

Obviously, additional explanations can easily be advanced for this *post hoc* serendipitous finding. It is apparent that a large number of important social psychological factors are involved. These need to be understood more thoroughly if we are to get a better grasp of individual differences in coping with stress and emotion in social interaction. Social psychological factors such as self-esteem, self-attribution and self-presentation need to be given a central place in the study of coping, and the dependent variables studied so far have to be complemented by the objective measurement of verbal and nonverbal interactive behaviour.

On the basis of these preliminary results, we launched a programme of research in our Giessen laboratory to study coping with stress and emotion from a more social psychological point of view, and with a special interest in nonverbal behaviour.

In a pilot study in the context of two diploma theses (Asendorpf 1978; Müller 1978) we studied the responses of two groups of subjects to both a cognitive and an emotional stressor. One group believed that they were unobserved during the experiment whereas the other group believed that they were watched by a group of psychology students in responding to the stressors. The results showed a very pervasive and highly significant effect of the observation condition: both body movement and vocal responses were highly affected by the presumed presence of observers, suggesting a strong influence of self-presentation concerns on the coping responses (Asendorp 1980; Scherer *et al.* 1978). Furthermore, there were interesting relationships between verbal trait anxiety report (as measured by the Repression-Sensitization scale) and the nonverbal behaviour patterns, as well as between the vocal and nonvocal behaviour patterns. The results of this pilot study showed that one of the most important tasks for future studies in this area should be a detailed investigation of the relationships between the various behavioural modalities, looking for synchrony and discrepancy as indicator of coping processes and control attempts.

Since there had been no study of the relationship between the verbal, vocal nonverbal and physiological responses to a stressful situation in the *same* group of subjects, we grudgingly set to work to add physiological recording to the complex and time-consuming objective measurement of vocal and nonvocal nonverbal behaviour. As it seemed impossible to study the relationships between these behavioural modalities in a social context (mostly because of the need for physiological recording), we designed a stress study following the classic paradigm of exposing subjects to various stressors in an individual testing situation in the laboratory. We studied the effects of easy vs. difficult arithmetic tasks (cognitive stressors) and a neutral film on pottery vs. a stress-inducing surgery film (emotional stressor) on verbal affect report variability in skin resistance, facial expression activity, and various vocal measures including $F_0$ and vowel formants for 18 high-anxious and 1 low-anxious subjects (selected from a group of 200 medical assistant students using the R–S scale).

The results of this study (Höfer, Wallbott & Scherer in press), while somewhat confusing owing to a number of extreme scores for some subject in some behavioural modalities, showed that while there were significant effects of both the cognitive and the emotional stressors on many of the behavioural modalities studied, there was almost no correlation (over subjects between the stress-related responses in the different modalities. In other words, subjects who responded strongly in the verbal domain, did not respond equally strongly in the physiological or nonverbal domain, and *vice versa* Thus, responses to stress seem to be modality-specific for different subjects Contrary to expectation, the trait-anxiety measure accounted for very little of the variance.

For the next series of studies, we used the Taylor Manifest Anxiety (MAS and the Crowne-Marlowe Social Desirability (SD) scales to select subjects with more specific coping styles from a pool of 374 students: repressors (low MAS high SD), sensitizers (high-anxiety subjects, high MAS, low SD), defensive high-anxiety subjects (high MAS, high SD), and low-anxiety subjects (low MAS, low SD). Two studies were conducted with the same set of subjects (except the defensive high-anxious) to assess the replicability of results concerning the effects of different types of emotional arousal in two different testing periods for the same individuals. In the first study, which was mainly conducted by Asendorpf for his doctoral dissertation, anxiety was induced by a phrase-association task modelled after a similar task used by Weinberger, Schwartz & Davidson (1979), and a funny film was used to induce happiness. The central thesis of this study was that the coping styles of repression and sensitization are specific to dealing with anxiety and that it is possible to make detailed predictions as to the differential response patterns of the different groups in the different behavioural modalities. These predictions are shown in table 1(a). The assumptions underlying these predictions are that repressors tend to suppress anxiety on the verbal level whereas they are 'generalizers' in terms of other behavioural modalities, i.e. reacting strongly on the physiological and all nonverbal behavioural modalities. The sensitizers or high-anxious, on the other hand, are predicted to be 'internalizers' (cf. Buck 1979; Jones 1950), i.e., in addition to reporting high verbal anxiety they should respond more strongly autonomically than in terms of observable nonverbal behaviour, particularly facial activity.

In addition to the usual verbal report measures of anxiety and arousal, heart rate and pulse volume amplitude were used to measure autonomic arousal, and ratings of facial activity to measure facial expressiveness. As shown in table 1(b), the predicted pattern of group differences for the phrase-association task was fully confirmed – except for the facial reaction of the high-anxious group, which was more intense than expected. Significant contrasts in an analysis of variance showed that repressors responded more strongly in the autonomic and facial expression modalities than in the verbal modality, whereas low-anxious subjects showed the opposite response. The high-anxious subjects, or sensitizers, reacted consistently high-anxiously in all three behavioural modalities. In addition, the prediction that the effects should be specific to the emotion of anxiety were also confirmed. They did not occur in verbal measures other than self-reported anxiety, nor in other experimental situations (i.e. the funny film and various other control conditions; for detailed results see Asendorpf & Scherer in press).

In the second study with the same subjects (except the defensive high-anxious), the classic stress paradigm was used to assess the reactions of the three different coping style groups to cognitive stressors (easy and difficult tasks from the Raven Progressive Matrices test) and emotional stressors (slides showing either slight skin blemishes or severe accident wounds). In addition

Table 1. *Predicted and actually found group differences in multimodal responding to an anxiety-producing task (reproduced from Asendorpf & Scherer in press)*

(a) Summary of the patterns of group means predicted for the phrase-association task

| Variables | Repressors | Low-anxious | High-anxious | Defensive high-anxious |
|---|---|---|---|---|
| Self-rated anxiety | Low | Medium | High | High |
| Autonomic response | High | Low | High | ? |
| Facial response | High | Low | Low | ? |

*Note:* ? = no hypothesis.

(b) Group means of standardized measures of anxiety for the phrase-association task

| Variables | Repressors | Low-anxious | High-anxious | Defensive high-anxious |
|---|---|---|---|---|
| Self-rated anxiety change[a] | −0.62 | 0.13 | 0.41 | 0.08 |
| Heart rate change[b] | 0.19 | −0.48 | 0.30 | −0.01 |
| Facial anxiety[c] | 0.23 | −0.44 | 0.00 | 0.19 |

*Note:* All three variables are z-transformed over all 48 subjects.
  [a] Baseline-corrected self-rated anxiety after completion of the phrase-association task.
  [b] Baseline-corrected heart rate average during all mixed phrases.
  [c] Average of facial anxiety ratings during all rated affective phrases.

to verbal measures of arousal, various objective measures of vocal behaviour, particularly computer extraction of $F_0$, spectral characteristics, formants and objective measures of facial activity were obtained for the nonverbal behaviour modalities, as well as skin resistance responses, heart rate, pulse, breath rate, and EMG measures for the autonomic modality.

There are first indications that, as in the earlier studies, there are important interaction effects between coping style, the nature of the emotional arousal, and the behavioural modalities studied. Clearly, it can be expected that further interaction effects will be observed if more 'social' paradigms can be used for studying emotional responses and coping style in more naturalistic social interactional settings. Once we understand better the relationships between the different components of the emotional response system, we can afford to return to research designs and situations that are closer to real life and social interaction in an attempt to capture various aspects of social control, self-presentation and emotion management.

Since it is almost impossible to measure physiological responses in the more naturalistic social interactional situations, nonverbal behaviour will have to play a major role as a dependent variable in such studies. For example, the question of whether the repressors' obvious denial of arousal and anxiety in the verbal modality is self-deceptive or other-deceptive – i.e., whether they delude themselves or whether they know better and just try to appear less anxious for self-presentation purposes – can only be settled by including an analysis of their nonverbal behaviour and possible control attempts. The present finding that repressors show quite a lot of anxiety in their facial expression seems to suggest that self-deception is a more likely explanation for the verbal repression of anxiety that characterizes this coping style (Asendorpf & Scherer in press). This and other results from the research conducted by our group in Giessen show quite convincingly that the inclusion of a variety of vocal and nonvocal nonverbal behaviours in the study of coping with stress and emotion constitutes an important advance on both the theoretical and the empirical levels.

## 2. Influence of attitudes and personality traits on behaviour

Among the major issues in social and personality psychology in the 1970s were heated controversies as to the utility of the concepts of attitude and personality. Those who thought that these psychological constructs were worse than superfluous argued mainly on the basis of the rather weak correlations between personality scores and attitude scales on the one hand, and behavioural measures on the other. The personality concept seems to have been saved by the emergent 'interactionism', i.e. the assumption that it is the interaction between personality traits and situation that exert the strongest influence on behaviour (Endler & Magnusson 1976; Mischel 1968). The concept of attitude, on the other hand, has been made more specific – and, one might add, less meaningful as a general construct – by measuring attitudes towards specific behaviours and showing that the predictability of the behaviour becomes more pronounced (Fishbein & Ajzen 1975; see also Chapter 18).

This is obviously not the place to discuss these developments in any detail. However, I would like to focus on one important issue that seems to have been somewhat neglected so far. In all of the discussions on the relationships between attitude and personality to behaviour it seems to have been assumed that it is not necessary to define behaviour, except in the sense of choosing a particular behavioural measure for particular correlational studies. Given that 'behaviour' is a very loose concept, this is hard to justify. It should be apparent to anyone that there are very many different units, types and modalities of behaviour and that attitudes and personality are more likely to

have an effect on some types of behaviour than on others. Thus, in order t
study the effect of attitudes and personality on 'behaviour', we have t
develop a 'theory of behaviour' which allows us to classify and operationaliz
different types and modalities of behaviour. Unfortunately, recent develop
ments in the direction of a 'psychology of action' do not seem to provid
much help in dealing with this important issue.

We (Scherer, U. & Scherer, K. R. 1977, 1980) have claimed that some type
of behaviour are more prone to be affected by attitudes and personalit
because they are less constrained by social norms and situational factors. W
have argued that types of behaviour or behavioural modalities that are of littl
goal relevance, that are very molecular, in terms of time and space, and tha
are highly negotiable, in terms of one's ability to deny the occurrence o
meaning of the behaviour, are less likely to be externally restricted. Verba
behaviour and task-related actions can generally be seen as molecular
non-negotiable in their occurrence and meaning and relevant for th
interactional goals. These behaviours are likely to be externally restricted b
situational expectations and social norms. Most nonverbal behaviours, bot
vocal and nonvocal, however, are molecular, negotiable, and not immediatel
goal-relevant, and thus less externally restricted. Thus, it immediately follow
that, contrary to the low correlations often found between personality score
or attitude measurements and task-relevant behaviour, one would expect ver
high correlations with different types of nonverbal behaviour.

Similarly, one would expect observers to focus on nonverbal behaviour i
their attempts to make inferences as to the attitudes and personality traits c
an actor. Naive observers know, probably better than most psychologists, tha
verbal task-related behaviour is heavily determined by situational factors an
self-presentation strategies. Therefore, they will tend to focus on thos
behavioural modalities that are less constrained and more likely to covary wit
attitudes, personality traits and affects of the actor. In terms of emotior
Ekman & Friesen (1969) talked about 'nonverbal leakage' and the literatur
on nonverbal communication is filled with references to the fact that th
nonverbal channel can serve as an important source of information abou
traits and states of the sender, as well as his relationship to other persons i
interaction.

Consequently, it seems reasonable to attempt to study the effect of attitude
and personality on a particular type or modality of behaviour, in this cas
on various types of nonverbal behaviour, and to assess the way in which suc
behaviours are used as important cues in person perception. Our group ha
studied this issue in a rather realistic social context – the interaction betwee
civil servants and citizens. In a long term research project we have conducte

a series of field and laboratory simulation studies to assess both the effect of personality and attitudes on behaviour and the nature of the nonverbal behavioural cues that influence the attribution of personality and attitudes by observers.

In a pilot study, conducted in the course of research for two diploma theses Herrmann 1977; Wirth 1977), post-office clerks were videotaped while dealing with clients across the counter. These video records were coded for a variety of gestural and body movement parameters, using a coding system based on Ekman & Friesen (1972) and developed further by our group (Scherer, Wallbott & Scherer 1979). Correlations between personality scores, based on tests that had been administered to the post-office clerks, and the nonverbal behaviour codes, showed that inhibited and excitable clerks showed little responsivity (few head emblems and few hand gestures) and little 'immediacy' (rarely leaning towards the client, for example: cf. Mehrabian 1972). Extraverted clerks, on the other hand, showed a high degree of immediacy (forward lean and eye contact) as well as a lot of responsivity (expressive facial activity, many head emblems and many gestures). Observers, who were shown these videotapes, attributed personality and attitudes accordingly: the post-office clerks were seen as friendlier, more sociable, more cooperative and less sullen and pig-headed the more hand illustrators they used, the more expressive their facial activity, the more they showed head emblems and the more often their gaze was directed toward the citizen (Scherer, K. R. & Scherer, U. 1979: 313–15).

We then videotaped a number of interactions between civil servants and citizens in municipal offices. Contrary to the short interactions in the post office, these were fairly lengthy and often quite important interchanges, e.g. in the social welfare office. Again, extraverted civil servants were more responsive in terms of a number of nonverbal behaviours, particularly head movements. In this field study, we measured Machiavellianism as one of the personality traits. There were a number of unexpectedly strong correlations with nonverbal behaviour. Civil servants with high Machiavellianism scores moved their hands very little and showed very few task-relevant hand movements, such as writing, leafing through documents, etc. However, they tended to change the resting position of their hands frequently and to move their fingers only. Observers, who rated these civil servants on the basis of the video records, saw them as measured, poised and not very enthusiastic (Scherer, K. R. & Scherer, U. 1979: 316–17).

While the results of these field studies were quite encouraging, particularly since the number of cases was fairly small and a large number of factors varied randomly, we felt that it would be important to examine the influence of attitudes and personality on the nonverbal behaviour of civil servants in a more controlled study. As a compromise between the need for experimenta control and the desire to be as realistic as possible, we devised an experimenta simulation (cf. Scherer & Ekman 1982). These simulations were part of socia skills training courses for civil servants lasting two days, which we ran in the interaction laboratory at the University of Giessen.[2] Thirty-nine male civi servants selected from over 400 civil servants on the basis of attitude scales (high and low on client orientation), from municipal social welfare agencies in several West German cities, holding the same type of job, namely dispensing monetary assistance to people with a monthly income below a certain limit all role-played the same two cases with two lay actors. The first case was an application for financial aid by an unemployed person. The second case basically constituted a request. The civil servant had to demand a contribution from the client, whose estranged elderly mother depended on financia assistance from the welfare agency.

The clients were played by two lay actors. Each actor showed either aggressive or submissive behaviour and played either a member of the middle or a member of the lower middle to lower class. Class membership was manipulated by dress and speech characteristics and behavioural differences by detailed instructions. The cases were varied slightly to allow for differences in social class. The arguments put forward in the interaction with the civil servants, however, were kept constant. The actors were requested to use all of these standard arguments and were not allowed to improvise new ones.

Thus, within a $2 \times 2 \times 2$ design (lower/middle social class, aggressive/submissive behaviour of citizen, low/high client-orientation of civil servant), 78 interactions – two for each civil servant, lasting from a minimum of approximately five to a maximum of 14 minutes – were audio- and videorecorded. On the basis of these records, objective measures of a large number of vocal and nonvocal behaviours were obtained, using trained coders and digital computer analysis (cf. Scherer, U. & Scherer, K. R. 1980).

As in some of the stress studies described above, fundamental frequency of the voice ($F_0$) seems to be a very useful, unobtrusive indicator of arousal. Figure 1 (and significant ANOVA effects) show that the civil servants' $F_0$ is generally higher when dealing with lower-class clients or aggressive clients. $F_0$ is particularly high (significant interaction effect) when the civil servants have to deal with aggressive lower-class clients, probably due to increased nervousness, anger, or other emotions. This tendency seems to be particularly pronounced for civil servants with low client-orientation. Thus, the use of $F_0$

2 The following description of the methods used in the simulations is adapted from Scherer U. & Scherer, K. R. 1980: 318–19.

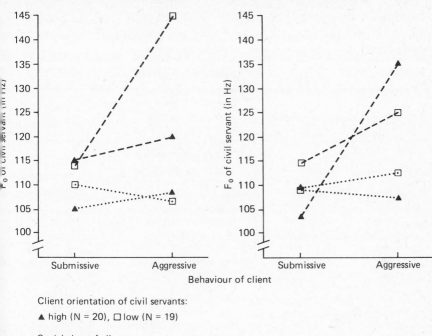

Client orientation of civil servants:

▲ high (N = 20), □ low (N = 19)

Social class of client:

.......... high, – – – – low

Figure 1. Voice fundamental frequency (means) of civil servants as a function of client characteristics and behaviour (adapted from Scherer, U. & Scherer, K. R. 1980: 32)

as an unobtrusive behavioural measure allows us to pinpoint emotional states and interpersonal attitudes that would be very difficult to assess differentially by verbal questioning or gross behavioural description.

The objective analyses yielded a large number of variables like $F_0$, representing microscopically small aspects or elements of the civil servants behaviour. In order to reduce the number of variables and to deal with more meaningful integrated behaviour patterns, we constructed a number of behaviour style scales, based both on theoretical considerations and on factor analyses of the data. These behaviour styles and the variables involved are shown in table 2.

Some of the results of this large-scale study, which is still being analysed, have been published elsewhere (Scherer, Scherer & Klink 1979; Scherer, U. & Scherer, K. R. 1977, 1980). As a summary, I would like to present regression analyses in which personality scores, attitude scores and experimentally manipulated situational factors have been regressed on to the major

Table 2. *Behaviour styles and objectively measured variables used to construct the respective scales (from Scherer, U. & Scherer, K. R. 1980: 320)*

| Behaviour style | Behaviour variables |
|---|---|
| Verbosity | Total verbal output in seconds |
| Domineering speech behaviour | Many interruptions *of* the client<br>Few interruptions *by* the client |
| Emotional manner of speaking | High pitch variability<br>Many head illustrators<br>Many hand illustrators (rhythmic or underlining speech production) |
| Many back channel signals | Many back channel head nods<br>Many verbal back channel signals |
| Immediacy | Head often oriented toward the client<br>Head rarely oriented toward the table<br>Body rarely upright or leaning backwards |
| Controlled expressive behaviour | Many positions with hands touching each other<br>Few repetitive adaptors<br>Few pointing illustrators<br>Relatively deep voice with low pitch variability |
| Preoccupation with records | Long pauses<br>Frequent handling of papers |

behaviour styles which we identified. Rather than present tables with details of the regression coefficients and multiple correlations, I chose a simplified presentation of the results as shown in figure 2, in which the amount of variance in the different behaviour styles accounted for by personality, attitude, and situational variables is represented by circle segments, and the strength of the corresponding effects by arrows of differential size.

The figure shows that the single most important factor that seems generally to affect the different behaviour styles, is the type of the client's behaviour, aggressive vs. submissive. In talking to clients who behave aggressively, the civil servants talk less, show less interpersonal orientation but exhibit a more emotional manner of speaking. The reduced speech activity is probably partly due to the fact that aggressive clients talk more than submissive ones – the civil servant has less opportunity to speak. Emotional manner of speaking seems to be a sign of arousal. As in the results for fundamental frequency reported above, the finding that aggressive behaviour increases the occurrence of this behaviour style seems to indicate that civil servants were aroused in dealing with aggressive clients. Emotional manner of speaking was also shown by civil servants with high scores on the personality scale 'rigidity'. This may

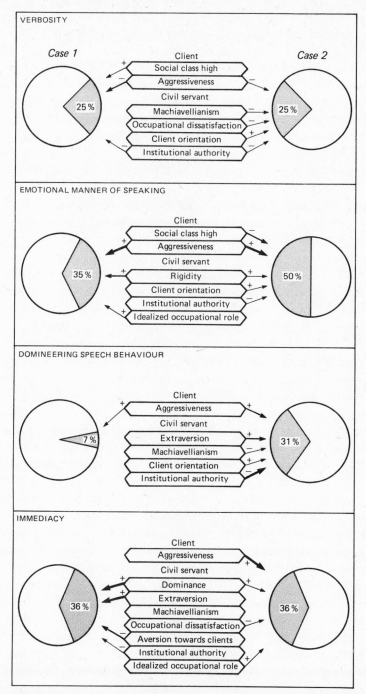

Figure 2. Effects of client and civil servant characteristics on four selected behaviour styles
*Note*: Circle segments represent percentage variance accounted for by variables connected by arrows; thickness of arrows represents strength; ' + ' and ' − ' represent direction of relationship.

indicate that rigid persons are more aroused in interacting with others, possibly because of their lack of flexibility in dealing with novel situations.

Interpersonal orientation or immediacy is generally seen as a sign of sympathy and attention towards the interaction partner. This behaviour style was shown more frequently, particularly in the first case, by dominant and extraverted civil servants, and less by civil servants with strong aversion against dealing with the public and a tendency to emphasize their institutional authority. Most of this seems to be in line with prior expectations, with the possible exception of dominance. In dealing with dominance, psychologists often imply that the behaviour style of dominant persons is generally aloof and distant. In this case, this impression is not supported. While the dominant civil servants in the study did take the initiative, they seem to have shown nonverbal behaviour that is normally seen as personal and friendly.

The data in figure 2 also show interesting differences between the two cases as far as the nonverbal behaviour of civil servants with high scores on the attitude scale 'emphasis on institutional authority' is concerned. In the first case, the unemployment case, in which they are in a position of power since they have the discretion to grant or not to grant financial aid, they talk less and show less interpersonal orientation towards the client than in the second case, in which they have to request something from the citizen and thus have less power over him. Taken together, these results show that, in line with the predictions, personality and attitude variables have a fairly strong influence on the nonverbal behaviour styles shown in a realistic social interaction.

In order to assess the extent to which these behaviour styles affect person perception, we showed the videotape records to judges to obtain attributions of personality and attitude characteristics to the civil servants. Forty-four secretaries, janitors and shop workers watched the videotapes and judged the behaviour of the civil servants in terms of 20 adjectives. The results showed that there were strong situational differences, since there were much stronger effects of the behavioural styles on attributions in the first case than in the second case. The results for the first case show that civil servants who are verbose, show frequent listening responses and controlled expressive behaviour are rated as kind and empathic, whereas civil servants speaking in an emotional manner are seen as aggressive and irritable, results which are generally in line with the findings from the field study.

Again, civil servants with high Machiavellianism scores yielded rather interesting results. There is consistent evidence that these persons seem strongly to control their expressive nonverbal behaviour. As in the field study, they showed fewer task-related movements and other expressive behaviours, whereas they seemed to change resting position more often and move their

ingers during resting position. In general, behaviour of this type is judged
by observers as kind, empathic and not aggressive. In the field study where
observers only saw one-minute excerpts from various interactions, Machiavellian civil servants were indeed described in these terms by observers, as well
as by the adjectives 'measured' and 'less enthusiastic'. In the experimental
simulation, however, where raters made attributions after having watched
the complete interactions, Machiavellians were not seen as particularly kind,
although they were still rated as less aggressive than others. It seems as if
Machiavellians were in fact rather adept at impression management but could
not prevent unfavourable attitudes towards the client (they are significantly
less client-oriented) from somehow 'leaking' in the long run and influencing
attributions considerably.

## 3. Implications for person perception and attribution research

Apart from documenting the important effects of personality and attitudes
on nonverbal behaviour, these studies have shown the viability of an
approach to person perception which stresses the study of nonverbal cues in
impression formation, as compared to the verbal label approach which has
dominated the area of interpersonal perception in recent years (Scherer, K. R.
& Scherer, U. 1981). In terms of the 'cue measurement approach' which we
have repeatedly advocated (Scherer 1979b; Scherer, K. R. & Scherer, U.
1981), we were able to show which nonverbal behaviour patterns seem to
produce certain types of impressions and attributions. In the light of the
interesting results on Machiavellianism, we decided to use the 'cue isolation
approach' to find out which communication channels mediate the nonverbal
cues shown by Machiavellian civil servants,

In her diploma thesis, Waldert-Lauth (1981) chose the eight most, and the
eight least Machiavellian civil servants from the experimental simulations and
presented judges with only two sentences from the interaction in the second
case of the study – which were fairly standard in content owing to the civil
servant having to acquaint the citizen with certain facts. These videorecords,
showing only the civil servant during these two utterances, were presented
to four groups of observers in different modalities: audio and video, audio
only, video only, and verbal transcript only.

As in other recent 'multichannel' studies (cf. Ekman *et al.* 1980), we find
that there is no general predominance of any one channel, but that the effects
of the different channels interact with a number of factors, particularly the
kind of personality or interpersonal relationship scale on which the judgment
is made (cf. Waldert-Lauth & Scherer 1983).

Significant ANOVA effects, with extraversion as a covariate, show that Machiavellian civil servants are judged as more 'superior' whenever they can be heard, i.e. whenever the vocal channel is available, such as in audiovisual or audio presentations, the effect being particularly strong in the audiovisual condition. The second major result is that non-Machiavellians, i.e. person scoring very low on the Machiavellianism scale, are seen as more sympathetic when dealing with aggressive clients but only in the 'video only' condition when they can only be seen but not heard, i.e. a significant interaction effect between Machiavellianism and behaviour of the client for the 'video only' presentation condition. These results show that Machiavellianism and the interaction of Machiavellianism with particular behaviour patterns of the interaction partners affect the civil servants' behaviour in such a way as to be differentially accessible in different communication channels. While this is interesting in itself, it does not tell us what behaviours are involved and what are the verbal and nonverbal cues that the judges use. Yet we need this information for a comprehensive account of the person perception process.

I have repeatedly argued for the Brunswikian lens model (Brunswik 1956) as a useful paradigm in trying to account for the effect of sender traits and states on observable behaviour (distal cues), and the effect of these distal behavioural cues on attributions made by observers on the basis of a proximal representation of these cues (e.g. Scherer 1978). Figures 3 and 4 show somewhat modified Brunswikian lens models for the data just discussed. This paradigm allows us not only to trace the effects of significant factors on observable behaviour, but also to evaluate the way in which these factors are communicated to observers via nonverbal behavioural cues in different channels.

Figure 3 shows two lens models for the 'superior' judgment in the audiovisual and audio conditions. Path analysis was used to estimate the adequacy of this model for the underlying person perception process (for details of the approach see Scherer 1978). The fairly strong direct paths in both cases show that the nonverbal behaviour styles included in the model do account for some of the variance in the 'superior' judgment but cannot adequately explain why Machiavellians are seen as more 'superior' than non-Machiavellians. Thus, it will be necessary to search further for mediating nonverbal behaviours.

In figure 4 the lens model for the results concerning sympathy judgment is shown. This model is more complicated, since both Machiavellianism and the behaviour pattern of the client, as well as the interaction of those factors played a role in the sympathy judgments in the 'video only' condition. Only the interaction effect has been entered into the model (using effect coding: cf

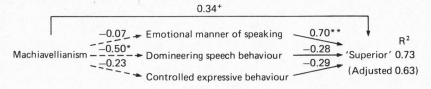

*Audiovisual condition*

0.34+

Machiavellianism

−0.07 → Emotional manner of speaking

−0.50* → Domineering speech behaviour

−0.23 → Controlled expressive behaviour

0.70**

−0.28

−0.29

'Superior' 0.73

$R^2$

(Adjusted 0.63)

*Audio only condition*

0.36*

Machiavellianism

−0.07 → Emotional manner of speaking

0.08 → Immediacy

0.18 → Backchannel signals

0.45*

0.46*

−0.51*

'Superior' 0.72

$R^2$

(Adjusted 0.61)

Figure 3. Path analysis models for the attribution of 'superior' in the audiovisual and audio only conditions
*Note*: Dotted arrows represent Pearson rs and full arrows represent regression coefficients (betas);
$\dagger p = 0.10$, $^*p < 0.05$, $^{**}p = < 0.01$.

Cohen & Cohen 1975). In this case, the absence of a strong direct path from the interaction effect to the sympathy judgment shows that the effect of this variable can be accounted for by the postulated paths in the model, i.e. the interaction affects interpersonal orientation or immediacy, and, to a lesser extent, controlled expressive behaviour, which in turn affect the sympathy judgment. As more detailed analyses of the results show, non-Machiavellian civil servants tend to show greater interpersonal orientation or immediacy towards aggressive clients than towards submissive clients. Since this behaviour style is mostly characterized by visual cues, such as leaning forward towards the client, judges using the standard inference patterns discussed above attribute positive attitudes to these civil servants and see them as sympathetic. However, this is only true in the 'video only' condition. Apparently the lack of indicators for positive attitudes in other nonverbal behaviour patterns 'leaks' if other communication channels are available.

Again, a detailed study of the nonverbal behaviour patterns allows us to provide much more specific explanations for the social psychological phenomena under study than would have been possible with the help of verbal material only. Given the importance of nonverbal cues in the person perception process, owing to the lack of external restriction (see discussion above), we cannot afford to study person perception without a strong emphasis on nonverbal behaviour and the cues it provides for impression formation.

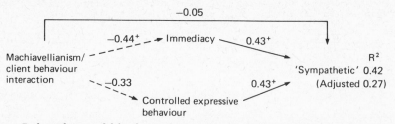

Figure 4. Path analysis model for the attribution of 'sympathetic' in the video only condition
*Note*: Dotted arrows represent Pearson rs and full arrows represent regression coefficients (betas);
p = 0.10, p = 0.05, p = 0.01. Interaction variable is formed by effect coding (cf. Cohen & Cohen
1975).

As in the area of coping with stress and emotion, it seems that the study
of behavioural effects of personality and attitudes as well as the study of
interpersonal attribution of personality and attitudes stand to benefit considerably from research paradigms which include the objective measurement of
various types of nonverbal behaviour. Given the limited scope of this
discussion, many theoretical considerations as well as empirical findings have
only been mentioned in passing. The streamlined summary of many years of
very complex, time-consuming, and expensive research may have suggested
to the reader that it is a trifling issue to introduce the objective measurement
of nonverbal behaviour into the empirical study of social psychological issues.
This is certainly not the case. As discussed elsewhere (Scherer & Ekman 1982),
the measurement of nonverbal behaviour, if it is done properly, ranks with
the most difficult and frustrating analysis techniques in the social and
behavioural sciences. Yet, I hope I have made the case for why it may be
fruitful, and even necessary, to take this thorny road if we are to move from
a strictly mental social psychology to a more comprehensive approach, which
includes cognition, emotion and behaviour, as well as their complex
relationships, in the social dimension.

## References

Aristotle. Ethica Nicomachea. In R. McKeon (ed.) 1941. *The basic works of Aristotle*.
New York: Random House.
Asendorpf, J. 1978. Bewegung und Erregung: Bewegungsstereotypien als Indikatoren
physiologischer Erregung. Unpublished diploma thesis, Universität Giessen.
1980. Nichtreaktive Stressmessung: Bewegungsstereotypien als Aktivierungsin-
dikatoren. *Zeitschrift für Experimentelle und Angewandte Psychologie*, 27, 44–58.
Asendorpf, J. & Scherer, K. R. in press. The discrepant repressor: differentiation
between low anxiety, high anxiety, and repression of anxiety by autonomic-
facial-verbal patterns of behavior. *Journal of Personality and Social Psychology*.

Brunswik, E. 1956. *Perception and the representative design of psychological experiments.* Berkeley and Los Angeles: University of California Press.

Buck, R. 1979. Measuring individual differences in the nonverbal communication of affect: the slide-viewing paradigm. *Human Communication Research, 6,* 47–57.

Cohen, J. & Cohen, P. 1975. *Applied multiple regression/correlation analysis for the behavioral sciences.* Hillsdale, NJ: Erlbaum.

Ekman, P. (ed.) 1982. *Emotion in the human face.* 2nd edn. Cambridge: Cambridge University Press.

Ekman, P. & Friesen, W. V. 1969. Nonverbal leakage and clues to deception. *Psychiatry, 32,* 88–105.

  1972. Hand movements. *Journal of Communication, 22,* 353–74.

  1974. Detecting deception from the body or face. *Journal of Personality and Social Psychology, 29,* 288–98.

Ekman, P., Friesen, W. V. & Scherer, K. R. 1976. Body movement and voice pitch in deceptive interaction. *Semiotica, 16,* 23–7.

Ekman, P., Friesen, W. V., O'Sullivan, M. & Scherer, K. R. 1980. Relative importance of face, body and speech in judgments of personality and affect. *Journal of Personality and Social Psychology, 38,* 270–7.

Endler, N. S. & Magnusson, D. (eds.) 1976. *Interactional psychology and personality.* Washington, DC: Hemisphere Publications.

Fishbein, M. & Ajzen, I. 1975. *Belief, attitude, intention, and behavior.* Reading, Mass.: Addison-Wesley.

Haan, N. 1977. *Coping and defending.* New York: Academic Press.

Harper, R. G., Wiens, A. N. & Matarazzo, J. D. 1978. *Nonverbal communication: the state of the art.* New York: Wiley.

Herrmann, D. 1977. Der Zusammenhang von Einstellungen und Persönlichkeitszügen mit der nonverbalen Kommunikation bei Schalterbeamten in der Post. Unpublished diploma thesis, Universität Giessen.

Höfer, I., Wallbott, H. G. & Scherer, K. R. in press. Messung multimodaler Stressindikatoren in Belastungssituationen: Person und Situationsfaktoren. In H. W. Krohne (ed.) *Angstbewältigung in Leistungssituationen.* Weinheim: Edition Psychologie.

Izard, C. E. 1971. *The face of emotion.* New York: Appleton-Century-Crofts.

Jones, H. E. 1950. The study of patterns of emotional expression. In M. L. Reymert (ed.) *Feelings and emotions.* New York: McGraw Hill. pp. 161–8.

Knapp, M. L. 1972. *Nonverbal communication in human interaction.* New York: Holt, Rinehart and Winston.

Lazarus, R. S. 1966. *Psychological stress and the coping process.* New York: McGraw Hill.

  1980. The stress and coping paradigm. In C. Eisdorfer, D. Cohen, A. Kleinman & P. Maxim (eds.) *Theoretical bases for psychopathology.* New York: Spectrum.

Mehrabian, A. 1972. *Nonverbal communication.* Chicago: Aldine-Atherton.

Mischel, W. 1968. *Personality and assessment.* New York: Wiley.

Müller, S. 1978. Bewegungsdauer als Indikator physiologischer Erregung in Abhängigkeit von Persönlichkeitsvariablen. Unpublished diploma thesis, Universität Giessen.

Scherer, K. R. 1978. Personality inference from voice quality: the loud voice of extraversion. *European Journal of Social Psychology, 8,* 467–87.

  1979a. Nonlinguistic vocal indicators of emotion and psychopathology. In C. E. Izard (ed.) *Emotions in personality and psychopathology.* New York: Plenum. pp. 493–529.

1979b. Voice and speech correlates of perceived social influence. In H. Giles & R. St. Clair (eds.) *The social psychology of language*. London: Blackwell. pp. 88–120.

1981. Wider die Vernachlässigung der Emotion in der Psychologie. In W. Michaelis (ed.) *Bericht über den 32. Kongress der deutschen Gesellschaft für Psychologie in Zürich, 1980*. Göttingen: Hogrefe. pp. 304–17.

Scherer, K. R. & Ekman, P. (eds.) 1982. *Handbook of methods in nonverbal behavior research*. Cambridge: Cambridge University Press.

Scherer, K. R. & Scherer, U. 1979. Nonverbales Verhalten von Beamten in der Interaktion mit dem Bürger: erste Ergebnisse. In K. R. Scherer & H. G. Wallbott (eds.) (1979). pp. 307–19.

1981. Nonverbal behavior and impression formation in naturalistic situations. In H. Hiebsch, H. Brandstätter & H. H. Kelley (eds.) *Proceedings of the XXIInd International Congress of Psychology, Leipzig, GDR, 1980, Social Psychology*. Berlin: VEB Deutscher Verlag der Wissenschaften.

Scherer, K. R. & Wallbott, H. G. (eds.) 1979. *Nonverbale Kommunikation: Forschungsberichte zum Interaktionsverhalten*. Weinheim: Beltz.

Scherer, K. R., Scherer, U. & Klink, M. 1979. Determinanten des Verhaltens öffentlich Bediensteter im Publikumsverkehr. In F. X. Kaufmann (ed.) *Bürgernahe Sozialpolitik*. Frankfurt: Campus. pp. 408–51.

Scherer, K. R., Wallbott, H. G. & Scherer, U. 1979. Methoden zur Klassifikation von Bewegungsverhalten: ein funktionaler Ansatz. *Zeitschrift für Semiotik*, 1, 187–202.

Scherer, K. R., Helfrich, H., Tolkmitt, F., Standke, R. & Wallbott, H. 1978. Psychoakustische und kinesische Verhaltensanalyse. Unveröffentlichter Zwischenbericht des DFG-Forschungsprojekts, Giessen.

Scherer, U. & Scherer, K. R. 1977. Bürgernähe im Publikumsverkehr: die Rolle des menschlichen Faktors in der Sozialplanung. In F. X. Kaufmann (ed.) *Bürgernahe Gestaltung in der sozialen Umwelt: Probleme und theoretische Perspektiven*. Meisenheim: Hain-Verlag. pp. 237–72.

1980. Psychological factors in bureaucratic encounters: determinants and effects of interactions between officials and clients. In W. T. Singleton, P. Spurgeon & R. B. Stammers (eds.) *The analysis of social skill*. New York: Plenum Press. pp. 315–28.

Schneider, D. J., Hastorf, A. H. & Ellsworth, P. C. 1979. *Person perception*. Reading, Mass.: Addison-Wesley.

Streeter, L. A., Krauss, R. M., Geller, V., Olson, C. & Apple, W. 1977. Pitch changes during attempted deception. *Journal of Personality and Social Psychology*, 35, 345–50.

Tomkins, S. S. 1962. *Affect, imagery, consciousness*. vol. 1: *The positive affects*. New York: Springer.

1963. *Affect, imagery, consciousness*. vol. 2: *The negative affects*. New York: Springer.

Waldert-Lauth, M. 1981. Machiavellisten im Amt: eine Multi-Kanal-Untersuchung zur Eindruckswirkung machiavellistischer Bediensteter. Unpublished diploma thesis, Universität Giessen.

Waldert-Lauth, M. & Scherer, K. R. 1983. Interpersonale Kommunikation von Machiavellismus: zur Bedeutung von Kommunikationskanälen und Situationsfaktoren. *Zeitschrift für Experimentelle und Angewandte Psychologie*, 30 (2), 311–55.

Weinberger, D. A., Schwartz, G. E. & Davidson, R. J. 1979. Low-anxious, high-anxious, and repressive coping styles: psychometric patterns and behavioral and physiological responses to stress. *Journal of Abnormal Psychology*, 33, 369–80.

Weitz, S. (ed.) 1974. *Nonverbal communication*. New York: Oxford University Press, 2nd edn 1979.

Wirth, T. 1977. Der kommunikative Aspekt nonverbalen Verhaltens bei Schalterbeamten in der Post: der Einfluss nonverbaler Verhaltensweisen der Schalterbeamten in der Post auf die Beurteilung der Interaktionszufreidenheit durch Studenten. Unpublished diploma thesis, Universität Giessen.

Zajonc, R. B. 1980. Feeling and thinking: preferences need no inferences. *American Psychologist*, 2, 151–76.

# 10. Aggression as an interpersonal phenomenon[1]

JACQUES-PHILIPPE LEYENS AND ADAM FRACZEK

Aggression and violence are a constant preoccupation of our societies; sometimes this is spontaneous and at other times provoked by special events. Two questions are frequently asked: 'Is our period more violent than others in the past have been?'; and: 'What are the factors responsible for the increase in violence?' To take a recent example, confined to one country: the French minister (at the time), Alain Peyrefitte, chaired a commission which produced a gigantic final report under the title: *Réponses à la violence* (Peyrefitte 1977). Its publication stirred as much public interest as is more usually the case for the award of one of the major literary prizes. At the same time a French senator, Jean Cluzel (1978), was publishing *Télé-violence* and several publishers were offering translations of American books on the subject (Winn 1979).

It is to be expected that a social phenomenon of this nature would become of interest to social psychologists; indeed, aggression has been one of the major fields of study in the subject. Unfortunately, it seems that the accumulated mass of research on aggression is directly proportional to the number of theoretical interpretations given to the findings. Rather than accept this abundance of empirical facts and theoretical outlines as a handicap, in view of the limitations of space in this book we shall concentrate on a few of the directions of research on interpersonal aggression, selecting those which appeared to us the most interesting and most representative of specifically European preoccupations.[2]

The scientific interest of social psychologists in the domain of aggression originated in 1939 with publication by the Yale group (Dollard, Doob, Miller,

[1] The preparation of this chapter was partly supported by a grant from the Fonds de Recherche Fondamentale Collective, No. 2.4561.75. We are most grateful to Ginette Herman for her extremely useful comments. The chapter was translated from the French by Henri Tajfel.
[2] Despite this selection, the two authors of this chapter have not always agreed about the formulations they are presenting to the readers. This must be attributed to the richness of the phenomenon of aggression and the complexity of its theoretical interpretations.

Mowrer & Sears) of the monograph on *Frustration and aggression*. This work was intended as a synthesis of psychoanalytic ideas and Hullian behaviourism; it led to many controversies and even more empirical research (cf. Berkowitz 1969). The fact that most of the subsequent research has considered aggression as an individual phenomenon which needs to be understood in terms of intra-individual processes must undoubtedly be attributed to these psychodynamic and strictly experimentalist origins. The same bias is still present in a more recent definition of aggression proposed by Geen (1976), which would receive a large degree of consensus amongst researchers studying aggression:

The delivery of a noxious stimulus by one organism to another with intent thereby to harm and with some expectation that the stimulus will reach its target and have its intended effect.

Three elements emerge from this definition: (i) the delivery of unpleasant excitations, (ii) with the intention to harm, (iii) independently of the success or failure of the undertaking. Implicit in this definition is the fact that these three elements are defined – at best – from the point of view of the person who delivers the unpleasant excitations, and, as is much more often the case, from the point of view of the experimenter, who determines the degree of aversion of the noxious stimuli and directly infers the intention to harm from the experimental situation which he has arranged.

It is our intention in this chapter to modify this traditional perspective and to consider aggression as an interactive and interpersonal phenomenon which is produced in a given social context. It is certainly not our aim, in doing this, to propose some kind of a differential psychology of social psychology which would take into account one type of environment after another (as natural independent variables) and would thus go on accumulating innumerable 'regional' conclusions. We simply wish to show that the replacement of an intra-individual perspective by one which is inter-individual and which stresses the social context, leads the researcher to ask different questions about aggression, to propose different concepts and, whenever possible, to formulate different theoretical orientations. Contrary to the views of some people, we do not think that this different level of analysis must necessarily result in theories which will differ in their *nature* from previous theories. The explanation will always *in fine* remain (intra)-psychological, but as a consequence of different questions being asked, it will be a different explanation. It must be hoped that it will also be more adequate than those which have found acceptance until now.

## 1. Conceptualizing aggression as an inter-individual phenomenon

When inter-individual behaviour is defined, various points of view must be considered: the point of view of the *actor* who initiates an action, or reacts, in relation to a *target* (normally referred to as a victim, since the actor has decided in advance that this target will be the object of aggression), the whole sequence happening in the presence of an eventual *observer*. The absence of distinctions of this kind has led to cases where behaviours referred to by some authors as aggression (e.g. Berkowitz 1973) were interpreted by others (e.g. Tedeschi, Smith & Brown 1974) as acts of reciprocity, and thus as not being aggressive.

We do not wish to suggest that the experimenters who accept the definition of Geen (1976) did not take steps to ascertain that the aversive nature of the stimuli and the intentions of the actor were obvious to everyone: the actor, the victim and the observer (the last being, usually, the experimenter). It still remains true that if one wishes to represent with economy and conceptual precision the interpersonal nature of aggression, the classic definition could be usefully replaced by the following one:

Aggression constitutes a (set of) reactive or planned or sometimes habitual behaviour(s) which violate(s) a commonly accepted norm with the aim, which may or may not succeed, of inflicting physical or psychic harm upon someone else.[3]

Amongst the European authors who based their work on this definition, da Gloria & de Ridder (1977, 1979) provided precise operationalizations of it and, in doing so, went beyond the traditional Aggression Machine of Buss (1961). A description follows.

The subjects, who cannot see each other, are confronted with a competitive task. When the signal to start is given, they must try to insert as rapidly as possible a stylus into a hole (see figure 1). The subject has three shock buttons at his disposal. They enable him to disrupt the performance of his opponent. It is clear to both that:

(1) pushing button no. 1 sends only a minimal electric shock into the stylus, so that the performance remains successful in 50 per cent of cases;

(2) pushing button no. 2 amounts to sending a more intense shock which is sufficient to disrupt the performance in 100 per cent of cases;

---

[3] Of course, a norm need not be necessarily shared by everyone; this is why we refer to a norm as 'commonly accepted'. Nevertheless, if the condition of 'a commonly accepted norm' is to be respected, the views of the various interacting individuals must be sought, and consequently account must be taken of the inter-individual aspects of the situation. In the same way, physical or psychological harm is subject to individual differences; but it is the aim that matters, and consensus about this should not be difficult to reach as it is the violation of collective norms which is at issue.

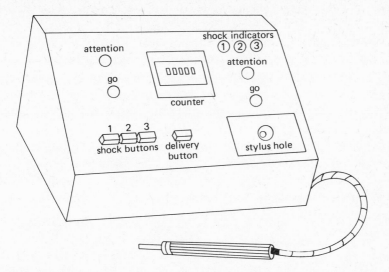

Figure 1. Aggression machine used in experiments by da Gloria & de Ridder (1977, 1979)

(3)  pushing button no. 3 delivers an even more unpleasant electric shock which, however, obviously has no greater effect on the performance than button no. 2.

In other words, the use of button no. 2 is considered as normal in the normative context of the competition. In contrast, the use of button no. 3 is a violation of the norm, to which the subjects in the experiments by da Gloria and de Ridder (1977, 1979) proved to be very sensitive.

Amélie Mummendey and her research team (1981) adopted a different strategy in validating the three elements of the new definition. Their subjects, who were schoolchildren, were asked to read descriptions of episodes assumed to be 'aggressive', in which the seriousness of the consequences, the intention to inflict harm and the extent of norm violation were varied. The children were then asked to judge how 'aggressive' was each episode. The first results clearly showed that all three variables had a significant effect and that the subjects responded with extremely high consensus. A few of the interactions are also worth noting: thus, the consequences of the act increase their impact when the intention to harm is not particularly explicit and the violation of the norm is not very clear. When the consequences are kept constant, the judgments that aggression has occurred become more marked when the intention is explicit and the norm totally misapplied. Until now, this research has been concerned only with judgments made from the point of view of the observer. It would be most interesting to compare these judgments with those made by a victim and an actor, and then to relate all these judgments to actual behaviour.

Whatever directions this research may take in the future, the value of this work by Mummendey and her collaborators (1981) has been to insist on the role of the social context: the same action is judged as aggressive or not depending upon the social context in which it is inserted. This is already a far cry from the dogmatic judgments of the past, expounded *ex cathedra* by the experimenters.

Camino & Troccoli (1980) took this analysis further. Rather than work according to the aseptic definition of the experimenter, they suggested that the determination of what is aggressive or not, of what is or is not reprehensible, is made by dominating groups who hold power:

In general, at the same time that societies propose to their members the concrete aims and goals to be obtained, they also legitimize some means in order to achieve the proposed goals, and at the same time, proscribe other means (Merton 1957; Cloward 1959). In a large number of societies it may be observed that the processes of legitimization and proscription of means are fundamentally related to the intention of the groups in power to perpetuate and consolidate the control of the social order. In most cases political violence is handled by the authorities in the same way that the common crimes are handled, thus denying the specificity of such an act. If we relocate social violence in its actual ecological space, that of social conflict, we may assume that the social process of categorizing what is 'violent' or 'non-violent' is already one aspect of the conflict, and by implication, exerts an important effect in its resolution. We may conclude, then, that groups engaged in conflict would possess different norms and perceptions of what is violent or not. (Camino & Troccoli 1980: 2)

In order to test their thesis, Camino & Troccoli (1980) asked professors and students in a Brazilian university to judge the degree of violence of various offences motivated in various ways (self-preservation, self-interest, social change, mere pleasure) and committed either in a legal framework (by a policeman) or in a non-legal framework (by an ordinary citizen). Each of the subjects also completed a Brazilian version of the 'just world' scale (Rubin & Peplau 1975). The hypothesis was that the subjects minimizing the degree of legal violence in relation to non-legal violence would be those who considered themselves to live in a just world, in which those who are well provided for deserve their privileges, where accumulated benefits are distributed *pro rata* through God's will, etc. In contrast, those who did not share this vision of a just world would tend to judge non-legal violence as being less aggressive than legal violence. The results clearly supported the hypothesis.

The study by Camino & Troccoli (1980) was not, however, confined to establishing relations between 'the perception of a just world' and 'legal or non-legal violence'. The authors drove their point home by demonstrating a

Table 1. *Mean scores of two measures of political activism as a function of three levels of belief in a just world. Numbers with a different subscript are significantly different at 0.05 (from Camino & Troccoli 1980)*

| Political activism | Just world belief | | |
|---|---|---|---|
| | Low | Medium | High |
| Verbal agreement | $38.5_a$ | $36.4_b$ | $34.1_c$ |
| Active participation | $6.25_{a'}$ | $2.38_{b'}$ | $2.54_{c'}$ |

correlation between the 'perception of a just world' and political activity. As such activity is fairly limited in Brazil, the authors made a distinction between merely verbal agreement and active participation in syndicalist activities. In both cases, the results were very clear: there is no need to act when the world is seen as just (see table 1).

Thus, some aggressions are more aggressive than others. The study by Camino & Troccoli (1980), undoubtedly the most audacious and spectacular to date, is not the only one to show this. For example, Forgas, Brown & Menyhart (1980) brought to light different interpretations of offences as a function of the contexts in which they were committed. Jorge Vala (1980) conducted a study in Portugal which was in some ways similar. He asked four samples of subjects to produce free associations to the word 'violence'. The resulting vocabularies were assessed for word similarities using multidimensional scaling analyses. Vala chose his four samples in such a way that he had people sharing or not sharing the dominant ideology and being members of majority and minority groups.[4] They were: high level managerial staff (dominant, majority); subordinate employees (dominant, minority); syndicalist leaders (non-dominant, majority) and common-law prisoners (non-dominant, minority). All the subjects were also requested to complete a Portuguese adaptation of Adorno's F-scale. Without going into the detail of the findings, let us note that the four samples differed in their fairly specific representations of violence. The high level managers were the only group who attributed positive value to a dimension placing the individual in opposition to society, but they were also the only ones not to value positively a dimension in which socio-structural violence was contrasted with a moral conception of violence. The results concerning authoritarianism were even more striking. When the

[4] By dominant groups, Vala refers to institutions upholding the prevailing ideology; opposition comes from the non-dominant groups. Within each category, there are the 'respectable people', the authorities and the experts – they are the majority groups – and, on the other hand, there are the 'humble folk', even the marginals – they are the minority groups.

authoritarian subjects talk about violence, they refer much more than do the liberal subjects to personal attributes, psychological states and individual moral values. The liberal subjects tend to invoke aspects of social reality, institutions and processes or phenomena which are external to individuals.

Having outlined our conception of aggression as an inter-individual phenomenon, we shall now examine the intra-individual processes traditionally used to explain aggression: emotional activation and cognitive elaboration. As far as possible, this will be presented in terms of the perspective outlined here, and some suggestions will be made about possible directions of research which would encompass the interpersonal aspects of aggression.

## 2. Emotional activation[5] and indices of violence

It has been abundantly proved that unpleasant stimulation provokes a state of physiological arousal. According to the theory of Hull (1943), which inspired the authors of *Frustration and aggression*, the existence of this state should be sufficient to provoke aggression, provided that this behaviour is available in the repertoire of the actor and that he is in a state of readiness to engage in it (i.e. when aggressive behaviour is dominant in the repertoire).

The explanation of aggression proposed by Bandura (1973) is faithful in all its aspects to the Hullian tradition. In brief outline, his views are as follows: unpleasant stimulation produces emotional activation which may lead to aggressive behaviour, but this is not always necessarily the case. Some individuals will react to an insult by submission, others by aggression, others still may show somatic effects or resort to drugs. The choice depends upon past experience, i.e. upon direct or vicarious social learning. In other words, the dominance of aggressive behaviour is related to past positive or negative reinforcements experienced by the individual.

Berkowitz belongs to the same theoretical school. He also assumes that unpleasant stimuli provoke emotional activation which predisposes the individual to respond in an aggressive manner. In contrast, however, to Bandura, Berkowitz does not resort explicitly to direct or vicarious positive reinforcements in order to account for the dominance of aggressive behaviour, but relies instead on the presence in the environment of indices associated with ideas of violence. Berkowitz's model has constantly been the object of criticism, possibly because of the theoretical status of his indices, or their operationalization which led to political and social repercussions, or perhaps his style, which accepts no compromise. We should first consider the empirical

---

[5] For a detailed discussion of this aspect, see Ekkers (1977).

status of the indices associated with violence, and then examine their theoretical validity.

The best known and most spectacular demonstration of Berkowitz's theory, as it applies to the effects of the mere presence of indices associated with the idea of violence, has traditionally been referred to as 'the weapons effect' (Berkowitz & Le Page 1967). There were two groups of subjects in the experiment; in one of them the subjects had been mistreated by a partner; in the other one, this was not the case. The subjects were supposed to administer to the partner electric shocks in the context of a task which involved solving a series of problems. In the case of some of the subjects, a gun and a revolver, supposedly belonging to the partner, were placed next to the shock-delivering machine. Other subjects found there a badminton racquet, or there was no additional object at all. The aggression was minimal in the case of the subjects who had not previously been irritated by the partner. The behaviour was very different after an initial unpleasant excitation. In this case, the mere presence of weapons increased the aggressivity of the subjects, as compared with the control conditions in which aggressive indices were not used. These results led Berkowitz to say that if it is true that the finger presses the trigger, it is also true that the trigger can lead the finger on.

It is easy to imagine the repercussions of this research in a country where the tolerance of the sale of weapons is the subject of public debate. Since the original study was conducted, other psychologists have tried to reproduce the effect; several succeeded, but others obtained results which went in a direction opposite to that reported by Berkowitz & Le Page (1967). The main criticisms concerned the 'demand characteristics' which were supposedly swarming in the original study: according to this view, the subjects, obedient to the presumed wishes of the experimenter, were showing themselves aggressive as and when they were supposed to do so. Understandably enough, this objection was forgotten when Turner & Simons (1974) were able to demonstrate *experimentally* that if 'demand characteristics' existed in the situation, they would have worked in the opposite direction: the subjects would have shown less aggression.

Leyens & Parke (1975) formulated a different hypothesis to explain the failures to reproduce 'the weapons effect': the weapons can simultaneously instigate and inhibit aggression. As the choice of the weapons serving as stimuli becomes determinant here, slides of weapons were used, since they are markedly less anxiety-producing than the real objects. In a study which was presented to the subjects as concerned with learning, Belgian university students were shown slides either of a gun or of a whistle or of a tin of chocolate milk (all three stimuli having been previously tested for the degree

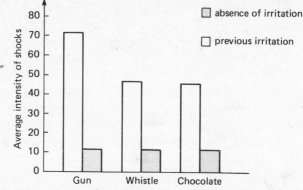

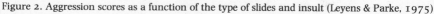

Figure 2. Aggression scores as a function of the type of slides and insult (Leyens & Parke, 1975)

to which they aroused aggression and interest). After the projection of the slides, half of the subjects were annoyed by a partner who was a confederate of the experimenter. Later, they were all given the opportunity to display aggression in deciding about the intensity of an electric shock which they wished to deliver to their partner during a learning task which was to follow. Figure 2 clearly shows that the three types of slides produced no difference in responses when there had been no previous irritation, but that amongst the insulted subjects the slide showing the gun incited more violence than did the other two. These results were replicated by Leyens, Cisneros & Hossay (1976) with Belgian soldiers, and by Turner *et al.* (1977) with children in natural field conditions.

Fraczek (1974, 1979) and his collaborators (Ciarkowska 1971, 1979) adopted another experimental paradigm in studying the same problem. In one of their studies, male university students were conditioned to associate the colour green with electric shocks. Afterwards, when a Buss Aggression Machine was to be used, half of the students found the machine to be green while the other half were confronted with a machine of a colour to which they had not been conditioned. As expected, the highest aggression was shown by those subjects who had to use the green BAM. The purpose of another study was to see whether the intensity of aggressive reactions is influenced by stimuli having a positive or a negative meaning. Male prisoners, aged 18–30, participated in this experiment. In a first phase, aggressive behaviour was measured in an emotionally neutral situation. In the second phase, the colour yellow was conditioned to either electric shocks or cigarettes. Effectiveness of this classical conditioning procedure was checked by means of GSR recordings. In the third phase of the experiment, aggressive reactions were again measured: half of the conditioned subjects worked with a grey BAM, half with a yellow one. There was also a group of subjects who did not undergo the conditioning procedure. The most intensive aggression took place in the groups confronted with the negatively conditioned apparatus. Not surprisingly, the positively conditioned BAM led to a significant decrease of aggression.

It can thus be seen that environmental indices associated with violence have their impact on aggressive behaviour. What is their theoretical status? Berkowitz (1973) favoured for a very long time an explanation in terms of classical conditioning. As he used to say, the trigger – so powerfully conditioned – leads on the finger. No doubt this explanation enabled him to account for totally impulsive or indeed automatic aggressions which are fairly different from actions controlled by reinforcements, which were the concern of Bandura's conception.

In a recent chapter, which is undoubtedly of considerable importance in his theoretical itinerary, Berkowitz (1982) seems to lean towards another explanation. Just as emotional excitation is capable of activating certain particular types of emotions, so indices associated with the idea of violence can elicit certain emotional schemata:

Emotional schemata, as representations of prior emotional experiences, can be evoked by many of the same stimuli that activate the expressive motor reactions (and also, I would add, by stimuli that have been associated with these reactions in the past). Leventhal's (1980) thinking here seems to resemble Bower's (1981) network conception of the relationship between emotional feelings and particular thoughts so that the evocation of certain images or ideas might then elicit the feelings that have been connected with these thoughts in the past. This general notion is compatible with the suggestion I offered some years ago (Berkowitz, 1973) that words and symbols having an aggressive meaning can evoke other ideas with the same meaning and even feelings conducive to the display of aggressive behaviour. (Berkowitz, 1982)

In fact, the same idea was proposed a few years earlier by Turner, an ex-student of Berkowitz. In the first of two experiments (Turner & Layton 1976), the subjects were requested to learn a list of words which were linked either to a high or to a low level of mental imagery and which either had or lacked an aggressive connotation. Immediately after this learning task, they had to punish the errors of a partner. Most aggression was shown by the subjects who had learned aggressive words linked to a high level of imagery, undoubtedly because these words evoked instances of aggressive events selected in memory. The second experiment (Turner & Fenn 1981) is even more convincing. In its first phase, the subjects had to memorize a list of pairs of words. In some of the pairs, one of the items had aggressive connotations with a high level of imagery (for example, 'cigar-*attack*'); in others, the connotation was not aggressive but also high in imagery (for example, 'table-*sky*'). In the next phase, all the subjects worked for 15 minutes at a puzzle so that the stimuli passed from active to passive memory. In the third phase, the experimenter presented half the subjects with an inducing word (such as 'cigar') which should cause the recall of an aggressive word; the other half were given words (such as 'table') which recalled another, non-aggressive, word. As this recall task proceeded, the subjects were listening to white noise, either intense or weak, so as to induce, or not induce, a state of physiological arousal. Finally, verbal aggression towards a partner was measured. This was much the strongest for the subjects who experienced 'aggressive cueing' while listening at the same time to intense white noise, as compared with the other three conditions, which did not differ from each other. The demonstration is elegant, in the sense that all the subjects had been confronted with exactly the same verbal material and that, as far as possible, all potential 'demand characteristics' were minimized. The study also shows that the effect of indices associated with the idea of violence need not be immediate but can be produced after some delay in appropriate circumstances, i.e. when the 'cueing' is present. The parallel with the 'weapons effect' is obvious; as the authors wrote: 'the presence of a weapon in the same room as a subject who is aroused and disinhibited may instigate an aggressive reaction because the weapon serves as a retrieval cue for a previously exposed-to aggressive incident' (Turner & Fenn 1981).

This interpretation in intra-individual terms must inescapably be supplemented by an inter-individual dimension. We do not live in an aseptic social world. There is always mutual influence between ourselves and other people; this is why a gun in the hands of a friend is not the same gun when it is held by an enemy. A simple comment by someone can be sufficient to modify our interpretation of the environment. A study by Cisneros, Camino & Leyens (1974) will provide an example. They projected a series of slides, some of which were aggressive and some neutral, for subjects who had previously been annoyed by a partner. Approximately half the subjects were given the task of judging the slides on aesthetic criteria; the others received no special instructions. The focusing on the aesthetic aspect caused the weapons shown in the aggressive slides to be judged as less violent, 'better', 'weaker', etc. than was the case in the control condition. In a subsequent experiment, Leyens, Cisneros & Hossay (1976) also showed that focusing on the aesthetic aspect of the aggressive slides weakened the aggressive behaviour of the subjects as compared with several control conditions. If one follows Turner's conception, it would appear that an aesthetic attitude towards the slides (not towards the weapons themselves), induced by the experimenter, elicited a different network of mnemonic associations. In other words, it is not simply a physical object present in the environment – a weapon – which affects an isolated individual: it is a cultural product inserted into a particular social context.

## 3. The cognitive elaboration

In discussing Turner's conception, as taken up by Berkowitz in 1982, we are already at the heart of the issues of cognitive elaboration, although the expression has not been generally used in this sense in the field of research on aggression. As was the case above for activation, we shall outline only a few aspects of this trend of research, showing again how the individual process cannot be dissociated here from the interpersonal dimension.

It was through the insertion of the criterion 'intention to harm' into the definition of aggression that the cognitive approach was introduced in this field of study. When later research on attribution became *en vogue*, it was to be expected that it would take hold of the phenomenon of aggression and deal with topics such as attribution of intention, perception of responsibility, etc. The cognitive dimension was thus being stressed at the same time as the interpersonal aspects, since the treatment of an issue such as, for example, the attribution of responsibility, depends upon its social anchorage: victim, actor, observer (see de Ridder 1980 for a detailed discussion of this point).

Undoubtedly, the best known exponent of this attributionist tendency in the research on aggression is Zillmann (1979). His conception is directly inspired by Schachter's theory of emotions. This can be very briefly outlined as follows: an individual who is in a state of physiological arousal is seeking an 'emotional label' for it. If the label which is found is 'angry' and if he considers the emotion to be appropriate, he might act aggressively. Obviously, as is the case in Schachter's research, 'misattributions' do occur and, accordingly, the individual will or will not accentuate his aggressive behaviour, depending upon whether he is mistaken about the source of the physiological activation. There is no doubt that cognitions have an enormous impact upon behaviour and that events are sometimes erroneously interpreted. It seems, however, that 'misattributions of emotions' do not happen as frequently as the theory predicts (Calvert-Boyanowsky & Leventhal 1975; Marshall & Zimbardo 1979; Maslach 1979); that the experiments by Zillmann are difficult to replicate (e.g. Ekkers 1977; Bornewasser & Mummendey 1981); and that Schachter's theory of emotions is now subject to assaults, fairly convincing as it appears, by Leventhal's (1980) model. A full chapter would not be sufficient to describe the controversy in detail; we shall therefore abandon it to its fate and veer towards another domain where there occurs a conjunction of the individual and the interpersonal; this is catharsis.

It may appear surprising that it is Konečni (Konečni & Doob 1972; Konečni 1975; Konečni & Ebbesen 1976), another leader of the attributional tendency in the research on aggression, who at present defends the existence of the cathartic phenomenon. It is true that Konečni (e.g. 1975) rejected the hydraulic model and proposed an explanation based on a Schachterian model. This went as follows: when a person is insulted or attacked, his emotional arousal increases (Kahn 1966), and the indices are sufficiently clear to interpret this arousal as anger. This anger determines, according to Konečni, the level of aggressive behaviour: the more intense the anger, the more aggressive the response. This aggressive response reduces the level of physiological activation (a reaction which, according to Hokanson, 1970 is fairly frequent) and in diminishing in this way the feeling of anger, it causes a decrease in the subsequent aggressive behaviour.

Very briefly described, the experimental paradigm used to verify this thesis looks as follows: in the first phase, a subject is either forcefully insulted or not insulted at all by a confederate of the experimenter; all counter-attack, which is potentially cathartic, is carefully prevented at that stage. In a second phase, the subject is requested to administer electric shocks to the confederate whenever the latter makes (contrived) errors in a learning task. These shocks are of a pre-arranged duration and their rhythm is fixed by the experimenter. Conditions which do not include shocks are manipulated in a variety of ways in different experiments. Finally, in a last task, the confederate must produce thirty word associations which the subject is supposed to judge for their degree of originality, deciding, for each case, whether to deliver or not one or several electric shocks to the confederate. Konečni maintains that the results of his numerous experiments confirm his original hypothesis.

Leyens (1977) undertook a detailed evaluation of this vast programme of research. The conclusions were less optimistic. Two problems in particular came to the surface. First, it is true that in conditions of cathartic activity, residual aggression (i.e. the number of shocks) is in general less high than in control conditions where no shock had previously been administered. It is, however, possible, even probable, that these results were due to a methodological artifact, namely the rhythm of shocks implicitly created by the experimenter during the cathartic activity (e.g. 14 shocks in 13 minutes, or 42 shocks in 7 minutes). In fact, when one brings together the different studies by Konečni, one notices that the *best predictor* of residual aggression is this pre-established rhythm; the correlation between the two is perfect: the more the rhythm of cathartic activity is raised, the more important is the residual aggression (e.g. 12 shocks following a rhythm of 42 shocks in 7 minutes, but only 6.3 shocks after a rhythm of 14 shocks in 13 minutes). Konečni himself recognizes this phenomenon when numerous shocks are sent, but he does not apply the argument to more intermittent shocks – that is, precisely for those which go in the direction of catharsis and which he usually employs. Is it not possible, therefore, to think that a slow rhythm brings about a cathartic effect precisely because it induces a smaller number of shocks than would be spontaneously given by a subject who is not influenced by a predetermined rhythm? The answer is simple: if the rhythm of the cathartic activity is increased, the alleged catharsis should disappear – and that is, in fact, what occurs.

The second difficulty has to do with the presumed decrease in the feeling of anger. Why is it that the subjects whose anger should have been reduced because of their opportunity to express physical aggression still report at the end of the experiment high levels of irritation and anger? As the delivery of 'cathartic' shocks was supposed to return their activation to its base level, those subjects should not have experienced further emotion, since they were no longer in a state of physiological arousal. How to explain the fact that a physical aggressive response reduces activation and the feeling of anger when, according to Ebbesen, Duncan & Konečni (1975), verbal aggressive reaction increases their level? The sources which Konečni (1975) quotes in support of his statements that a physical expression of aggression reduces emotional arousal show that this is equally true of verbalization (e.g. Kahn 1966).

It can thus be seen that, once again, the cathartic phenomenon has been envisaged in this work exclusively from an individual point of view. And yet, aggression involves two persons and two different views of the same situation. In what ways have these two antagonistic views anything to do with a chastisement dictated from the outside by the experimenter?

Leyens (1977) suggested a different way of approaching the problem of catharsis. Aggression must be considered as an interaction which acquires a meaning for the protagonists, a meaning which depends upon the attributions which come into play. If the experimenter encouraged an exchange of attributions between the partners rather than imposing behaviours which he had defined *a priori*, and if this exchange – violent to begin with – resulted at the end in a less aggressive reinterpretation of the situation, one could assume that true catharsis was taking place. This is, at any rate, the view adopted by psychoanalysts (Laplanche & Pontalis 1967). They do not consider that a simple abreaction is sufficient to abolish a traumatizing affect; a perlaboration is also needed, which consists of a repetition being modified by *interpretation*. This is also suggested by studies such as those of Mallick & McCandless (1966) and Green & Murray (1975). In both these experiments, the authors devised a 'cathartic' condition which could lead to a reinterpretation of the original situation that caused the irritation; in both cases this proved to be effective. We still need to know whether a reinterpretation is sufficient on its own (Mallick & McCandless 1966) or whether it necessarily needs to be associated with an expression of aggression (Green & Murray 1975).

## 4. Filmed violence and the social context of viewing

To conclude this outline of aggression as an interpersonal phenomenon, one should refer to one of the favourite themes in this domain: the effects of violence in cinema and television.

Almost all of the experiments on this subject have shown that, in appropriate conditions (Leyens & Herman 1979), filmed violence increases the aggressive behaviour of the spectators. The conclusion – which really was a starting-point as a postulate – has thus become that individuals are influenced in a direct and immediate way, rather than indirectly and through some mediation, by the violent films which they see. This postulate can be reformulated by stating that all spectators are duplicates of one another and that an audience is no more than the sum of isolated and equivalent individuals. It should be noted that this postulate was not questioned even when studies were conducted in the field, and when observations were made not of isolated subjects but of groups of children or adolescents who were continually interacting as members of a group (cf. Leyens, Herman & Dunand 1982).

In fact, this postulate is far from certain. We rarely go alone to the cinema; most of the time we watch television with the family; our choice of films depends upon our membership group and the comments we hear; we discuss films before, during and after they are shown, etc. Let us imagine two brothers who watch together an instalment of *Kojak*. The elder reacts immediately in torturing the cushions of the couch on which he sits – using toys within his grasp as projectiles and applying an approximate judo hold to his younger brother. The younger one, who remained calm at the beginning of the show, begins also to try his hand at judo, to transform toys into bullets, etc. What happened to him? Has he also succumbed to the surfeit of filmed violence and been influenced directly and immediately by the scenes shown on the screen? Or was it the activity of his elder brother which drew his attention to the filmed violence? Is he imitating his brother? Or did his brother's judo hold hurt him to the point where he wants to exact vengeance? We cannot provide answers of any precision to these questions, just as we were not able to do so in a quasi-experimental field study (Leyens *et al.* 1975). Whatever the case may be, the validity of a postulate of direct and immediate influence is highly dubious.

What is the origin of this postulate? It must be remembered that the two main pioneers of studies on the effects of filmed violence – Bandura and Berkowitz – were not, to begin with, interested in these effects *per se*. Bandura saw a filmed aggressive model as a methodological improvement on a real

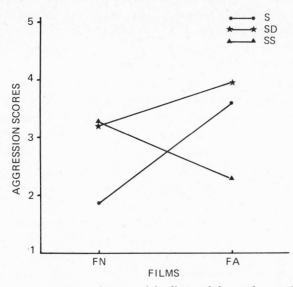

Figure 3. Aggression scores as a function of the films and the co-observer (Leyens, Herman & Dunand 1981)

live one for his studies on the imitation of a model by *one* subject. As for Berkowitz, he used aggressive films as one index, amongst others, associated with the idea of violence, the impact of which on *one* individual predisposed towards aggression needed to be observed. The influence of their experimental paradigms was, however, so powerful that those who really wished to study the effects of mass media violence were caught in the trap of this individualistic perspective.

At the laboratory of Louvain-la-Neuve, Leyens and his research group began work some years ago (see Leyens, Cisneros & Hossay 1976) on a research programme intended to throw some light on the effects of the social context of viewing aggressive films. As in the field study mentioned above (Leyens *et al.* 1975), we noticed that the dominant members of a group reacted immediately and in a relatively aggressive manner to violent films which they were seeing, while the less dominant members only reacted after some delay. We decided to engage in systematic studies of the effects on the audience as a function of the variable dominance–submission. For practical reasons, we worked with preschool boys (Leyens, Herman & Dunand 1981).

As can be seen in figure 3, the children who were tested in the presence of one female experimenter did respond in a definite way after viewing an aggressive film: they were not afraid to cause considerable annoyance to a stranger who was present in an adjacent room. It cannot therefore be said that, in order to react, they needed a large dose of stimulation from violent films – the film lasted for about ten minutes. The results look totally different when pairs of children – submissive–dominant or submissive–submissive – watch the films together and are frustrated by an unknown partner. When one of the submissive children of the pair is tested first, with a dominant companion present at his side, the level of his aggression is slightly increased after a violent film as compared with a neutral film. In fact, we know from other evidence that this reaction is very similar to the reaction shown by a dominant child tested individually. This reaction is reversed, at a level which is statistically nearly significant, when a submissive subject is tested in the presence of another submissive subject; the difference in reactions after a violent film between these two types of submissive subjects is statistically significant. This last result seems to be of particular importance with reference to the traditional literature. Its significance is that the viewing of an aggressive film can lead either to an increase or a decrease in aggression as a function of the social context of the viewing. Unfortunately, we are nowhere near being able to articulate an explanation for these phenomena: verbal communication and nonverbal behaviour which disinhibit in one case (Dunand, Berkowitz & Leyens 1981) and exert a double inhibiting role in another; changes in the meaning of the situation; social comparisons, etc. It remains, however, that despite this temporary uncertainty, there is a *rapprochement* between the study of the effects of violent mass media and the classic field of research on 'co-presence' (Paulus 1980).

We hope to have shown in this chapter that aggression is an interpersonal phenomenon. Our hope has also been that this level of explanation will be increasingly adopted to provide a better understanding of the problem. But we still insist on the fact that the *nature* of this explanation will not be different from those which preceded it. It is only the questions which are changed.

### References

Bandura, A. 1973. *Aggression: a social learning analysis.* Englewood Cliffs: Prentice-Hall.
Berkowitz, L. 1969. *Roots of aggression: a re-examination of the frustration–aggression hypothesis.* New York: Atherton Press.
    1973. Words and symbols as stimuli to aggressive responses. In J. F. Knutson (ed.) *Control of aggression: implications from basic research.* Chicago: Aldine-Atherton.
    1982. The experience of anger as a parallel process in the display of impulsive, 'angry' aggression. In R. G. Green & E. Donnerstein (eds.) *Aggression: theoretical and empirical reviews.* New York: Academic Press.
Berkowitz, L. & Le Page, A. 1967. Weapons as aggression-eliciting stimuli. *Journal of Personality and Social Psychology,* 7, 202–7.

Bornewasser, M. & Mummendey, A. 1981. Effects of arbitrary provocation and arousal on aggressive behavior. *First Congress of the European section of ISRA*, Strasbourg.

Bower, G. H. 1981. Mood and memory. *American Psychologist*, *36*, 129–48.

Buss, A. H. 1961. *The psychology of aggression*. New York: Wiley.

Calvert-Boyanowsky, J. & Leventhal, H. 1975. The role of information in attenuating behavioral responses to stress: a reinterpretation of the misattribution phenomenon. *Journal of Personality and Social Psychology*, *32*, 214–21.

Camino, L. & Troccoli, B. 1980. Categorization of violence, the belief in a just world and political activism. Unpublished MS, University of Paraíba.

Ciarkowska, W. 1971. Znaczenie emocjonalne bodźca jako czynnik modyfikujący zachowanie agresywne. (Emotional meaning of stimulus as a factor modifying aggressive behavior.) M.A. dissertation, Institute of Psychology, Warsaw University.

1979. Znaczenie emocjonalne bodźca a natężenie czynności agresywnej. (Emotional meaning of stimulus and intensity of aggressive act.) In M. A. Fraczek (ed.) *Studia nad psychologicznymi mechanizmami czynności agresywnych*. Warsaw: Ossolineum.

Cisneros, T., Camino, L. & Leyens, J. Ph. 1974. La décentration: auto-contrôle de l'influence de la violence filmée. *Revue de Psychologie et des Sciences de l'Education*, *9*, 301–16.

Cloward, R. A. 1959. Illegitimate means, anomie, and deviant behavior. *American Sociological Review*, *24*, 164–76.

Cluzel, J. 1978. *Télé-violence*. Paris: Plon.

Da Gloria, J. & de Ridder, R. 1977. Aggression in dyadic interaction. *European Journal of Social Psychology*, *7*, 189–219.

1979. Sex differences in aggression: are current notions misleading? *European Journal of Social Psychology*, *9*, 49–66.

De Ridder, R. 1980. Agressie in sociale interactie: waarneming en reactie. Unpublished Ph.D. thesis, University of Tilburg.

Dollard, J., Doob, L. W., Miller, N. E., Mowrer, O. H. & Sears, R. R. 1939. *Frustration and aggression*. New Haven: Yale University Press.

Dunand, M. A., Berkowitz, L. & Leyens, J. Ph. 1981. Audience effects when viewing aggressive movies. Unpublished MS, University of Wisconsin.

Ebbesen, E. B., Duncan, B. & Konečni, V. J. 1975. Effects of content of future verbal aggression: a field experiment. *Journal of Experimental Social Psychology*, *11*, 192–204.

Ekkers, C. 1977. Aktivatie en agressie. Unpublished Ph.D. thesis: University of Leiden.

Forgas, J. P., Brown, L. B. & Menyhart, J. 1980. Dimensions of aggression: the perception of aggressive episodes. *British Journal of Social and Clinical Psychology*, *19*, 215–27.

Fraczek, A. 1974. Informational role of situation as a determinant of aggressive behavior. In W. W. Hartup & J. de Wit (eds.) *Determinants and origins of aggressive behavior*. The Hague: Mouton.

1979. Functions of emotional and cognitive mechanisms in the regulation of aggressive behavior. In S. Feshbach & A. Fraczek (eds.) *Aggression and behavior change. Biological and social processes*. New York: Praeger.

1980. Aggressive actions: a topic in experimental social psychology studies. *Polish Psychological Bulletin*, *2*, 99–110.

Geen, R. G. 1976. *Personality: the skein of behavior*. Saint Louis: Mosby.

Green, R. A. & Murray, E. J. 1975. Expression of feeling and cognitive reinterpretation in the reduction of hostile aggression. *Journal of Consulting and Clinical Psychology*, 43, 375–83.

Hokanson, J. E. 1970. Psychophysiological evaluation of the catharsis hypothesis. In E. I. Megargee & J. E. Hokanson (eds.) *The dynamics of aggression: individual, group and international analyses*. New York: Harper.

Hull, C. L. 1943. *Principles of behavior*. New York: Appleton Century.

Kahn, M. 1966. The physiology of catharsis. *Journal of Personality and Social Psychology*, 3, 278–86.

Konečni, V. J. 1975. Annoyance, type, and duration of postannoyance activity, and aggression: the 'cathartic' effect. *Journal of Experimental Psychology: General*, 104, 76–102.

Konečni, V. J. & Doob, A. N. 1972. Catharsis through displacement of aggression. *Journal of Personality and Social Psychology*, 23, 379–87.

Konečni, V. J. & Ebbesen, E. B. 1976. Disinhibition versus the cathartic effect: artifact and substance. *Journal of Personality and Social Psychology*, 34, 352–65.

Laplanche, J. & Pontalis, J. B. 1967. *Vocabulaire de psychanalyse*. Paris: Presses Universitaires de France.

Leventhal, H. 1980. Toward a comprehensive theory of emotion. In L. Berkowitz (ed.) *Advances in experimental social psychology*, vol. 13. New York: Academic Press.

Leyens, J. Ph. 1977. La valeur cathartique de l'agression: un mythe ou une inconnue. *L'Année Psychologique*, 77, 525–50.

Leyens, J. Ph. & Herman, G. 1979. Cinéma violent et spectateurs agressifs. *Psychologie Française*, 24, 151–68.

Leyens, J. Ph. & Parke, R. D. 1975. Aggressive slides can induce a weapons effect. *European Journal of Social Psychology*, 5, 229–36.

Leyens, J. Ph., Cisneros, T. & Hossay, J. F. 1976. Decentration as a means for reducing aggression after exposure to violent stimuli. *European Journal of Social Psychology*, 6, 459–73.

Leyens, J. Ph., Herman, G. & Dunand, M. A. 1981. The influence of an audience upon the reactions to filmed violence. Unpublished MS, University of Louvain.

1982. Towards a renewed paradigm in movie violence research. In P. Stringer (ed.) *Confronting social issues: applications of social psychology*. European Monographs in Social Psychology. London: Academic Press.

Leyens, J. Ph., Camino, L., Parke, R. D. & Berkowitz, L. 1975. The effects of movie violence on aggression in a field setting as a function of group dominance and cohesion. *Journal of Personality and Social Psychology*, 32, 346–60.

Mallick, S. K. & McCandless, B. E. 1966. A study of catharsis of aggression. *Journal of Personality and Social Psychology*, 4, 591–6.

Marshall, G. D. & Zimbardo, P. G. 1979. Affective consequences of inadequately explained physiological arousal. *Journal of Personality and Social Psychology*, 37, 970–85.

Maslach, C. 1979. Negative emotional biasing of unexplained arousal. *Journal of Personality and Social Psychology*, 37, 953–69.

Merton, R. K. 1957. *Social theory and social structure*. New York: Free Press.

Mummendey, A., Bornewasser, M., Loschper, G. & Linneweber, V. 1981. Defining interactions as aggressive in a specific social context. *First Congress of the European section of ISRA*, Strasbourg.

Paulus, P. B. (ed.) 1980. *Psychology of group influence*. Hillsdale, NJ: Erlbaum.

Peyrefitte, A. 1977. (Rapport du comité d'études présidé par) *Réponses à la violence*. Paris: La documentation française.

Rubin, Z. & Peplau, L. A. 1975. Who believes in a just world? *Journal of Social Issues*, *31*, 65–89.

Tedeschi, J. T., Smith, R. B. III & Brown, R. C. Jr. 1974. A reinterpretation of research on aggression. *Psychological Bulletin, 81*, 540–62.

Turner, C. W. & Fenn, M. R. 1981. The instigating effects of associated retrieval cues and white noise on delayed verbal aggression. Unpublished MS, University of Utah.

Turner, C. W. & Layton, J. F. 1976. Verbal imagery and connotations as memory induced mediators of aggressive behavior. *Journal of Personality and Social Psychology, 33*, 755–63.

Turner, C. W. & Simons, L. S. 1974. Effects of subject sophistication and evaluation apprehension on aggressive responses to weapons. *Journal of Personality and Social Psychology, 30*, 341–8.

Turner, C. W., Simons, L. S., Berkowitz, L. & Frodi, A. 1977. The stimulating and inhibiting effects of weapons on aggressive behaviour. *Aggressive Behaviour, 3*, 355–78.

Vala, J. 1980. Violence filmée et comportements agressifs. La représentation sociale de la violence. Unpublished M.A. dissertation, University of Louvain.

Winn, M. 1979. *T.V. drogue?* Paris: Fleurus.

Zillmann, D. 1979. *Hostility and aggression*. Hillsdale, NJ: Erlbaum.

# 11. Justice and fairness in interpersonal relations: thoughts and suggestions[1]

## GEROLD MIKULA

The notions of 'justice' and 'fairness' were neglected for a long time in empirical social psychology despite their importance in everyday life. It was only at the beginning of the 1960s that they began to emerge as the subject of various theoretical conceptions and empirical studies. Since then, the situation has drastically changed. Justice and fairness have become central themes in social psychological research, and the number of relevant publications has rapidly grown (cf. books by Berkowitz & Walster 1976; Folger in press; Greenberg & Cohen 1982a; Lerner 1975a; Mikula 1980a).

Following the main theme of the author's own research and the general trend of the relevant research in social psychology, the present chapter will focus upon problems of 'interpersonal justice', while issues pertaining to 'social justice' will be hardly touched upon. In other words, we shall be primarily concerned with justice in interpersonal relations (as it functions inside a homogeneous social milieu) and not with relations between social groups or with the large-scale phenomena of social justice.[2] As will be seen in the course of the discussion, even the term 'interpersonal justice' is overstretched in some respects. This is due to the fact that the research on justice has been mainly concerned with the role played by the notions of

[1] I would like to thank Hans-Werner Bierhoff, Egon Kayser and Thomas Schwinger for their helpful comments on an earlier version of this chapter. This chapter was translated from the German by Henri Tajfel.
[2] Tajfel (1982; see also Chapter 33 in this book) has recently presented a convincing argument that the present perspectives dominating the psychological study of justice are not appropriate for an analysis of the large-scale phenomena of social (in)justice. This is the case because of their individualistic assumptions and in spite of some recent attempts, made within these same perspectives (e.g. Austin & Hatfield 1980), to redress the balance. We are in full agreement with this view. It remains to be seen whether Tajfel's requirement that we need a theory of justice which would encompass both these areas can be met. To quote from Tajfel (1982: 158): 'A future theoretical framework for a social psychology of justice must be capable of taking into account both the inter-individual relations within a socially homogeneous milieu *and* the relations – inter-individual and collective – which obtain across a variety of barriers dividing social categories of people who perceive themselves as belonging to different "communities"'.

ustice in the actions and judgments of single individuals, following in this
way the individualistic assumptions dominating much of contemporary social
psychology. As a result, the significance of the concepts of justice in the
control and dynamics of interpersonal relations, the formation of interpersonal
consensus about what should be conceived as being just, and the consequences
of the corresponding disagreements, have all been seriously neglected.

This chapter deals with three themes of central importance in the psychological research on interpersonal justice: (i) the nature of concerns with
justice; (ii) feelings of injustice and their consequences; and (iii) rules of
distributive and procedural justice. On each of these topics, after a brief review
of the present state of research, some proposals will be made about promising
directions of future research. With regard to concerns with justice and
feelings of injustice, a theoretical perspective which uses motivation for
control as the basic explanatory concept will be proposed and sketched out
in its main outlines. Regarding the third theme, preference will be given to
those theoretical approaches which assume that several different rules with
specific ranges of appropriateness exist in the individuals' naive conceptions
of justice.

Although justice is the central theme of this chapter, no definition of the
concept will be provided in the course of the discussion. According to the
author's view, this is not the business of psychological studies of justice
phenomena. Rather, they have to analyse the manner in which people use
the concept of justice and deal with it in their everyday lives.

## . Concerns with justice

### .1. Justice as a motive. In the two theories which dominate today's social
psychological conceptions about justice–equity theory (Adams 1965; Walster,
Berscheid & Walster 1973; Walster, Walster & Berscheid 1978), and the
justice motive theory (Lerner 1975b, 1977; Lerner, Miller & Holmes 1976)
- the human preoccupation with questions of justice is seen as a consequence
of a motivation for justice. Although the assumptions about the nature of this
motivation and its roots differ in the two theories, they are in agreement that
the implementation of justice and avoidance of injustice are of central
significance as a goal of action in human life.

The origins of concerns with justice are explained in the following way by
Walster and her colleagues (1973, 1978) in their equity theory. Human
beings are selfish by nature and seek to maximize their outcomes. As
everyone's unlimited pursuit of individual selfish goals would be totally
disruptive for social systems, principles and rules of the distribution of goods

and conditions are developed in order to maximize the collective outcome. Because of the application of rewards for rule-following behaviour and punishments for rule-breaking behaviour, the participants in a social system learn to keep to these rules and finally come to internalize them; as a result, a violation of the rules causes distress and is followed by cognitive or behavioural attempts to restore a state of affairs which is just. Thus, concern with justice is explained by equity theorists in terms of a socially learned motivation for justice which is seen as a reactive phenomenon (cf. van Avermaet, McClintock & Moskowitz 1978): the actual goal is not to achieve justice *per se* but to avoid injustice.[3]

In contrast, Lerner's justice motive theory uses a pro-active concept of motivation: it is not the avoidance of injustice which is the basis of human concern with justice, but an active striving to establish just states of affairs and conditions. The roots of this justice motivation are not to be sought, according to Lerner (1975b, 1977; Lerner, Miller & Holmes 1976), in the processes of social learning but in the individual cognitive development. In the course of this development, the child acquires the ability to anticipate various alternatives for action and their consequences, and thus is in a position to plan and to choose. It also gains experience showing that it is often advantageous to sacrifice the immediate satisfaction of a need for the sake of a delayed but greater satisfaction. Simultaneously, it develops a conception of entitlement and deserving, which provides the basis for the 'personal contract' and, subsequently, for the concerns with justice. The personal contract is expressed in the individual's readiness to do certain things and leave others undone on the assumption that, as a result, certain expected consequences will follow. It is only if an individual believes in a just world where everybody gets what he deserves and is entitled to receive, that the adherence to the personal contract can make sense to him. Any information about someone who has been struck by undeserved misfortune undermines the validity of this belief. Therefore, an individual's concern is also for others being treated according to their entitlements, and this accounts for the origin of the striving for justice.

---

[3] As van Avermaet, McClintock & Moskowitz (1978) correctly pointed out, it is only Adams' conception of equity theory which can be considered as relying on a purely reactive motivational concept, since Walster and her colleagues (1973, 1978) discuss in their Proposition 2 not only punishments for inequitable behaviour, but also rewards for equitable behaviour: '...not only may inequity operate as a negatively valued state, but equity can operate as a positive value' (van Avermaet, McClintock & Moskowitz 1978: 435). It remains true, however, that Walster *et al.* hardly take this possibility into account in their subsequent discussion.

**1.2. Justice as a goal or a strategy?** Other authors have been less interested in the etiology of the concerns with justice than in the role played by these concerns in the actions and judgments of individuals, and in social interaction. Since both equity theory and Lerner's theory give the impression that the striving for justice is the exclusive motivating force of action in social situations, other researchers stressed that justice is only one of many goals which can be pursued (e.g. Homans 1976; Leventhal 1980). This view is particularly clear in the models concerning allocation preferences and allocation decisions put forward by Leventhal, Karuza & Fry (1980) and Mikula (1980c).

It is also argued that very often justice is not the real goal of actions, but is much more likely to represent strategic means used in order to achieve other goals (e.g. Greenberg & Cohen 1982b; Leventhal 1980; Mikula 1980b, c; van Avermaet, McClintock & Moskowitz 1978; Reis 1981, in press). There exists a very large variety of goals the achievement of which can be attempted through the means of just behaviour. Avoidance of conflicts, furthering of harmony within a group, legitimization of self-seeking behaviour, favourable presentation of self and the achievement of recognition are but a few examples.

It seems useless to ask the question as to which of the viewpoints outlined above is likely to be the most adequate. A theoretical construct such as the concept of motivation does not lend itself to empirical validation. It is also quite impossible to reach a conclusion which would be generally applicable as to whether justice functions as a goal or as a means to other goals, since both can be assumed to occur. Many actions which are guided by considerations of justice may indeed have as their exclusive goal the achievement of justice, but just as often the instrumental functions of such behaviour will come to the foreground.[4] In addition, an action may be consonant with the rules of justice without being guided in any way by considerations of justice on the part of the acting individual. Thus, all these possibilities must be taken into account in an adequate assessment of the role played by concerns with justice. Moreover, an observation that an action fits in with a rule of justice does not allow any inference about underlying concerns with justice and their functions (cf. Cohen 1978; Leventhal 1980; Reis in press; van Avermaet, McClintock & Moskowitz 1978).

---

[4] It also needs to be mentioned that, in the last analysis, in many concrete occurrences, it may be very difficult to decide whether what appears as the (ultimate) goal of an action should not be seen as a means for the achievement of another goal.

**1.3. Justice as serving the motivation for control.** The instrumental and strategic character of concerns with justice has been stressed by several authors who have proposed independently of each other that these concerns can be conceived as one of the expressions of the general motivation for control (Kayser *et al.* 1980; Reis in press). Man is seen in this perspective as striving for control in order to achieve desired outcomes and to avoid undesired ones. Stimulated by some of the arguments of these authors, a control motivational conception of concerns with justice will be developed and outlined below.

The basic assumptions of this conception are similar to those of Lerner (1975b, 1977). In the course of his development a human being acquires the ability to identify causal associations between his own behaviour and the events which happen in his environment. This enables him to construct explanations for these events, to foresee them and to control, at least in part, his outcomes through the planning of his actions. Certain beliefs, which may be more or less firm, determine this planning. Generally speaking, these beliefs are of the general form that in particular situational conditions particular effects can be obtained by means of particular actions. These beliefs originate partly from the experience accumulated in various (social and non-social) areas of an individual's life, and in part they are taken over from other people in the course of socialization. As these beliefs imply the expectation of security and control of outcomes, an individual acts according to them. In addition, he expects others to act similarly, because they are assumed to have developed similar beliefs.

Using these arguments, concerns with justice can be described as being connected with a certain sub-category of beliefs which apply to the exchange and distribution of resources and the corresponding procedures. From early childhood, individuals confront the concept of justice and accumulate manifold experiences with this concept. They come to know justice as a social value having regulating and legitimizing functions within social systems. They discover that there exist a great number of different rules of justice which are considered appropriate and are used in specific conditions. Additionally, they learn that actions which are not considered to be just by the social environment of an actor are generally not accepted but rather criticized and punished. As a consequence of these experiences, people will make use of the rules of justice, as they provide a sense of control over one's outcomes and a sense of security regarding the modes of action which are pertinent to the exchange and distribution of resources. Based on the experience that actions which are considered unjust by the social environment usually result in negative and undesired consequences, people will try to justify their actions by making reference to a rule of justice to which their actions correspond. The knowledge of the various rules of justice and their ranges of validity will lead to the development of assumptions about what actions can be successfully justified in one's environment and about what actions are to be expected from other persons in certain situations.

It is important at this point to raise two issues which follow from the above discussion. In the first place, there are differences between the conception as just outlined and alternative views of concerns with justice, whether considered solely as the results of a social learning process (as in Walster's version of equity theory) or solely as the result of cognitive development (as is the case for Lerner's justice motive theory). In the above argument, a distinction is made between, on the one hand, the *acquisition* of the concept of justice and of the various rules of justice and, on the other, the *utilization* of the concept of justice. It is assumed that a process of socialization is responsible for the former, while the latter is explained from a theoretical basis of motivation for control.[5] Secondly, it is proposed that the actual goal of people's concerns with justice is not to achieve justice *per se* but to avoid the negative consequences which are usually associated with events which are considered to be unjust by the social environment. It follows from this that the primary issue in concerns for justice is to be able to *justify* one's actions, decisions and claims (cf. Reis in press; Tajfel 1982; see also Chapter 33) in the eyes of others as well as for oneself.

*1.3.1. Justifications to others.* To provide justifications to others of one's actions and claims becomes particularly important in situations of social interdependence, at least when there exists amongst the participants a minimum level of readiness to cooperate. Justifications can be understood in such cases as attempts to bring the partner to the point of acknowledging the appropriateness of one's actions and claims. It is only when this succeeds that one can hope to ensure the desired and expected outcomes, since in cases of interdependence they are brought about not only by one's own actions but also by those of the partner. Conceived in this way, justice is an argument which individuals can use (in real or in anticipated discussions with the partner) in order to legitimize their interests (cf. Kayser *et al.* 1980; Reis in press).

[5] The argument of Lerner (1977) that a human being is bound to reach a concept of justice even without undergoing socialization appears neither very important nor convincing. In the first place, all human beings go through a process of socialization; secondly, unlike the concepts of 'deserving' and 'entitlement', the concept of justice is only relevant in a social context (see Cohen 1979).

A few examples will illustrate this function of referring to justice. Justifications of already performed actions and decisions can be used to stress an actor's impartiality. At the same time, personal responsibility for the action (or decision) is played down, and transferred, at least in part, to the impersonal authority of the norm of justice. When someone makes claims and, in doing so, argues with reference to justice, he tries in this way to present his personal wishes as justified deserts, or as Reis (in press) puts it, 'the stated desire for a just resolution often adds a greater degree of justifiability to a claim – that is, stating that one deserves a particular outcome imbues it with a greater degree of worthiness or legitimacy than merely wanting it'. A similar situation obtains when someone characterizes an action or a decision as 'unjust'. Rather than stressing personal dissatisfaction, the individual points to the infringement of the social value 'justice', and simultaneously, by referring to the norm of justice, requests a change or a compensation, or, at the least, stresses the objectionable character of what has happened.

It may be worthwhile to mention at this point that there exist two sets of questions concerning justifications offered to others, which should be kept apart although they are not entirely independent of each other. The first set, which applies to the examples described above, is centred upon the individual even if it concerns justifications made to other people. In what conditions and by what means does an individual attempt to justify his actions, decisions and claims? The second set of questions is centred upon interaction. What are the conditions underlying the acceptance by others of the attempted justifications? The first of these issues will be discussed in some detail before the second is briefly considered.

The basic prerequisite which is necessary for offering a justification to others is the correspondence of the action being justified with some rule of justice. But this is undoubtedly not sufficient. The actor must also see to it that his justification is accepted. As the available rules of justice are not equally appropriate for all situations (see section 3 of this chapter; also Mikula 1977, 1980c), he must also take into account the special features of the situation and the presumed expectations of the partner in whose eyes the justification is supposed to succeed. Unfortunately, not much research has been directly concerned with the use made of concepts of justice in the justification of one's actions presented to other people. One must therefore rely on speculation and indirect empirical evidence taken from research concerned with allocations. Studies of this kind (for reviews, see Leventhal 1976a, b; Mikula 1980c, 1981b) have consistently shown that, in general, allocation decisions are made in accordance with well-established allocation rules which, under certain circumstances, are considered as just. The findings suggest, in addition, a highly flexible use of the rules, also that they are applied for justifications of allocations serving a very great variety of aims and purposes. Three examples of findings will help clarification. They all come from studies in which the allocator also functioned as a recipient of one part of the reward which was being distributed. The experimental situation was such that an allocation conforming to rules could mainly be made either according to the contribution rule (to each according to his contributions) or corresponding to the equality rule (to each the same).

Reis & Gruzen (1976) were able to show that when partners could be expected to have different types of preferences, different allocations were made. Subjects who were led to expect that the experimenter would be informed of their allocation decisions, and accordingly that this decision (if at all) would have to be justified in his eyes, distributed the reward according to the contribution rule. In contrast, subjects who expected their decision to be known to the other recipients, and who therefore had to justify their decision (if at all) only to those recipients, followed in their allocations the rule of equality.

Research with children (cf. Mikula 1972a, 1980c: 148ff; Schwarz in preparation) demonstrates the use of rules of justice in the justification of self-serving allocations. In experimental studies conducted with children of preschool age, allocations guided by rules usually were not observed. The subjects claimed more than half of the reward for themselves, independently of whether they had contributed more or less than the partner to the attainment of the reward which was to be distributed. In contrast, the decisions of children of primary school age were already guided by rules. However, the allocations corresponded predominantly to the rule which was of greatest advantage to the allocator: the subjects who had contributed more than their partner distributed the reward according to the contribution rule; those who had contributed less decided for the equality rule. As the assignment of the subjects to the experimental conditions of contribution size was made randomly, the differences in the allocation decisions of these children of primary school age cannot be attributed to different stages of development or different conditions of socialization.[6] These findings are best interpreted as showing attempts to obtain what is, in the circumstances, the largest possible part of the reward which can also be claimed as justifiable.

The application of rules can also be used to justify allocations which seek aims other than self-interest; this is a finding which has repeatedly emerged

---

[6] In addition, there exist studies which show that even children of preschool age are already capable of making allocations corresponding to the contribution rule, when as allocators they are not themselves recipients of a part of the reward (cf. Hook & Cook 1979; Mikula 1980c).

from experiments with adult subjects (cf. Mikula 1977, 1980c, 1981b; Mikula & Schwinger 1978; Schwinger 1980). In these studies, as in the previous ones, different allocation principles were also used by allocators who differed in the amounts of their input. But as distinct from the behaviour of the children, the rule which was chosen presented a disadvantage to the allocator and an advantage to his partner; the subjects who had produced more than their partners opted for the rule of equality, and those who produced less opted for the contribution rule. This behaviour is most probably based on the wish of the allocator to show unselfishness, generosity, modesty, politeness, etc. The correspondence of the allocation with a rule of justice makes it easier in these cases, as in those described above, to justify a decision. Indeed, it was shown in post-experimental interviews that the subjects explicitly claimed their preceding allocations to be 'just'. The subjects who acted according to the rule of equality stressed that their partner worked for as long as they themselves had done, that the partner's effort was equal to theirs, they underestimated the existing differences in input, and attributed these differences to external causes. The subjects who chose the contribution rule produced arguments of a similar kind in support of their decisions (Mikula 1972b, 1974).

Some authors (Cohen 1978; Mikula 1981a; Reis in press) have recently pointed out that the findings from the allocation experiments throw little light on the role and importance of concerns with justice in allocation decisions. This is so because the subjects in a typical allocation experiment are not explicitly instructed to make fair allocations. The results are, however, of some interest for the problem of the justification functions of justice which concerns us here. They show convincingly that allocation decisions are strongly guided by rules, which is a basic prerequisite for the subsequent justifications of these decisions. Moreover, the results suggest that the rules of just allocation are not applied inflexibly but are used instead as planned strategies aiming at the achievement of certain goals. This is particularly clear in the finding that individuals who find themselves in different positions, as compared with their partner, with respect to their contribution to the gaining of reward, adopt in allocations different rules which all serve the same aim. Although the studies were not conducted for the purpose of looking at this particular problem, it seems plausible to conclude from them that the observed behaviour represents attempts to keep alive the possibility of using justifications for allocations which have been made.

Let us now look briefly at the conditions underlying the acceptance by a partner of an attempted justification. The treatment of this problem will have to be even more speculative than was the above discussion. This is why no more can be done here than to present a fairly unsystematic enumeration of conditions which cannot by any means claim to be exhaustive. In addition, the conditions to be listed are likely to be limited in their general applicability.

One condition upon which the probability of success of a justification depends is the degree of impartiality which can be attributed to the actor. This in turn depends on how much profit accrues to the actor as the result of his action.[7] Further, a justification is more likely to be acceptable when the personal interests of the partner who must be convinced by it have not been affected, or at least not damaged, by the action. But more interesting are the instances, which contain a potential conflict, when the bias of the actor is taken for granted and the interests of the partner are affected. This will be discussed next.

If justifications are to be made acceptable in such situations of conflict of interests, a consensus must be reached between actor and partner as to how the situation should be interpreted, which rules of justice are applicable to it, and how these rules should be implemented in this particular instance. Consensus of this kind is more likely to be reached inside a homogeneous social milieu where norms exist (which may be explicit or implicit) about the appropriate choice of a rule and the manner of its application (see section 3). Agreements of this nature should be much more difficult to reach – if they can be reached at all – between people belonging to different social milieus (see Chapter 33).[8]

When the normative basis for such consensus is little developed or is lacking altogether, a negotiation between the partners becomes necessary. Whether or not an agreement is reached, and what is its nature, will depend here – as in other instances of negotiation – upon the extent of the existing discrepancies, upon the quality of the affective relations between the partners, their readiness to cooperate, their interest in continuing the relationship, and, last but not least, upon the existing balance of power. In relation to this last point, the 'justification theory' which Tajfel briefly formulates in Chapter 33 of this book includes the following important proposition: when a power differential exists between two parties, the justifications put forward by the more powerful party need to be less plausible the greater is the power

[7] One of the courses of action of tactical advantage to the actor could be to point out that there exists an alternative to what he has done which also corresponds to a rule, from which he could have obtained greater advantages for himself, and which he did not choose. In this way he can 'prove' that his main preoccupation is not his own gain but a just solution.

[8] As intergroup phenomena are not the subject of this chapter, the role played by justifications in intergroup conflicts can be discussed only marginally. Generally, in such situations actions do not have to be justified to the outgroup but only to the members of the ingroup, which should be fairly easy to manage. Sometimes, however, it may also be necessary to provide justifications to neutral third parties.

differential; when these differentials become very large, a point can be reached when no justifications of any kind are required.

*1.3.2. Justifications for oneself.* Until now, the discussion has been concentrated on the justifications an actor offers to others. What remains to be discussed is the necessity for an actor to convince himself that his actions and claims are justifiable. Tajfel (see Chapter 33) has pointed out the possibility that people who are motivated solely by rational interest have no need at all to provide justifications for themselves. This idea makes sense. Nevertheless, considering the experiences people gain with the concept of justice and its functions during their socialization, it seems reasonable to assume that it is important for most persons to be able to believe that their actions are just. Learning theorists would explain this fact as a consequence of internalization processes. From a theoretical perspective stressing the role played by motivation of control, justifications for oneself are important in giving an actor the feeling that he has done everything possible to avoid negative consequences of his actions. It must be admitted, however, that there may exist marked individual differences with regard to the necessity felt to justify one's actions and claims for oneself.

From the point of view adopted here, the important issue for an individual is not so much to gain control *per se* as the need for control in order to achieve desired outcomes and to avoid undesired ones. It can therefore be expected that when an individual engages in justifying his actions to himself (i.e. in full privacy), frequently he will choose that option which is the most favourable to him and can be made consistent at the same time with a rule of justice.[9] Reis (1981) has reviewed empirical findings which provide, at the least, indirect support for this notion (although his purpose was slightly different). Therefore, it will be sufficient to provide here only one example. Reis & Gruzen (1976) were able to show that, in a condition of anonymity, individuals responsible for allocation claimed for themselves a greater proportion of the rewards than was the case when they were expecting to have to justify their decisions to others; nevertheless, in the former condition they were nowhere near claiming for themselves the total amount of the available rewards. A clearer indication of the tendency of justifying one's actions to oneself was provided in the ratings obtained from the allocators of the abilities and efforts of the members of the group amongst whom the rewards were to be shared out. Although these ratings were presented as fully private, and

---

[9] In view of the ambiguity inherent in the concept of justice, the large number of justice rules, and their high level of abstraction, this should not be too difficult to manage.

were experienced as such, they corresponded to the relative shares of the rewards allotted to the individual recipients by the allocators.

1.3.3. *Concluding remarks.* The theoretical perspective stressing the role played by motivation for control in concerns with justice has not until now been worked out in detail in many respects; and there are no empirical studies specifically designed to test it. Despite this, it is an approach which seems to present in many ways a promising start. As compared with Lerner's justice motive theory, which it resembles in many respects in its basic assumptions, the control motivation theory assigns a less central role in human life to the concerns with justice, and it attempts to clarify them in a more general theoretical framework. A distinct advantage of the theory is its stress upon the strategic nature of the concerns with justice. Further, it allows for integration within the same conceptual perspective of both the phenomena of justice and justification (cf. Reis in press). Although the present discussion has mainly concentrated upon the problems of distributive justice, it also seems possible to consider the themes of procedural fairness from the point of view of the control motivation theory. Finally, as will be seen in the following section, this approach allows for the development of a new perspective about the sense of injustice.

## 2. Feelings of injustice

The experience of injustice results from the perception that a given action or the consequences resulting from it do not correspond to the rule of justice which seems appropriate in the given circumstances. In the psychological literature on justice, the theme of injustice finds its fullest and most explicit treatment in the writings of equity theorists (cf. Adams 1965; Walster, Walster & Berscheid 1978). In the view of these authors, the experience of injustice is based on the perception that the principle of equity has been infringed, i.e. the parties involved in the situation have not obtained equal relative gains from the situation. Each perception of this kind (whether made by the individual who is advantaged by the state of affairs, by the disadvantaged one, or by an impartial observer) leads to distress, which becomes greater as the perceived discrepancy increases. In order to remove the distress, attempts are made to restore the state of equity, and these attempts become more marked the greater is the existing inequity and the stronger is the distress associated with it. The restoration of an equitable state of affairs can be done through changing either the inputs or the outcomes of the participants ('restoring *actual* equity') or through a perceptual distortion of these amounts ('restoring *psychological* equity'), i.e., in the last analysis, either through compensation or through justification.

Apart from the problems (which will be discussed in the next section) raised by the postulation in equity theory of one, and one only, rule of justice, the equity principle, a number of authors have also questioned the assertion made in equity theory that each perception of inequity causes distress and leads to attempts to restore equity. Some authors (e.g. Greenberg in press; Tajfel 1982) are doubtful of the need to postulate distress or tension as an intervening variable between a case of injustice being noticed and the reactions following this perception. Other authors have argued that attempts to restore actual or psychological equity cannot be assumed to constitute the only consequences of experiences of injustice. For example, Utne & Kidd (1980) stress that the perception of inequity is generally followed by a search for information which, in turn, can serve as a basis for a more correct assessment of, and an explanation for, the events which took place. According to Utne & Kidd, the results of such information-seeking, as well as of attributional processes, are of considerable importance in determining the degree of the consequent distress, the decisions as to whether equity should be restored and, if so, by what means.[10]

The assumption that the perception of an injustice need not lead immediately and unconditionally to distress and to attempts to restore justice, also appears plausible when the experiences of injustice are analysed from the point of view of the control motivation theory. In this perspective, the perception that a rule of justice considered to be appropriate has been infringed means, first of all, the refutation of an existing expectation. Since this expectation has been derived from more basic (and more or less firmly established) beliefs regarding the appropriate modes of exchange and distribution of resources, its disconfirmation causes insecurity. The individual's ability to predict social events and thus to achieve control over his outcomes becomes doubtful when this happens. Considered in this way, the perception of an injustice is equivalent to the experience of loss of control (cf. Reis in press). Various factors are responsible for the intensity of this experience and the nature of its consequences. Two of these factors, namely attributions and the role assumed by an individual in the context of an injustice being committed, will be discussed below in some detail. Examples of other variables are the extent of the discrepancy between expectation and event and the degree of confidence in

---

[10]  Other authors, such as Cohen (1982) and Kayser (1979; Kayser & Lamm 1980; Kayser & Schwinger 1982) have also pointed out the need to take into account subjective attributions in order to achieve a better understanding of the psychological phenomena of justice.

the disconfirmed belief, which should depend upon the frequency of its previous confirmations (Kayser *et al.* 1980).

It can be expected that the perceived discrepancy between an expectation and an event, and the resulting insecurity, will motivate an individual to seek an explanation (cf. Kayser & Schwinger 1982). It can also be expected that, in many cases, causal attributions which will then be made will not change the perception that an injustice has occurred. They can, however, endow the event with various meanings, and in this way influence the extent to which the situation is experienced as threatening and distressing. They can also affect decisions about whether and how the situation should be reacted to (cf. Utne & Kidd 1980, for a detailed discussion of the many possibilities which may be involved here). Sometimes the individual can also make, during his attributions, a re-assessment of the situation, leading to the conclusion that no injustice has occurred. As distinct from the view held by equity theorists, this latter possibility is considered here as no more than one amongst many; it is not by any means seen as inevitable, unless the injustice has in fact been removed. Utne & Kidd (1980: 75) were right in stressing that there are plenty of examples in everyday life of people being able to live with the awareness of injustices, 'and when they can do nothing to change them, they do not pretend that the injustices never occurred'.

The second significant factor determining the intensity of the experience of loss of control is the role an individual assumes in relation to a perceived injustice. Does it present for him an advantage or a disadvantage, or does he simply acknowledge it as a non-participating observer (cf. Kayser *et al.* 1980; Reis in press)? As was said earlier, the striving for control is not an aim itself; it aims at the achievement of desired outcomes and the avoidance of undesired ones. Therefore, the sense of control of individuals who have been disadvantaged is not only impaired by the recognition that their expectations (and eventually the underlying beliefs) have been wrong. They also have to realize that, as a matter of fact, they were not able to achieve a desired and expected outcome. Advantaged individuals and non-participating observers, on the other hand, do not have this experience. The satisfaction of their wishes and desires is endangered only to the extent that they must take into account the possibility that at some later time they may themselves become victims of a similar injustice. Whether they do or do not consider this to be a possibility will obviously depend upon the explanations to which, based on their attributions, they will have resorted in any particular case. When the contingency that a similar fate might befall them does not seem likely, their sense of control will be impaired only in so far as their expectations and beliefs have been disconfirmed. It follows from this discussion that disadvantaged persons would experience stronger feelings of loss of control and would be more likely to feel distressed than those who obtained advantages or did not participate in the unjust situation. In consequence, their reactions would be quicker and more intense. Everyday observations and empirical findings from research based on equity theory support these assumptions (cf. Walster, Walster & Berscheid 1978).

These considerations lead to the assumption that disadvantaged, advantaged and non-participating third-party individuals will prefer and adopt different methods in order to reduce the experience of loss of control (and eventual distress) when they are confronted with a perceived injustice. The advantaged individuals and the neutral observers must first of all deal with the threatening idea that at some time they may themselves become victims of a similar injustice. The first requirement for the disadvantaged individuals is to change the existing state of affairs. It follows that the former would generally produce justifications of the perceived situation, while the latter might try active intervention, perhaps by using justice arguments for support. Unfortunately, there are no studies as yet which aim to provide a direct test of these predictions.

To conclude this section, the point should be made that feelings of injustice and unfairness do not relate only to issues of distribution; they may also relate to the procedures which are applied in connection with a distribution (see section 3). This presents no theoretical difficulty for an approach based on the control motivation theory. In all these cases, the experience of injustice is based on a disconfirmation of expectations originating from beliefs regarding the appropriate modes of exchange and distribution.

## 3. Rules of distributive and procedural justice

This final section deals with the theoretical points of view and empirical findings regarding the rules of justice, and the circumstances in which these rules are considered as appropriate for adoption as a basis for actions and assessments of justice. Rules of justice refer either to the exchange and distribution of resources (rules of distributive justice) or to the related procedures (rules of procedural fairness). Since the psychological research on justice has concentrated until now mainly on distributive justice, and only in recent times focused on issues of procedural fairness, we shall begin with a discussion of the rules of distributive justice.

**3.1. Rules of distributive justice.** The basic texts on equity theory (Adams 1965; Walster, Berscheid & Walster 1973; Walster, Walster & Berscheid

1978) were concerned solely with one single justice rule, the equity principle, which is based on the proportionality of inputs and outcomes of the participants. Other authors (representatives of the so-called multi-principle approaches) have insisted that, in addition to the equity (or contribution) principle, there exists a considerable number of other rules of justice (cf. Deutsch 1975; Kayser & Schwinger 1982; Lerner 1975b, 1977; Leventhal 1976b, 1980; Leventhal, Karuza & Fry 1980; Mikula 1977, 1980c; Mikula & Schwinger 1978, 1981; Sampson 1969, 1975; Schwinger 1980). These authors also draw attention to the fact that the relevance and appropriateness of various rules of justice change with historical, cultural, situational and dispositional conditions.[11] Protracted discussions have consequently developed between equity theorists and the representatives of multi-principle approaches with regard to the usefulness and necessity of the assumption that several different rules of justice exist within the individuals' conceptions of justice. As this discussion is documented elsewhere (Lerner 1975a; Mikula 1980a), and it can be interpreted as having been settled in favour of the multi-principle theorists, it will not be pursued here.

The rules of justice considered as important by the proponents of multi-principle approaches differ to some extent regarding their number and content; all these conceptions share, however, their stress on the contribution principle ('to each according to his contributions'), the equality principle ('to each the same'), and the need principle ('to each according to his needs'). Considering the large number of rules of allocation which can be shown to relate in a variety of cases to the notions of justice, it seems unwise to try and reach any definite conclusions about exactly how many such rules there are. The multi-principle theories of justice become interesting and significant primarily through research attempting to specify the conditions in which the different rules of justice appear appropriate and are actually adopted as a basis for actions and assessments of justice.

There exist at present a number of classificatory schemes aiming to relate various rules of justice to distinct types of social situations. According to Deutsch (1975), Leventhal (1976b), Mikula (1977, 1980c), Mikula & Schwinger (1978) and Schwinger (1980), the perception of particular rules as being appropriate in one situation or another is mainly determined by the primary orientation or goal-setting of a social system (economic, solidarity or

---

[11] Many of the studies referred to above present a view stressing the instrumental and strategic character of concerns with justice. Accordingly, they also make assumptions about the specific and differing consequences which follow for social systems from the application of each of the rules. As is the case for appropriateness, however, one should not expect these consequences to remain the same irrespective of situational, structural, cultural and historical conditions.

welfare) and by the nature of the relationships obtaining amongst the participants.[12] For Lerner (1975b, 1977), it all depends on the perception of a relationship with another person (such as identity, unit and non-unit relationships) and also whether a partner is seen as a person *per se* or as occupying a social position. Greenberg & Cohen (1982b) used as the criteria for their classification the variables of 'outcome interdependence' and 'intimacy', which combine into a single unifying dimension of 'potential conflict over resources'.

More complex models were recently proposed by Deutsch (1982) and Kayser *et al.* (1980). Deutsch drew for his typology of situations on the dimensions of 'cooperation vs. competition', 'equal vs. unequal division of power', 'task vs. social-emotional orientation' and 'formal vs. informal'. These dimensions were conceived by Wish, Deutsch & Kaplan (1976) as being fundamental in interpersonal relations. Kayser *et al.* (1980; cf. also Kayser & Schwinger 1982) based their classification of social situations on three variables: the cognitive-motivational orientation of the participants; the quality of the affective relationship between the participants; and the kind of resources which are mainly transmitted, exchanged or distributed within the relationship. The two conceptions just outlined differ from the models mentioned earlier, whose sole concern was the ordering of justice rules with reference to specified social situations. The latter two conceptions consider the subjective notions about the situation-specific appropriateness of rules as being no more than one aspect of a more general orientation (consisting of cognitive, motivational and moral components) with which an individual approaches his social environment.

Despite the fact that nearly all the proponents of multi-principle approaches acknowledge in their discussions of the appropriateness of justice rules that their statements have a validity which is limited to one particular socio-historical context, the historical, cultural and structural variables have not been considered by them in any detail. The articles by Sampson (1975) and Schwinger (1980) which deal explicitly with these influences are welcome exceptions. There has also been, for too long, too little work on the dispositional and person-specific variables with which covary the subjective ideas of what should be considered as just (but see articles by Major & Deaux 1982; Sampson 1980; also remarks on the subject in Mikula 1980c, 1981b). When one considers the empirical research relating to the issue just

---

[12] In his three-stage model of allocation decisions, Mikula (1980c: 142ff.) discusses 'the specific nature of the goods to be allocated, and their function for the system' and 'the way in which the goods were acquired' as additional variables which can be significant for the choice of a justice rule. Moreover, he points to the importance of personality variables.

mentioned, it turns out that this research confined itself until recently almost exclusively to the use and testing of the allocation paradigm, through which it attempted to determine whether the variation in certain situational and person-specific variables leads to the application of different rules of allocation. Although the results generally confirmed the hypotheses which were formulated (see Leventhal 1976a, b; Mikula 1980c, 1981b, for reviews of the research on allocations), the explanatory power of this research is questionable. As was pointed out earlier, in most of these experiments the subjects were not explicitly requested to make fair allocations.[13] Therefore, the only conclusion which follows from these studies is that different distribution rules are applied in connection with different situational and person-specific variables. Whether this means that ideas of what is fair also vary remains an open question.

Independent of this difficulty, which could easily be overcome in future studies, the empirical testing of the assumptions inherent in the multi-principle approaches has suffered from the almost exclusive use in these studies of the allocation paradigm. If these assumptions could also find support when other paradigms are applied (such as justice judgments or re-allocations of already existing distributions), confidence in their validity would markedly increase. Relevant to this point is a study by Schmitt & Montada (1982). The subjects were presented with short descriptions of 114 allocation decisions varying according to the orientations dominating the social situations which were described, the object of the decisions, and the rules governing the decisions. These descriptions were then assessed on six-point rating scales which yielded judgments about the perceived degree of fairness of the various allocation decisions. The details of the complex findings, which were generally congruent with the hypotheses, cannot be described here (see a report in Mikula 1981b). Despite the well-known difficulties usually encountered in questionnaire studies and within-designs, the procedures suggested by the authors can be considered as a significant widening of scope of the hitherto available research methods.[14]

In addition to the nature of the paradigms which were being used, another problem connected with this research needs to be discussed. It has been mainly limited until now to the 'classic' rules of justice and the range of their application. In practice, this meant that studies were conducted about the contribution and equality principles, to which very recently the need principle has been added (e.g. Lamm & Schwinger 1980; Schwinger & Lamm 1981).

[13] One of the few exceptions is the recent study by Lamm & Schwinger (1981).
[14] Some other methodologically interesting studies recently have been reported by Bierhoff (1982) and Kayser, Schwinger & Kramer (1981).

It is possible that these three principles are, in fact, particularly important as rules of justice. Presumably, however, there are still other distribution rules which are adopted by individuals as a basis for their actions and assessments about justice, or for the justification of their claims, and whose infringement can lead to experiences of injustice. If one considers the gaining of insight into the ways individuals conceptualize justice as one of the tasks of the psychological research on justice, then these other rules must also be identified and their relevance assessed. However, it appears that the methods which have been used until now are not very suitable for these purposes. As a first step, studies could be undertaken which would deal with subjective statements about injustice and arguments used in justifications as they occur in everyday social situations. These statements and arguments could then be analysed with reference to the rules on which they are based, and this could be followed by ascertaining the situational conditions in which each of the rules is used. The subjectivity of judgments about justice would then be taken into account more fully in the research than has been the case until now. It remains to be seen whether, as a result, statements could be produced having a wider range of validity.

An entirely different procedure was recently adopted by Reis (in press). In order to determine how people understand and structure various rules of justice, he presented to his subjects 17 different rules for an assessment of their similarity, and analysed these assessments using multi-dimensional scaling. In addition to the finding that there existed three basic dimensions, he was also able to establish interesting relationships with some person-specific variables (such as sex and Protestant ethics). Although research of this kind is only in its beginnings, it points to further possibilities of gaining insights about the ways people understand the concept of justice and its numerous and varied rules.

**3.2. Rules of procedural fairness.** To conclude this section, we shall briefly consider the issues relating to procedural fairness. It is entirely obvious that ideas of justice are not only concerned with the distribution of resources but also extend to the procedures which are applied in connection with the allocations. We still know very little about the various aspects of the decision procedures which are assessed according to their fairness, and what rules and standards are used for this purpose. Apart from the studies dealing with procedural fairness in connection with institutional methods of conflict resolution (e.g. Thibaut & Walker 1975), there are very few which take an explicit position on this issue, and the empirical findings are sparse (cf. Deutsch 1975; Folger 1977; Lerner & Whitehead 1980; Leventhal 1980).

The most detailed proposals have come at present from Leventhal (1976b, 1980; Leventhal, Karuza & Fry 1980). He distinguished between seven procedural components of the allocative process which can be made the object of judgments about fairness. Furthermore, he enumerated six different rules of procedural fairness (consistency, bias suppression, accuracy, correctability, representativeness and ethicality) which can be applied to these components; but the conditions in which this happens are not specified. As Leventhal has himself admitted, his proposals are rather speculative: 'Because there are few relevant studies, descriptions of organizations by other commentators, and the author's own observations of groups and organizations, constitute the primary evidence for the theoretical proposals' (1980: 39). An urgent requirement here seems to be an empirical analysis of the rules and standards of procedural fairness individuals use in their everyday lives, their validity and range of application. It is to be expected that in this case the cultural, historical, structural, situational and person-specific variables will also play a significant role. In addition, research on the likely complex sets of reciprocal relations between distributive and procedural justice would be worthwhile. The points of view represented in the literature regarding this latter question are fairly divergent.

If future research were to address itself more directly to both the dimensions of justice, the distributive and the procedural, it is likely that the nature of the processes involved in justice phenomena would become better understood than it is now. The actual allocation which stands at the end of a sequence and is in the foreground of the analysis of distributive justice is no more than a small component (although admittedly it is salient in perception, cf. Leventhal, Karuza & Fry 1980: 172) of a long chain of actions, evaluations and decisions which are all interdependent.

## 4. Concluding remarks

The concern of this chapter has been with three themes which appear to me to be of central importance in the psychological research on justice. The present state of research on the subject was critically reviewed, and some proposals made about the promising directions of future research. In partial agreement with Kayser *et al.* (1980) and Reis (in press), a theoretical perspective stressing control motivation as a background of concerns with justice and feelings of injustice was proposed, and its main outlines were sketched out. According to this approach, the primary aspect of concerns with justice is the justification of one's own actions and claims. Justifications offered to one's partner are particularly required in situations of social interdependence in which personal goals cannot be achieved without support from the social environment. Subsequently, the justification of actions and claims may also become important for the individual himself, as it allows him to feel that he has done everything that was required for the achievement of his desired outcomes. It is possible that there exist significant individual differences in the subjectively felt need to present justifications to oneself.

Feelings of injustice were interpreted as experiences of insecurity and loss of control. The conceptions of control motivation theory provide here plausible explanations for the diverse consequences which may follow a perception of injustice. The variables seen as important in this context, and discussed in some detail in the chapter, were the role which an individual plays in connection with a perceived injustice and his attributions about the perceived state of affairs. Presumably, these variables are mainly responsible for a perception of injustice leading, or not leading, to distress, and also for the occurrence of other reactions shown by the individual.

It is hoped that it has been possible to demonstrate in this chapter the fruitfulness of the control-motivational point of view for the analysis of individual concerns with justice and feelings of injustice.[15] The requirement at present is to prove the usefulness of these conceptions in studies specially designed for this purpose. Naturally, it would not be possible to decide between the competing theories on the basis of empirical findings or of an *experimentum crucis*. Their elaboration is far from sufficient, and their formulation far from sufficiently exact, for this purpose. Which of the theories is given preference is always, at least in part, a matter of the personal taste of individual researchers and of their implicit preferences for a certain model of Man. But beyond this, a basis for decisions should also be provided by the utility, parsimony and range of application of a theory.

In the treatment of our third theme – the rules of justice – the control-motivational conception was abandoned, as it did not appear to offer any direct contributions. Despite this, the presently prevailing view that different rules exist in the individual's conception of justice, having their specific range of application, accords well with the control-motivational perspective. This is so because a functional view is adopted by most representatives of the multi-principle theories of justice: the definition of what distributive and procedural rules are just in which circumstances is assumed to depend finally on what is advantageous and useful for a social system of a certain kind and for its members (see Mikula 1980b: 17). These definitions, which are acquired

---

[15] Although the notion of motivation for control can be meaningfully applied only in approaches dealing with justice on an individualistic (or interpersonal) level, it seems to the present author that many of the arguments brought forward in this chapter make sense also in psychological analyses of large-scale phenomena of justice.

by the individual, together with the various justice rules, in the course of socialization, provide the fundamental basis from which originate the beliefs and expectations according to which an individual adjusts his actions in order to achieve desired outcomes and to avoid undesired ones. Beyond this, individual ideas as to what constitutes justice in any concrete situation will always remain to some extent idiosyncratic. It is this curious mixture of the objective and the subjective, so typical of the whole area of the study of justice, which causes research on the subject to be complex and difficult but at the same time full of interest.

## References

Adams, J. S. 1965. Inequity in social exchange. In L. Berkowitz (ed.) *Advances in experimental social psychology*, vol. 2. New York: Academic Press.

Austin, W. & Hatfield, E. 1980. Equity theory, power and social justice. In G. Mikula (ed.) (1980a).

Berkowitz, L. & Walster, E. (eds.) 1976. *Equity theory: towards a general theory of social interaction. Advances in experimental social psychology*, vol. 9. New York: Academic Press.

Bierhoff, H. W. 1982. Sozialer Kontext als Determinante der wahrgenommenen Gerechtigkeit: absolute und relative Gleichheit der Gewinnaufteilung. *Zeitschrift für Sozialpsychologie, 13*, 66–78.

Cohen, R. L. 1978. A critique of allocation research on distributive justice. Unpublished MS, Bennington College.

1979. On the distinction between individual deserving and distributive justice. *Journal for the Theory of Social Behaviour, 9*, 167–85.

1982. Perceiving justice: an attributional perspective. In J. Greenberg & R. L. Cohen (eds.) (1982a).

Deutsch, M. 1975. Equity, equality and need: what determines which value will be used as the basis of distributive justice? *Journal of Social Issues, 31*, 137–49.

1982. Interdependence and psychological orientation. In V. Derlega & J. L. Grzelak (eds.) *Living with other people: theories and research on cooperation and helping behaviour*. New York: Academic Press.

Folger, R. 1977. Distributive and procedural justice: combined impact of 'voice' and improvement on experienced inequity. *Journal of Personality and Social Psychology, 35*, 108–19.

(ed.) in press. *The sense of injustice: social psychological perspectives*. New York: Plenum.

Greenberg, J. in press. On the apocryphal nature of inequity distress. In R. Folger (ed.) (in press).

Greenberg, J. & Cohen, R. L. (eds.) 1982a. *Equity and justice in social behaviour*. New York: Academic Press.

1982b. Why justice? Normative and instrumental interpretations. In J. Greenberg & R. L. Cohen (eds.) (1982a).

Homans, G. C. 1976. Commentary. In L. Berkowitz & E. Walster (eds.) (1976).

Hook, J. G. & Cook, T. O. 1979. Equity theory and the cognitive ability of children. *Psychological Bulletin, 86*, 429–45.

Kayser, E. 1979. Kognitive Algebra bei Aufteilungsentscheidungen. *Zeitschrift für Sozialpsychologie, 10*, 134–42.

Kayser, E. & Lamm, H. 1980. Input integration and input weighting in decisions on allocations of gains and losses. *European Journal of Social Psychology*, *10*, 1–15.

Kayser, E. & Schwinger, T. 1982. A theoretical analysis of the relationship among individual justice concept, layman's psychology and distribution decision. *Journal of the Theory of Social Behaviour*, *12*, 47–51.

Kayser, E., Schwinger, T. & Kramer, V. 1981. Soziale Beziehung, Ressourcenart und Gerechtigkeit: eine erkundende Fragebogenuntersuchung. Unpublished MS, SFB24, University of Mannheim.

Kayser, E., Köhler, B., Mikula, G. & Schwinger, T. 1980. Intrapersonale Kontrakte und interpersonale Gerechtigkeit: Entwurf einer Theorie. Unpublished MS, SFB24, University of Mannheim.

Lamm, H. & Schwinger, T. 1980. Norms concerning distributive justice: are needs taken into consideration in allocation decisions? *Social Psychology Quarterly*, *43*, 425–9.

1981. Need considerations in allocation decisions: Is it just? Unpublished MS, FB24, University of Mannheim.

Lerner, M. J. (ed.) 1975a. The justice motive in social behaviour. *Journal of Social Issues*, *31*, (3).

1975b. The justice motive in social behaviour: introduction. *Journal of Social Issues*, *31*, 1–20.

1977. The justice motive: some hypotheses as to its origins and forms. *Journal of Personality*, *45*, 1–52.

Lerner, M. J. & Whitehead, L. A. 1980. Procedural justice viewed in the context of justice motive theory. In G. Mikula (ed.) (1980a).

Lerner, M. J., Miller, D. T. & Holmes, J. G. 1976. Deserving and the emergence of forms of justice. In L. Berkowitz & E. Walster (eds.) (1976).

Leventhal, G. S. 1976a. The distribution of rewards and resources in groups and organizations. In L. Berkowitz & E. Walster (eds.) (1976).

1976b. Fairness in social relationships. In J. W. Thibaut, J. T. Spence & R. C. Carson (eds.) *Contemporary topics in social psychology*. Morristown: General Learning Press.

1980. What should be done with equity theory? New approaches to the study of fairness in social relationships. In K. Gergen, M. Greenberg & R. Willis (eds.) *Social exchange theory: advances in theory and research*. New York: Plenum.

Leventhal, G. S., Karuza, J. & Fry, W. R. 1980. Beyond fairness: a theory of allocation preferences. In G. Mikula (ed.) (1980a).

Major, B. & Deaux, K. 1982. Individual differences in justice behaviour. In J. Greenberg & R. L. Cohen (eds.) (1982a).

Mikula, G. 1972a. Die Entwicklung des Gewinnaufteilungsverhaltens bei Kindern und Jugendlichen: eine Untersuchung an 5-, 7-, 9- und 11 Jährigen. *Zeitschrift für Entwicklungspsychologie und Pädagogische Psychologie*, *4*, 151–64.

1972b. Die Berücksichtigung der Leistungskompetenz bei der Gewinnaufteilung in geschlechtsheterogenen Dyaden. *Psychologische Beiträge*, *14*, 283–91.

1974. Nationality, performance and sex as determinants of reward allocation. *Journal of Personality and Social Psychology*, *29*, 435–40.

1977. Considerations of justice in allocation situations. *Berichte aus dem Institut für Psychologie der Universität Graz*, *6*.

(ed.) 1980a. *Justice and social interaction*. Bern: Huber; New York: Springer.

1980b. Introduction: main issues in the psychological research on justice. In G. Mikula (ed.) (1980a).

1980c. On the role of justice in allocation decisions. In G. Mikula (ed.) (1980a).

1981a. Konzepte der distributiven Gerechtigkeit als Grundlagen menschlichen Handelns und Wertens: ein Überblick über den Forschungsgegenstand. In W. Michaelis (ed.) *Bericht über den 32. Kongress der Deutschen Gesellschaft für Psychologie in Zürich, 1980.* Göttingen: Hogrefe.

1981b. Concepts of distributive justice in allocation decisions: a review of research in German-speaking countries. *The German Journal of Psychology, 5,* 222–36.

Mikula, G. & Schwinger, T. 1978. Intermember relations and reward allocations. In H. Brandstätter, J. H. Davis & H. Schuler (eds.) *Dynamics of group decisions.* Beverly Hills: Sage.

1981. Equity-Theorie. In H. Werbik & J. Kaiser (eds.) *Kritische Stichwörter zur Sozialpsychologie.* München: Fink.

Reis, H. T. 1981. Self-presentation and distributive justice. In J. T. Tedeschi (ed.) *Impression management theory and social psychological research.* New York: Academic Press.

in press. The multi-dimensionality of justice. In R. Folger (ed.) (in press).

Reis, H. T. & Gruzen, J. 1976. On mediating equity, equality and self-interest: the role of self-presentation in social exchange. *Journal of Experimental Social Psychology, 12,* 487–503.

Sampson, E. E. 1969. Studies of status congruence. In L. Berkowitz (ed.) *Advances in experimental social psychology,* vol. 4.

1975. On justice as equality. *Journal of Social Issues, 31,* 45–64.

1980. Justice and social character. In G. Mikula (ed.) (1980a).

Schmitt, M. & Montada, L. 1982. Determinanten erlebter Gerechtigkeit. *Zeitschrift für Sozialpsychologie, 13,* 32–44.

Schwarz, E. in preparation. Alter, Geschlecht und Selbstinteresse als Determinanten von Aufteilungsentscheidungen durch Kinder. Unpublished doctoral dissertation, University of Graz.

Schwinger, T. 1980. Just allocations of goods: decisions among three principles. In G. Mikula (ed.) (1980a).

Schwinger, T. & Lamm, H. 1981. Justice norms in allocation decisions: need consideration as a function of resource adequacy for complete need satisfaction, recipients' contributions, and recipients' interpersonal attraction. *Social Behaviour and Personality, 9, 235–41.*

Tajfel, H. 1982. Psychological conceptions of equity: the present and the future. In P. Fraisse (ed.) *Psychologie de demain.* Paris: Presses Universitaires de France.

Thibaut, J. & Walker, L. 1975. *Procedural justice: a psychological analysis.* New York: Erlbaum.

Utne, M. K. & Kidd, R. F. 1980. Equity and attribution. In G. Mikula (ed.) (1980a).

Van Avermaet, E., McClintock, C. & Moskowitz, J. 1978. Alternative approaches to equity: dissonance reduction, pro-social motivation and strategic accommodation. *European Journal of Social Psychology, 8,* 419–37.

Walster, E., Berscheid, E. & Walster, G. W. 1973. New directions in equity research. *Journal of Personality and Social Psychology, 25,* 151–76.

Walster, E., Walster, G. W. & Berscheid, E. 1978. *Equity: theory and research.* Boston: Allyn and Bacon.

Wish, M., Deutsch, M. & Kaplan, S. J. 1976. Perceived dimensions of interpersonal relations. *Journal of Personality and Social Psychology, 33,* 409–20.

# 12. Towards a comprehension of friendship development and breakdown

STEVE DUCK AND DOROTHY MIELL

For many years now the research literature on interpersonal attraction has been limited, turgid and unprovocative. In their search for laboratory manipulable effects, researchers have probed more and more deeply into an increasingly arid set of phenomena – some of which are highly replicable, but theoretically minute and unexciting to an intolerable degree. In contrast to the dry realities of the experimental work, large, expansive and interesting claims have often been made, promising the reader an explanation of human personal relationships which will lead to satisfying marriages, deep and varied friendships, and many social or sexual advantages derived from that explanation. Disaffection with the area itself has been one predictable consequence of the discrepancy between the claims and the realities.

Since the late 1970s however, a general maturation of the perspective in such research makes one more optimistic that research on personal relationships will become more convincing and acceptable to social psychologists as a whole. It is now much clearer that the familiar research on initial attraction is not even the tip of the iceberg of the problem: it is the tip of the tip. Of course, personal relationships of many kinds start with attraction to a stranger, such that an understanding of the dynamics of attraction is a fundamental component of the larger task of understanding personal relationships. Yet so many other processes begin once initial attraction has been expressed; so many enterprises have to be initiated once one feels initially attracted; and so many other social processes become necessary to preserve a relationship; that an explanation of relationships merely *in terms of* initial attraction would be so fundamentally over-reaching itself as to be unacceptable. Until recently, researchers exploring the development of relationships looked with amazement and dismay at the claims of researchers of initial attraction, and yet in many cases they saw the value of incorporating similar explanatory principles into their own general perspective. With the publication, first of Hinde's (1979) seminal work and, second, of the series on *Personal relationships* (Duck 1982, in press; Duck & Gilmour 1981a, b, c), however, it has become clearer that workers in many fields have reached a stage of development where they could now collaborate constructively on the task of understanding personal relationships, since the ultimate goals and their associated problems are now much clearer than they were in the early 1970s. It is now clear also that the fundamental task of such research is to describe and account for the present state and past or future *development* of relationships – including their decay, dissolution, and repair – rather than merely their starting-point or initiation.

Recognition of such a task fundamentally alters the aims and methodology of the work, whilst also restructuring the preliminary and preparatory work that requires resolution. It also makes one look afresh at the role of laboratory work in this field and prompts new ways of exploring initial relationships. The present chapter will outline an approach to some of the newly explored issues and will illustrate some consequent methodological developments. Essentially, the focus of the work is upon an understanding of the influence of personal and social characteristics on attraction and on a grasp of the emergent properties of relationships. (Emergent properties are those properties that are of neither individual alone but which eventuate from their relationship and interaction, such as similarity or intimacy – see Hinde 1979, 1981; so 'emergent' here does *not* refer simply to things that take time to come into the open, as, for instance, Levinger, Senn & Jorgensen 1970 use the term.) The work also relies on a theory of the ways in which relationships develop and a set of advanced methodological techniques for assessing the growth of relationships and intimacy.

## 1. A selective review of interpersonal attraction research

Despite the fact that research in IPA (interpersonal attraction) has grown exponentially since the early 1970s, it has nonetheless been a product of its times and has reflected the emphases, biases, weaknesses and strengths of the surrounding social psychological subculture. At a time when the predominant theme in social psychology was consistency, theories of IPA were based on a cognitive consistency or balance approach; when the emphasis fell on real-life applicability, so IPA research began to apply itself; attribution theory influenced social psychology and IPA alike; the tide of case-study and ethogenic styles washed over IPA research in particular, as it did over social psychology as a whole.

It would be absurd to represent IPA research as having only one style, one history, one present and one future. However, the predominant styles of thinking in the area – the banks and channels of the river of change – have had characteristic features of their own. For example, the earliest work on attractiveness was a search for the properties of individuals that made them attractive to other people, whether physical properties (Perrin 1921) or behavioural features (Thomas & Young 1938) or personality and opinion characteristics (Richardson 1939). It was quite a long time – and after much vigorous research on IQ, socio-economic status and demographic characteristics (Festinger, Schachter & Back 1950) – before researchers took up the idea that the main influence on attractiveness was not simply the pre-existing properties of the individuals in a dyad but the relationship of these properties to one another. Thus grew up venerable and productive traditions of research into personality similarity, complementarity of needs, levels of correspondence in physical appearance, matching of self-esteem with other features of partner, and role congruence of the dyad (see Berscheid & Walster 1978; Duck 1977, for reviews).

As often happens in these cases, research issues in such topics were found to be both local and global. Thus, whilst there was much discussion of the high-level theoretical principles involved in acceptance of a reinforcement interpretation of attitude similarity and attraction relationships (Byrne 1971; Levinger 1972), there were also vigorous debates on the apparent conflicts between the attitude similarity and the need complementarity findings (Tharp 1963). Many valueless, and some useful, points were made in the course of these often vitriolic but career-facilitating debates. One valuable piece of advancement in our thinking was the Kerckhoff & Davis (1962) suggestion that different factors may be relevant at different times in a courtship's growth, and that partners are hence faced with sequences of decisions about their attraction to a partner. This appealing notion is sometimes misrepresented as a general theory of friendship growth, sometimes attacked through failures to replicate and sometimes dismissed (Levinger 1974; Levinger, Senn & Jorgensen 1970). What is usually overlooked is the probability that in first stating the position, Kerckhoff & Davis (1962) simply offered rather thin data for an essentially correct idea, and that many adjustments to the scope of their suggestion can be made and have been supported by subsequent research (Duck 1977; McCarthy 1981). The fact that the original suggestion was correct in outline rather than in detail should not encourage us to dismiss it too freely, and the fact that it was restricted to courtship must not lead us to assume it has been disconfirmed in respect of the entirely different relationship of friendship. The 'filtering' notion, as Kerckhoff & Davis vividly described the idea, makes two important contributions to thinking about IPA: first, it emphasizes the continuity of the processes involved in building a relationship (i.e. that decisions about staying in the relationship and about its future form are continually being made – especially in the earlier stages – and there is no simple once-and-for-all decision about attraction based on single cues or characteristics); second, it stresses that the features of a partner which are relevant to the process of continual re-evaluation are different from time to time (i.e. that partners attend, probably sequentially, to different features of one another at different times, in order to assess their desire to remain related). Hence partners who fail to satisfy one of the points in the criterial sequence are 'filtered out' of the population of potential friends.

Until such notions had been proposed and had placed greater emphasis on the social significance of the interactions between individuals' properties, one might very well have found it hard to argue that research on IPA had a distinctively social dimension. Features of social partners had been explored, but not social features of partners – and certainly not the social significance of the social processing of the features. Individuals had been divided, as if by John Wayne's scriptwriters, into two kinds of people in the world: them as are targets and them as are perceivers. One person was always represented as an active processor making judgments and evaluations of the properties of the other. Judgments were presumed to be absolute and universal: thus spectacles just did indicate intelligence and intelligence simply is attractive – and for all people at that. This nonsensical view persisted for some thirty years and, what is more surprising, voluble amazement greeted its overthrow by Argyle & McHenry (1971). Not until 1976 were formal approaches proposed to represent and account for the reciprocity of such judgments and the mediating effects of their creation and transmission in the context of real social interaction (Berger & Calabrese 1975; Duck 1976).

It is also true that the nature of the environment in which the research ideas on IPA were tested was rather more vacuous than realistic. Many studies were conducted in the laboratory on student subjects; careful manipulation of isolated variables was the general norm. However, critics who attack the area on this point usually overstate it (see, e.g. Eiser 1980), or actually get the research wrong (see, e.g. Gergen 1980; Harré & Secord 1972), and are usually guilty of failing to point out to readers the large number of studies that were addressed specifically to the criticism (see Duck 1980b, for a discussion). Workers who had established reliable laboratory effects made considerable efforts to reproduce similar effects in the real world, often with notable success (e.g. Byrne, Ervin & Lamberth 1970; Golightly, Huffman & Byrne 1972). However, whilst this does temper the criticism, it is no substitute for a systematic study of real-life relationships, and even studies on real-life friends (e.g. Duck 1973b) tended to use limited methodologies or to reproduce laboratory methods in a less unrealistic way (McCarthy 1981). Whilst such studies were a step forward, they were a small one and omitted, as previous research had done, such influences as the social networks in which relationships occurred in real life, the position in the life cycle of the subjects (and hence the exterior influences on their relationships), and subjects' own reports of what they thought they were doing and why.

What, then, can be concluded from this brief and highly selective reporting of the literature on IPA? Several things – but first of all it should not be concluded too hastily that nothing has been learned. Certainly the earliest research took a naive view of the nature and processes of attraction and ignored or omitted most of the important *social* processes that are also overlooked in commonsense views of relationships. But it did build up a useful picture of both the strengths and the weaknesses of such views and it is doubtful whether we would be in as strong a position to advance if the previous developments had not occurred.

One useful step forward has been the recognition that 'similarity' and 'personality' need to be understood in complex ways, some of which have been outlined above. Thus, if one seeks to establish that personality similarity is relevant to personal relationships and friendships, one's first intuition would be to measure personality in populations of friends and non-friends to compare the relative similarity levels. Researchers did exactly this, but in so doing they failed to recognize the very considerable and inviting traps concealed in that apparently simple enterprise. It is hardly surprising, therefore, to find that, even up to 1978, the research literature was thoroughly confused and inadequate. At first glance one finds that there are some 25 studies showing that personality similarity causes attraction, some 25 showing that it does not, an equal number showing that one cannot decide one way or the other and a few books of studies showing that some form of oppositeness is attractive. However, this is not one of those areas that can be improved by the usual claim that more research needs to be done. Since researchers have previously fallen with great flourishes into a variety of traps, there is no reason to suppose that they will stop doing so merely because they flourish more vigorously.

What traps are there here? There are three main traps: first, researchers have failed to recognize that similarity between personalities can be measured in a number of ways and that the choice of measure actually represents not a mere methodological decision but a theoretical statement about the researcher's view of what is the important sort of relationship between the two personalities. Second, researchers have blithely assumed that personality is an entity that can merely be measured in a variety of ways. It did not occur to us until quite late on that different measures of personality at worst may be measuring entirely different social constructs and, at best, are assessing social phenomena with different social significance to people interacting in the real social world. In other words, someone's assessment about a partner's introversion–extraversion, for example, may have entirely different social significance in interaction from his ratings of a partner's conformity, achievement motivation, psychological mindedness, or femininity. Yet both sorts of measure are found on different personality tests and both are measures of 'personality' in some sense. It is not commendable – but not surprising either –that researchers and reviewers persistently compared, and gave equal treatment to, studies using these entirely different personality tests. The third trap in this literature was the failure to recognize that the different relationships tested in the research may be *significantly* different, or may perhaps represent different stages in the development of relationships. Thus studies of groups acquainting for 11 weeks or 40 minutes are not truly comparable, either with each other or with studies of courtship pairs of 18 months' standing. Yet such heedless comparisons occur in all reviews of the literature in pursuance of a test of the relationship between personality similarity and liking.

By taking account of the actual social dynamics of relating and putting recognition of all these three traps together one can derive a perspective on the literature which makes it all less confusing. This argument goes as follows. In the real world, acquainting individuals are, with the passage of time, enabled to make increasingly precise interpretations of one another's personality. Thus one would predict that global characterizations of a partner's personality have their place in acquainting at an earlier point than do more specific and detailed understandings of him or her. Individuals simply are more able to assess a partner's introversion–extraversion at an earlier point than they can 'place' his or her views on detailed attitudes or personality components. The appropriate test for a personality-similarity hypothesis is thus a test which allows for the different social significance of the different grades of measuring personality similarity at different points in the growth of relationships. Tests of this hypothesis are uniformly supportive (Duck 1973a, b, c, 1977; Duck & Craig 1978). 'Personality', 'similarity' and 'friendship' each have many different facets and features, such that any simple test of relationship between them is bound to be productive of confused and ridiculous results. The inclusion of a *social* dimension for interpreting the relationship simultaneously leads to a more sophisticated, and to a more useful, approach.

Although the position outlined above can help to reformulate and clarify a particular portion of the IPA research literature, it should be noted that there remains the problem of accounting for intimacy development. The above view merely points out that there are likely to be stages in its development and that each stage will be associated with a different level and type of facilitative forces. However, the growth of relationships in a social context is far more complicated than this and, as noted at the start of this chapter, it would be misleading and unconstructive to be seen to suggest that this is all that there is to it. Relationship development is a complex of many independent features, both cognitive and social, involving the growth of knowledge about one another, the growth of liking, growth of intimacy (both of knowledge and of behaviour), growth of commitment, and a variety of other things (including alterations in the way in which partners *perceive the relationship*). Nor should relationship development be seen merely in terms of *growth* of its constituents, if this is taken to imply simple linearity of progress to the exclusion of the concept of change in the type of components involved. The growth of liking, for example, includes not only an increase in its intensity but also changes in its form, both in the forms of its feelings and in the forms of its expression as well as in the form of the cues that stimulate or evoke it.

The above formulation is limited by its focus on the cognitive processes involved and by its narrowness of concern. Personality similarity – even personality similarity of different types and analytical levels at different stages of relationships – is a sophisticated but dry abstraction of research psychologists that actually has to be translated into (or epitomized in) some form of vital, vibrant *social activity*. It is still a concept based on the pre-existing properties which partners bring to a relationship, and it somehow has to 'be allowed to appear' that such similarity exists. In the earliest formulations of the model here described, there was still an element of the error contained in previous views of initial attraction: namely, the emphasis fell strongly on the ways in which each individual individually processed information about the partner. The social processes were regarded as occurring essentially in the heads of the two partners involved, and it was only a small advantage over previous views that the proposal recognized that sociality requires two heads rather than just one. In this approach, as in most American work, the emergence of such social processes in and through interactions was largely ignored. How *do* people indicate similarity? How *do* they structure their behaviour in such a way as to bring out similarities, to indicate their recognition and acceptance of similarity with others? How *do* they conduct acquaintances in ways that ultimately generate the kinds of impact for similarity and other cues that the research tells us are important in acquainting?

## 2. The social dimension in relationships

These questions point to the need for specific types of improvement in the styles of research that are required to illuminate the social dimension of behaviour in relationships, and to move research away from the emphasis on mere social cognition. Clearly the weight of useful clarifications of such social processes will fall, at least in part, on contemporaneous recording of the *actual* rather than the hypothesized development of relationships. Thus a movement towards a comprehension of friendship development involves us in establishing a coherent descriptive base from which to account for the complex pattern of the growth (and decline) of relationships. This base must reflect such aspects of the development as the multi-dimensional nature of intimacy growth, the emergent properties of a relationship (in the sense outlined on page 229), and the causes and consequences of development of a relationship (even if this results in its breakdown or decline) as perceived by both participants. Such aspects have been unexplored by, and inaccessible to, the researcher in this area up until quite recently, but contrived laboratory-based studies of brief, initial encounters with strangers remain a poor substitute, since they have been able to afford insights into only a very thin cross-section of the full complexity of relationship development. What are clearly needed are advances in research methods, which would be sensitive to the complex nature of the changes taking place as a friendship develops.

**2.1. Initiating and developing relationships.** There is little research to guide an investigator who has these meritorious aims! Few investigations have been directed at the day-to-day analysis of social interaction, and our understanding of natural interaction patterns remains thoroughly limited and uninformed. Notable exceptions are the studies by Wheeler & Nezlek (1977) and Reis, Nezlek & Wheeler (1980), who explored the daily social participations of their subjects. Using daily record sheets for a two-week period, Wheeler & Nezlek (1977) provided pioneering data concerning the amounts of time that persons spend in social activity, and the forms of participation across which the time is characteristically distributed. Reis, Nezlek & Wheeler (1980) took this further by exploring the role and influence of physical attractiveness on the general pattern of social participation.

Illumination of the characteristic patterns of social participation is an important requisite in research and the Wheeler-Nezlek-Reis studies are pioneering efforts of great significance. In the present context (i.e. in relation to friendship growth), what is needed is a similar style of approach to such questions as how subjects distribute their time with potential friends, what they do with them, how intimacy is conveyed by social participation patterns, and how these patterns change. In short, we need to focus on persons' accounts of their social behaviour in friendship and their decisions about intimacy, rather than simply where they met, how long the interaction lasted and what they *talked* about. Accordingly, several new approaches have recently been employed in the programme of research at Lancaster, England, mainly involving self-report measures and longitudinal studies of naturally-occurring friendships, but also cross-comparison of such novelties with each other and with other methods. Some of these methods will now be outlined, and we shall show that several of the previously unexplored features of the natural course of friendship development can be excitingly illuminated using these techniques.

The emphasis of these new studies is on charting naturally-occurring relationships, with concurrent detailed investigation of several aspects of the relationships as they develop and change. As the relationship progresses, so the nature of the decisions constantly being made by partners about its future form change, and provide one such aspect for investigation (Duck 1977; Kerckhoff & Davis 1962). The longitudinal approach allows us to examine more readily how and when these decisions are made and what their consequences are. Investigations of the course of courtship development (e.g. Huston *et al.* 1981) have relied heavily on retrospective accounts in which couples explain the current status of their relationship (e.g. marriage or breakdown) in terms of the sequence of events during courtship. The obvious drawback of retrospective accounts for yielding reliable information on the actual day-to-day decision making is that the known final outcome of a relationship will inevitably colour the retrospective accounts given by the subjects in specifiable and predictable ways (Duck 1980a; Huston *et al.* 1981). On the basis of only these highly selective histories as data, the psychologist may be led to incorrect evaluations of the importance of factors which, unknown to, or subsequently forgotten by, the partners, were nonetheless actually influential at the time. However, by asking the partners for regular and frequent description of what is happening in their relationship as it develops, we should be able to determine more clearly the complex nature of the decisions made by the partners as to how (if at all) the relationship should proceed.

In several recent studies designed to establish continuous monitoring of the relationship in order to yield exactly this kind of data, subjects kept detailed diary records of their two most significant social interactions of each day for ten weeks. They recorded details of their interaction partners, their similarity with, and liking for their partners(s), and how this interaction had affected their impression of, or liking for, the other(s). Subjects were first-year university students, and were asked to keep the diaries during different terms of their first academic year at Lancaster. Different studies had different aims, of course, but, taken together, the series allowed us to chart not just one isolated relationship, but many friendships from their initiation through the somewhat turbulent early weeks where several relationships break down or strengthen rapidly. Also, by using the extended period of ten weeks, particular relationships could be followed in detail, with the partners' reactions to important decisions being recorded at the time they were made. In other studies, particular relationships were charted intensively, with both partners recording their views of the relationship, their partner, the decisions involved in its growth, the influence of key events, and their beliefs about the future of the relationship. We also took measures of subjects' beliefs about the influence of such data collection upon the relationship. We found, as did Wheeler & Nezlek (1977), that subjects reported that the measurements did not disrupt, and may actually have *improved*, their relationships, because they made the partners more aware of the other person's views and needs in the relationship. The diaries of progress actually seem to facilitate the growth of the friendship rather than to pollute it.

These diaries, besides providing day-to-day records of the current state of several relationships, also generate a good deal of data on the 'normal' interacting pattern and social participation of such a subject pool. This latter information is thus very useful in building up a more complete picture than we currently have of the basic components of everyday interactions, and can supplement the data obtained by Wheeler & Nezlek's (1977) similar diary study of different questions. What is new in the present approach is the focus on friendships and friendship growth rather than, as in Wheeler & Nezlek's study, mere social participation.

It now becomes an interesting question as to how subsequent retrospective reports distort this objectively established sequence. Retrospective interviews were conducted with samples of the same subjects in order that comparisons might be made between the contemporary day-to-day accounts and subsequent retrospective accounts of the same events. However, it is instructive before reviewing this study to comment on two pseudo-methodological issues. First, trivially, it may be argued that the diaries themselves constitute retrospective records of the interactions of any one day, as the subjects were asked to decide at the end of each day which were their two most significant interactions, which they would then record – and this is obviously different from asking their opinions at the time of interaction. This may have altered the objective assessment of the interaction, made as it actually took place. However, what appears to be a methodological problem, on closer inspection casts an interesting theoretical light on the processes operating during an interaction. Might it not be the case that, even at the time of the interaction, the subjects are reviewing the information available to them, and trying to place any incoming information about the partner or the relationship into the broader context of its history and expected future? Furthermore, it is likely that one glaring absurdity of much past research is the overlooking of the reflective activity that takes place betimes in friendship (Duck 1980a). Researchers have overlooked the importance of individuals' time *out* of relationships, when they review, evaluate, interpret and assess the day's events or the trends and developments in their experiences with other people. The present method often is exactly timely for capturing these important features of relationship development (or breakdown).

A second and more instructive pseudo-methodological problem arose during the retrospective interviews conducted with the sample of subjects at the end of a ten-week period of diary keeping. Subjects were interviewed either alone, or with a friend who had also been keeping the diaries, and it appeared that the amount and type of obtained information differed importantly with the nature of the interview. Friends interviewed together seemed to aid each other's memory of specific events; they talked about a wider range and number of particular incidents than did subjects interviewed alone. However, the depth of the discussion of these incidents, and how the events related to their views of each other and of the relationship as a whole, appeared to be dependent on the current state of their relationship. In the case of the interviews conducted with one subject alone, the type of information revealed in different interviews was fairly constant, but the pair interviews yielded information with varying levels of intimacy. Again, this seemingly methodological problem leads us to examine more closely the processes which may be operating in the pair interviews. Throughout the diary study the subjects had been requested to analyse their relationships and chart their development. Here, in these pair interviews, the subjects were required to disclose their own thoughts and feelings on the relationship's development in the presence of their partner. Hence, the partners could disclose to the interviewer only what they felt was appropriate to disclose *to their partner* rather than to a confidante or outsider, and this varied with the level of intimacy characteristic of their relationship. With this approach, the differences noted between the couples in the types of revealed information would be accounted for by the differences in their degree of intimacy, thus reflecting not so much a methodological flaw as a more significant result only to be expected from our knowledge about the appropriateness of self-disclosure (Chaikin & Derlega 1974; Chelune 1977; Miell, Duck & La Gaipa 1979).

A further theoretical assumption underpinning our use of the diary technique has been that people can, and habitually do, analyse their involvement in their relationships, and that it is not, therefore, unnatural to ask them to do so in our research. This raises the whole question of whether and to what extent, partners are, through such analysis, able to structure their behaviour and conduct their relationships in ways that ultimately generate their desired outcomes. For example, the subjects in the retrospective interviews seemed to be carefully controlling the amount and style of their disclosures to match what they believed to be the picture that their partner already had of their relationship. This form of negotiation of intimacy is perceived by both partners as problematic and is not merely a habitual response made without awareness of 'social norms' for disclosure. Partners are therefore continually involved in assessing and evaluating all relevant information; for example, what their partner's view of the relationship might be, and what topics to disclose in such a way as to reveal only the details of the relationship which would accord with their partner's view, and so on.

It can be postulated that these conscious, or strategic, attempts to structure their comments so as not to transgress the agreed level of intimacy, are operating to varying degrees throughout the development of a relationship and do not manifest themselves only in the pair interview where the partners are explicitly analysing their relationship with a researcher present.

Although such a position is a speculative one at present, an investigation of these forms of relational strategies has been undertaken by one of the present authors (Miell). The focus of this research is on one aspect of the self-report data – that of the strategic use of self-disclosure in developing a relationship. It is suggested that people frequently use purposeful strategies in order to structure the course of development of a relationship: decisions are continually being made as to whether, for example, to increase or maintain the intimacy level, or possibly to bring about the dissolution of the relationship; and, once these decisions have been made, deliberate action may be taken to effect the desired changes. An example of the type of action that would result in the maintenance or increase in the level of intimacy in a relationship can be found in the norm of reciprocity (Altman & Taylor 1973; Gouldner 1960), which involves the recipient of a disclosure feeling obliged to reciprocate with a disclosure of information at a comparable level of intimacy and of similar topic content. This phenomenon has been fully researched *as a social norm* operating especially at early stages of a relationship's development (for reviews, see Chelune 1979; Cozby 1973), but it is rarely viewed *as a social tool* to be used strategically by one partner to elicit desired information from the other.

Such an intriguing notion is entirely consistent with our present emphasis on the social dimension of relationships. Miell's argument is that self-disclosure reciprocity has been too often regarded in purely affective-cognitive terms, almost as a pre-programmed cognitive response to the disclosure of information about the cognition of the partner. Such self-disclosure, however, should also be seen as a vibrant force in the development of relationships, with strategic impact and social force upon the *behaviour* of the partners and calculated influence on the progress of the relationship. It is *used* to affect intimacy levels – whether to increase them, contain them at present levels or to decrease them – and intimacy levels are not simply an automatic consequence of some haphazard interaction. Of course, to establish whether or not the reciprocity norm is used strategically and whether other possible strategies are indeed used to manage, or structure, the course of a relationship's development, we must employ a new research focus to a new research question and use different methods from those used up until now, and we must examine the changing role of such strategies throughout the development of the relationship.

In our present investigations, several complementary research methods were employed in combination to build up a comprehensive account of the form and function of these relational strategies. As in the diary study, this involved measures being taken at several stages throughout the subjects' first year at University and many naturally-occurring friendships were charted from their initiation onwards. Data were available from several friendship pairs within the subject pool, and provided contrasting perspectives on the same relationship which thus yielded valuable information about the development of each friendship.

Interviews attempted to establish the nature of the link between experiences of the use of disclosure strategies and the subsequent effect on the relationship. These interviews were conducted at various times over the duration of the study (a) to encourage the subjects to discuss the current state of the relationship in the context of its development to date, and to talk about the strategies employed to effect that development, and (b) to attempt to predict the future course of the relationship's development. This prediction can be compared to the subject's later description of the actual outcome.

Questionnaires of various types were also employed to elicit particular examples of disclosure strategies, to allow for the discussion of the experience of the breakdown of a relationship, and also to establish the pattern of intimacy growth and disclosure rates for a relationship as it developed. As the subject sample included several friendship groups (mainly dyads), the information relating to these actual disclosure patterns in a relationship permitted a detailed examination of the degree of correspondence between the partners' assessments of this pattern.

From the difference between the partners' records of the type and extent of the disclosure made in a relationship, it would appear that a model of intimacy growth which assumes an unproblematic, inevitable advance towards greater intimacy is untenable. Closer emphasis must be placed on the systematic, private negotiation involved in the development towards a more intimate relationship, and on an understanding of the properties of the negotiation process itself. In short, more emphasis is needed on the social dimensions, especially in its communicative forms.

A third method employed in this study required the subjects (in friendship pairs) to talk about a topic which they had not previously discussed in detail. This discussion was videotaped, and then the subjects were asked individually to look through the tape and to point out any instance where they discovered something new about their partner, or where they felt their partner had learnt something new about them. They were then asked to say what effect they felt this new knowledge would have on their impression of each other. This method highlights once again the degree of mismatch between the partners' perceptions of what constitutes novel information, and is also useful in eliciting discussion of how the subjects typically structure an interaction, by providing them with a particular interaction to analyse. This information will be invaluable in assessing the nature of relational disclosure strategies, and is elicited most effectively by the type of research methods outlined here in the context of established or developing friendships. Similar methods can also be used to gain a firmer grasp of the understanding or representation that partners have of their relationship. Just as partners reveal to an interviewer those things that are strategically relevant to the perception of partner, and particularly those that the partners feel are common knowledge between them, so too, partners make strategic use of their beliefs about their partner's knowledge of them. David Miell, a further member of the Lancaster Research Programme on Friendship Development, has encouraged pairs of friends to converse and then to switch places and pretend to be one another, starting sentences with 'I' and generally role-playing the other person. In such a way, intriguing revelations of knowledge and feelings about one another are made. Whole systems of communications are revealed, and replay to the partners of videotapes of these interactions has shown even more of the depth at which strategic interactions and strategic use of this recursive knowledge takes place (D. K. Miell 1982).

Perhaps the concept of strategic interaction can, however, be extended back in time and cast some light also on the initial interactions between strangers. After all, if the previous years of laboratory research into IPA have shown anything, they ought to provide us with a basis for predicting the *sorts* of information that need to be disclosed to a stranger in order to promote attraction. We are not thinking here so much of the level of intimacy in disclosure which is required, but the sorts and type of information evaluated in another dimension than intimacy. For example, Byrne's (1971) model for initial attraction suggests that similarity of attitudes is attractive. We could deduce from this that effort in establishing those areas where one is attitudinally similar to a partner will be effort well invested, if one wishes to provide a base for initial attraction or to create in a partner a greater willingness to contemplate future relationship. Alternatively, other work in IPA suggests that complementarity, oppositeness, stimulus and dissimilarity may be attractive (e.g. McCarthy & Duck 1976; Winch 1958), and so a different strategy would be predicted to be most attractive on such a model. Filtering models of friendship growth, on the other hand, suggest that the nature of the information and the timing of its release are as important as its gross similarity to, or differences from, information supplied by the partner – that is, information about physical features must be released before information about roles and attitudes to interaction, and information about psychological evaluation of other people is best reserved until later (Duck 1973b, 1977).

In brief, our idea is that individuals need to complete certain social actions in order to become attracted to one another in real life. An experimenter may well be able to give two strangers relevant pieces of paper showing that they are, in fact, similar or complementary in personality or in attitudes but we think that does not reflect what people have to do in acquaintance to make best use of those similarities or complementarities. In real life, we suggest, people want to find these things out for themselves, and we further suggest that this process of discovery is an *essential* part of the process of acquaintance. By analogy, it is theoretically possible to train soldiers merely by describing the rifle and its workings, explaining how to aim, and so on; however, an essential part of its effective employment is practice in handling it and finding out for oneself the practical effects of some of the theoretical preparations.

Accordingly, we reasoned that actual conduct of acquaintance, guided by an effective strategy, would enhance subjects' liking for their partner. So we tried these ideas experimentally by presenting pre-selected, unacquainted pairs of subjects with one of the above strategies derivable from the research literature and instructing them to get acquainted using that strategy. Since we were attempting to assess the relevance of such strategies to first encounters, our subjects were given only 30 minutes to get acquainted. This might be seen as a drawback of the study, even given our intention to apply, in circumstances comparable to those from which they were derived, such strategies concerning initial acquaintance. A follow-up study accordingly extended this period, but results are not reported here since they substantially support those to be described below. Two criteria for the success of a strategy emerge: on one criterion a strategy is successful to the extent that it approximates normal processes (as assessed by a simple 'Get acquainted' condition, which we termed 'No strategy'). On a separate criterion, that strategy is most successful which produces in the partners the highest ratings of liking for one another and the greatest desires to continue a relationship. In order to protect the study from the charge of artificiality – even though in using the laboratory we are simply reproducing the situation from which the strategies stem – we compared two areas for testing the acquainting: the laboratory, under supervision; a coffee bar.

In general it can be said that if you want to get to know someone well and quickly, then choose a female. Females were likely to give higher ratings to their partner on many different scales that concern liking, for example, how much do you like partner? How much do you think partner likes you? How interested are you in continuing a relationship with your partner? How interested do you think your partner is in continuing a relationship with you? The context (laboratory vs. coffee bar) had a relatively predictable simple effect on feeling of comfortability in the task (lab significantly less comfortable) but also had some less predictable effects on perceived similarity, honesty and openness (coffee bar significantly increased perceived similarity, own authenticity and honesty; but significantly decreased partner's perceived authenticity. Evidently one's own feelings of comfort increase one's own feelings of honesty, but the sense that both partners are observed, because one views the laboratory as more of a stage, increases one's trust of partner).

The results contain many more effects which are presented in detail elsewhere (Miell & Duck 1982). At present we are inclined to interpret many of the outcomes by reference to findings that females feel generally more observed than males. Thus, in conditions where observability is stressed, males 'do worse' and show less enjoyment or less interest in continuing the interaction. Male–male pairs on the whole do worst of all, especially in the laboratory, although, paradoxically, that is precisely where they express the strongest belief that the task was useful.

The study makes a number of intriguing suggestions at both a detailed and a more global theoretical level. It is clear that the individual strategies do not uniquely and uniformly improve acquainting in all circumstances. Of course, it could be objected that the strategies could not be *expected* to work, given their derivation from relevant but perhaps 'artificial' empirical or laboratory studies; or that we merely failed to find the best universal strategy. This latter, we concede, is a possibility that remains to be explored, although the former is probably indefensible, if it is not actually absurd. The theoretical principle embodied in each strategy is precisely that culled from many laboratory experiments on acquaintance. We merely added a social dimension by making the subjects *use* the principles. To argue that we derived the strategies undeservedly is implicitly to argue that the strategies do not apply even to the laboratory environment from which they were derived, whilst the usual complaint is that the laboratory does not reflect real life. If they are derived from the laboratory, they should *at least* work there when 'reversed' as in the present case and used in the laboratory.

This new style of method to the study of initial encounters thus could be developed to offer the promise of identifying those situations and those circumstances which are best suited to certain styles of strategy in acquaintance with certain types of partner (since no important simple effects were observed). Whilst this promises ultimate practical application for some of the work, it also prompts the intriguing theoretical thought that much of the reason why much of the previous work in IPA has been wasted is that workers have been too stoutly absolutist. Perhaps there are no valuable steps which can be taken from the basic position that, say, similarity of attitudes, or reinforcement, or complementarity is invariably attractive. Indeed, another of our team (Martin Lea) has found that there are those subjects for whom reinforcement works best and those for whom complementarity is most effective (Lea & Duck 1982).

The key point that has been missed is a simple extension of the filtering notion outlined earlier. Instead of applying to acquainting, the notion here applies to the investigation, description and explanation of acquainting! This simple extension says: the factors which promote growth of acquaintance at given points are different *and the theories which are relevant to explaining this growth are also relevant at different points and, perhaps, to different people.* Thus, some theoretical principles will be relevant at some stages in relationship growth and others at others, depending on a variety of variable factors describing the relationship. As in the case of establishing that personality similarity is relevant to acquaintance once one can establish the important differences between the stages of relationship, types of personality test, and measures of similarity that have erstwhile been confounded (see Duck 1977: chapter 6) so too it may be possible to show the relative importance of different theoretical principles at different points of acquainting.

Over and above these possibilities, which stem from the importing of a *social* dimension to add to the emphasis on social cognition and to develop its possible social reality, the set of studies and the style of work described above point out the distinct advantages of studying real relationships with some of the techniques that we have developed. The utility of studying initial encounters, on the other hand, should not be overlooked either, merely because, in the past, workers have hitherto lacked or failed to employ the most useful approaches, or have not seen the best ways of clarifying the real-life importance of this earlier work. The important omission in such work has been the omission of the relationship as an entity in the minds of the partners and a failure to try and understand what happens when people are really trying to develop one.

**2.2. Relationship decline and dissolution.** Further work in the Lancaster programme has explored breakdown of relationships using both retrospective and contemporaneous accounts. It is astonishing that theoretical accounts of friendship breakdown are a recent development and that generalization from theories of courtship or marital breakdown is the best that social psychology had to offer until recently (Duck 1981, 1982).

We recognize that the problems of retrospective accounts are particularly acute in the context of relationship breakdown, and that people are especially likely to be subject to distortion of memory over their failed relationships. In Western cultures, at least, notions of success and failure are strongly attached to the concept of friendship, and people are inclined to measure their success as a person in terms of their 'success' in relationships. We recognize this drawback in the study to be reported briefly here, but we console ourselves with the thought that if anyone else has better data (s)he has so far failed to produce it. More constructively, however, we are presently conducting, as part of the aforementioned longitudinal studies, some studies of breaking relationships (indeed, a few have already broken during the course of the studies).

In an attempt to explore the causes which individuals perceive as explanations for the dissolution of different sorts of friendship, Duck & Tweedale (1980) conducted a study of accounts of dissolved relationships. A distinction between fast and slow dissolving relationships was also felt intuitively to be one with possible psychological importance to individuals, and this too was explored. A simple point running through the rationale of the study was that relationships are complex social entities that differ in type, one from another, and hence have complex forms of deterioration that are not explicable merely in terms of intimacy decline (Duck 1981). Results were complex, as expected, but showed significant sex differences in respect of accounts for the decline of both same-sex friendships and cross-sex friendship. Females, but not males, were also significantly different in their accounts of same-sex friendship breakdown compared to cross-sex friendships. It is hence clearly *not* the case that females, at any rate, have an approach to relationship decline that is general, consistent and irrespective of the sex of the partner with whom the relationship is formed. This echoes findings from the 'strategy study' of early acquainting described above. One hidden confound that this present study illuminates therefore is that, for females, same-sex friendships are with other females, whilst for males they are with other males, and, conversely, cross-sex pairs taken from the point of view of females are differently composed from those looked at from the point of view of males! Hence lumping together of 'same-sex friendships' and, perhaps (but not absolutely) also of 'cross-sex friendships' is, at best, risky and, at worst, likely to be downright misleading – yet we found studies that make this easy mistake (e.g. Wheeler & Nezlek's 1977 study of participation). Duck & Tweedale conclude that there are many dimensions on which the study of relationship breakdown needs to be differentiated, and Duck (1981) lists some dozen.

It is clear that the topics of relationship disorder, breakdown and dissolution have been unduly neglected, and we trace this to the fact that they are difficult topics to study in the compass of a laboratory. We draw comfort from the fact that the newly developed methods for studying development of relationships are equally applicable to deteriorating ones, and that, fortuitously, in the course of studying developing relationships *in vivo* one invariably records some that are ultimately doomed to dissolve. Unfortunately, at present, too few researchers are collecting data on the naturalistic growth of relationships and consequently too few fortuitous records of dissolving relationships have been completed.

There are, nevertheless, multitudes of research possibilities here and the only text on dissolving personal relationships (Duck 1982) records the speculations and suggestions of workers from several different theoretical backgrounds who have applied themselves to this issue. For instance, Miller & Parks (1982) point to the many research hypotheses about dissolution of relationships that lie scattered through the literature on nonverbal communication and on sociolinguistics. Certain very clear predictions about the signalling of reduced intimacy, withdrawal from relationship and diminution of immediacy lie fallow in these separate research literatures. Equally, the attribution theorists have so far had little to say about the disruption of personal relationships until Harvey *et al.* (1982) provided us with some stimulating proposals. Symbolic interactionists (McCall 1982) and sociologists (Johnson 1982; La Gaipa 1982) have thoughts about the conduct of dissolving relationships which remain to be tested. Now that methods for testing some of these proposals can feasibly be developed from the kinds of methods that we have employed by exploring the social dimension to the study of friendship, there are grounds for believing that the terrors and distress of relationship problems can be better understood. Records of daily conduct of relationships and their ups and downs are practically useful as well as methodologically challenging and theoretically stimulating.

## 3. Conclusions

A general conclusion from all of the above work is that a topography of relationships is both necessary and possible. Types of relationships, relationship growth and relationship decline are as much in need of clarification as are the subjective experiences of these phenomena. New methods can be developed along the above lines and we can begin to explore some important social problems. Only by the development of our methodological armoury can we begin to build up the topography of relationship growth which is so badly needed (Hinde 1979, 1981). We believe that the above has given some idea of the developments that we see to be needful and productive. Such development is, frankly, essential if the area of personal relationship research is to become more fruitful, more *social* and more challenging to the fertile and active minds of those young psychologists that any field needs to attract in order to expand. Only from such baselines will we be able to extend our work towards the goals of assisting those with clinically pathological relationships, and understanding those persons, such as adolescents, who experience turmoil and distress in their personal relationships.

### References

Altman, I. & Taylor, D. A. 1973. *Social penetration: the development of interpersonal relationships*. New York: Holt, Rinehart and Winston.

Argyle, M. & McHenry, R. 1971. Do spectacles really affect judgements of intelligence? *British Journal of Social and Clinical Psychology*, *10*, 27–9.

Berger, C. R. & Calabrese, R. J. 1975. Some explorations in initial interaction and beyond: towards a developmental theory of interpersonal communication. *Human Communication Research*, *1*, 99–112.

Berscheid, E. & Walster, E. 1978. *Interpersonal attraction*, 2nd edn. Reading, Mass.: Addison-Wesley.

Byrne, D. 1971. *The attraction paradigm*. New York: Academic Press.

Byrne, D., Ervin, C. R. & Lamberth, J. 1970. Continuity between the experimental study of attraction and real-life computer dating. *Journal of Personality and Social Psychology*, *16*, 157–65.

Chaikin, A. L. & Derlega, V. J. 1974. Variables affecting the appropriateness of self-disclosure. *Journal of Consulting and Clinical Psychology*, *42*, 588–93.

Chelune, G. J. 1977. Disclosure flexibility and social-situational perceptions. *Journal of Consulting and Clinical Psychology*, *45*, 1139–43.

248    Steve Duck & Dorothy Miell

Chelune, G. J. *et al.* (eds.) 1979. *Self-disclosure.* San Francisco: Jossey-Bass.
Cozby, P. C. 1973. Self-disclosure: a literature review. *Psychological Bulletin, 79,* 73–91.
Duck, S. W. 1973a. *Personal relationships and personal constructs: a study of friendship formation.* London: John Wiley & Sons.
    1973b. Personality similarity and friendship choices: similarity of what, when? *Journal of Personality, 41,* 543–58.
    1973c. Similarity and perceived similarity of personal constructs as influences on friendship choice. *British Journal of Social and Clinical Psychology, 12,* 1–6.
    1976. Interpersonal communication in developing acquaintance. In G. R. Miller (ed.) *Explorations in interpersonal communication.* Beverly Hills: Sage.
    1977. *The study of acquaintance,* Farnborough: Gower Press.
    1980a. Personal relationships research in the 1980s: towards an understanding of complex human sociality. *Western Journal of Speech Communication, 44,* 114–19.
    1980b. Taking the past to heart: one of the futures of social psychology?. In R. Gilmour & S. W. Duck (eds.) *The development of social psychology.* London: Academic Press.
    1981. Towards a research map for the study of relationship breakdown. In S. W. Duck & R. Gilmour (eds.) 1981c. *Personal relationships 3: Personal relationships in disorder.* London: Academic Press.
    (ed.) 1982. *Personal relationships 4: Dissolving personal relationships.* London: Academic Press.
    in press. *Personal relationships 5: Repairing personal relationships.* London: Academic Press.
Duck, S. W. & Craig, G. 1978. Personality similarity and the development of friendship: a longitudinal study. *British Journal of Social and Clinical Psychology, 17,* 237–42.
Duck, S. W. & Gilmour, R. (eds.) 1981a. *Personal relationships 1: Studying personal relationships.* London: Academic Press.
    (eds.) 1981b. *Personal relationships 2: Developing personal relationships.* London: Academic Press.
    (eds.) 1981c. *Personal relationships 3: Personal relationships in disorder.* London: Academic Press.
Duck, S. W. & Tweedale, S. 1980. A study of two sorts of breakdown of friendship. Unpublished MS.
Eiser, J. R. 1980. Developments in application: prolegomena to a more applied social psychology. In R. Gilmour & S. W. Duck (eds.) *The development of social psychology.*
Festinger, L., Schachter, S. & Back, K. 1950. *Social pressures in informal groups: a study of human factors in housing.* New York: Harper and Row.
Gergen, K. 1980. Developments in theory: toward intellectual audacity in social psychology. In R. Gilmour & S. W. Duck (eds.) *The development of social psychology.*
Golightly, C., Huffman, D. M. & Byrne, D. 1972. Liking and loaning. *Journal of Applied Psychology, 56,* 521–23.
Gouldner, A. 1960. The norm of reciprocity. *American Sociological Review, 25,* 161–78.
Harré, R. & Secord, P. 1972. *The explanation of social behaviour.* Oxford: Blackwell.
Harvey, J., Weber, A., Yarkin, K. L. & Stewart, B. E. 1982. Attribution and relationship breakdown. In S. W. Duck (ed.) 1982.
Hinde, R. A. 1979. *Towards understanding relationships.* London: Academic Press.
    1981. The bases of a science of interpersonal relationships. In S. W. Duck & R. Gilmour (eds.) (1981a).

Huston, T., Surra, C. A., Fitzgerald, N. M. & Cate, R. 1981. From courtship to marriage: mate selection as an interpersonal process. In S. W. Duck & R. Gilmour (eds.) (1981b).

Johnson, M. 1982. Social and cognitive features of dissolving commitment to relationships. In S. W. Duck (ed.) (1982).

Kerckhoff, A. C. & Davis, K. E. 1962. Value consensus and need complementarity in mate selection. *American Sociological Review*, 27, 295–303.

La Gaipa, J. J. 1982. Rituals of disengagement. In S. W. Duck (ed.) (1982).

Lea, M. & Duck, S. W. 1982. A model for the role of similarity of values in friendship development. *British Journal of Social Psychology*, 21, 301–10.

Levinger, G. 1972. Little sand box and big quarry. *Representative Research in Psychology*, 3, 3–19.

    1974. A three level approach to attraction. In T. Huston (ed.) *Foundations of interpersonal attraction*. New York: Academic Press.

Levinger, G., Senn, D. J. & Jorgensen, B. W. 1970. Progress toward permanence in courtship: a test of the Kerckhoff-Davis hypothesis. *Sociometry*, 33, 427–43.

McCall, G. 1982. Becoming unrelated: the management of bond dissolution. In S. W. Duck (ed.) (1982).

McCarthy, B. 1981. Studying personal relationships. In S. W. Duck & R. Gilmour (eds.) (1981a).

McCarthy, B. & Duck, S. W. 1976. Friendship duration and responses to attitudinal agreement–disagreement. *British Journal of Social and Clinical Psychology*, 15, 377–86.

Miell, D. E. & Duck, S. W. 1982. Charting the development of personal relationships. Paper presented to the International Conference on Personal Relationships, Madison, Wisc.

Miell, D. E., Duck, S. W. & La Gaipa, J. J. 1979. Interactive effects of sex and timing in self-disclosure. *British Journal of Social and Clinical Psychology*, 18, 355–62.

Miell, D. K. 1982. The intimation game. Unpublished Ph.D. thesis, University of Lancaster.

Miller, G. R. & Parks, M. 1982. Communication in dissolving relationships. In S. W. Duck (ed.) (1982).

Perrin, F. A. C. 1921. Physical attractiveness and repulsiveness. *Journal of Experimental Psychology*, 4, 203–17.

Reis, H. T., Nezlek, J. & Wheeler, L. 1980. Physical attractiveness and social interaction. *Journal of Personality and Social Psychology*, 38, 604–17.

Richardson, H. M. 1939. Studies of mental resemblance between husbands, wives and friends. *Psychological Bulletin*, 36, 104, 20.

Tharp, R. 1963. Psychological patterning in marriage. *Psychological Bulletin*, 60, 97–117.

Thomas, W. F. & Young, P. T. 1938. Liking and disliking persons. *Journal of Social Psychology*, 9, 168–88.

Wheeler, L. & Nezlek, J. 1977. Sex differences in social participation. *Journal of Personality and Social Psychology*, 35, 742–54.

Winch, R. F. 1958. *Mate selection: a study of complementary needs*. New York: Harper and Row.

# 13. When love dies: an integration of attraction and bereavement research

WOLFGANG STROEBE AND MARGARET S. STROEBE

It may seem obvious to an outside observer that the study of interpersonal attraction, marriage, and bereavement should form an inter-dependent set of research problems hardly in need of integration. However, this is not the case. Until very recently, these areas had been investigated independently and by researchers belonging to different disciplines, employing different theoretical approaches, who rarely took any notice of each other's work. Interpersonal attraction has been a major area of social psychology, examining the impact of variations of the perceived characteristics of one person (the 'object' of attraction) on the perceiver's attitudes towards that person. Social context variables, such as the demands on the relationship by the 'external world', their role and reward structures, were disregarded. These were, however, exactly the variables which sociologists considered important for the maintenance of marital relationships. They studied the family as a social organization or social system whose survival depends on members' effectiveness in coping with the demands imposed by the outside world, while at the same time maintaining good interpersonal relations within the family. The work of family sociologists on the division of labour within the marital relationship and on other functions marital partners perform for each other seems to be highly relevant to an assessment of the stress of partner loss. Nevertheless, their findings have been completely disregarded by psychiatrists, who have been responsible for most of the studies on the consequences of bereavement. They regard the loss experience as a traumatic emotional event which has been linked to steep increases in the occurrence of depression, physical ill health and mortality among the recently widowed and separated. Explanations of the loss effect have focused on individual emotions and ignored the fact that marriage not only constitutes an emotional bond but is also a social organization.

Only recently have both attraction and bereavement research begun to move towards a more sociological approach. Attraction researchers have become interested in the structure and development of intimate relationships (for recent summaries, see Burgess & Huston 1979; Duck & Gilmour 1981; Huston & Levinger 1978; and Chapter 12 of this book), and sociologists (e.g. Berardo 1968, 1970; Gove 1972b, 1973; Lopata 1973) and social psychologists (e.g. W. Stroebe *et al.* 1980, 1982) have entered the field of bereavement research, applying sociological and social psychological concepts to explain the consequences of bereavement on psychological and physical well-being.

In the tradition of this more recent work, this chapter attempts to integrate the body of theorizing and research on interpersonal attraction, marriage, and bereavement, interpreting attraction and grief as social as well as emotional events. Starting with the general question of why individuals join groups, section 1 analyses the motives underlying group formation from different theoretical perspectives. Applying these perspectives, section 2 examines, in the context of mate selection, some of the factors which influence individual preferences for specific others, i.e. partner choice. In section 3, on the structure of the marital relationship, the functions that marital partners perform for each other are discussed. Since losing a partner implies the deprivation of all the services that the partner performed, the fact that women carry a greater share of the marital load, with the present division of roles within marriage, suggests that, contrary to assumptions made by many researchers in the area of bereavement, men should be worse off than women after losing their partner. Section 4 both reviews the evidence on health-related effects which substantiates our hypothesis, and develops this interpretation into a social psychological theory of the loss effect.

## 1. The motivational basis of group formation: three theoretical perspectives

The question as to why people form groups is answered differently depending on the theoretical perspective one applies to this problem. As bereavement research uses a different theoretical framework from that adopted by attraction or marriage theorists, it seems essential to discuss the implications of these different theoretical perspectives before presenting their application to the various content areas.

**1.1. The ethological approach.** The ethological approach conceives of human attachment behaviour as based on an instinct that serves the evolutionary function of keeping the individual attached to a group. As animals and men have always had a better chance of survival as part of their herd or group rather than in isolation, it seems not unreasonable to assume that some instinctual tendency towards the formation of social attachments developed in the course of evolution. Although an instinctual basis of sociability was already assumed by William James (1890), McDougall (1908) was probably the first psychologist to discuss explicitly the evolutionary advantage of such an instinct. In his introduction to social psychology, McDougall (1908) emphasizes the 'gregariousness instinct' as an essential basis for the development of human social organization.

McDougall's (1908) approach had little influence on the development of psychological theory. Behaviourism preferred to account for attachment as a secondary drive resulting from the reduction of primary drives such as hunger or thirst (e.g. Dollard & Miller 1950; Sears, Rau & Alpert 1965). More recently, related ideas have been suggested by John Bowlby (1969, 1973, 1980), who formulated an ethological theory of the development of attachment. Although Bowlby is mainly concerned with attachment in children, he maintains that his theory also applies to the development of emotional bonds in later life. While in Bowlby's theory the *connection* between adult attachment and childhood attachment formation has at least been explicitly stated, the *nature* of adult attachments remains unclear. How do early attachments become supplemented or replaced by new bonds during the course of development? What processes underlie the formation and maintenance of adult attachments? While it is clear, for example, that attachment in the infant is likely to focus on the figure with whom he has most experience of social interaction (Bowlby 1979), it is less obvious how these early experiences relate to close emotional ties in adulthood. Thus, it is hardly surprising that this theory has had no impact on attraction research.

However, although it does not permit the prediction of specific attachments in adult life, Bowlby's theory gives some insight into the consequences of the disruption of attachments as they occur on loss of a partner. In contrast to psychoanalytic theory, which regards grief as serving the function of detaching the individual from the loved one, Bowlby believes that, in the case of permanent separation, the mechanisms for restoring proximity (e.g. crying, searching) are redundant and dysfunctional. Grief has the biological function of promoting reunion and thus, in the case of an irrevocable separation such as death, it is a redundant response. Another interesting deduction from Bowlby's theory is that the disruption of a long-standing attachment should lead to negative consequences, regardless of whether strong emotional bonds existed.

**1.2. Social comparison theory.** Social comparison theory sees group formation motivated by the human need to validate cognitions about reality. To the extent that such validation can only be accomplished by means of comparison with other persons, the need for validation is a force acting on persons to belong to groups, to associate with others. Basic to the theory of social comparison processes is the assumption that people like to have confidence in their ability to deal effectively with their environment. Since such success in dealing with one's environment depends to a large degree on the correctness of one's cognitions about one's own abilities and about the structure of reality, Festinger (1954) postulated the existence in the human organism of a 'drive' to evaluate his beliefs and his abilities.

The correctness of beliefs about the physical nature of our environment can typically be tested against 'physical reality'. Value judgments or evaluations of one's relative ability, or beliefs about the social nature of our environment, on the other hand, have no 'objective' basis for their validity. The only way one can have confidence in the correctness of the latter type of beliefs is if there are other people around who share one's opinion. Thus, to the extent that 'objective, non-social means are not available' (Festinger 1954), people will have to associate with others, join groups to evaluate their opinions and abilities.

In his well-known extension of social comparison theory, Schachter (1959) argued that social comparison processes are involved not only in the assessment of one's beliefs and abilities but also in the evaluation of one's emotional response to novel or ambiguous emotion-arousing situations. However, since all experiments that ostensibly demonstrated a need for social evaluation of emotions involved the threat of painful stimulation, their results could also be explained in terms of the ethological theory of group formation. Since the survival chances of an individual under physical threat are greater in his group than in isolation, it would follow from an ethological approach that physical danger elicits an 'instinctual' tendency to join one's group.

**1.3. Economic and exchange theories.** The basic assumption of the economic theory of group formation (e.g. Olson 1965) is that groups will only be formed when goals cannot be reached through individual action:

There is obviously no purpose in having an organization when individual, unorganized action can serve the interests of the individual as well or better than the organization; there would, for example, be no point in forming an organization simply to play solitaire. (Olson 1965: 7)

Although we are not aware of any solitaire clubs, the existence of such would be quite likely from a psychological perspective. While the economic analysis of collective action is useful in stressing the importance of group tasks, it completely fails to consider the more 'social' aspects of group formation.

This oversight has been corrected by the development of exchange theory (e.g. Thibaut & Kelley 1959) which, though considering small groups analogous to economic markets, acknowledges the fact that many of the rewards exchanged in groups are of a psychological nature, e.g. anxiety reduction, social validation. Whether individuals enter into a relationship and remain in it will depend on the adequacy of the outcomes they receive from that relationship. However, the adequacy of outcomes cannot be determined in any absolute sense, but is evaluated against levels of comparison the individual brings into the relationship. A relationship is likely to dissolve when outcomes fall below that offered by potential alternatives available to the individual.

**1.4. Implications.** According to economic theory, interpersonal relations are not an object in themselves: people associate merely because they can mediate goals for each other. This assumption runs counter to the firmly held conviction of many psychologists that, as Schutz (1960) once put it, people need people, even if they can do things by themselves. William James (1890) already emphasized the basic need for social contact when he stated:

As a gregarious animal, man is excited both by the absence and by the presence of his kind. To be alone is one of the greatest evils for him. Solitary confinement is by many regarded as a mode of torture too cruel and unnatural for civilized countries to adopt. (James 1950: 430)

That loneliness is a painful experience has been demonstrated in more recent research (e.g. Peplau, Russell & Heim 1979; Shaver & Rubenstein 1980) which links it to feelings of self-hate and to clinical depression, alcoholism and suicidal tendencies. Although loneliness, being a subjective state, is not identical with social isolation, the extreme negative consequences of loneliness substantiate the assumption that there is some basic need for social contact.

The existence of such a need is naturally a central assumption of the ethological approach, although Bowlby (1969) dislikes the concept of need and uses other constructs. According to social comparison theory, social contact is not quite an end in itself, but it is essential to satisfy a need to validate one's construction of reality, a need which can *only* be satisfied in interpersonal relations. Since a lack of confidence in the validity of one's construction of reality can be linked to anxiety and depression (Kelly 1955), social comparison theory could also account for some of the negative consequences of social isolation. The assumption of a need for social contact is, finally, no problem for exchange theory. If isolation is costly and social contact rewarding, exchange theorists would argue that people will be prepared to exchange other things to realize this particular reward.

## 2. Determinants of mate selection

The previous section attempted to offer an answer to the basic question, why do people form groups, i.e. our apparent preference for social interaction rather than social isolation. In this section we will apply these theoretical perspectives to the issue of interpersonal attraction, i.e. to account for our preferences for *specific* others. However, since somewhat different persons tend to be preferred for different purposes, we will not attempt to deal with attraction in general but rather analyse it in the context of mate selection.

Most treatments of the determinants of mate selection have been formulated in terms of a social exchange framework (e.g. Berscheid & Walster 1969; Murstein 1970; Winch 1958). The basic assumption shared by these researchers has been stated by Edwards (1969): 'Within any collectivity of potential mates, a marriageable person will seek out that individual who is perceived as maximizing his rewards' (p. 525). Making this basic assumption, attraction theorists have been confronted with three related research problems: (1) the identification of characteristics which might be perceived as rewarding in a potential partner; (2) the theoretical explanation of the nature of these rewards; and (3) the analysis of the decision processes that lead up to the choice of a marital partner. We will start this section with an analysis of the last problem, since it will allow us to develop a theoretical framework for the discussion of the determinants of mate selection.

Some years ago, Kerckhoff & Davis (1962) developed an influential model, describing the process of mate selection as a sequence of choice points, with different 'filtering factors' operating at each of the stages of the selection period. Social homogamy was assumed to be the first filter. Value consensus and need complementarity were hypothesized to have second and third positions. It is assumed that in passing through these filters increasing numbers of individuals are eliminated until finally only the ideal 'match' remains.

Although this model is over-simplified, the assumption of a sequential process seems very reasonable in the light of recent developments in decision theory. The assumption of filtering factors is structurally similar to the 'eliminations-by-aspects' model of Tversky (1972), which suggests that decision making is essentially a 'sequential narrowing-down process, similar to the logic employed in the popular game "Twenty Questions"' (Janis & Mann 1977). Starting with the most important requirement, all potential alternatives that do not contain the selected aspect are eliminated. The process continues for each requirement in turn, until a single object remains.

Since information about alternatives varies not only in importance but also in accessibility, the decision maker will have to balance his need for information against his search costs. This problem is aggravated in mate selection by the fact that certain information is not available unless a number of commitments have been made. For example, while the socio-economic background or the physical attractiveness of a person can be ascertained without interaction, information about psychological characteristics which determine compatibility can only be collected in the course of extended interaction. As increasingly more intimate information is gained about the other, partners also become more and more committed towards a permanent relationship.

The filter model of Kerckhoff & Davis (1962) has been elaborated by Duck (1973), Levinger & Snoek (1972), Lewis (1972) and Murstein (1970). However, rather than present these various models, we will use the notion of filtering factors as a heuristic framework and discuss determinants of attraction in terms of the filtering processes of availability, desirability and compatibility.

**2.1. Availability.** The minimum requirement for a relationship to develop between individuals is their availability for interaction. This limits the field of potential partners to those persons whom one is likely to meet in situations which are conducive to the development of informal relationships. The one determinant of availability investigated most extensively in studies of mate selection has been propinquity. It has typically been found that in any given sample studied, the frequency of marriages decreased with increasing distance between the residences of potential partners (e.g. Bossard 1932; Katz & Hill 1958). Obvious explanations of this relationship assume that the probability that two people meet decreases with increasing distance or that conducting affairs becomes more costly in time and effort (Catton & Smircich 1964). However, like social psychologists, sociologists mistrust the obvious. Thus, Katz & Hill (1958) with their 'norm-segregation' theory suggest an explanation which does not imply a direct causal link between propinquity and marriage frequency but attributes the correlation to a third factor, the norms defining the sociological characteristics of potential partners. If we assume the existence of norms restricting the field of eligible spouse-candidates for any individual to others of similar sociological characteristics (e.g. socio-economic status, race, religion) and if we further assume that individuals who are similar with regard to these characteristics are likely to share the same neighbourhood, this could account for the positive relationship between propinquity and marriage frequency.

**2.2. Desirability.** There are social and physical characteristics of spouse-candidates that are highly valued within a given society. For example, most people would prefer a partner who is physically attractive to one who is unattractive. Similarly, high socio-economic status, high educational attainment and good health are highly desirable characteristics. If we assume that each marriageable individual is out to get the most desirable spouse possible, we would expect marital partners to be highly similar to each other with regard to these variables. This similarity would not be due to a *preference* for similar others but to the competitiveness of the marriage market.

Let us take the case of physical attractiveness as an example. A moderately good looking woman might be asked out by a number of men, some physically more attractive and some less. She is likely to prefer offers from the better looking males but she might find that these relationships typically end with the men leaving her for some other more attractive woman. In such moments of distress, she is likely to accept offers of friendship from men who make up in adoration what they lack in good looks. Again, she might find that these affairs never last, this time because she is tempted away by some better looking male. This process of trial and error, which used to be called 'dating', goes on until finally the 'right' man comes along with whom she is happy ever after.

On the basis of this analysis one would expect that heterosexual relationships should be the more stable, the more similar partners are in their physical attractiveness. Thus, married couples should be more similar than dating couples and couples going steady should be more similar than short-term dates. Consistent with this hypothesis, Cavior & Boblett (1972), who compared the physical attractiveness of dating and marital couples, found a markedly higher correlation between marital couples' attractiveness than between that of dating couples.

However, physical attractiveness is merely one of many characteristics desired in a mate. Apart from good looks, potential partners should have personality, a good education and good health. Preferably, one would want a partner who has all these characteristics, but those are hard to come by, and the final choice is likely to involve some compromise. If one values wealth in a partner, one might not be able to strike the best bargain with regard to physical attractiveness or educational attainments. Economists call this 'substitution' and assume that individuals are always willing to sacrifice some of any good for some more of any other good. The maximum reduction of any good that a person is willing to incur to get one unit more of some other specified good can be expressed as a ratio or rate of substitution.

The concept of substitution could be heuristically fruitful for attraction research. Our analysis would suggest that there need not be a high degree of similarity between marital partners for any given valued characteristic, as long as discrepancies compensate each other (i.e. add up to zero). One should also look at typical rates of substitution for specific characteristics. There is at least indirect evidence that women are more willing than men to trade off physical attractiveness for some other characteristics (e.g. W. Stroebe *et al.* 1971; Walster *et al.* 1966). It is unclear which other characteristics are typically involved in this substitution, but as in traditional role differentiation a wife's status is determined by her husband's achievements in the socio-economic sphere, it would not be unreasonable if women traded beauty for socio-economic promise.

**2.3. Compatibility.** While propinquity or physical attractiveness exert their influence on mate selection even before any interaction has taken place, the determinants of compatibility affect attraction only during interaction. Research in this area has mainly concentrated on two classes of variables, attitudes and personality traits. With regard to attitudes there seems to be widespread consensus that attraction is increased by similarity and decreased by dissimilarity. The situation is less clear-cut in the case of personality traits.

*2.3.1. Attitude similarity and attraction.* The prediction that individuals prefer others who share their beliefs, opinions and attitudes to those who do not, can be derived from social comparison theory in a number of different ways. While Festinger's (1954) own explanation is less than satisfactory, Byrne & Clore (1967) argue quite persuasively that the major reason why disagreement is perceived as punishing is that it frustrates the individual need for cognitive clarity and lowers confidence in one's ability to interact effectively with one's environment. Agreement is rewarding because it increases one's confidence in the validity of one's cognitions about reality.

The evidence for a positive effect of attitude similarity on attraction is actually less clear-cut than is typically suggested in social psychology textbooks. Although studies by Byrne (1969) and co-workers consistently support the similarity–attraction relationship, this work can be criticized for its exclusive reliance on the rather artificial 'simulated stranger' paradigm. Field studies of the similarity–attraction relationship have been conducted by Curry & Emerson (1970), Griffitt & Veitch (1974), Levinger (1972) and Newcomb (1961). Although Newcomb's (1961) classic study of attitude similarity and liking in a student dormitory seemed to support the similarity–attraction relationship, the statistical analysis of his data has been criticized by Levinger & Breedlove (1966). One's trust in Newcomb's results is further reduced by the fact that two replications of the study (Curry & Emerson 1970; Levinger 1972) failed to find any evidence of a positive effect of attitude similarity on attraction. Thus, the only field study which supports the relationship is a study by Griffitt & Veitch (1974) conducted in a simulated air raid shelter. Since subjects in this study spent ten days in a room measuring 28 m², it is likely that they discussed their responses to the 44 items of the attitude questionnaire, which had been administered to them at the outset of the study to measure attitude similarity. This would make the procedure of this study rather similar to the 'simulated-stranger' design. It does suggest, however, that one of the reasons for the failure of other field studies to demonstrate any effect of attitude similarity on attraction may have been that subjects never interacted sufficiently to discuss the attitude issues on which the assessment of their similarity had been based.

*2.3.2. Partner personality and attraction.* Research on the effect of partner personality on attraction has been less theory-guided than investigations of the attitude-similarity–attraction relationship. After dark ages of theory-lessness, the situation was only slightly improved when Winch (1958), with his need-complementarity hypothesis of mate selection, developed a theoretical framework in which the effect of personality traits on attraction could be studied. Need complementarity has the unique feature that it allows individuals to satisfy their partner's need while satisfying their own at the same time. As both partners can produce behaviour which is rather valuable to the partner at low cost to themselves, their relationship should result in better outcomes than that of partners whose need constellations are not complementary.

Winch's theory had such intuitive appeal that it survived two decades with a minimum of empirical support. There are a number of reasons for the repeated failure to find empirical support for the need-complementarity hypothesis. One problem is Winch's (1958) conceptualization of complementarity. He maintains, for example, that complementarity exists with regard to the same need dimension (Type I complementarity), if the need of one partner is strong and that of the other partner weak. While the assumption of such a negative relationship makes sense in the case of a need for dominance, it would make no sense in the case of a need for sexuality. A second problem is that Winch gives equal weight to all complementary need constellations, although it seems only reasonable that the satisfaction of some needs is more important to marital stability than that of others. A third problem is that the theory of complementary needs neglects the existence of cultural norms which prescribe marital role behaviour. A fourth problem is that any successful empirical study of the theory presupposes that the personality questionnaire employed to test the theory really predicts behaviour of partners in the marital situation. However, such an assumption seems hardly justifiable (Mischel 1968). It is at least indicative that the strongest support for the need-complementarity hypothesis comes from the study of Lipetz *et al.* (1970), who use personality items which were specifically formulated to assess behaviour in the marital situation.

**2.4. Love, choice and constraints.** Social critics and parents alike often used to feel that it was foolhardy to leave an important decision such as the choice of a marital partner to children who, to make things worse, employed 'blind love' as a reputedly irrational decision rule. It is not surprising that only with the decline of the extended family system did the elders hand the privilege of this decision over to the young ones, partly because, with the emergence of the nuclear family, they at least did not have to *live with* their children's choices, but also partly because they had lost the power of control.

As things turned out, they would not have had to worry. Already the differential availability of individuals for interaction in our society makes the partner choice likely to be a homogamous one (Kerckhoff 1974). In addition to segregating unmarried males and females into more delimited non-interacting sub-populations, society instills them with a value system which makes such characteristics as position, income and educational attainments desirable. Thus, market competition will act as a further force toward homogamy. Although this would not prevent individuals from giving themselves away below value, social pressures from peer groups and parents arise as soon as marked deviations are detected.

Only after having been sorted into homogeneous segments by these filters are individuals free to love. It is at this choice point that the further selection is guided by psychological principles, of which the most important ones are probably the comparison of cognitive structures in social validation processes and the mutual rewards of behaviour determined by the compatibility of partner needs and interests.

Although we finally managed at least to mention the concept of love, people often object that love is not conceded its proper place in attraction research. This has to be admitted. While interest in love as a scientific concept has increased over the last decade (e.g. Berscheid & Walster 1974; Rubin 1974; Walster 1971) the explanatory power of these love theories has been rather minimal. This is perhaps not surprising, considering the role emotion plays in cognitive social psychological theories (e.g. Schachter 1964). As long as we conceive of emotion as an epiphenomenon, as a mere *result* of our interpretation of reality, we cannot concede love, the emotion *par excellence*, a causal role as a *determinant* of marital partner choice. Naturally, this does not preclude the possibility that we may feel affection for, be romantically attached to, or even infatuated by and sexually dependent on, our partners.

## 3. The structure of the marital relationship

In the previous section we were mainly concerned with the question of which characteristics or constellations of characteristics determine who is recruited into marriage and with (or by) whom. In this section we are interested in the factors which determine the survival of the marital group. When two individuals give up the informality of the dating relationship and become committed to each other in marriage, their relationship typically moves towards a greater involvement with task-related problems and away from the preoccupation with social-emotional issues which characterizes most romantic relationships. The demands imposed by the outside world force marital partners to come to some agreement about how to divide the various tasks within the marital group. Although the problems the couple is now faced with could theoretically be shared equally by both, marital partners usually adopt some division of labour, with each partner becoming mainly responsible for some of the tasks. This role differentiation is not decided upon anew by each couple. Rather, they enter the marital relationship with culturally determined expectations about the kind of role differentiation that is normal for a marital relationship. It removes a great deal of conflict potential if both partners hold expectations that are compatible. The matching of role expectations is therefore seen by theorists of mate selection (e.g. Murstein 1970) as the last decisive stage in the courtship process.

**3.1. The differentiation of marital roles.** The classic analysis of marital role differentiation has been made by Parsons & Bales (1955), based on earlier work by Bales (1949) on leadership roles in small groups. According to Bales, the survival of any group depends on its ability to solve two types of problems: problems involving goal achievement and adaptation to demands on the group from the outside world, and problems involving internal integration and the expression of emotional tensions. The first group of issues which demand activity in the task area was called 'adaptive-instrumental' problems by Bales. The second group of problems which demand activities in the social emotional area was called 'integrative-expressive'.

In observations of leadership behaviour in small groups, Bales & Slater (1955) described a fundamental role differentiation, divorcing the task functions from the social emotional functions. While the task specialist moved the group towards a solution of the task, the social emotional specialist helped the group to maintain good intermember relations. Bales & Slater (1955) saw as the main reason for this type of role differentiation the fundamental incompatibility of the task and social emotional roles.

Applying these concepts to marital role differentiation, Parsons & Bales (1955) argued that in most industrialized societies, the husband is the goal-oriented leader and as such is the task specialist on the relationship between the family and the outside world. He concentrates his skills on the socio-economic sphere and serves as the breadwinner for the family. The wife, on the other hand, is mainly concerned with the internal workings of the family, serving the social emotional needs of the family members while at the same time fulfilling her role as a housewife.

Sociologists no longer accept Parsons & Bales' (1955) belief in the functional inevitability of this type of traditional role differentiation. However, although evidence has been accumulating which indicates a gradual shift in attitudes concerning traditional marital role differentiation (Scanzoni & Fox 1980), it appears that *actual* household division of labour patterns have been changing less rapidly. In a recent study of the distribution of household tasks among cohabitating and married couples, Stafford, Backman & Bona (1977) observed that these couples were still dividing their household chores along traditional lines, with the women doing the lion's share of the work.

Very many sociologists (e.g. Bernard 1972; Gillespie 1971; Laws 1971; Safilios-Rothschild 1976; Scanzoni 1972), and not all of them women, feel that this type of role differentiation is not very equitable. More specifically, they argue that women are worse off in marriage than men. Because access to the socio-economic sphere was blocked, or at least made difficult, for women, due to the prevalence of sexist attitudes in society, they had to take over the less desirable tasks in the marital partnership. As Safilios-Rothschild explains:

because of social structural and sociopsychological barriers to women's economic independence, the cost of divorce to them is so high (in absence of adequate legal alimony provisions) that any other cost incurred is lower, as long as they are supported by their husbands and enjoy the social status bestowed upon them...This differential value of exchanged resources explains how marriages can be stable when the one spouse appears to be offering little (only economic support and status) and the other a lot of resources. (Safilios-Rothschild 1976: 356)

3.1.1. *The differentiation of instrumental role functions.* Of the two major instrumental role functions distinguished by sociologists, provider and housekeeper, the husband typically occupies the more powerful provider role. The importance of this role is indicated by the fact that male income is an excellent predictor of marital stability (Cutright 1971), with high income families having more stable marriages. While this correlation could be due to the fact that the successful performance of the provider role helps to maintain mutual affect between husband and wife, feminist sociologists (e.g. Safilios-Rothschild 1976) prefer an explanation in terms of constraints against separation. The higher the husband's income, the more the wife has to lose in leaving the relationship.

While the husband's instrumental function consists in the provider role, women's instrumental function is mainly directed inwards, towards the family. Women are largely responsible for household duties in the traditional fashion, including the care of children. The list of tasks making up the household duties (e.g. cooking, dusting, dishwashing, vacuum cleaning, laundry washing, scrubbing, garbage disposal) makes very uninspiring reading. Since most of these tasks do not require a great deal of skill and since their successful performance is not rewarded by a great deal of social esteem, it is hardly surprising that women find marriage more difficult than men do, and that women perceive their marriage role more limiting and frustrating (Bernard 1972; Gurin, Veroff & Feld 1960).

It could be argued that women are compensated for any frustration they might experience in performing their household chores by the joyful task of bringing up their children, while the husbands' duties in the socio-economic sphere cruelly restrict the frequency of their interaction with the little ones. It is sobering, therefore, to learn that most researchers have found that childless individuals report a higher level of marital adjustment and satisfaction than do people with children (e.g. Feldman 1971; Renne 1970). Even when couples were matched for socio-economic background, participation in the labour force, and a number of further sociological characteristics, married women who stayed childless reported a higher degree of happiness in their marital relationship than did mothers of children (Houseknecht 1979). These findings are complemented by results of studies on marital satisfaction over the family life cycle (e.g. Rollins & Feldman 1970), which suggest that marital satisfaction declines for wives with the advent of children and begins to increase again when children leave the home.

*3.1.2. The differentiation of expressive role functions.* Are these inequities in instrumental role functions compensated by expressive role functions: do males shower their downtrodden spouses with more social and emotional support, with more frequent reassurances of their personal worth than their wives give them? This is not quite the picture that emerges from the literature on marital role differentiation. It seems to be the wife who, in her prime role as the 'expressive hub of the conjugal family' (Scanzoni 1972), is expected to support and nurture her husband for the performance of his economic role obligations.

While social psychological research, which has mainly focused on premarital relationships, has little to contribute to our understanding of the causes and consequences of marital role differentiation, the determinants of attraction studied by social psychologists add to our evaluation of the competence of marital partners in performing the expressive functions of group maintenance. Thus, the partners' physical attractiveness and their similarity in sexual drive level may affect mutual sexual satisfaction, while similarity in attitudes and interests as well as need-complementarity are likely to increase the mutual enjoyment of companionship in intellectual as well as leisure activities (Adams 1979; Lewis & Spanier 1979).

A more important contribution of social psychology, however, is to our understanding of the kinds of expressive functions marital partners perform for each other. Our analysis of the motivational basis of group formation presented earlier would lead us to emphasize the following functions of marital partnership in the integrative-expressive area: *social protection, social* and *emotional support*, and *social validation*. We would argue that the need for these services forms the major basis for our need for social contact and companionship.

*Social protection.* The studies by Schachter (1959) on the determinants of affiliation demonstrate that fear elicits affiliation. While Schachter (1959) interpreted these findings in terms of a need to evaluate one's emotions through a process of social comparison, we suggested in section 1 of this chapter that an alternative interpretation of these findings could be derived from the ethological approach (e.g. Bowlby 1969; McDougall 1908). The assumption that physical danger motivates individuals to join the group for social protection is not only consistent with Schachter's findings that fear elicits a need for affiliation, but also with evidence indicating that the presence of others indeed serves a stress-reducing function (Cottrell & Epley 1977), although the mechanisms which mediate social stress reduction have not yet been clearly identified.

*Social and emotional support.* There is a great deal of agreement among personality and clinical psychologists (e.g. Erikson 1963; Rogers 1968) about the importance of positive self-regard for optimal human functioning. Thus, it is the basic assumption of the theory of therapy developed by Rogers (1968) that the problem motivating individuals to seek therapeutic consultation most frequently stems from a depleted feeling of self-regard. The partner's expression of regard or love, his or her indications of trust or communication of praise may therefore serve an important function in bolstering one's feelings of self-worth or self-esteem.

Sociologists have been well aware of the importance of this aspect of expressive marital functioning. Nye & Berardo (1973) have termed it the 'therapeutic role' which partners perform for each other. Although the sociological literature provides more discussion of the performance of this role by females, there is reason to assume that wives need therapeutic services as much as husbands. Brown, Bhrolchain & Harris (1975) found that general level of intimacy with one's spouse and amount of social support from him made a critical difference in the occurrence of depression in working class wives under stress. Similarly, Weissman & Paykel (1974) found that acutely depressed women reported more difficulties in communicating with their spouses and in marital intimacy than controls. Finally Kotlar (1965) found that among high marital adjustment couples both were higher in expressive characteristics than were both members of low adjustment couples.

*Social validation.* Effectiveness in dealing with one's physical and social environment depends on the validity of both the evaluation of one's competence and of one's beliefs about the structure of that environment. Since the evaluation of one's ability and the validation of one's beliefs often have to take place under highly ambiguous circumstances (Festinger 1954), they can be expected to depend mainly on social comparison processes. Similar conclusions can be derived from Kelley's (1967) covariance model of attribution, which states that social consensus is as important for a valid attribution of stable characteristics to the environment as it is for characteristics of the person himself/herself. Recent failures to support this assumption (e.g. Hansen & Donoghue 1977; Nisbett & Borgida 1975) are probably due to these investigators overlooking the fact that consensus-information should only be applicable if the comparison person is similar with regard to dimensions relevant for the specific comparison. It seems likely, therefore, that, owing to the closeness of the marital relationship and owing to their similarity in many social characteristics (Lewis & Spanier 1979), spouses serve mutually as important bases of social reality.

**3.2. Implications.** With regard to *instrumental role functions*, there can be no doubt that men are better off than women. In traditional partnerships wives are dependent on their husbands not only for economic but also for social (and even legal) status. In return for these provisions they are expected to perform a number of highly mundane, low prestige chores, a situation from which they can hardly escape without worsening their lot even more.

This sex difference in instrumental role functions is reflected in mental health: married women have more symptoms of distress, are more depressed and have a higher incidence of mental illness than their male counterparts (Bloom, Asher & White 1978; Gove 1972a). This is not surprising for, despite the changing roles, such social and economic discrimination makes it difficult for a married woman to achieve success through her own talents or by her own intervention. It is only a short step from this state of affairs to chronically low self-esteem, psychological distress and depression. The parallel between an acceptance of such traditional values with the learned helplessness paradigm is apparent.

As we have seen, these inequities in instrumental role functions are not compensated for by the distribution of the expressive role functions. Again, it is the wife who is expected to support and nurture the husband, although as we noted, women need the social and emotional support of their husbands as much as husbands need 'therapeutic services' from their wives.

In contrast to feminist sociologists (e.g. Bernard 1972; Safilios-Rothschild 1976), who argue that women are *forced* into marriage because *direct* access to socio-economic resources is blocked to them, due to prevalent sex discrimination and sexist attitudes, we would suggest that *both* wives and husbands profit from a mutual performance of expressive functions. Thus, as in most groups, the maintenance of the marital group does not only depend on members' competence in performing task-related functions but in mutually satisfying their need for social protection, social and emotional support and social validation.

Unfortunately, there is evidence to support either position. With societal barriers to women's economic freedom being rapidly broken down, feminist supporters would predict that fewer women should choose marriage and that divorce rates should go up. This is exactly what seems to be happening: while rates of first marriages have been showing a slow decrease since 1950, divorce rates have been increasing at an accelerating pace for the last two decades (e.g. Carter & Glick 1976). There is some evidence on the other hand, to support our position as well. Analyses of marital status differences in physical and mental health (e.g., Bloom, Asher & White 1978; Gove 1972a; M. S. Stroebe & W. Stroebe 1983) report a consistent pattern: compared to unmarried members of the same sex, both married men and married women show fewer symptoms of mental and physical distress and have longer life expectancies. Thus, while there is little doubt that marriage is better for men than for women, it still seems to be the healthiest, if not the best, option for both sexes.

## 4. The consequences of bereavement

The death of a spouse is not only a traumatic emotional event for the surviving mate, it also means the end of a social organization consisting of two partners sharing many instrumental and expressive role functions. As women seem to carry the greater share of the marital load, we would expect men to be affected more negatively than women by the death of a spouse. This prediction contradicts the firmly held opinions of many health professionals working with the bereaved. For example, Greenblatt (1978: 43) concluded that 'Loss of a spouse presents serious risks to the psychological and physical health and well-being of the survivor. This is particularly true for women', and similarly, Carey (1977: 125) stated that 'Widowers were significantly better adjusted than widows.' Two factors are responsible for such claims: firstly, there are far more widows than widowers, and secondly, there are main effects on mental and physical health. In the following section we will demonstrate that when appropriate within-sex married controls are used, widowers are worse off than widows on all indices of mental and physical health as well as mortality.

**4.1. Health-related consequences of partner loss: empirical evidence.** With only one or two exceptions, in cases where other controls are used, the research to which we here refer enables comparisons of the widowed with same-sex married controls. Thus, for each measure of mental and physical illness, and for mortality indices, widowed to married ratios can be calculated by dividing the age and sex specific rates for the widowed by the comparable rates for the married. Coefficients greater than 1.00 indicate a relative excess among the widowed. It should be noted that in general the rates presented are based on data from white citizens only.

*4.1.1. Mental illness.* With high consistency, research has shown that women are more likely to be mentally ill than men and, generally, that married individuals have lower rates than any other marital status group (see reviews by Bloom, Asher & White 1978; Gove 1972a). The widowed population (i.e. not specifically the recently bereaved) – and this is the case for both males and females – have intermediate rates between the married and the divorced/separated (the latter, particularly the separated, have exceptionally high rates). However, large-scale surveys indicate higher excess rates for widowers than for widows, compared with their married counterparts. In most investigations, not only these ratios but even the rates per 100,000 widowers, exceed those for widows. Also, despite some indication that general trends in sex differences in mental illness may be changing (see Bloom, Asher & White 1978) it is noteworthy that the male excess among the widowed is still consistently greater than the female.

Though not longitudinal in a strict sense, a study by Stein & Susser (1969) was undertaken on a sufficient scale, and with adequate controls, to provide some support for this cross-sectional data, which must be interpreted with caution (see M. S. Stroebe & W. Stroebe 1983). In this study, widower to married men's inception rates into psychiatric care were higher (2.74) than widow to married women's (1.66). A separate set of data on the same population related to the time interval between bereavement and first entry into psychiatric care, and found clustering of inception to psychiatric care in the months immediately following bereavement.

4.1.2. *Depression.* Information on diagnostic-specific mental illness rates by marital status cannot be included here (indeed, very little is available). Depression is, however, a special case as it is an integral part of grief and furthermore, particularly among the bereaved, may not be so extreme as to be classified as a mental illness. The majority of the recently widowed who have symptoms of depression do not receive medical or psychiatric treatment. It seems that depression is accepted as a normal reaction to loss and is fatalistically endured (Briscoe & Smith 1975; Clayton, Desmarais & Winokur 1968).

The evidence again indicates that women preponderate in rates of depression, and marriage seems to be associated with low rates. It is, however, surprising, considering the relevance of information on depression across marital status groups to the question of the contribution of marriage to male and female well-being, that neither reviewers of the area (e.g. Weissman & Klerman 1977) nor feminists (e.g. Bernard 1972) deal adequately with the suggestion that widowed, divorced/separated, and, even more importantly, the never-married are all *worse* off than married men and women – as most surveys have found.

Fairly detailed information on depression by sex and marital status group is contained in a community survey by Radloff (1975). Marriage was reported to be associated with low depression scores for both men and women, though here again the advantage of marriage is much more striking for males than for females. Married females were more depressed than males. The widowed groups had relatively high depression scores, and the interaction effect was observed: widowed men were more depressed than widowed women. In this study the never-married were also more depressed than the married, and like the widowed, single men were more depressed than single women. So here too, marriage seems to be a mental health advantage for men and women, but more so for men.

Some have claimed that there are no sex differences in depression among the bereaved (e.g. Clayton 1974; Weissman & Klerman 1977) and some (e.g. Carey 1979) that widows are more poorly adjusted than widowers. Frequently the reason for such claims is a failure to adjust for the total numbers of widows and widowers and the omission of married controls (M. S. Stroebe & W. Stroebe 1983). As Parkes (1972) observed, although widows adjusted more poorly in the first year, there were large differences between the married men and women in his control group. When this was taken into account, widows showed no greater *decline* in adjustment than widowers. In fact, widowers took longer to recover than widows. Thus, in the case of widowed depression, we again have evidence of a male excess.

*4.1.3. Physical health.* Klerman & Izen (1977), in a major review on the effects of bereavement and grief on specific medical disorders, noted shortcomings of many potentially useful investigations purporting to link losses to physical illness, and consequently focused on causes of death among the bereaved. Indeed cross-sectional investigations on physical health provide scant evidence on sex and marital status differences. Most reports (e.g. Bloom, Asher & White 1978; Carter & Glick 1976) draw on a survey by the National Center for Health Statistics (1976). Generally, as in the mental health area, indications are that widowed, divorced and separated persons have higher rates of illness and debility than the never-married and the married. The sex main effect is again found; females generally report more illness and debility than males. But there is an important reversal: reports from males exceed those of females (regardless of marital status) for the indicator 'limitations in activity due to chronic conditions'. Other recent data (see Gove & Hughes 1979) support this small but inconsistent pattern: men are more likely to have serious chronic illnesses than women. The excessive rates of females in morbidity are due, it seems, to milder transitory disorders, but men are more prone to serious debilities.

These data do not permit a thorough analysis of sex differences in the health of the widowed as compared to married persons (cf. Bloom, Asher & White 1978). A few longitudinal studies provide further information. Gerber, Rusalem & Hannon (1975) included an analysis of physical health in a study of elderly widowed, and reported significant differences after bereavement between widowers and widows of spouses who had died of prolonged chronic illnesses, with widowers more vulnerable to physical deterioration, though no sex difference was found among those whose spouses had died of a shorter, sudden illness (physical health was generally better for this sample). In a second study (Heyman & Gianturco 1973), however, no differences between widowers and widows were found in the number of physical symptoms. In fact, in this study, no significant decrease in physical health on bereavement was reported at all. Demographic features may account for this: Heyman & Gianturco's (1973) sample was drawn from a relatively small, stable community in North Carolina, Gerber, Rusalem & Hannon's (1975) from the Bronx, New York.

Parkes & Brown (1972) included an analysis of physical symptoms in their comprehensive investigation of the sample of young widowed. While widows achieved high values on acute symptoms, these were not significantly different from means for married women, whereas the rate for widowers, though lower than either the widow sample or married women control group, was significantly excessive compared with the married men control group.

To summarize, it seems that, if there is a sex difference in physical health of the bereaved at all, it is the health of widowers that is more severely affected than that of widows.

4.1.4. *Mortality*. If people do not actually die 'of grief', they are certainly prone to die 'during' it, as Engel (1961) prefers to put it. This is the conclusion that we came to after reviewing the evidence on mortality among the bereaved (M. S. Stroebe *et al.* 1981), despite shortcomings of the investigations, lack of detailed information, and a series of artifacts which could conceivably account for some of the mortality patterns. The striking feature about these mortality patterns is the consistency with which they are found, but though the regularities parallel those for mental and physical illness, there is one major difference: the sex main effect is reversed. Whereas women have higher rates for mental and physical illness, men's death rates are invariably excessive compared with women's. While the weaker sex ails, the stronger dies.

Nationwide, even worldwide, surveys for well over a hundred years have been unequivocal about mortality patterns: not only do males have higher death rates, but marital status patterns seem stable too. Married males and females have the lowest mortality rates of all, but married women's rates are lower than married men's. While the never-married are intermediate, the widowed and divorced have some of the highest sex ratios among death rates. Being widowed is a high risk for males and females, but again, widowers are relatively worse off than widows, compared with their married counterparts. Notable too are the extreme excesses for young widowed groups, and here again the excesses are even more extreme for males (see, e.g., Kraus & Lilienfeld 1959).

No further discussion of these atypically clear-cut observations would be necessary, were it not for a number of problems in interpreting such epidemiological data. For example, remarriage rates of widowers are far in excess of widows (does this select out the healthiest widowers?), and joint accidents or infections could increase the proximity of death dates of spouses (particularly, deaths from accidents in the young bereaved). So we need to look at mortality patterns among the recently and relatively recently bereaved, among whom there should be the highest excess risks, for confirmation of the relationship between bereavement and mortality.

The classic longitudinal study of widowers' mortality (Young, Benjamin & Wallis 1963; and the follow-up by Parkes, Benjamin & Fitzgerald 1969) testifies to an elevated risk in the first six months following death of a spouse in widowed men over 54 years of age. One of the few sufficiently large investigations of the opposite sex, by Cox & Ford (1964), found an elevation in risk for widows in the second year of bereavement, but not immediately following the loss. There is further evidence from other studies that males are more vulnerable immediately on the death of their spouses, and widows somewhat later (cf. Ekblom 1963; McNeill 1973; Niemi 1979; Ward 1976). Studies which fail to find an excess mortality risk in the recently bereaved have usually employed samples too small for statistical significance to be likely (e.g. Clayton 1974).

Clearly, a comprehensive, large-scale, longitudinal survey of relative risk for widowed males and females is overdue. When a new study by two epidemiologists Helsing & Szklo (1981) hit the news headlines in the United States, with the announcement of widower excesses over widows in death rates, the answers to a lot of questions were expected. The study, using census information, was large and included married controls. Contrary to cross-sectional and the other longitudinal studies, no differences between the female widowed and married were found, though somewhat higher rates for the younger widows were observed which was 'suggestive'. Male widowed persons had higher rates than controls. The risk appeared to be more excessive for younger widowers though numbers were too small for this to reach significance. So far these findings do not differ too dramatically from previous ones, though this is the first study of sufficient size that fails to find an excess among widows. However, even more unexpected are Helsing & Szklo's observations on the duration effect: they found little evidence of higher mortality in the first six months or twelve months of bereavement for either males or females.

The last word has obviously still not been had about a causal relationship between bereavement and mortality, and we can offer little explanation of the contradiction of the Helsing & Szklo (1981) findings on duration of the effect with, notably, the Young, Benjamin & Wallis (1963) and Parkes, Benjamin & Fitzgerald (1969) results. Information on causes of death, not included in Helsing & Szklo's investigation, would be enlightening. But basically the thesis of the present chapter stands firm: widowers are more vulnerable to the loss effect than widows.

*4.1.5. Suicide.* The most extreme indication of a loss effect in the bereaved, an index of the absence of any desire to live on without the spouse, is self-annihilation. Since Durkheim's (1897) pioneering work, it has become well established that self-destruction is higher among the widowed than among the married. Further, MacMahon & Pugh (1965) found that, at least in part, the high suicide rate among the widowed was due to the excessive risk in the early years of widowhood. There is also evidence that widowers are more likely to take their own lives than widows (e.g. Bock & Webber 1972; Carter & Glick 1976; Gove 1972b). A further significant result for our present argument was reported by Bojanovsky & Bojanovsky (1976). In a study of suicide among the widowed and divorced, they found excesses in suicide rates for widowers particularly in the first half year of bereavement, whereas for widows there was not such a dramatic peak risk period initially after the spouse's death: the excesses were observable, and only gradually declining, across a period of ten years. This pattern underlines the differences that we reported above for non-suicidal mortality among bereaved males and females.

**4.2. Health-related consequences of partner loss: theoretical analyses.** There are basically two types of explanation for the health deterioration following the loss of a partner. On the one hand, it would seem reasonable that marriage, due to the various role functions partners perform for each other, serves as a 'screen' that 'protects' married individuals from a number of negative health consequences, which then tend to occur once this protective screen is removed. This 'social-protection-through-marriage' interpretation would be consistent with most of the evidence reported above: since marriage is assumed to serve as a support system for both husband and wife, we would expect individuals who are married to be better off than the never-married, divorced or widowed, as is indeed the case. Furthermore, since marriage appears to be a more effective support system for men than for women, we would also expect a sex by marital status interaction, with women being relatively less affected than men by the loss of their partner. Again, this expectation is borne out by empirical data. There is one piece of evidence, however, which would fit less readily within the framework of a protection interpretation, and that is the peak in mortality shortly after bereavement.

If the health-related consequences of bereavement are merely due to a removal of the 'protective screen' of marriage, one would expect the mortality rates of the widowed to decrease *slowly* from the level of the married to that of the groups not married.

This peak in mortality following bereavement would be more consistent with a second and more popular type of interpretation in terms of a 'loss effect' or 'broken heart syndrome' which sees extreme loneliness (Lynch 1977) or hopelessness (Melges & Bowlby 1969; Schulz 1978; Seligman 1975) as the cause of health deterioration following bereavement. Seligman (1975) argues persuasively that hopelessness and depression follow repeated experience of loss of control. When an individual loses a spouse, a decreased sense of outcome control may be generated, which in turn could lead to depression and hopelessness. Since there is evidence for an effect of hope (e.g. Alderson 1975; Phillips 1972) or hopelessness (e.g. Schmale & Iker 1966) on life expectancy, Seligman's (1975) interpretation of the loss effect is quite convincing. Unfortunately, however, this interpretation cannot offer any ready explanation for the marital status main effect or the sex by marital status interaction on physical and mental health reported earlier. While it would be expected that the bereaved are worse off than the married, one would need additional assumptions (e.g. selection effect: the healthy are more likely to marry) to account for the relatively poor health of the never-married. Even more problematic would be the explanation of the marital status by sex interaction. Why should women be less affected by the hopelessness experienced after the loss of a partner? One potential reason might be that since there are more widows than widowers, women encounter a more extensive 'social support network' (Walker, MacBride & Vachon 1977) than men in bereavement. Thus, social support from other widows might help women over the first shock after losing their partner. The work of Lopata (1973) offers tentative support for this assumption.

By integrating some of the assumptions underlying the 'social-protection-through-marriage' hypothesis with some of the processes suggested by an explanation in terms of 'learned helplessness' (Seligman 1975), we (W. Stroebe *et al.* 1980, 1982) have recently attempted to develop a social psychological interpretation of the loss effect, which could account for the pattern of health findings reported above. This approach shares with the social protection hypothesis the conviction that, as a marital relationship constitutes a small group in which members fulfil certain functions for each other and have certain tasks to perform, the health deterioration following the loss of a partner must somehow be related to the loss of these functions. We would also agree with Seligman's argument however, that the loss of a partner may be a traumatic experience of lack of control which is likely to result in hopelessness and depression. In line with the more recent attributional interpretation of 'learned helplessness' (Abramson, Seligman & Teasdale 1978) we would argue that this initial feeling of loss of control and helplessness should be aggravated by the deficits the death creates for the surviving spouse in the areas of social validation, social and emotional support and task performance. The surviving partner is likely to experience problems in socially validating a wider range of his or her judgments, he or she should suffer marked deficits in social and emotional support and, furthermore, will have to take over those parts of the group task which had formerly been performed by the partner.

To summarize then, we suggest that marriage has a protective function which can probably be explained in terms of social anxiety reduction and other role functions of marital partners such as social validation, social and emotional support and companionship. This assumption would be consistent with the finding that marital status is typically associated with better mental and physical health than any of the non-married statuses. We further argued that marriage serves as a better social support system for men than for women. We substantiated this argument with evidence from the work of family sociologists on the traditional distribution of labour and power within marital relationships, which indicated a number of inequities with regard to the distribution of instrumental as well as expressive role functions. This inequity, or more precisely, the women's feeling of being treated inequitably, could be responsible for the fact that the health consequences of marriage are less positive for women than they are for men.

The death of a partner not only removes this 'protective screen', it also leaves the surviving spouses worse off than the never-married for two further reasons: firstly, a married couple may have taken on a number of tasks such as children, a large house, etc., with which any single person would have problems in coping. More importantly, however, marital partners serve as each other's major source of social validation, companionship, and social and emotional support. The sudden deprivation of these services is likely to aggravate the feeling of helplessness and hopelessness already caused by the uncontrollable loss of a loved person. Since the widowed are likely, in time, to find alternative relationships which partly fulfil these functions and thus (at least to some extent) replace the spouse, this perspective would lead one to expect the health-related consequences of partner loss to be worst in the first few months of bereavement, and to be worse if the loss were sudden and unexpected rather than occurring after a long illness (which has also been consistently found, see e.g. Parkes 1975).

Our perspective has finally no difficulty in explaining the fact that, compared to widowers, widows are less negatively affected by bereavement. There are probably two reasons for such a sex difference: on the one hand, there is evidence that women carry the greater share of the marital load. This has the positive consequence that they lose less in bereavement. There is, secondly, evidence (e.g. Berardo 1968, 1970; Bock & Webber 1972) that widowers have greater difficulty than widows in making effective substitutions for the loss of a spouse and typically experience greater social isolation in widowhood.

## 5. Implications for applied social psychology

Making a case for a more social social psychology, one of the authors (Stroebe 1979) criticized the fact that, although social psychology was supposed to occupy a mediating position between the sociological and the psychological points of view, it *de facto* stayed within the limits of a psychological approach. We feel that the theoretical analysis of sex differences in bereavement developed in this chapter not only illustrates the value of taking a more sociological perspective but also demonstrates the unique mediating position of social psychology. While psychiatrists studying the widowed present valuable analyses of the processes responsible for health deterioration in bereavement, they typically offer only rough estimates about the prevalence and distribution of such problems in a given society. Thus, with regard to widowed depression, the fact that, for reasons discussed earlier, there are more depressed widows than widowers, misled many psychiatrists to conclude that bereavement is more likely to lead to depression in women than in men. Demographers, epidemiologists and sociologists, on the other hand, by analysing the characteristics of the distribution of such health problems, allow us to refute such erroneous notions and to identify the subgroups which are most at risk. The weakness of these disciplines, however, is that they cannot offer theories to account for their patterns which would be acceptable to, or of use for, psychiatrists or clinical psychologists. It is here that the social psychologist trained to be at home in both worlds has a unique opportunity to carve out a new field of applied social psychology.

## References

Abramson, L. Y., Seligman, M. E. P. & Teasdale, J. D. 1978. Learned helplessness in humans: critique and reformulation. *Journal of Abnormal Psychology*, *87*, 49–74.
Adams, B. N. 1979. Mate selection in the United States: a theoretical summarization. In W. R. Burr, R. Hill, F. I. Nye & I. L. Reiss (eds.) *Contemporary theories about the family*, vol. 1. New York: Free Press.

Alderson, M. 1975. Relationship between month of birth and month of death in the elderly. *British Journal of Preventive and Social Medicine, 29,* 151–6.

Bales, R. F. 1949. *Interaction process analysis: a method for the study of small groups.* Cambridge, Mass.: Addison-Wesley.

Bales, R. F. & Slater, P. E. 1955. Role differentiation in small decision making groups. In T. Parsons & R. F. Bales (eds.) (1955).

Berardo, F. 1968. Widowhood status in the United States: perspectives on a neglected aspect of the family life-cycle. *The Family Coordinator, 17,* 191–203.

1970. Survivorship and social isolation: the case of the aged widower. *The Family Coordinator, 19,* 11–25.

Bernard, J. 1972. *The future of marriage.* Harmondsworth: Penguin.

Berscheid, E. & Walster, E. H. 1969. *Interpersonal attraction.* Reading, Mass.: Addison-Wesley.

1974. A little bit about love. In T. L. Huston (ed.) *Foundations of interpersonal attraction.* New York: Academic Press.

Bloom, B. L., Asher, S. J. & White, S. W. 1978. Marital disruption as a stressor: a review and analysis. *Psychological Bulletin, 85,* 867–94.

Bock, E. W. & Webber, I. L. 1972. Suicide among the elderly: isolating widowhood and mitigating alternatives. *Journal of Marriage and the Family, 34,* 24–31.

Bojanovsky, J. & Bojanovsky, A. 1976. Zur Risikozeit des Selbstmordes bei Geschiedenen und Verwitweten. *Nervenarzt, 47,* 307–9.

Bossard, J. H. S. 1932. Residential propinquity as a factor in mate selection. *American Journal of Sociology, 38,* 219–24.

Bowlby, J. 1969. *Attachment and loss,* vol. 1. *Attachment.* London: Hogarth Press.

1973. *Attachment and loss,* vol. 2. *Separation: anxiety and anger.* London: Hogarth Press.

1979. *The making and breaking of affectional bonds.* London: Tavistock Publications.

1980. *Attachment and loss,* vol. 3. *Loss: sadness and depression.* London: Hogarth Press.

Briscoe, C. W. & Smith, J. R. 1975. Depression in bereavement and divorce: relationship to primary depressive illness: a study of 128 subjects. *Archives of General Psychiatry, 32,* 439–43.

Brown, G., Bhrolchain, M. & Harris, T. 1975. Social class and psychiatric disturbance among women in an urban population. *Sociology, 9,* 225–54.

Burgess, R. L. & Huston, T. L. (eds.) 1979. *Social exchange in developing relationships.* New York: Academic Press.

Byrne, D. 1969. Attitudes and attraction. In L. Berkowitz (ed.) *Advances in experimental social psychology,* vol. 4. New York: Academic Press.

Byrne, D. & Clore, G. L. 1967. Effectance arousal and attraction. *Journal of Personality and Social Psychology Monograph, 6* (638).

Carey, R. G. 1977. The widowed: a year later. *Journal of Counseling Psychology, 24,* 125–31.

1979. Weathering widowhood: problems and adjustment of the widowed during the first year. *Omega: The Journal of Death and Dying, 10,* 163–74.

Carter, H. & Glick, P. C. 1976. *Marriage and divorce: a social and economic study,* rev. edn. Cambridge, Mass.: Harvard University Press.

Catton, W. R. & Smircich, R. J. 1964. A comparison of mathematical models of the effect of resident propinquity on mate selection. *American Sociological Review, 29,* 522–9.

Cavior, N. & Boblett, P. J. 1972. Physical attractiveness of dating versus married couples. *Proceedings of the 8th Annual Convention of the American Psychological Association, 7*, 175–6.

Clayton, P. J. 1974. Mortality and morbidity in the first year of bereavement. *Archives of General Psychiatry, 30*, 747–50.

Clayton, P. J., Desmarais, L. & Winokur, G. 1968. A study of normal bereavement. *American Journal of Psychiatry, 125*, 168–78.

Cottrell, N. B. & Epley, S. W. 1977. Affiliation, social comparison and socially mediated stress reduction. In J. M. Suls & R. L. Miller (eds.) *Social comparison processes: theoretical and empirical perspectives.* New York: Wiley.

Cox, P. R. & Ford, J. R. 1964. The mortality of widows shortly after widowhood. *Lancet, 1,* 163–4.

Curry, T. J. & Emerson, R. M. 1970. Balance theory: a theory of interpersonal attraction? *Sociometry, 33,* 216–38.

Cutright, P. 1971. Income and family events: marital stability. *Journal of Marriage and the Family, 33,* 291–306.

Dollard, J. & Miller, N. E. 1950. *Personality and psychotherapy.* New York: McGraw-Hill.

Duck, S. W. 1973. Personality similarity and friendship choice: similarity of what, when? *Journal of Personality, 41,* 543–58.

Duck, S. & Gilmour, R. 1981. *Personal relationships 1: studying personal relationships.* London: Academic Press.

Durkheim, E. 1951. *Suicide: a study in sociology.* Glencoe, Ill.: The Free Press; first published in 1897.

Edwards, J. N. 1969. Familial behavior as social exchange. *Journal of Marriage and the Family, 31,* 525–40.

Ekblom, B. 1963. Significance of psychosocial factors with regard to risk of death among elderly persons. *Acta Psychiatrica Scandinavia, 39,* 627–33.

Engel, G. L. 1961. Is grief a disease? *Psychosomatic Medicine, 23,* 18–22.

Erikson, E. H. 1963. *Childhood and society.* New York: Norton.

Feldman, H. 1971. The effects of children on the family. In M. Andrée (ed.) *Family issues of employed women in Europe and America.* Leiden: Brill.

Festinger, L. 1954. A theory of social comparison processes. *Human Relations, 7,* 117–40.

Gerber, I., Rusalem, R. & Hannon, B. A. 1975. Anticipatory grief and aged widows and widowers. *Journal of Gerontology, 30,* 225–9.

Gillespie, D. L. 1971. Who has the power? The marital struggle. *Journal of Marriage and the Family, 33,* 445–58.

Gove, W. R. 1972a. The relationship between sex roles, marital roles and mental illness. *Social Forces, 51,* 34–44.

1972b. Sex, marital status and suicide. *Journal of Health and Social Behavior, 13,* 204–13.

1973. Sex, marital status and mortality. *American Journal of Sociology, 79,* 45–67.

Gove, W. R. & Hughes, M. 1979. Possible causes of the apparent sex differences in physical health: an empirical investigation. *American Sociological Review, 44,* 126–46.

Greenblatt, M. 1978. The grieving spouse. *American Journal of Psychiatry, 135,* 43–7.

Griffitt, W. & Veitch, R. 1974. Preacquaintance attitude similarity and attraction revisited: ten days in a fall-out shelter. *Sociometry, 37,* 163–73.

Gurin, G., Veroff, J. & Feld, S. 1960. *Americans view their mental health.* New York: Basic Books.

Hansen, R. D. & Donoghue, J. M. 1977. The power of consensus: information derived from one's own and other's behavior. *Journal of Personality and Social Psychology*, 5, 294–302.

Helsing, K. J. & Szklo, M. 1981. Mortality after bereavement. *American Journal of Epidemiology*, 114, 41–52.

Heyman, D. K. & Gianturco, D. T. 1973. Long-term adaptation by the elderly to bereavement. *Journal of Gerontology*, 28, 359–62.

Houseknecht, S. K. 1979. Childlessness and marital adjustment. *Journal of Marriage and the Family*, 41, 259–65.

Huston, T. L. & Levinger, G. 1978. Interpersonal attraction and relationships. In M. R. Rosenzweig & L. W. Porter (eds.) *Annual Review of Psychology*, 29. Palo Alto: Annual Reviews Inc.

James, W. 1950. *The principles of psychology*, vol. 2. New York: Dover; originally published by Holt, 1890.

Janis, I. L. & Mann, L. 1977. *Decision making*. New York: Free Press.

Katz, A. M. & Hill, R. 1958. Residential propinquity and marital selection: a review of theory, method and fact. *Marriage and the Family Living*, 20, 27–35.

Kelley, H. 1967. Attribution theory in social psychology. In D. Levine (ed.) *Nebraska symposium on motivation*. Lincoln: University of Nebraska Press.

Kelly, G. A. 1955. *The psychology of personal constructs*. New York: Norton.

Kerckhoff, A. C. 1974. The social context of attraction. In T. L. Huston (ed.) *Foundations of interpersonal attraction*.

Kerckhoff, A. C. & Davis, K. E. 1962. Value consensus and need complementarity in mate selection. *American Sociological Review*, 27, 295–303.

Klerman, G. L. & Izen, J. E. 1977. The effects of bereavement and grief on physical health and general well-being. *Advances in Psychosomatic Medicine*, 9, 63–104.

Kotlar, S. L. 1965. Middle class marital role perceptions and marital status. *Sociological Social Research*, 49, 283–93.

Kraus, A. S. & Lilienfeld, A. M. 1959. Some epidemiological aspects of the high mortality rate in the young widowed group. *Journal of Chronic Diseases*, 10, 207–17.

Laws, J. L. 1971. A feminist review of the marital adjustment literature: the rape of the Locke. *Journal of Marriage and the Family*, 33, 483–516.

Levinger, G. 1972. Little sand box and big quarry: comments on Byrne's paradigmatic spade for research on interpersonal attraction. *Representative Research in Social Psychology*, 3, 3–19.

Levinger, G. & Breedlove, J. 1966. Interpersonal attraction and agreement: a study of marriage partners. *Journal of Personality and Social Psychology*, 3, 367–72.

Levinger, G. & Snoek, J. D. 1972. *Attraction in relationship: a new look at interpersonal attraction*. Morristown, NJ: General Learning Press.

Lewis, R. A. 1972. A developmental framework for the analysis of premarital dyadic formation. *Family Process*, 11, 17–48.

Lewis, R. A. & Spanier, G. B. 1979. Theorizing about the quality and stability of marriage. In W. R. Burr, R. Hill, F. I. Nye & I. L. Reiss (eds.) *Contemporary theories about family*, vol. 1.

Lipetz, M. E., Cohen, I. H., Dworin, J. & Rogers, L. S. 1970. Need complementarity, marital stability, and marital satisfaction. In K. J. Gergen & D. Marlowe (eds.) *Personality and social behavior*. Reading, Mass.: Addison-Wesley.

Lopata, H. Z. 1973. *Widowhood in an American city*. Morristown, NJ: General Learning Press.

Lynch, J. J. 1977. *The broken heart: the medical consequences of loneliness.* New York: Basic Books.

MacMahon, B. & Pugh, T. F. 1965. Suicide in the widowed. *American Journal of Epidemiology, 81,* 23–31.

McDougall, W. 1960. *An introduction to social psychology.* London: Methuen; originally published 1908.

McNeill, D. N. 1973. *Mortality among the widowed in Connecticut.* MPH Essay. New Haven: Yale University.

Melges, F. T. & Bowlby, J. 1969. Types of hopelessness in psychopathological process. *Archives of General Psychiatry, 20,* 690–9.

Mischel, W. 1968. *Personality and assessment.* New York: Wiley.

Murstein, B. I. 1970. Stimulus, value, role: a theory of marital choice. *Journal of Marriage and the Family, 32,* 465–81.

National Center for Health Statistics 1976. Differentials in health characteristics by marital status: United States, 1971–1972. *Vital and Health Statistics, 10,* 104.

Newcomb, T. M. 1961. *The acquaintance process.* New York: Holt, Rinehart and Winston.

Niemi, T. 1979. The mortality of male old-age pensioners following spouse's death. *Scandinavian Journal of Social Medicine, 7,* 115–17.

Nisbett, R. E. & Borgida, E. 1975. Attribution and the psychology of prediction. *Journal of Personality and Social Psychology, 32,* 932–43.

Nye, F. I. & Berardo, F. M. 1973. *The family: its structure and interaction.* New York: Macmillan.

Olson, M. 1965. *The logic of collective action.* Cambridge, Mass.: Harvard University Press.

Parkes, C. M. 1972. *Bereavement: studies of grief in adult life.* London: Tavistock Publications.

1975. Unexpected and untimely bereavement: a statistical study of young Boston widows and widowers. In B. Schoenberg, I. Gerber & A. Wiener (eds.) *Bereavement: its psychosocial aspects.* New York: Columbia University Press.

Parkes, C. M. & Brown, R. 1972. Health after bereavement: a controlled study of young Boston widows and widowers. *Psychosomatic Medicine, 34,* 449–61.

Parkes, C. M., Benjamin, B. & Fitzgerald, R. G. 1969. Broken heart: a statistical study of increased mortality among widowers. *British Medical Journal, 1,* 740–3.

Parsons, T. & Bales, R. F. (eds.) 1955. *Family, socialization and interaction process.* Chicago: The Free Press of Glencoe.

Peplau, L. A., Russell, D. & Heim, M. 1979. The experience of loneliness. In I. H. Frieze, D. Bar-Tal & J. S. Caroll (eds.) *New approaches to social problems.* San Francisco: Jossey Bass.

Phillips, D. 1972. Deathday and birthday: an unexpected connection. In J. M. Tanur (ed.) *Statistics: a guide to the unknown.* San Francisco: Holden-Doug.

Radloff, L. 1975. Sex differences in depression: the effects of occupation and marital status. *Sex Roles, 1,* 249–65.

Renne, K. S. 1970. Correlates of dissatisfaction in marriage. *Journal of Marriage and the Family, 32,* 54–66.

Rodgers, R. H. 1964. Toward a theory of family development. *Journal of Marriage and the Family, 28,* 262–70.

Rogers, C. 1968. The significance of the self-regarding attitudes and perceptions. In C. Gordon & K. J. Gergen (eds.) *The self in social interaction.* New York: Wiley.

Rollins, B. & Feldman, H. 1970. Marital satisfaction over the family life cycle. *Journal of Marriage and the Family, 32,* 20–8.

Rubin, Z. 1974. From liking to loving: patterns of attraction in dating relationships. In T. L. Huston (ed.) *Foundations of interpersonal attraction.*

Safilios-Rothschild, C. 1976. A macro- and micro-examination of family power and love: an exchange model. *Journal of Marriage and the Family, 38,* 355–62.

Scanzoni, J. 1972. *Sexual bargaining: power politics in the American marriage.* Englewood Cliffs, NJ: Prentice Hall.

Scanzoni, J. & Fox, L. G. 1980. Sex roles, family and society: the seventies and beyond. *Journal of Marriage and the Family, 42,* 743–56.

Schachter, S. 1959. *The psychology of affiliation.* Stanford: Stanford University Press.
   1964. The interaction of cognitive and physiological determinants of emotional state. In L. Berkowitz (ed.) *Advances in experimental social psychology,* vol. 1.

Schmale, A. H. & Iker, H. P. 1966. The affect of loneliness and the development of cancer. *Psychosomatic Medicine, 28,* 714–21.

Schulz, R. 1978. *The psychology of death and dying.* Cambridge, Mass.: Addison-Wesley.

Schutz, W. C. 1960. *FIRO: a threedimensional theory of interpersonal behavior.* New York: Holt, Rinehart and Winston.

Sears, R. R., Rau, L. & Alpert, R. 1965. *Identification and child rearing.* Stanford: Stanford University Press.

Seligman, M. E. P. 1975. *Helplessness: on depression, development and death.* San Francisco: Freeman.

Shaver, P. & Rubenstein, C. 1980. Childhood attachment experience and adult loneliness. In L. Wheeler (ed.) *Review of personality and social psychology.* Beverly Hills: Sage.

Stafford, R., Backman, E. & Bona, P. J. 1977. The division of labor among cohabitating and married couples. *Journal of Marriage and the Family, 39,* 43–58.

Stein, Z. & Susser, M. W. 1969. Widowhood and mental illness. *British Journal of Preventive and Social Medicine, 23,* 106–10.

Stroebe, M. S. & Stroebe, W. 1983. Who suffers more? Sex differences in health risks of the widowed. *Psychological Bulletin, 93,* 279–301.

Stroebe, M. S., Stroebe, W., Gergen, K. J. & Gergen, M. 1981. The broken heart: reality or myth? *Omega: The Journal of Death and Dying, 12,* 87–105.

Stroebe, W. 1979. The level of social psychological analysis: a plea for a more social social psychology. In L. H. Strickland (ed.) *Soviet and western perspectives in social psychology.* Oxford: Pergamon Press.

Stroebe, W., Insko, C. A., Thompson, V. D. & Layton, B. 1971. The effects of physical attractiveness, attitude similarity, and sex on various aspects of interpersonal attraction. *Journal of Personality and Social Psychology, 18,* 79–91.

Stroebe, W., Stroebe, M. S., Gergen, K. J. & Gergen, M. 1980. Der Kummer Effekt: psychologische Aspekte der Sterblichkeit von Verwitweten. *Psychologische Beiträge, 12,* 87–106.
   1982. The effects of bereavement on mortality: a social psychological analysis. In J. R. Eiser (ed.) *Social psychology and behavioral medicine.* Chichester: Wiley.

Thibaut, J. W. & Kelley, H. H. 1959. *The social psychology of groups.* New York: Wiley.

Tversky, A. 1972. Elimination by aspects: a theory of choice. *Psychological Review, 79,* 281–99.

Walker, K. N., MacBride, A. & Vachon, M. L. 1977. Social support networks and the crisis of bereavement. *Social Science and Medicine, 2,* 35–41.

Walster, E. 1971. Passionate love. In B. I. Murstein (ed.) *Theories of attraction and love*. New York: Springer.

Walster, E., Aronson, V., Abrahams, D. & Rottmann, L. 1966. Importance of physical attractiveness in dating behavior. *Journal of Personality and Social Psychology*, 4, 503–16.

Ward, A. W. 1976. Mortality of bereavement. *British Medical Journal*, 1, 700–2.

Weissman, M. M. & Klerman, G. L. 1977. Sex differences and the epidemiology of depression. *Archives of General Psychiatry*, 34, 98–111.

Weissman, M. M. & Paykel, E. S. 1974. *The depressed woman: a study of social relationships*. Chicago: University of Chicago Press.

Winch, R. F. 1958. *Mate selection: a study of complementary needs*. New York: Harper.

Young, M., Benjamin, B. & Wallis, C. 1963. Mortality of widowers. *Lancet*, 2, 454–6.

# Part III
# Social contexts of individual actions

# 14. The social dimension of goal-directed action[1]

## MARIO VON CRANACH AND LADISLAV VALACH

The purpose of this chapter is to present the view that goal-directed action is basically social in nature and that, as such, it constitutes a legitimate, even a fundamental, object of study in social psychology. If one accepts this to be the case, then it seems paradoxical that social psychologists have hardly ever been concerned with goal-directed action, and that quite often they are not even clear about the meaning of the term.

What is goal-directed action? Does it constitute a scientific psychological problem, does it really contain a social dimension, and is it justifiable to locate research about it in the context of social psychology? The aim of this chapter is to answer these questions. *Action – the behaviour of a human actor which is consciously and purposefully aimed towards a goal –* is above all individual. Nevertheless, it is also truly social, and this is so for three reasons: it is of social origin, it has social consequences and, most of all, it provides the material from which is constructed the fabric of social life. This sentence already contains the structure of our argument. In the first place, we shall clarify, with reference to the psychological theory of action, some of the organizational principles of action. Next, we shall discuss the social origins of action from a perspective in which the actual formation of action is seen as both phylogenetic and historical as well as ontogenetic, and finally we examine its unfolding in the specific case. (It is true that we should also point to, and describe, some of the social consequences, as they contribute to creating social structures and functions, but this would go beyond the scope of a brief psychological discussion.)

In our presentation, we shall confine ourselves to our theory and empirical results, even if it is true that the latter are still preliminary and by no means abundant; in doing so, the discussion will rely mainly on the work done by

---

1 This chapter was translated from the German by Henri Tajfel.

our research group in Berne[2]; but occasionally it will also take into account research done elsewhere. In conclusion, an attempt will be made to show that the basic assumptions of the psychology of action must constitute, explicitly or implicitly, an essential component in the construction of modern social psychological theories. On all these points, assertions will be made which will then be defended.

Action, in the sense of its definition proposed above, plays an important role in our daily lives. The reader might try to recall all that he or she has done today: a very large part of it will be goal-oriented action, or at least embedded into a larger context of such actions. Many of these actions are social: *interaction* is acting amongst people. The time is ripe for taking up the challenge that the ensuing problems represent for social psychology.

## 1. Outlines of our theory of action[3]

'Theory of action' is a term which can have a great variety of meanings. The theory to be described here claims, at least in principle, to include the most important assumptions of other theories. A consideration of various prototypes of contemporary theories of action shows that they differ considerably in their emphasis. In some of them the accent is on freedom of action, in others on its predetermined nature; in some, on its inner-directedness, in others on its outer-directedness. In some theories the impulse (in the sense of the decisive or impelling moment) is in the foreground, in others it is the 'course of action' ('the organization of action'). Sometimes the individual aspects are considered in more detail, and sometimes the social aspects.

Still relevant today are the so-called 'behaviour theories', based on a behaviourist model in which behaviour is understood mainly in terms of responses to external stimuli. This view has struck deep roots in psychological conceptions, so that many psychologists (mainly of the Anglo-American tradition) talk about 'reactions' when what they really mean are 'actions'. More differentiated are those theories which, incomplete as they are in their present state, attempt to relate the course of human action to a diversity of situational factors (e.g. Argyle 1980). Action is considered as internally caused but somewhat lacking in flexibility in 'script theory' (Abelson 1976, Langer 1978), a theory which starts from the assumption that actions are

---

2  This chapter is based on work done within a research project supported by the *Schweizerisch* *Nationalfonds*. Vincent Brunner, Katrin Indermühle, Urs Kalbermatten, Elfi Mächler and Ver Steiner have all contributed to our work. We also wish to thank the students participatin in our 'Working group on action' for their many helpful suggestions.

3  Detailed information can be found in von Cranach (1982a, b); von Cranach & Kalbermatten (1982); von Cranach *et al.* (1980); Kalbermatten & von Cranach (1981, 1982).

directed by learned and fairly solid 'scripts' or plans. The 'role–rule model' (Harré 1972, 1974) stresses the social nature of plans which are acquired through experience. The so-called theories of 'regulation of action' (Hacker 1973/78; Miller, Galanter & Pribram 1960; Tomaszewski 1978) refer to the sequential and hierarchical aspects of action, which they interpret in terms of information-processing. These theories are closely related to contemporary cognitive psychology and the psychology of memory, and also to research on so-called 'artificial intelligence' (cf., e.g., Aebli 1980). A special position is held by 'value-expectation' theories (Heckhausen 1982; Lewin 1938), which are primarily interested in the role of motivation in the release of action as the 'point of change of direction in the course of action' (Heckhausen 1982).

It is evident that all these points of view are important. Real action is obviously an active accomplishment which also presupposes and includes reactions to situations. Actions depend in part upon pre-established plans, but at the same time they are continually developed and adjusted to take account of social circumstances. And who can doubt that they arise from motives and are accompanied by emotions? The problem is that a theory must be developed which can take into account, or at least allow for, many diverse influences and processes, and which at the same time can be sufficiently articulated as to ensure a transition to empirical research. Modern psychological theories also aim at prediction; but this is a criterion which we cannot satisfy in view of the complex and diverse aspirations to which claim has been laid above. In addition, we still know far too little about action. This is why the aim of our theory is to construct an open system which can become as precise and empirically useful as possible in its concepts and statements, and which will also leave room for further expansion.

To come to the outlines. At the core of the theory is a postulate which already contains its social psychological implications.

**1.1. The theorem of action.** In action, manifest behaviour is guided by cognitions which are, in part, conscious, and which are, in part, of social origin; so that society[4] generates and controls the action of its individual members through their cognitions, while at the same time those individuals, through their actions, create the societal structures. All this happens in the framework of a social and material environment, mediated, once again, through individual cognitions of social origin which influence all other contributing factors; all individuals are each other's environment.

Thus, information-processing and control are at the core of the theory. Four

4 We use the term 'society' almost as a shorthand, to denote all the social systems and sub-systems which affect at a given time the actions of individuals.

fundamental directions of influence are to be distinguished (the feedback from individual cognitions to social meaning is not considered here):

(1)   from 'social meaning' to individual and partly conscious cognition;
(2)   from individual cognition to (individual) manifest behaviour;
(3)   feedback from manifest behaviour to cognition;
(4)   influence of environmental factors on all these components of the system.

Consequently, the action theorem links the theory with all three categories of notions, mentioned above, which are concerned with *manifest behaviour*, (partly) *conscious cognition* and *social meanings*, respectively. They include altogether approximately 50 constructs, which are linked with each other conceptually as well as empirically. The most important constituent parts of the theory are as set out in (i)–(vi), below.

(i) *The definition of action.* Action designates the behaviour of the person performing the action (an actor[5]), which is consciously goal-directed, planned and intentional, socially directed and controlled.

(ii) *Two-dimensional organizations.* In action, behaviour is organized along two dimensions: sequence and hierarchy. The sequential organization concerns the temporal ordering of the constituent units of behaviour, that is the course of an action, which is analysed with the help of such constructs as starting-point, end-point, a step in an action, node, network, etc. The hierarchical organization concerns the pattern of super- and sub-ordination: units of higher order differ from units of lower order with regard to their range, function and quality. In parallel with these differences, we distinguish between different levels of organization.

(iii) *Cognitive steering and control.* This is a result of specific cognitive processes which are described in concepts such as the search and input of information, goal, plan, strategy, decision, etc. Feedback loops which function as parts of feed-forward processes[6] combine the various levels of cognitive functioning. These levels of cognitive organization are, in general, represented to varying extents in consciousness.

The two-dimensional structure of action is therefore based upon a two-dimensional organization of the flow of information.

(iv) *Conscious representation and the processes of attention.* A classification of the levels of consciousness has been developed in order to characterize the concept of conscious representation. We assume that conscious cognitions represent a higher order of information-processing since they have the

5 An actor is a person who has at his or her disposal self-cognitions related to action (such as identity, autonomy, competence) and who (as a rule) is made responsible by society for his or her actions.
6 Feedback loops evaluate existing states in relation to previous representations; feed-forward processes compare existing states with future ones.

properties of selectivity, reflexivity and symbolic representation which fulfil special functions in the regulation and control of action. To a lesser extent this is also true of subconscious cognitions. We also assume that cognitions become conscious through the operation of attentional processes. The attention theorem ('The attention of an actor is directed wherever it is needed or stimulated in the context of the action.') provides a basis for predictions as to which of the cognitions linked to action will become conscious.

(v) *Emotions and affects, motives and volitional processes.* These will be described with the help of constructs such as emotion, resolution and effort. They influence the processes of attention, generally determine the direction of the cognitive steering of action, and serve as the energizing foundation of its execution.

(vi) *Social steering and control* are exerted via the actors' cognitions, which themselves, in turn, direct and instruct action. This is referred to more precisely in three theorems, concerned respectively with convention, attribution and retroaction. The cognitive processes which are derived from these theorems are represented with the help of constructs such as knowledge, convention, rule, norm and value. Action attitudes (as distinct from judgment attitudes) are cognitive processes in which a value is introduced as a criterion for decisions about the existing alternatives for action.

## 2. Individual action rests upon a social foundation

We start from the principle that cognitions guide action; many of the important cognitions are conscious and can therefore be reported by the actor. These conscious cognitions form a significant part of the great information-processing system, which is important here because of the function it fulfils in guiding action. Many properties of manifest behaviour, for example its sequential-hierarchical structure, can be derived from the cognitive processes on which they are based (cf. Volpert 1982).

We have made the assumption that cognitive processes are of social origin and that their form and content can be conceived as being based on social factors. The sections which follow are devoted to these issues.

**2.1. Action requires conscious representations; consciousness is of social origin.** We consider human consciousness to be a self-monitoring system which differs from other aspects of the cognitive system through its properties of selectivity, reflexion and abstraction (cf. von Cranach 1982a, b). Under what conditions is consciousness generated? As in any analysis of a course of development, its phylogenetic, historical, ontogenetic and organizational aspects can be separately identified as constituting the actual processes which determine the course taken by a given specific action. The first three of these processes will be discussed in this section.

*2.1.1. Phylogenetic and historical development.* Statements about phylogenetic and historical development of consciousness cannot but remain speculative. Two of the many attempts to clarify them will be emphasized here: the ethological and the Marxist perspectives. For example, Lorenz (1973), starting from ethological conceptions, saw the origin of consciousness as resulting from a co-ordination between certain of its characteristic features and the social conditions in which they operated. As our ancestors used their hands for grasping when they were climbing, they achieved a high level of space perception and a considerable development of voluntary movements. The fact that objects which were grasped were most often manipulated within the field of vision also turned out to be advantageous:

In the moment when our ancestor recognized for the first time his grasping hand and the object it grasped as features of the real outside world, and understood their mutual effects, his understanding of the process of grasping became comprehension, and his knowledge about certain features of the thing which he grasped developed into a concept. (Lorenz 1973: 203)

Further development can be understood (p. 230):

from the assumption that the highly organized communal social life enabled the sudden emergence not only of the integration of cognitive achievements but also of conceptual thinking together with syntactic language and cumulative tradition.[7]

Within psychology, fundamental conceptions concerning the phylogenetic and historical aspects of development have been mainly worked out by the Marxist psychology of action (*Tätigkeitspsychologie*). The phylogenetic origins are seen in socially organized work activities. Action plays a special role in this development:

The beginning of the history of mankind signifies a step in development which is qualitatively new, as it is fundamentally different from the previous biological developments of modes of life. New forms of social existence also engender new forms of the psyche which are fundamentally different from those found in animals: human consciousness is generated. (Rubinstein 1977: 173)

In work activity which is designed to produce an object rather than to satisfy directly a need, there is, on the one hand, the object which represents the aim of action, and on the other, the drive or incentive. The latter ceases to operate as a direct spring of

7 Lorenz uses in German the term *fulgurisation*. This is, in the quotation provided by von Cranach & Valach, 'the sudden emergence of new system characteristics' (Lorenz 1973: 48) [Translator's note].

action. The relationship between the subject and the environment is gradually unfolded from this combination of object and drive. In order to satisfy their personal needs, the human individuals must adopt their social needs as direct aims of their actions. In this way, the goals of human activity become separated from needs. It is only through activity that needs can be represented as such in consciousness. Human activity becomes *conscious* activity. Human *consciousness* is expressed in the unfolding of activity, both in the *reflection* of the independent object and in the relationship to it of the subject. (Rubinstein 1977: 196)

The origin of consciousness is closely bound up with the development of language.

The genesis of consciousness requires language with which it is formed simultaneously in the activities of work... Individual human consciousness... presupposes the existence of social consciousness. Consciousness is, as it were, a reflection of reality seen through the prism of socially created word meanings, representations and concepts. (Leontiev 1977: 214)

In many ways, the views of Lorenz, Rubinstein and Leontiev are very similar.

*2.1.2. Ontogenetic development.* In this field, we are on firmer ground than in the previous section, since some empirical work is available (cf. Lunzer 1981); but even here, there is but a narrow basis from which inferences can be made. Therefore, the few empirical findings must be generalized in their interpretation and finally brought together in a somewhat risky synthesis.

A start can be made with the work of Bruner and his collaborators. Studies based on naturalistic observation have shown how mothers transmit to small children the *schemata of action* through play and daily social intercourse. Several strategies can be identified here: 'modelling', the indication of new action possibilities ('cueing'), the guaranteeing of provision of help ('scaffolding'), the continual setting of higher aims ('raising the ante'), and finally, when the child can already master the activity, verbal instruction.

The conclusion to which I am forced is that the mother is operating as if the child had intentions in mind, as if he were trying to deploy means to its realization, as if he were out to correct errors, as if he had a finished task in mind – but that he is not quite able to put it all together in a fashion to suit him or his mother. She imposes regularity on the task, takes account of his channel capacity for information processing, and keeps him activated by managing to keep full affectance just out of reach. I can come to one of two conclusions. Either the mother is a victim of common sense and does not really understand action, else she would put her charge into a Skinner box and devise a schedule of reinforcement for her operant responses. Or she is behaving appropriately toward an immature member of the species who does in fact operate along the lines of intentional action I originally proposed. (Bruner 1982)

Thus, action develops from interaction. Directly converging with these views is one of the basic concepts of the Geneva school which has always been stressed by Piaget and his students: consciousness develops from action.[8] Two studies will be singled out here as examples. In their investigation of the development of images, Piaget & Inhelder (1966) concluded from a number of studies that images are formed in the course of interaction through imitation. Imitation is, of course, based on perception: it is a representation of the model in action and in its presence. The transition from perception to image is achieved through the interiorization of this representation. One can distinguish between various types of images, some of which correspond to our 'cognitions which guide action'. From the point of view of the psychology of action, it is most interesting and enlightening to see that anticipatory images which are of the type of 'produits des résultats' – i.e. goals in the terminology adopted here – are formed significantly earlier than the 'anticipation des modifications (des processus)', i.e. plans and strategies in our use of the terms; goals are the essential aspect of action.

In a later monograph, Piaget (1974) described how certain cognitive processes become conscious ('prise de conscience'). Starting from the general hypothesis

que la prise de conscience est fonction des réglages actifs comportant des choix plus ou moins intentionnels, et non pas des régulations sensori-motrices plus ou moins automatiques (p. 11)

Piaget refers to a large number of related studies conducted by his students which lead to the following general conclusion:

la loi générale qui semble résulter des faits étudiés est que la prise de conscience procède de la périphérie au centre, si l'on définit ces termes en fonction du parcours d'un comportement donné. (p. 263)

If one attempts a concluding synthesis, the following could be maintained: action is developed and brought to completion in interaction; consciousness develops from, and in, action. This clearly converges with the previously discussed phylogenetic and historical considerations.

### 3. The principal contents of action-related cognitions originate in society

The concern in this section is with the notion formulated in our 'theorem of action': the social steering and control of individual actions through conscious cognitions. We differ in this from authors who assume that, prevalently, rules (Harré 1972, 1974) or scripts (Schank & Abelson 1977) regulate action. However important may be these lasting and socially founded guiding

8 Many contributions to this theme can be found in Aebli (1980).

prescriptions for action, we found in our investigations that the constantly new and (partly) conscious cognitions, adjusted in an *ad hoc* manner to the changing circumstances, remain in the foreground. In this way, we begin to define the scope of our assertions: they are mainly concerned – on methodo-logical grounds – with cognitions which accompany action and unfold during action. These cognitions are only in part parallel with action. In the case of *action-related cognitions*, distinctions can be made among cognitions which serve the functions of *steering action*, *controlling action* and *evaluating action*.

To come to our principal theme. The first and basic notion of the theorem of action can be sub-divided into three further theorems (see section 1.1, (vi)).

*The convention theorem:* members of social communities share social representations which acquire their meaning according to circumstances; these are the 'social conventions'.

*The attribution theorem:* social conventions influence the perception, exper-ience and judgment of one's own and other people's actions, as well as the definition of the situation.

*The retroaction theorem:* self-perceptions of actors, which are based on social conventions, affect in turn their own actions.

We are already in a position to provide partial empirical support for these assumptions. Further research is in progress.

**3.1. The attribution of action-related cognitions on the basis of social conventions.** This research is based upon the convention and attribution theorems.[9] All the studies consisted of two phases. In the first, naive observers were shown videotapes of concrete actions, interactive in most cases, and were asked to interpret what they saw; then these reports were analysed in terms of relevant cognitions, using the definitions adopted in our theory. Within this general scheme, there were many variations in the methods of presentation and questioning. The actions included mother–child interactions, quarrels about toys amongst children, drinking behaviour of alcoholics and the arrangement of a room.

To come to the findings: in the naive interpretations, the action-related cognitions of the actors, as well as their emotions and motives, play generally a more important role than their more permanent dispositions and personality characteristics. The action-related cognitions which, according to our theory, are important, were in fact used in the attributions, often with considerable

---

9 The findings reported here are based on the research done by some of our students (A. Ammann, Ch. Grichting and M. Herrmann, E. Mächler, F. Nüesch and L. Valach), con-ducted as part of the activities of our 'Working Group on Action'.

inter-observer agreement (up to 100%). By noting the degree of this agreement, it is possible to assess which of the attributions rely on social conventions, and which derive from idiosyncratic cognitions. The attributed constructs present a meaningful pattern in which the outlines of naive theories of action seem to be reflected. Goals are particularly important in the articulation of perceived action; moreover, hierarchies of goals are also being attributed. It is shown in several studies that the attribution of goals in interactive actions relies above all upon interactive connections. The resulting structures correspond to those which emerge when the naive observers simply attempt to provide an articulation for the stream of behaviour. Finally, attribution seems to tend towards economy and thus it manages to present actions of higher order which are as meaningful and complete as is possible in the circumstances. It is only when the observed behaviour offers no foothold allowing an ordering of this kind that the observers fall back on simple descriptions of behaviour.

In sum, we find that the important action-related cognitions are used with high agreement in the naive explanations of action. This can be considered as providing support for the convention and attribution theorems.

**3.2. The regulation of action through social conventions.** These findings relate to the retroaction theorem. The results originate in part from observational studies in which action-accompanying cognitions were inferred from conditions prevailing and remarks made at the time of the action, and also from subsequent reports. Most of the results were obtained, however, in studies which aimed at gaining a direct grasp of the action-accompanying cognitions of the actor.[10] This was done as follows: the actors were shown films of their own actions; subsequently, they were questioned about their action-accompanying cognitions in structured and partly open-ended interviews. A content analysis of the replies was made, based on the constructs of our theory.[11]

Only indirect conclusions about the theory can be reached from those replies; particularly relevant are the contexts of the action-accompanying cognitions reported by the actors. These reports contain many indications pointing to the action-related functions of the cognitions which accompany actions. It can be inferred from these reports that the hierarchical-sequential organization applies not only to the observable behaviour, but also to the cognitions themselves. When these cognitions reported by the actors are arranged according to their frequency, the resulting rank-order is very close

10 This research was done mainly in collaboration with V. Brunner, K. Indermühle, U. Kalbermatten, J. Lang, Ch. Morgenthaler, H. Müller, K. Kühne and V. Steiner.
11 For the methodology of these studies, see items in the bibliography referring to our work.

to the order of the cognitions *attributed* by the naive observers. The regulation of action is, to a large extent, affected by goals and plans; we found in one of the studies that the goals reported by the actor coincided exactly with those which were the most often attributed.

Conscious action-accompanying cognitions seem to become most evident, in accordance with our attention theorem (see 1.1, (iv)), when the organization of action encounters difficulties which need to be overcome. Thus, cognitions which regulate speech tend to become conscious in connection with mistakes in speech which can be traced back to conflicts between goals or between norms. Observational studies also show that norms and norm conflicts can affect observable behaviour even to the point of influencing the fine detail of motricity. Rules and norms are, by definition, social conventions.

Cognitions, which can likewise be conceived as being basically social conventions, exert a powerful influence upon actions, and particularly upon those individual decisions which are of special strategic significance. The function of value and knowledge in decisions must be emphasized; our findings were that decisions proceed in the form of an ordered series of individual cognitions in which knowledge and value are inserted to serve as criteria. From this perspective, attitudes are seen as a form of cognitive process (see section 4.).

All these findings cannot prove that action-related cognitions are of social origin; at most, they can establish a probability that this is the case. A direct validation of the assumptions contained in our action theorem, particularly as they concern the operation of retroaction, would require testing of the hypotheses about the connection between, on the one hand, social conventions inferred from naive interpretations and, on the other, the action-related cognitions of the actors and the observable behaviour unfolding during the action. Research on this issue is now nearing completion. In other studies we take as our point of departure the structure and function of social conventions in their form of social representations, in order to determine how they assimilate into the cognitive system of an actor ('individual social representations') and finally become translated into action.[12]

It can be said in conclusion that, although a number of findings seem to support globally the validity of the retroaction theorem, direct confirmation is still lacking. There is little doubt, however, about the validity of the assertion that 'the principal contents of action-related cognitions are of social origin'.

---

12 These studies are being conducted in collaboration with V. Aebischer, S. Moscovici, B. Thommen and Rolf Ammann.

## 4. Goal-oriented action is a fundamental concept in social psychology

The aim of this section is to show that assumptions about goal-oriented action underlie, explicitly or implicitly, many social psychological theories; and that therefore this notion can be appropriately used for the integration of various areas of social psychology which until now have remained unrelated.

Let us begin with attitudes. The question of how attitudes are manifested in behaviour has been considered until now with the help of inappropriate notions about the properties of behaviour or action respectively, and, as a result, the findings have been meagre (Meinefeld 1977; Six 1975). In one of the studies conducted by our working group, Morgenthaler (1980) found two clearly distinct and regularly occurring cognitive processes when he undertook an analysis of interviews in which his respondents had to confront their own actions. One of these types, which could be called a 'judgment attitude', appears predominantly as a reaction to the judgment of another person. As soon as a statement from someone else, most often a judgment, is perceived as having a value connotation, it becomes itself an object of judgment for the actor. This is followed by providing reasons for one's own judgment, reasons which are generally supported by the relevant knowledge. Next, the corresponding attitude is formed in the judge's mind; this contains an evaluation and it is affectively loaded. Finally comes the decision, which is the only action-relevant cognition in this sequence, whether the actor will or will not *express* his own attitude.

The second type, which can be designated an 'action attitude', appears in the course of goal-oriented action within the context of decisions which are relevant to the action. It starts with the perception, during an action sequence, of alternative courses of action (a 'node'); this is followed by processes of cognitive search, such as interpretations, attributions, etc. Then the goals and plans of action are reconsidered. As a fourth step, the choice of an appropriate decision is met, account being taken of rules, values and knowledge. Finally, a decision is taken whether to terminate the action or to carry it out. The last phase of the judgment attitude – the decision as to whether it should be expressed or not – can, to varying extents, consist of part of a fully completed action attitude.

These initial results will continue to be tested in further research. Despite the fact that they remain tentative, we shall hazard a few conclusions. In the first place, it is worth remembering that all cognitive transactions and factors must be considered as *processes*. Processes cannot be represented through one simple characteristic value, as is the case for points on attitude scales. It further appears that the traditional research probably manages to do no more than to activate, through its use of items from attitude scales, the judgment attitudes which do not relate to action and have no direct consequences for action. In our opinion, action attitudes can only be activated in situations of real action. It is no wonder, then, that Six (1975: 270) reached the following conclusion: 'It appears that, as compared with numerous concepts of set which, for many reasons, stand in urgent need of revision, we do not have at our disposal as yet a usable conception of behaviour.'

Further conclusions, however, can also be drawn in connection with the findings discussed above. The uncovering of systematic cognitive processes in decisions gives grounds for hope that it may be possible to construct a decision theory which would become less formalistic and more realistic. Even more important appears the fact that decisions in action attitudes are taken with the view of fulfilling special criteria, such as those of values, rules and knowledge. Values in particular provide a link between the theory of attitudes and the area of self-concepts (cf. Fillipp 1979).

We have introduced (see section 3) three theorems in order to clarify the effects that social cognitions have upon actions. This is not, however, sufficient. Values, rules, norms and knowledge constitute at the same time social representations. The theory of social representations[13] (Moscovici & Farr 1984) contains assumptions about the origin and function of social representations, but it also comes to the conclusion that social representations influence individual actions. It is still unknown how this happens.

Other areas also need to be mentioned. Many theories concerned with the operation of social influence (e.g. Moscovici, Mugny & van Avermaet, in press) state, explicitly or implicitly, that the aim of the sender of a message is to cause a change of behaviour on the part of the receiver of the message. We are dealing here with communicative actions inserted into a context of actions which have a larger scope; therefore, they also need to be investigated in that larger context. In the area of social perception, the hypothesis theory postulates that expectations lead to readiness to select certain perceptual categories and that, in this way, they influence perception; the goals of action are the strongest of expectations. Group psychology is concerned with group goals and group actions; but until now these collective actions have not been investigated in detail. The analysis of so-called 'pro-social behaviour' starts from an implicit assumption about goal-oriented actions. The relationship between the psychology of action and research on attribution has already been discussed above. Recent research on socialization lays great stress upon the acquisition of action competence (Bruner 1982; Eckensberger & Silbereisen

13 The linking of this theory with the theory of action is the aim of a joint research project which has been planned together with Moscovici.

1980; Waller 1978). In brief, it is difficult to find almost any area of social psychology to which the concept of action is not directly relevant.

## 5. Conclusions

We have tried to show in this chapter why the psychology of action must be considered as a core area of social psychology.

(i)   Action requires conscious representations, and this consciousness is of social origin;

(ii)   the contexts of the important cognitions which guide action stem from society;

(iii)   action is (implicitly or explicitly) a fundamental category of social psychology.

## References

Abelson, R. P. 1976. Script processing in attitude formation and decision making. In J. S. Carroll & J. W. Payne (eds.) *Cognition and social behaviour*. Hillsdale, NJ: Erlbaum.

Aebli, H. 1980. *Denken: das Ordnen des Tuns*. vol. 1. *Kognitive Aspekte der Handlungstheorie*. Stuttgart: Klett-Cotta.

Argyle, M. 1980. The analysis of social situations. In M. Brenner (ed.) *The structure of action*. Oxford: Blackwell.

Bruner, J. 1982. The organization of actions and the nature of adult–infant transaction. In M. von Cranach & R. Harré (eds.) *The analysis of action: recent theoretical and empirical advances*. Cambridge: Cambridge University Press.

Eckensberger, L. H. & Silbereisen, R. K. 1980. *Entwicklung sozialer Kognitionen*. Stuttgart: Klett-Cotta.

Fillipp, S. H. 1979. *Selbstkonzept-Forschung*. Stuttgart: Klett-Cotta.

Hacker, W. 1973/78. *Allgemeine Arbeits- und Ingenieurpsychologie*. Berlin: Deutscher Verlag der Wissenschaften; Bern: Huber, 2nd edn, 1978.

Harré, R. 1972. The analysis of episodes. In J. Israel & H. Tajfel (eds.) *The context of social psychology: a critical assessment*. European Monographs in Social Psychology, No. 2. London: Academic Press.

   1974. Some remarks on 'rule' as a scientific concept. In T. Mischel (ed.) *Understanding other persons*. Oxford: Blackwell.

Heckhausen, H. 1982. Models of motivation: progressive unfolding and unremedied deficiencies. In W. Hacker, W. Volpert & M. von Cranach (eds.) *Cognitive and motivational aspects of action*. Amsterdam: North Holland.

Kalbermatten, U. & Von Cranach, M. 1981. Hierarchisch organisierte Beobachtungs-systeme zur Handlungsanalyse. In P. Winkler (ed.) *Methoden zur Analyse von face-to-face Situationen*. Stuttgart: Metzler.

   1982. Attribution of action-related cognitions. Paper presented at the XXII International Psychological Congress, Leipzig.

Langer, E. J. 1978. Rethinking the role of thought in social interaction. In J. H. Harvey, W. Ickes & R. F. Kidd (eds.) *New directions in attribution research*. Hillsdale, NJ: Erlbaum.

Leontiev, A. N. 1977. *Tätigkeit, Bewusstsein, Persönlichkeit.* Stuttgart: Klett-Cotta.

Lewin, K. 1938. *The conceptual representation and the measurement of psychological forces.* Durham, NC: Duke University Press.

Lorenz, K. 1973. *Die Rückseite des Spiegels.* München: Piper.

Lunzer, E. A. 1981. The development of consciousness. In G. Underwood & R. Stevens (eds.) *Aspects of consciousness.*

Meinefeld, W. 1977. *Einstellung und soziales Handeln.* Hamburg: Rowohlt.

Miller, G. A., Galanter, E. & Pribram, K. H. 1960. *Plans and the structure of behaviour.* New York: Holt.

Morgenthaler, Ch. 1980. Handlungsbegleitende Kognitionen. Unpublished doctoral Dissertation, University of Berne.

Moscovici, S. 1981. On social representations. In J. P. Forgas (ed.) *Social cognition.* London: Academic Press.

Moscovici, S. & Farr, R. M. (eds.) 1984. *Social representations.* Cambridge: Cambridge University Press.

Moscovici, S., Mugny, G. & van Avermaet, E. (eds.) in press. *Perspectives on minority influence.* Cambridge: Cambridge University Press/Éditions de la Maison des Sciences de l'Homme.

Piaget, J. 1974. *La prise de conscience.* Paris: Presses Universitaires de France.

Piaget, J. & Inhelder, B. 1966. *L'image mentale chez l'enfant.* Paris: Presses Universitaires de France.

Rubinstein, S. L. 1977. *Grundlagen der allgemeinen Psychologie.* Berlin: Volk und Wissen.

Schank, R. C. & Abelson, R. P. 1977. *Scripts, plans, goals and understanding.* Hillsdale, NJ: Erlbaum.

Six, B. 1975. Die Relation von Einstellung und Verhalten. *Zeitschrift für Sozialpsychologie,* 6 (4), 270–94.

Tomaszewski, T. 1978. *Tätigkeit und Bewusstsein: Beiträge zur einführung in die polnische Tätigkeitspsychologie.* Weinheim und Basel: Beltz.

Volpert, W. 1982. The model of hierarchic-sequential organization of action. In W. Hacker, W. Volpert & M. von Cranach (eds.) *Cognitive and motivational aspects of action.*

Von Cranach, M. 1982a. The psychological study of goal-directed action: basic issues. In M. von Cranach & R. Harré (eds.) *The analysis of action: recent theoretical and empirical advances.*

1982b. The organization of goal-directed action: a research report. In M. Brenner & M. von Cranach (eds.) *Discovery strategies in the psychology of action.* London: Academic Press.

Von Cranach, M. & Kalbermatten, U. 1982. Ordinary interactive action: theory, methods and some empirical findings. In M. von Cranach & R. Harré (eds.) *The analysis of action: recent theoretical and empirical advances.*

Von Cranach, M., Kalbermatten, U., Indermühle, K. & Gugler, B. 1980. *Zielgerichtetes Handeln.* Bern: Huber.

Waller, M. 1978. *Soziales Lernen und Interaktionskompetenz.* Stuttgart: Klett-Cotta.

# 15. Social rules and social rituals

ROM HARRÉ

Common observation suggests that social life is full of *rituals*, some minute, some grand, some insignificant, some fraught with long-term consequences for the participants. Performing rituals often involves, at least for novices, the following of *rules*. It seems natural to treat these as correlative notions. How can these commonsense notions be worked into a scientific analysis of certain features of social interaction? And if successfully worked in, what do they imply about the nature of that interaction and the relation of individuals to it?

I want to show (i) that of all possible concepts available to a social psychologist, 'ritual' and 'rule' fit most easily into a theory fulfilling the general prescriptions for a scientific approach to a field of social phenomena, as that approach has developed in the natural sciences; (ii) that the success of the use of these concepts offers a very direct illustration of the way social representations, rather than individual cognitions, provide the deepest explanatory level for an understanding of social action.

To make clear how the scientific versions of the commonsense concepts of rule and ritual have been developed for the purposes of my own research, it is essential to begin with a preliminary exposition of the multiple role of models and analogues in developing a scientific account of a phenomenon. Commonsense understandings can be, indeed must be, the ultimate sources of scientific concepts, but the scientific version of a concept is usually developed as an analogue of the basic commonsense notion. The structure of such analogies must be carefully, even painstakingly, spelled out.

In general, a scientific theory is related to its subject matter through three analogy relations; the commonsense source(s) serving to provide models (concrete analogues) for three distinctive theoretical activities.

1. The analysis of experience: patterns in observable phenomena are not given, they are extracted from experience. In general, the extraction is controlled by an analytical model. For instance, Darwin used the commonsense concept of 'the family' as an analytical model for organizing and abstracting

certain patterns of relationships from the world of plants and animals as he had experienced it. He picked descent relationships as central, out of all the relationships that could have been identified in the organic world. Descent chains were not literally 'families' in the sense that the Darwins and the Wedgwoods were families, but were in certain respects *like* them, and in others unlike.

2. The explanation of abstracted patterns: in general, the productive processes that engender observable patterns cannot be observed by the same kind of empirical techniques that reveal the patterns. Something has to be *imagined*, a productive process that would engender patterns sufficiently similar to those actually observed, with the help of the analytical models necessary to abstract them from a complex reality. This 'something', the explanatory model, is constructed to *behave* analogously to the way the real but unobservable productive 'mechanisms' behave. Molecules, as imagined by Clausius and Maxwell, behave so as to produce, *en masse*, patterns of behaviour very similar to those gases can be made to exhibit, patterns which are produced by happenings in the unknown inner constitution of gases.

3. The maintenance of plausibility: explanatory models, analogues of the unobservable real productive entities, must be developed under some sort of *constraint*, to ensure their plausibility. This constraint is exercised through a source model to which the explanatory model bears some degree of material analogy – thus molecules were thought to be quite *like*, but not wholly like, ordinary Newtonian material things, and are imagined to obey very similar laws.

In ethogenic psychology, the commonsense concepts of 'ritual' and 'rule' function as progenitors of scientifically powerful models which involve closely analogous concepts, which I shall write as '*ritual*' and '*rule*'. The scientific concepts are constructed by analogy within three types of contexts I have identified in the physical sciences – analysis, explanation and plausibility control.

## 1. Social 'ritual'

The scientific concept of *ritual* can be seen to be functioning relative to the scheme I have outlined in the introduction, in two quite distinct ways, depending on whether it is being used in the formulation of psychological or sociological hypotheses.

**1.1. Psychological application.** The idea of a social *ritual* as a concept for analysing social activity relative to our psychological interests has an immediate application as an analytical model. By looking for analogues of social rituals in the activities of everyday life, we, as observers, are enabled to tease out of undifferentiated social reality certain processes, features, structured sequences of events, social outcomes, social meanings, etc., which we would not otherwise readily observe as integrated wholes. When should we use this concept? A test for the propriety of applying the notion of a *ritual* as an analytical model can be reduced to three criteria, as defined below.

(i) A social activity is like a ritual if there is a conventional relation between the performance of a sequence of social actions and some social consequences or effect which the performance of that sequence brings about. For example, the performance of the sequence of actions – 'presentation of candidate by college dean' – 'recital of ritual formula beginning *"Insignissime Vice-cancellarie..."'* – 'acceptance of candidate by Vice-Chancellor' – 'recital by him of admission formula beginning *"Ego admitto te ad gradum..."'* – 'change in the status of a member of Oxford University', leads, by convention, to a He or She who *was* a Bachelor, being now and *from henceforth* a Master of Arts. The conventional relation between action and upshot should be seen in contrast to a natural relationship. In a natural relationship actions have upshots or effects via the operation of some causal mechanism, whose behaviour can be described in a causal law. For example, the death of an individual is brought about by the action of sticking a knife in an appropriate place. The relationship between the actions involved in an assassination and the effect of those actions, the death, is mediated by a natural process. But rules and conventions begin to enter in when deaths are considered as part of a social process and interpreted as acts. It is a matter of convention whether a particular killing should be called an act of assassination rather than, say, an act of manslaughter.

(ii) A sequence of actions interpreted as acts is like a ritual if the actions *must* be repeated in the same form, in the same order, on every occasion of use in order to have their conventional effect: a structural analysis will be needed to identify what counts as the rite, i.e. sequence of actions, with which the ritual, i.e. sequence of acts, is performed. Henceforth I shall take the rite and the *ritual* together as an act–action sequence.

(iii) A structured sequence of act–actions is like a ritual if it is possible to partition the whole into action-units whose meaning as acts can be seen to contribute to the meaning of the whole. Meaningful act–action-units need not necessarily be contributions by single individuals, though they may be on certain occasions. The rite, as a sequence of actions, is defined and identified by reference to the *ritual*, the action-sequence seen as meaningful, i.e. as acts, which is itself identified in terms of the social upshots of the correct performance of the ritual.

An immediate consequence of (iii) is that the *social* nature of the act–action sequence, in particular its social upshot, must be known prior to analysis. The three criteria above derive from the analysis of events which are literally rituals. Since literal rituals function as analogues in each of the contexts (analysis, explanation and maintenance of plausibility) that I have identified above, we must examine the literal concept of a ritual more closely. So a catalogue of the essential elements, however identified, without reference to the social force of the component actions and the social upshot of the whole event, would be entirely worthless.

In the kind of cases with which I propose to begin, there is no question of any problem of subjective interpretation or misinterpretation on the part of the actors. Social rituals of the most formal kind provide us with the analytical basis, i.e. they *are* the analytical models upon which are based the analyses such as that which I have sketched above. The component parts of the Oxford degree ceremony do not have to be discovered by some empirical procedure. They are laid down in advance in the statutes which define the ceremonial aspects of the degree giving. Such and such bowings, sayings, walkings and touchings, are specified as the rite, and so defined as constitutive of the ritual. Their order of sequence is controlled by regulative rules which lay down which should occur first, which should follow, and so on. There is no place for an empirical investigation to decide how to partition that fragment of social reality which occurs in the Sheldonian Theatre of Oxford University three times each term. It is given. Furthermore, it is given in terms of assigned meanings. A pamphlet is provided for the graduands, which offers a definitive *a priori* interpretation of those meanings according to a scheme which includes both historical and contemporary references. Each part of the ceremony is shown to contribute something towards the total meaning of the events in question.

When we use such a ceremony as an analytical model for bringing out features, say of the actions and acts required to introduce a stranger to a host, indeed in any application of an analytical model to social reality, it is essential to grasp that nothing has been explained by the use of the idea of a ritual or ceremonial, with the correlative notions of constitutive and regulative rules. The effect of applying this model has been to force an opaque social reality to reveal a structure. It is like staining a cell for microscopical examination. Choosing a particular stain will bring out certain structures, while others remain unnoticed. One has no option but to choose to see a degree ceremony in accordance with the views of the university. But one should notice that even the literal use of the concept serves to obscure some of what went on in the episode in question. For instance, nothing of the emotional flux that is affecting graduands, deans, Vice-Chancellor and Proctors, parents, university marshals and the like can be picked out with this analytical model. The pattern of emotions is a researchable reality, but it cannot be identified from out of the complex social reality by the use of the concept of social ritual. To study the emotional flux another analytical model would be required.

To illustrate the analytical use of the concept of ritual I have taken a case where it is literally true that the event we are studying is a ritual. When we apply the notion of a social ritual to the analysis of other, more mysterious forms of social reality, let us say to the behaviour of football fans at matches, the issue of whether or not there is *really* a ritual embedded within those actions cannot be answered directly and simply. The use of the idea of ritual is analogical, metaphorical and analytical. It is being applied to a complex and mysterious social reality in order to see whether by using it certain features can be made to stand out, exposing a limited structure, having certain conventional effects. But in analysing 'aggro' as if it were a ritual (Marsh, Rosser & Harré 1978), other features and effects will be concealed by the use of that particular analytical model. When the 'fights' which football fans engage in are seen in terms of the ritual *model*, that is, as analogous to rituals, this draws attention to certain features of those fights which are analogous to features of formal ceremonies, such as the Oxford graduation ceremony. Referring to the three criteria above, i.e. that there should be a conventional upshot, that there should be a structured sequence of act-bearing actions, and that these actions should be defined in terms of the ceremonial necessity itself, the fights, looked at through the lens of the analytical model, do show these features to a satisfying degree. Much that is going on in 'aggro', however, is not represented in the structure yielded by the use of this particular analytical model. But the model does bring out the conventionality of the relation between the result of a 'fight' and the change in social status achieved by the winner. It serves to highlight repeatability of the sequence of actions which go to make up the *ritual* event. Finally, the appropriateness of particular actions and the irrelevance of others to the aggro-sequence can also be empirically demonstrated by reference to the necessities of the *ritual*. In this way one can see how a model, an analogue, functioning analytically, abstracts something we might reasonably call 'data'.

**1.2. Sociological application.** I argued above that social ritual as an analytical model is peculiar to a psychological investigation. It is no help to an understanding of how a sequence of actions is produced to say that it is like a ritual. We shall have to deploy explanatory and source models to look into that matter, and I shall return to them later on. However, it is worth noticing that from a *sociological* point of view, the concept of social ritual, used analogically, does provide one with an explanatory model. It embeds football aggro, for example, in a view of society which sees the continuing maintenance of social structure and social power in terms of *rituals* which ratify, maintain and sometimes marginally modify, the social order. This could be elaborated by incorporating the explanation in a Darwinian framework. *Rituals* continue to exist which are actually effective in maintaining the social order, and only in so far as they continue to be effective are they copied and repeated generation by generation by the novices of the society. In the sociological or anthropological context, we can see that the social *ritual* notion has good explanatory power within a generally functionalist account of society. One finds this explanatory use, for instance, implicit in Mary Douglas' application of a notion of ritual to family meal-structures to *explain* the way meals are organized in British households (Douglas 1972). Meals are both nourishing and ritualistic, and by virtue of the latter they serve to reproduce and sometimes restructure the social order. This is a sociological *explanation* of meal-structures and not just a sociological analysis.

Some confusion has been engendered by this double feature of the use of ritual as a model for social action in general. To look upon events in the social world, such as marriage ceremonies, degree ceremonies and judicial proceedings, as rituals, is a literal application of the notion of ritual, because marriages, degree ceremonies and judicial proceedings are, literally, rituals. But whereas the psychological application is analytical and by itself has no explanatory force, the sociological application of the analogy is explanatory, and we would do well not to confuse the two. In social psychology the notion of a social ritual provides us with a 'staining' technique, by the use of which certain parts of the anatomy of the social world become visible at the expense of others.

## 2. Social 'rules'

In outlining the features of a social event which is literally a social ritual, I drew attention to the existence of both constitutive and regulative rules which are recorded in authoritative documents such as prayer books, statutes, etc. These rules do literally control the performance of rituals and actually ensure that their repetitions are within the permitted bounds of variation. In our understanding of events which are literally rituals we have an explanatory concept whose use is quite transparent, namely that of 'rule', both constitutive and regulative (Searle 1969). In order to bring off a ceremony, one consults the prescribed rule-book and follows the appropriate rule. The psychological phenomenon that is involved in the production of literal ceremonies and rituals is exactly that of rule-following. The rules are known, the processes conscious and psychologists might take some interest in understanding how consciousness, awareness, attention, etc. are brought to bear in controlling action and how interpretative procedures, practical syllogisms and so on, are used to identify the proper rule. This is a branch of cognitive psychology in the conscious mode. At the beginning of this chapter I discussed the *desiderata* for an investigation to count as scientific. I introduced the notion of explanatory and source models which provide the intellectual capital to create explanations in those contexts in which the generative process itself cannot be observed. For those kinds of social events where the analytical model (*ritual*) is being used analogically and the concepts (rite, role) metaphorically, the social rule notion should also be taken as an analogue. Rule-following considered literally becomes a source model. The source model is developed by showing how rules are literally used for explaining the structure of real rituals. But as an explanatory model '*rule-following*' and '*rule*' are used only analogously to the way the literal concepts 'rule-following' and 'rule' are used for explaining real rituals.

In making use of a source model to generate concepts by analogy or metaphor for formulating a theory in terms of an explanatory model, the basic methodology of science requires us to presume that the explanatory analogue is some form of representation of the unobservable real productive processes by which people produce patterns of behaviour identified by analytical models. To get the empirical force of the models we have to look closely at the analogy relations by which they are created from the literal uses. Analogy is best understood in terms of three relations between source and analogue or model:

(i)   Positive analogy: in which likenesses are catalogued;
(ii)  Negative analogy: in which unlikenesses are catalogued;
(iii) Neutral analogy: in which attributes of the source which have not yet been explored for their analogical force, are catalogued.

To study the use of an analogy is to pursue the question of the strength of the positive, negative and neutral analogy. Looking at the uses of the notion of rule and of rule-following in the explanatory model, as representing our ideas of the processes by which events analytically analogous to rituals are generated, we are clearly dealing with transformations of a concept from literal to figurative application, metaphor or simile. The distinction between metaphor and simile is rather subtle and need not detain us at this level of analysis. All that should be noted is that the application of the term 'rule' in explaining conduct which is only analogous to performing rituals is itself non-literal. To explore this aspect of the matter I shall turn to a fairly detailed example of the use of the rule notion in these non-literal contexts. *Mutatis mutandis*, the account ought to apply too to the use of the rule notion by mathematicians, grammarians and others in their understanding of, for example, how calculations are performed, how grammatical sentences are spoken, and so on. In these contexts, too, the use can hardly be literal (Shwayder 1965).

The fundamental test for whether or not to apply a rule notion, literally or indeed analogically, indeed whether to use any normative concept whatsoever in understanding the engendering of action, is to examine the treatment of error. If error is treated as an infraction and perhaps in extreme cases as punishable, then the appropriate concept to employ for understanding the regulative aspects of the production of the action, is '*rule*'. If, at the other extreme, error is treated as some kind of malfunction, then the appropriate notion is that of natural law as the description of the regular working of a natural mechanism. It may be that social practices which treat error as infractions are themselves normatively determined and are part of the process by which the workings of natural mechanisms are domesticated, so to speak, and transformed into social and, hence, normatively assessable activities of human agents. That too occurs. In human affairs there is no hard and fast line between what is the result of the working of a natural mechanism and what is action under *rule*. The efforts of practitioners of yoga to bring all kinds of processes, which are normally considered natural and treated non-normatively, under conscious control, is precisely an example of transforming the natural into the cultural and bringing it under *rule*. Digestion, heart-beat and the like, can become *rule*-governed activities rather than causal sequences to be explained in terms of natural laws. Though a powerful criterion, the treatment of error should be used only on a case-by-case basis, since which irregularities count as infractions and which as malfunctions is historically, technically and culturally conditioned. Think if you will of pregnancy.

It should also be noticed that in the metaphorical application of the notion of *rule* to create an explanatory model, concepts of motivation, intention, project, etc. are not automatically applicable at this level of analysis. The justification for using the *rule* notion, then, must turn on whether it can be shown that in a particular case error is treated as infraction. The test for that will be what sorts of statements appear in accounts relative to a socially defined form of activity. Clearly, errors which are treated as infractions are accountable, and their commission can call for justification or excuse by reference to various normative principles. Clearly, this whole procedure *must* be a function of *représentations sociales*, since accounting is, above all, an activity of the collective. But if the statements which appear in accusations and accounts (a) mention the activity and its normatively preferred alternative, and (b) have a universal necessitarian form (e.g. use modal qualifiers like 'must' or 'should'), then we are being presented, literally, with rules. The first justification, then, for saying that *rules* in the metaphorical sense are involved in the production of a social activity, is if rules in the literal sense appear in the accounting, which is related to the activity. But what do these rules express – I mean, considered psychologically? Are they anything more than *représentations sociales*?

Their presence in accounts can be looked at in two ways. First of all, they are part of the practical activity of criticizing bad performances, of drawing the attention of an actor to a failure of some sort. By citing the rule in the form of what an actor should have done, the actor is brought to see his failure as the adoption of a worse alternative than that which is required in the situation. But these practical uses of rule material in discourse depend upon everyone privy to the event agreeing that the literal rules, as cited in the discourse, do indeed express accurately the social norms of that culture relative to that particular kind of activity, i.e. are really social representations of proper action. So they must be taken to be wholly exemplary of social knowledge. As such, *inter alia*, they must be statements of social knowledge. It is under that aspect that a social psychologist can draw upon them in formulating his psychological hypotheses about the causal mechanisms or productive processes involved in the action. Since representations of social knowledge are public ways of demonstrating and exemplifying what linguists call 'competence', it is not surprising that when competence is expressed in discourse it appears in the form of rules. Rules state the conditions under which an action should occur, and what action it should be, and also establish the modality of the social imperative. They make clear whether the action as act is necessary, desirable, obligatory, and so on. As a source model rule-following is taken literally. If the genesis of social action is literally rule-following one supposes that an agent is conscious of following a rule, a rule to which he or she is actually attending in acting. Considering only an individual's contribution to collective (many-person), structured action sequence, we would look for cognitive processes like practical syllogism. It is by no means clear that one can create a performance theory by ascribing some analogue of rule-following to the actors in cases where the act–action sequence is picked out by the use of a non-literal concept of *ritual*. The kind of concepts that seem unproblematic when transferred from a literal use in the analytical stage to set up a competence theory, may be rather far from the mark when used in thinking of the means by which people act. Various suggestions have been made as to how a non-literal notion of '*rule*' might be developed for performance theories.

In thinking of the use of the concept of 'agent-following-rules' as a source model for controlling the formulation of an explanatory model of performance processes, the most natural metaphorical generalization of concepts from the source model would be to that of means and ends. In commonsense terms we would treat the actor as having an intention defining an 'end', and knowing the means to realize his intention, for instance, knowing an appropriate *rule*. Then he or she goes ahead and realizes the intention in the action specified in the *rule*. There are problems with the dynamics of this account, but the theory makes no pretence at being complete, particularly in the matter of motivation. Means–end hierarchies could be conceived as a specific application of the *rule*-following model, taken metaphorically. As a further and natural derivation from the source model, one might conceive the follower as a human being, that is, as an agent formulating intentions and searching his/her social knowledge for means of realizing them – that is, actively engaged in the construction of a means–end hierarchy. But what is the psychological status of whatever it is that is represented as a means–end hierarchy? The idea of means–end pairs as intention–*rule* pairs was derived from a source model of human functioning which implies consciousness. But our applications of these concepts as a theory of performance precludes references to consciousness since people, as a matter of fact, are not aware of following *rules*. 'Intention–*rule*' concepts in this application must be analogical. In those cases where people are acting out their social lives or practical activities in real time, it seems very unlikely that there are many cases in which they are actively and consciously following rules.

Our general methodology of science, as outlined at the beginning of this chapter, follows the physical sciences in treating the question of the plausibility of a model and its representational quality as distinct issues. The power of a means–end hierarchy as a simulacrum or model of the real process as productive of action is undeniable (von Cranach & Harré 1982). Means–end hierarchies, when imagined as guiding action, lead to activities very similar indeed to the patterns of behaviour people actually put on. The question as to representational quality of the model is more difficult, partly because there is some obscurity in the question itself.

In order for the accounts of actors to be relevant to the understanding of real-time generative processes one must have some way of relating those accounts to the action that is currently taking place – in particular to the goal-setting and means-choosing which would be involved if the means–end hierarchy were a realistic representation of a real psychic mechanism. The work done by von Cranach, Kaminsky, Hacker and others (see von Cranach & Harré 1982) suggests that the breakdown of smooth performance of a task already mastered, or the troubles encountered in learning a manual skill, are amongst the occasions under which people do consciously represent both means and ends. Linguists have noticed that during hesitation the speaker often pays explicit and conscious attention either to what he intends to say or to the means by which he intends to say it. So there is little doubt that under the conditions where a forced error or some other form of breakdown of smooth functioning occurs, as e.g. in von Cranach and Steiner's perambulator-wrapping experiment, there is conscious representation of means–end structures. This does not establish that the cognitive process, if there is such a thing, which is not being attended to when action is proceeding smoothly, has a similar structure, or indeed is properly to be described in means–end terms. My own view is that the means–end hierarchy method of representation should be treated explicitly as a model derived from the source model of conscious human functioning and assessed for its plausibility rather than its representational quality. The rules which appear in the means term in means–end hierarchies as expressed in the discourse of those engaged in the action, are then to be seen as elements in a discourse which is addressing the events in question but not necessarily describing them.

How, then, can we pass from such a model to a form of representation which does not imply any analogue of conscious functioning? In systems theory and cybernetics, we have a form of representation of means–end hierarchies, goal-setting processes, etc., which is ideally suited to stand between the use of '*rule*-in-an-explanatory-model' based on the anthropomorphic source model and whatever it is in a human being (and it might just be a physiological process) that is actually engaged in real time in producing the activity in question. What is cognitive about the cybernetic representation of physiological processes is that the structure of that cybernetic representation is produced not by reference to physiology, speculative or empirical, but by reference to the explanatory model as it appears in terms of features of the discourse with which human beings express themselves when they are consciously representing the underlying cybernetic structure. This means that in its broad outline a cybernetic model is derivative from prior *représentations sociales*. It is no part of my intention to argue that there are *rules* in *rerum natura* in the human being, so to speak, for that would be just the kind of individualistic mentalism one wishes to avoid. Legitimate mentalism includes, for example, the way people talk to themselves, the feelings that they experience and express, and so on. It need not include any speculation about hypothetical mental processes which are beyond the reach of conscious attention.

What are criteria for plausibility of an explanatory model?

(i) Either in its concrete means–end form including *rules* and intentions, or in its abstracted cybernetic form, including goal-setting and feedback, memory store and the like, the explanatory model should behave in the same way, or at any rate in a sufficiently similar way to the way real people behave in producing the patterns of action revealed by the use of the co-ordinate analytical model. The patterns, as elicited by applying the appropriate analytical model, in this case 'ritual', to the undifferentiated social reality, are the products of the activity of the processes people engage in. The hypothetical processes in the model must produce simulacra or analogues of these patterns. So if we can think of a means–end structure with the appropriate *rules* and intentions, which if it were implemented would produce patterns similar to those produced by social actors in generating *rituals* of the informal kind, then, of course, our model is so far plausible.

(ii) But plausibility also requires some kind of ontological grounding. One must be able to show that there are structures in a human being which are indeed as the explanatory model says they are. This introduces a mapping relation between the model and that which it represents, rather than between the behaviour of the model and the behaviour of what it represents, our first criterion. But this mapping relation must, in the first instance, hit 'thin air' so to speak, since we have no direct idea other than from the model itself as to what is the entity or structure in the real world which the model is simulating. But having constructed the model, we can then make some shrewd guesses as to where we might find evidence for the structure, processes and properties of that real-world 'something'. Psychological theorizing in the rule model, then, comes to an end with a cybernetic representation which is the abstract formulation of an intention–*rule*, means–end hierarchy, which is itself an analogue of the formal rule–intention means–end structure which lies behind the production of ceremonies and other consciously constructed rituals by agents knowingly following the rules, of which they are fully aware and to which they are attending.

## 3. The non-transparency of language

The point I have been making in the last section could be put another way: our cognitive processes ought not blithely to be ascribed as attributes to the individual human being who creates this discourse. Psychologists tend to treat cognitive processes individualistically, presuming that they can unproblematically infer from the properties of a discourse, say from its logical structure or its rationality, corresponding properties of the human mind that produced it. Wittgenstein (1953) pointed out long ago, and it has been reiterated recently by Coulter (1980) and others, that discourse may be the very seat of cognition. By that is meant that the kinds of property which we take as characteristically cognitive, such as mode of reasoning, structures of know- ledge and belief, and so on, may be primarily properties of the discourse and only secondarily, if at all, ascribable to individual human beings. The language may not be transparent. Now this has all kinds of different consequences in different fields. As far as this discussion is concerned, one should notice that intention–rule pairs and means–end hierarchies appear in real life as features of discourse. I have presumed that the discourse in which I am interested is wholly public. In the public discourse, accounts are offered to members of the relevant collective, accusations of moral impropriety or incompetence are rebutted, defences are proposed in advance of accusation, and so on. But, of course, human beings learn very quickly to conduct much of their discourse *sotto voce*, so to speak. I am inclined to think that it is this fact that has led to the focus of cognitive psychology on individual processes. But, if I am right, these individual processes are a kind of illusion, a trick with mirrors. To take cognitive processes as individual is to confuse the images with which individuals reflect social processes with the substantive reality, the public discourse. Talkings to oneself are framed in terms of the constraints on *public* discourse because that is, after all, the source of the material one uses in talking to oneself. A person may develop idiosyncratic features in his privatized discourse in his own time, for his own purposes. Vygotsky (1962) discovered that though the *sotto voce* discourse of young children was almost wholly intelligible in terms of public-collective vocabulary and grammar, that of older children had already taken on individualistic characters. This suggests that the original social constraints on that kind of speech are gradually supplemented by, and perhaps even in certain cases displaced by, idiosyncratic features which are the invention of the individual for him or her self.

## 4. Summary

I have argued that the use of the concepts, social rule and social ritual, provides a powerful entry to certain restricted kinds of social activity. These concepts have a literal application in social science in identifying and analysing patterns of collective behaviour, as well as in studying public documents such as etiquette books, instruction manuals, etc., on which the orderliness of collective action often depends. By introducing the idea of an analytical model, I was able to show how it is that the notion of a social ritual can be generalized beyond its explicit formal and literal application to elicit the structures of other forms of patterned co-ordinative interaction. As an analytical model, the *ritual* functions differently relative to psychological contexts where its role is purely analytical, from its use in sociological contexts where, in a functionalist sociology, its role may be explanatory. In psychological contexts the associated explanatory notion is arrived at by metaphorically transforming the concept of a rule. We saw that this leads to an analysis of action–production in terms of means–end hierarchies, but we must take great care in passing from means–end hierarchies as hypothetical referents of the discourse of humans in action to claims about productive processes 'in' individual people. If we take care to notice the non-transparency of the language of action-related discourse, we could set up a research programme to examine how far real cognitive processes are indeed reflected in the kinds of talk which people use to get themselves 'off the hook'.

## References

Coulter, J. 1980. *The social construction of mind*. London: Macmillan.

Douglas, M. 1972. Deciphering a meal. *Daedalus, Winter*.

Marsh, P., Rosser, E. & Harré, R. 1978. *The rules of disorder*. London: Routledge and Kegan Paul.

Searle, J. 1969. *Speech acts*. Cambridge: Cambridge University Press.

Shwayder, D. S. 1965. *The stratification of behaviour*. London: Routledge and Kegan Paul.

Von Cranach, M. & Harré, R. (eds.) 1982. *The analysis of action: recent theoretical and empirical advances*. Cambridge: Cambridge University Press.

Vygotsky, L. S. 1962. *Thought and language*. Cambridge, Mass.: MIT Press.

Wittgenstein, L. 1953. *Philosophical investigations*. Oxford: Blackwell.

# 16. Social differentiation and non-differentiation[1]

JEAN-PAUL CODOL

Sciences, and particularly the human and social sciences, do not develop in airtight compartments, unaffected by what happens around them. The fact that particular questions are asked at particular times is never just a matter of chance.

Experimental social psychology has been preoccupied for a long time with the *standardizing* effects on individuals of their social habitat. Whatever approaches to the study of differentiation existed were made either in terms of *deviance* or of *hierarchies* of power and influence. It is notable that in both cases the problems were defined in a general perspective of social non-differentiation. Seen in terms of its negative connotations, deviance was conceived only against a background of 'normality'; the hierarchical systems of power and leadership were envisaged in terms of their relation to the phenomena of communication and influence through which were expressed the organization of a group, its ordered functioning, its cohesion and permanence. A science, in order to be recognized as such, must prove that it is capable of establishing general laws of universal validity. Thus, discarding the particular, social psychologists strove to study and describe points of encounter, concordances, homogeneities and similarities.

The dream of unity was born in Europe, a continent exploded and torn by many wars, where in many nations the foundations of unity were still fragile or hardly established, where empires began to break up under the pressures of new forms of nationalism. This dream, which also affected social psychology, found its real expression in the United States, where the discipline was exported, found its new roots and its prodigious development. The ideology of the 'melting pot' became the crucible in which all the differences of race, class, religion and birth were to be dissolved and the new human being was to be born.

---

[1] This chapter was translated from the French by Henri Tajfel.

The way ahead appeared easy for social psychologists. The questions about the social bond found their answers in imitation and suggestion, negotiations and the establishment of consensus, acceptance of social norms and conformity, reciprocity and the equality of rights and duties, equity and equilibrium. But the dream turned out to be a chimera and, despite the long period of gestation, the new human being of the melting pot was never born. Thus, today's social psychology is beginning to ask other questions: about social deviation (which is not necessarily deviance), polarization in groups, influence of minorities, intergroup conflict, etc. For even if it is true that normalization and achievement of uniformities are characteristic of social life, it is just as true that one finds in it collective and individual expressions of claims to establish or maintain differences from others for oneself or one's group. To try to attract attention, to make oneself visible, is inherent in social life just as much as are anonymity, search for group consensus or the affirmation of similarity between oneself and others. Social psychology is now discovering that the social bond is forged not only through convergence and similarity: the establishment of differences is also a basic constituent of the processes of socialization and of the formation of social relations.

This is not a new hypothesis. Psychologists with viewpoints as diverse as Baldwin (1897), Cooley (1902), James (1909), Janet (1929), Mead (1934), Allport (1937) and Wallon (1941) have all stressed in their various ways the importance, for the creation of social bonds, of differences between oneself and others. As is often the case, these early lessons have been somewhat forgotten.

To begin with, I shall illustrate, using a few examples, the central role that the idea of similarity has been playing – and continues to play – in the explanation of a large number of social psychological phenomena. This will be followed by a description of some research which contests, in a number of ways, the model of a social psychology centred upon the achievement of uniformity. There are still not many of these studies, and some of them are not well known (see also Chapters 17, 23 and 24); but with varying success, and in their various ways, they all represent interesting attempts to account for the phenomenon of differentiation.

## 1. Similarities: the social bond and non-differentiation

It is possible to identify in social psychology two general orientations of theory and experimental research directly related to the notions of similarity and non-differentiation.

(i) The first of these is concerned with similarities of conduct, of ways of doing things, of thinking and of engaging in relations between people. The central idea is that, *in all their forms of communication, social relations inevitably lead to homogeneity, unification, the achievement of uniformities in behaviour – and consequently to objective similarity.* The relevant themes here are those of social influence and pressures towards uniformity.

(ii) In the second perspective, the same social psychological process is tackled from an opposite point of view: similarity is not considered here as a consequence of social relations but as their cause. *Individuals enter into relationships and associate with each other because they are similar (or think that they are).* In this perspective, it is not so much the degree of objective similarity between persons that matters but rather the subjective view of that similarity, which may or may not correspond to reality.

**1.1. The social bond: a determining factor in non-differentiation.** The first of these research orientations has been the subject of a great deal of theoretical and research work over a period of several decades. There has also been a substantial number of texts attempting to present a synthesis of this work.[2]

It is surprising to discover, when one reads these general reviews, that the widely accepted conception of an all-powerful social influence which, whatever the circumstances, succeeds in shaping and making uniform modes of thinking and acting, owes in fact more to myth and to observation biased by theoretical and cultural assumptions than to a serious examination of the results obtained in the innumerable studies. A global analysis of these results shows, in fact, the very considerable complexity of the variables intervening in the processes of social influence. Undoubtedly, influence exists when individuals interact; but this does not mean – far from it – that this influence always works to produce conformity. On the contrary, there exist many situations in which resistance to conformity in behaviour is much more massive than submission to it.

A group or an individual, who are members of a social entity, are not only targets of influence reaching them from elsewhere. One is always the *alter* of someone else, and always as much a *source of influence* as a recipient of it. Social life is a battlefield, in which diverse and contradictory influences permanently confront each other and where there is no such thing as a stable equilibrium of forces. It is not the case that the majorities always succeed in imposing their points of view. In a series of studies, Moscovici and his colleagues (Faucheux & Moscovici 1967; Moscovici, Lage & Naffrechoux 1969; Moscovici & Faucheux 1972; Moscovici & Nemeth 1974) were able

---

[2] See, for example, the well-informed review by de Montmollin (1977).

to show that minorities can be influential, and that they can modify the attitudes and behaviour of a majority (see Chapter 24).

Finally, and above all, social influence has been too often and too one-sidedly conceived in terms of pressures towards uniformity. The phenomena of influence can, in fact, fulfil diverse functions, take on different characteristics, and achieve different outcomes, depending upon the social contexts in which they take place. Thus, Moscovici (1976) was able to show that although uniformities of conduct undoubtedly exist in situations marked by conformity and normalization, it is just as true that there are many other influence situations in which the prevailing tendency is that of differentiation. After all, in the last resort, everyone needs some social recognition by others of his existence. Everyone wishes to be liked, chosen or respected; but to achieve this, one must be 'visible'. Social visibility requires in turn the adoption of points of view which are original, and which are maintained with constancy and vigour (see Chapter 17).

Thus, many of the results obtained in the research on social influence lead to the conclusion that both *conformity and resistance to conformity are fundamentally linked to the image of oneself that one wishes to present to others* (and undoubtedly also to oneself). In other words, if the positivity of this image depends upon a submission to the influence of another person, conformity will result. If, on the contrary, this positivity depends upon resistance to influence, there will be no conformity.

**1.2. Non-differentiation as a foundation of the social bond.** In parallel to the research orientation stressing the idea that social relations lead to uniformities of conduct and inter-individual similarity through the operation of communication and influence, other trends of work started from the opposite premise: people are generally different from each other. In this perspective, similarity was considered as the foundation of social bonds. Individuals enter into relationships and association when they discover – or assume – that they have something in common and are similar, at least in some respects.

The notion of direct relations between interpersonal similarity, a positive evaluation of others and interpersonal attraction runs like a thread through the long development of social psychology, and there is much empirical evidence for it (for a few examples, see Berkowitz 1957; Bleda 1972; Eiser & Taylor 1972; Exline 1957; Newcomb 1961; Precker 1952; see also Chapter 12 in this book).

In order to exemplify this view, some of the most influential social psychological approaches and theories in this area will be very briefly reviewed.

(i) One of the most interesting and coherent attempts to establish a link between similarity and other social psychological phenomena is due to Festinger. In his theory of social comparison (1954) he postulated that human beings have a tendency to evaluate as precisely as possible their opinions and attitudes. In the absence of objective means of assessment, comparisons with the opinions and attitudes of others serve as a basis for evaluation, which, in order to be precise, must rely on comparisons with others who are as similar as possible to oneself. As a result, *individuals will be attracted to situations and groups exhibiting opinions and attitudes which are close to their own.*

It is clear that in Festinger's theory interpersonal similarity is related to attraction for individuals or for groups as a whole. But in addition to the consequences, formulated in the theory, which these views have for the formation of groups, there are also other consequences for behaviour in collective situations and for the internal functioning of groups. *Individuals will engage in behaviour aiming to bring closer to them those with whom they are comparing themselves.* In other words, everyone tries to reduce divergences in the comparisons which he makes. Several strategies are possible here: for example, individuals may change their own position so as to be closer to others; or, conversely, they may try to influence others so as to move their position nearer to themselves, etc. This is how pressures towards uniformity work in groups. The strategy which is actually employed will, however, vary, depending on whether it is implemented by members of a group who are close to its centre or those who are at the periphery. The former will show the strongest tendencies to try and change the positions of others, relatively weaker tendencies to limit the areas of comparisons, and even weaker tendencies to modify their own positions.

It can therefore be said, from this perspective, that the direction of pressures towards uniformity is defined by the existing 'power relationships': *it is those who are the most different who must make the required effort to get closer to others.* A clearer statement could hardly be made about the links between similarity, uniformity and conformity.

Attraction and rejection, the formation of groups, communication and influence, changes in attitudes – all these can be explained within this framework by invoking the relationship between similarity and attraction. As is well known, Festinger's theory had a considerable impact in a large number of areas of social psychology.

(ii) The theory just described had very global aims and ambitions. Other, less ambitious, theories focused their efforts almost exclusively upon the relationship between similarity and attraction (although, in most of this work, this relationship is also supposed to mediate a larger area of social psychological phenomena). Some of these views originated from a background of cognitive theories, others from reinforcement theories. Amongst the former, one finds 'balance' (Heider 1946), 'symmetry' (Newcomb 1953) and 'consonance' (Festinger 1957) functioning in interpersonal systems where those who are perceived as 'similar' are also 'liked' and seen as 'agreeing', and those who are 'liked' are also perceived as 'similar' and 'in agreement'. Typical of the second kind of theory is the research of Byrne and his collaborators (e.g. Byrne 1961, 1962, 1969, 1971; Byrne & Nelson 1965; Clore & Byrne 1974). A remarkably consistent finding from these studies has been the existence of a *direct linear relationship between the proportion of attitudes similar to those held by others and the degree of attraction to them.*

(iii) There exists, however, a number of observations and results which throw doubt on the generality of the relationship between similarity and attraction.

A large majority of the studies supporting this relationship have used exclusively the similarity of attitudes or opinions. In the experiments manipulating physical similarity or similarity of personalities the results, when they appeared at all, were much weaker (e.g. Bleda 1974; Singh 1973). These exceptions are important: agreement about attitudes and opinions is undoubtedly gratifying, since it is a mark of social approval. A similarity in personalities is much less gratifying since it goes counter to one's feelings of personal singularity, uniqueness and identity. In addition, the proposition that similarity engenders attraction is probably true for some characteristics and not for others. There are cases when attraction seems more closely related to complementary than to similar characteristics of others (Jones, Bell & Aronson 1972).

Finally, a careful examination of all the research in this area shows that the *social desirability* of what is similar can explain, at least in part, the similarity–attraction relationship (Ajzen 1974; Bleda 1974; Fishbein & Ajzen 1972; Grush, Clore & Costin 1975; Lerner & Agar 1972; McLaughlin 1971; Novak & Lerner 1968; Posavac & McKillip 1973; Posavac & Pasko 1974; Stalling 1970; Taylor & Mettee 1971, etc.). In sum, *similarity appears to be linked to interpersonal attraction only so far as the consequences of this relationship are psychologically rewarding.*

As far as the dual relationship between similarity and the social bond is concerned, it appears that we are confronted here with a *general representation of social functioning* which is accepted by most of our contemporaries. Here, as in many other domains, social psychologists do not easily escape the common rule and readily accept the stereotypes inherent in the naive psychologies. But this representation is not without its significance. There does seem to exist a cognitive bias applying to the relationship between similarity and attraction. This consists of a *favourable prejudice* about those who are perceived as similar to oneself; and, as we know, there is a tendency to perceive as similar to oneself the people one likes.

The origins of this cognitive schema could be sought in the fact that another person perceived as similar to oneself represents *a priori* a safety anchor to which some degree of trust can be attached. In an experiment in which the social desirability of similarity was controlled, I was able to show that, for example, the subjects confided more, and about more intimate issues, to those strangers who appeared as relatively more similar to themselves (Codol 1979: 64–74).

## 2. Social differentiation and non-differentiation

The problem which is created by a social psychology centred upon non-differentiation is due as much to the fact that interest is shown in one only of the aspects of social life as to the general 'ideology' resulting from the limited scope of these conceptions. Seen as a foundation and a result of all social relations, similarity in modes of thinking and acting is inescapably considered as indispensable and sufficient for the establishment of a satisfactory social order. Similarity is seen as reducing anxiety, favouring positive mutual feelings amongst individuals, facilitating collective organization and the formation of groups, raising the morale of their members, increasing the efficiency of their functioning, etc. In its explicit or implicit form, this ideology pervades much of the research in social psychology and is at the centre of many theories.

There have been some authors, however, who have questioned the validity of this model, since they were interested in the processes of differentiation as well as non-differentiation.

**2.1. De-individuation.** Far from rejecting the reality of the trend towards social uniformity, there have been some researchers who have acknowledged it as a fact, and in their concern about it, they have attempted to clarify its causes and some of its harmful social and individual consequences. Research on de-individuation can be seen in this perspective (e.g. Cannavale, Scarr & Pepitone 1970; Festinger, Pepitone & Newcomb 1952; Singer, Brush & Lublin 1965; Zimbardo 1969). In brief, its conclusions were that when people cease to feel that they are perceived by others in terms of their individuality (a state referred to as de-individuation), there ensues a disinhibition of behaviour which can lead to social and psychological difficulties.[3] Individuation and social differentiation are seen in this research as counteracting the consequences – considered to be noxious – of the collective trend towards uniformity.

**2.2. The quest for individuation and singularity.** There are, however, other views in which the notion of a trend towards social uniformity is contested more directly. There is in these views no denial that such a trend exists. But at the same time attempts have been made to show that the majority of people seek individuation, that they wish to be socially visible and to achieve from others a recognition of what they see to be their own special characteristics. In this trend of research it is *individuation* which becomes the centre of interest. The principal questions are: why, in what circumstances, and how do people try to achieve their differentiation from others?

(i) Starting from this perspective, Ziller (1964) provided some elements of a theoretical model of individuation. According to him, it has been shown in many studies that individuation, far from being an obstacle to socialization, is a constituent of it. Having suggested a long list of social and organizational variables associated with individuation, Ziller put forward some general propositions. A few examples of these propositions follow.

Individuation and de-individuation are the two poles between which behaviour moves in a permanent oscillation. From this generalization, Ziller derived the hypothesis of *cyclical variations*: behaviour tending towards individuation and de-individuation is assumed to alternate in the course of everyone's life. Starting from this point, Maslach (1974) formulated subsequently an alternative hypothesis, that there is a continual search for the achievement of an equilibrium between these two poles. Again according to Ziller, it seems that, generally speaking, 'individuation is desirable when the social climate is favourable to it, but anonymity is sought as a means of defence in a threatening environment'. He also maintained that similarity between persons who are forced to be in a close personal relationship encourages opposites in modes of behaviour, so as to avoid confusions in self-perception and in the perception of oneself by observers. Other work by Maslach (1974) shows that people who had been previously de-individuated by the experimenter tended to adopt modes of behaviour which were more

---

[3] In a critical evaluation of this research (Codol 1979: 78–123), I have tried to show that the relationship between disinhibition and de-individuation is not a direct one. It seems that it is an *alteration of the cognitive functioning* which results simultaneously in de-individuation and disinhibition of behaviour. Thus, it appears that they are both determined by the same background factor and, when related to this common origin, they can both be seen as being at the same time the cause and the consequence of one another.

markedly singular than those of others who had not gone through this experience. In general, much of this work indicates the existence of *a quest for the social recognition of differences*.

(ii) Studies by Fromkin and his collaborators (1968, 1970, 1972; Snyder & Fromkin 1980) are fairly close in their conception to the work just described. They show that marked similarity, like anonymity, lack of distinctiveness or de-individuation, is a situation from which people try to escape. These studies seem, however, to demonstrate at the same time that extreme singularity is also rejected. This is shown in the finding, which was replicated in all the experiments by Fromkin, that it was impossible to induce this state of mind in the subjects. Beyond a certain threshold, difference becomes deviance, and this tends to be avoided.

(iii) Some research I conducted independently (Codol 1979: 165–200) can be interpreted as similar in its results. The aim was to establish a relationship between an individual's wish to adopt differentiating modes of behaviour and the opportunities he had in a particular situation to become singularized by his entourage. The study was done in a two-by-two design. The ease or difficulty of being socially singled out by others was one of the variables. This depended upon a combination of criteria of a personal and situational nature. (In the former case the subject was or was not objectively different in a few salient characteristics from people around him; in the latter case, he was surrounded either by a small, or by a large, number of other people.) The second variable consisted of the implementation, or its absence, of this potentiality to be singled out. In one of the situations the subject remained anonymous; in the other he was noticed by those who were present and thus made 'visible' to all of them. The results, derived from questionnaire measures, clearly showed that in situations in which the subjects were *difficult to single out and not effectively noticed* and in those in which they were easy to single out *and were consequently noticed*, their wish to be differentiated was stronger than in the two other situations.[4]

Although other explanations are possible,[5] these data can be simply interpreted in terms of psychological 'comfort': *the search for differentiation appears to be stronger in situations which are 'comfortable'*. The experience of being noticed when one is easily noticeable, and of not being so when this is difficult, may appear as habitual, expected and coherent. This is obviously not the case in the other two situations. Why should one remain anonymous

---

[4] On an index of which the maximal value was 100, the mean figure for the first two conditions was 80, and about 50 for the two other conditions.
[5] Another explanation might be that when a person is not taken notice of, he will try to draw attention to himself; if he is, he will try to justify it.

when one knows that one can easily be noticed? And why should one be the object of everyone's attention for reasons one ignores when one should have remained unnoticed? In this case visibility may appear as compromising and fraught with insecurity. It is understandable that, in such cases, the tendency will be to become less visible, to get lost in the crowd. Therefore, the quest for visibility has its limits despite the wish to have the others recognize one's differences from them.

(iv) In situations which appear threatening, other forms of differentiation are possible. This is shown in the research by Lemaine and his collaborators on the subject of 'avoidance of comparability' (Jamous & Lemaine 1962; Lemaine 1966, 1974; Lemaine & Kastersztein 1972; Lemaine, Kastersztein & Personnaz 1978; Lemaine, Matalon & Provansal 1969; Personnaz, Kastersztein & Lemaine 1977).

According to Lemaine's observations, agents who find themselves in a position of inferiority can adopt one of two modes of behaviour, depending upon the perceived importance of their inferiority. If the handicap is not insurmountable, they will engage in competition without attempting a differentiation from others; the effect will be to catch up, or get ahead if possible. If the handicap appears to be serious, the attempt at differentiation from the competitors will take the form of trying to become non-comparable. Three different strategies for such avoidance of comparability are then possible: simply to abandon the competition; to reject comparisons with others and, using a temporal perspective, to confine comparisons to oneself ('I am doing better now than I used to'); or finally, to introduce criteria for evaluation which are different from those currently serving as a basis for comparisons.

It is this last strategy which was the main subject of the research done by Lemaine and his colleagues (see Chapter 17 for a description by Lemaine of research based on these views, as it applies to competition for priority and recognition amongst scientists). They have shown in field observations and laboratory studies that when competition and handicap go together, the resulting behaviour is not confined to the usual attempts at catching up. People who find themselves in a position of inferiority begin to invoke criteria which are different from those used by their competitors. They change the rules of the game and introduce new modes of evaluation.

Lemaine's research originated in his interest in the processes of competition. It must be stressed, however, that as his empirical work developed it became progressively clearer that competition in the strict sense of the term (i.e. the efforts made by several agents to obtain a single reward) is by no means a necessary condition for the appearance of behaviour aiming at the avoidance of comparability. The experiments reported by Lemaine & Kastersztein (1972) and by Personnaz, Kastersztein & Lemaine (1977) show quite clearly that when no more than just *comparison* between two agents is involved, and as soon as this appears unfavourable from the point of view of one of the agents, avoidance of comparability can be observed in the ensuing behaviour. This can happen even when the comparison is not explicitly declared, or when it does not lead to the establishment of a socially acknowledged hierarchy. Even when no rewards or social recognition are involved, it is enough that the comparison be subjectively real for the person who sees his position as unfavourable for the avoidance of comparability to make its appearance in behaviour.

As is the case for all instances of the quest for social differentiation, modes of behaviour aiming at the avoidance of comparability are related here to the risk, as perceived by individuals or groups, of seeing their image devalued in their own eyes and in the eyes of others. These modes of behaviour can thus be interpreted as constituting a search for conditions which would allow for a positive *social re-evaluation*.

**2.3. Assertion of difference and acceptance of similarity.** To summarize so far: the studies described above show the existence – in appropriate conditions – of differentiating modes of behaviour. According to circumstances, this behaviour may take various forms, such as the quest for social visibility and the search for non-comparability. Two situations are particularly important here: when the individual feels that his uniqueness is under threat; and when this uniqueness is socially recognized and it is felt that it needs to be justified.

But this quest for differentiation is neither blind nor limitless. Situations, such as those described above, in which visibility entails a variety of risks for the maintenance of a positive self-image, produce a search for non-differentiation. It can thus be said that *differentiation is sought for its own sake* (because a feeling of uniqueness is central to the self-image), *while modes of behaviour aiming at the achievement of non-differentiation are only adopted in situations in which they help to avoid psychological discomfort.*

Ziller's (1964) hypothesis, according to which individuation is a state sought after in a supportive climate while a threatening environment determines a search for anonymity, seems based on a well-founded intuition: there exists a dissymmetry between the search for differences and the search for similarities. The former is essential for the definition and social expression of the self; the latter appears to be no more than a protective strategy. This assertion is based not only on a detailed examination of research results. It also finds a good deal of support in the freely expressed statements of the subjects on the theme of their resemblances to, and differences from, other people.

For example, a content analysis of open-ended questionnaires concerned with these themes (conducted by a 'judge' who was ignorant of the aims of the research) showed (Codol 1979: 241–4) that nearly all of the subjects' responses envisaged the search for similarity as a means of defence against a threat. This included: not to be noticed too much; not to be perceived by others as marginal; to avoid responsibility; to contribute to the cohesion of a group and show solidarity in the face of a threat from the outside – as in conflicts, strikes, competing teams in games, etc. In contrast, when the search for differences is involved, the responses mainly demonstrate the wish to be able to express oneself as a person and to achieve a positive evaluation of oneself in the eyes of others. Examples of such responses were: because one does not like to be or act like everybody else; to become visible in the eyes of people one likes; to distinguish oneself from people one dislikes; to achieve personal success; to defend one's views; to prove something to oneself, etc.

*2.3.1. Sensitivity to the theme of differences.* There is no doubt that the search for differences is more highly valued in our culture than the search for similarities, and that people are highly sensitive about the issue of their differences from others. Psychologists who are familiar with questionnaires concerned with self-descriptions know that claims of the individuals' differences from others and their singularity are expressed very frequently, while it is exceptional to find people claiming that they are similar to others. It is also the case that respondents stress much more, and at greater length, their personal differences from others than their similarities to them (Codol 1979).

This is reflected in the linguistic forms of the pronouncements on the subject. In one study (Codol 1981), a preliminary questionnaire was administered and the subjects were divided into two groups according to its results. One of the groups consisted of those who showed themselves to be more sensitive to their differences from others (and who were, by far, the majority); the subjects in the second group were more sensitive to their similarities to others. Our interest was in the modes of verbal expression employed by the subjects in the two groups.

The subjects who saw themselves as different produced many more assertions of differences than denials of similarities. (For example, they used statements such as 'we are different from each other' more often than 'we do not resemble each other'.) Conversely, the subjects who saw themselves as similar to others asserted these similarities less often than they denied the differences (using statements such as 'we are not different from each other' rather than 'we resemble each other').

The importance attached nowadays to the quest for social differentiation is clearly reflected in many forms of publicity – the mirror of our desires. Advertisements proclaim in all kinds of ways: 'Use our product and be different'. A study was conducted (Codol 1979: 248–54) in order to find out whether this was really an important theme in advertising, and if this was the case, whether advertisements hold the attention of the potential customers by reflecting this implicit wish, and thus manage to sensitize people to a product and its brand. The subjects were asked to read advertisements which were comparable in their form and length and contained, in addition to a few lines praising the quality of the product, an advertising slogan which informed the readers either that the use of the product would make them personally different from other people (e.g. 'a product which will make people notice you'; or 'for those who wish to be distinctive'), or that, on the contrary, the purchase of the product would make the person similar to a great number of other people (e.g. 'a product designed for all and appreciated by everybody'; or 'the best choice for all Frenchmen'). In a third condition, the advertisements included slogans which had no relation to the socially differentiating or non-differentiating functions of the product for the customer (as, for example, 'exceptional quality at a reasonable price'). The results showed a decrease in the remembering of the brand names, the advertised products and the slogans in the order of the conditions as described above.

There are other findings which also indicate that there is some resistance to accepting one's similarity to others and that the notion of difference is important. Several studies have shown that there exists a tendency to overestimate the perceived differences between oneself and others, as compared with the real differences, and correspondingly to minimize the objective similarities. This underestimation of similarity becomes more marked as the degree of objective similarity increases (Jarymowicz & Codol 1979).

All these studies lead to the conclusion that sensitivity to the theme of personal uniqueness is of particular significance in our contemporary society. It also appears that this quest for uniqueness derives in turn from a more general and more powerful determinant of behaviour: the assertion of the self-image. In this perspective, the search for non-differentiation need not always be understood, as was implied earlier, in terms of a simple reaction of defence and as a protective strategy. *Similarity can be accepted (or even sought) when it enables an individual to assert himself in his own eyes and in the eyes of others.*

*2.3.2. Self-assertion and the acceptance of similarity.* When a detailed examination is made of the experimental conditions in the studies in which there is an acceptance of similarity, and of the conditions in which this is not the case, two phenomena emerge which accompany (or perhaps explain) the differences in the degree of this acceptance. The first of these concerns the locus of the assertion of similarity. Has this been done by the subject himself or by someone else? An examination of several sets of data leads to the conclusion that subjects are less disposed to accept being considered as similar to others when this assertion comes from the outside. For example, when in research on social influence the subjects are asked questions after the experiment about 'what happened', many of them admit spontaneously that they were influenced by the responses of other participants. In contrast, when the experimenter questions them directly about the increasing similarity of their responses to those of others, the majority refuse to accept the idea that they could have been influenced by others even when their statements contradict the evidence available from their behaviour.

The second phenomenon appears in relation to the points of reference of the comparison which leads to an assertion of similarity: is it the subject who is similar to someone else, or is it someone else who is similar to the subject? Many findings lead to the conclusion that similarity is more easily accepted in the latter case than in the former. Indeed, in the second of these two cases, the comparison 'confirms' the individual and defines someone else in relation to him. The opposite is true for the first case. When the subject is taken as the point of reference of the comparison, the feeling of personal identity is not affected in any way; in the other situation, there is the possibility of a threat to personal identity.

It is interesting to note that the opposite happens in the assertions of differences. Research results show that, on the whole, individuals consider that they themselves are more different from others than others are different from them. Here again, self-assertion seems to be at the core of these findings.

No doubt other factors also intervene in the acceptance of similarity, as, for example, when similarity to others is associated with an increased positivity of the self-image.

## 3. Similar and different: the PIP effect

All the studies described so far consider the search for differentiation and non-differentiation as separate phenomena, occurring at different points of time. The task in all these cases was to specify the conditions in which the one or the other appeared. Differentiation and non-differentiation cannot, however, be considered solely as two poles between which the conduct of individuals ceaselessly oscillates. In many social situations, difference and similarity are sought simultaneously. This is so in behaviour which has been referred to as the 'superior conformity of the self' (or the 'PIP effect').[6]

This is the behaviour, observed in a very large number of social situations, by means of which individuals tend to assert that *they conform more closely to the norms which are appropriate in a situation* (norms which are experienced or perceived as such) *than is generally the case for other participants*. One example comes from experiments in which an attempt was made to induce for groups of subjects a representation of their task which centred either upon cooperation or upon competition. In the groups in which cooperation was perceived as the norm for the work to be done, the subjects showed a tendency to consider themselves as more cooperative than other members of their group; the same was true of perceived competitiveness in situations where the norm of competition was adopted (Codol 1969). Similar results were obtained in a study in which the attention of some subjects, working as members of a group, was focused on creativity, and of others on the methodical solution of problems. In the former case, individuals tended to see themselves as more creative than others; in the latter, as more methodical. The details of a large number of observations and experimental studies about the PIP effect have been described elsewhere (Codol 1971, 1973a, b, 1974a, b, 1975, 1976a, b; Codol & Flament 1971; syntheses are available in Codol 1975, 1979).

The explanation of the behaviour involved in the superior conformity of the self postulates the existence of a conflict of which the two sides are contradictory and complementary at the same time.

(i) The wish to present to others a favourable image of oneself leads to a general tendency to assert one's conformity to the norms which prevail in a situation.

(ii) At the same time, however, as this conformity is experienced or asserted, the systems of reference will often be perceived or experienced as a source of anxiety. This is so because they are seen as engendering uniformity and/or constraints and, in this way, creating threats for an individual's personal identity (on which is based his originality and distinctiveness), as well as reducing the degree of personal autonomy which appears available.

This conflict between a wish to please others (which leads to conformity achieved by means of non-differentiation) and the determination to protect

---

[6] PIP from *primus inter pares* (first amongst peers or equals).

the self (which results in attempts at social differentiation) can find a satisfactory solution in the superior conformity of the self. This is indeed the only way to present oneself as different from others while respecting the requirement to conform to social norms: the assertion that one's conformity to these norms exceeds that of other people. In this way, a synthesis can be achieved of the wish to be different and the wish to be similar.

It is worth mentioning at this point some research findings which show that the PIP effect is present even in social situations where the pertinent norms are not considered as desirable by the individuals involved. This is why the PIP effect cannot be understood simply as an attribution to oneself of characteristics which are perceived as positively valued. It is based simultaneously on a search for a positive *social* evaluation of oneself (which is achieved through conformity to norms) and the wish to achieve a positive *self*-evaluation (achieved through the claim that one occupies a special and distinctive position). It can therefore be seen as a form of self-assertion.

## 4. Identity: the quest for differentiation and non-differentiation

**4.1. The dimensions of the feeling of identity.** The self-image is thus central in the determination of behaviour tending towards both differentiation and non-differentiation. An attempt to clarify some aspects of the notion of identity is therefore necessary (cf. Codol 1979, 1981, 1982) in order to provide a theoretical background for this dual phenomenon. This cannot be done fully in this chapter (but see various chapters in Volume II, Part VI); we shall present, however, a rough outline of the ways in which the behaviour of differentiation and non-differentiation is associated with the notion of identity.

At the source of all feelings of identity there is, of course, an awareness of oneself which results from a subjective organization and transformation of the available information about the self. It can be assumed that the cognitive processes underlying the conception of self do not differ from the cognitive processes operating in other forms of human functioning. *Identification* and *recognition* are as fundamentally important here as they are elsewhere. The identification and recognition of an object implies above all: (i) that the *similarities* and *differences* of that object in relation to other objects can be determined; and (ii) that the object is endowed with characteristics which are invariant, i.e. that it presents a certain *coherence* and *stability* over time. It is also known that cognitive processes tend towards simplification, in the sense that most often what is registered must have some significance. This is based on links, close or remote, which can be established with objects already familiar and which have acquired, either through individual experience or through social transmission, a meaning and a value connotation. In this perspective, the feeling of identity can be considered as deriving from a complex compounding of the various dimensions of the self-image such as the conception of one's difference from others, of unity and permanence, and of positivity.

More needs to be said about the positivity of the self-image. If it is true that, in the last analysis, adaptation is the ultimate goal of all activity, then it follows (and there is a good deal of evidence in support) that the self-image must generally contain a positive value connotation. A certain *value* must be attached to the self which correlates with the satisfaction of the basic physiological and biological needs – such as ensuring one's survival. The positive evaluation of the self is a complex cognitive elaboration of this 'price' attached to oneself. But this consists not only of the attribution to oneself of a variety of positive characteristics (such as kindness, attractiveness, patience, tolerance, etc.): even more important is probably the attribution to oneself of a certain *power* over the material and social environment. The conception of oneself as the origin of certain effects, the feeling that one can influence things and people, the ability to guide or master, at least to some extent, the events in the surrounding world – all this is directly associated with a positive self-image.

**4.2. The content of the feeling of identity.** Self-image cannot be conceived only in terms of a *structure* based on distinctions between self and others, a certain coherence and permanence, and a positive evaluation. The characteristics which are attributed to the self provide the content of the self-image and maintain the feeling of identity. These characteristics are essentially the result of a cognitive integration by an individual of all the information received in the course of transactions with the environment. This information originates from the following sources:

(i) Insertion in the social world, and in particular, *membership of communities, groups and social categories* (see Tajfel 1981 for a discussion of this insertion as it affects intergroup relations). The fundamental process here is that of *introjective identification*[7] through which the individual attributes to himself

---

[7] This term has had a long history in psychology; but it has always contained some ambiguity. It has two connotations. 'Identification' can mean the activity by which an object is identified and recognized, and thus *distinguished* from other objects, invested with an identity which is its own. It can also mean, in a pronominal sense, the action through which an object becomes identical to another object, and thus it implies *similarity*. It is perhaps this ambiguity that reflects the difficulty in circumscribing identity which is located at the intersection of identity as difference and identity as similarity.

the characteristics which he attributes to other people and to groups. The converse phenomenon, which is complementary, can also be associated with this process. Through *projective identification*, the individual attributes to others – persons and groups – the characteristics which he attributes to himself. Projection and introjection are therefore the two processes through which an individual establishes a similarity between himself and others. But this establishment of similarity does not have the same meaning in the two cases. In projection, similarity is conceived in terms of oneself as the point of reference. As was argued earlier, similarity is more easily accepted in this case, since this contains a stronger assertion of one's own individuality. (See Chapter 25 for a related discussion of the processes of group formation seen in terms of identification.)

(ii) *The feedback obtained by the individual from the social environment.* The social images of individuals (i.e. the views about them held in their entourage), and their perception of these images, play a fundamental role in the construction of the self-image. At least in part, those images are built up in ways which are similar to introjective identification. The social milieu most often attributes to individuals the traits and characteristics which are those of the social categories to which they belong. One form of cognitive simplification is particularly important here: the phenomena of accentuation linked to categorization. *The classification of objects as belonging to the same category accentuates their perceived similarity; when they are classified in distinct categories, there is an accentuation of differences between them* (Tajfel 1959).[8]

The fact that the 'objects' can be people and the categories social does not modify this process – as was shown, for example, in the study by Tajfel, Sheikh & Gardner (1964). Stereotypes are the reflection, on the social plane of the attribution of common characteristics to different members of the same group. In a complementary fashion, social discrimination is associated with an exaggeration of differences between individuals belonging to different social categories (cf. among others, Billig 1972; Billig & Tajfel 1973; Tajfel *et al.* 1971; see also Volume II, Part VI of this book).

**4.3. Identity and the quest for social recognition.** It is not enough, however, for an individual to have a personal feeling of his identity. This must also be socially recognized.

---

[8] There exist in the literature many confirmations of this phenomenon (e.g. Marchand 1970; Tajfel & Wilkes 1963; also see Tajfel 1981). In an unpublished research study, in which people were interviewed about various professional groups, I also found clear evidence that members of *other* professions were perceived as more similar to each other, and less different from each other, within their group than was the case for the subjects' own membership groups. (For a description of several instances of convergent evidence, see Tajfel 1982.)

The self-image, partly constructed as it is from what one knows about the perception of others, which never remains entirely stable, is constantly under threat. There is always a gap, which the individual will try to bridge, between the conceptions he has of his own identity and the conception of it held by others. It is this which leads to the attempts to present the self, as it is seen by oneself, socially known in its attributes of uniqueness, coherence, stability and positive value.

Everyone is normally able to establish a cognitive discrimination between self and others, and also between different 'others'. It is, however, most probable that the former kind of discrimination is much clearer than the latter. This is not only because the experience one has of oneself is considerably richer, and of a different kind, but also because – as we have seen – all categorization entails a simplification reinforcing the appropriate differences and similarities. The result is that each individual has a much clearer idea of his own singularity than can be had by people in his social environment; and that there is a gap between the idea individuals have of their own specificity and the perception of it by others. Consequently, *the search for identity is made through the assertion of difference and its recognition by others.* Some of this search was described earlier in the discussion of social visibility, avoidance of comparability, etc.

Personal coherence and stability are often affected and endangered in the course of life. They are, however, so essential to the assertion of identity that they become normatively enshrined as a value. Many individual activities can thus be interpreted as expressing the wish to present an image of oneself which has coherence and stability, and to impress upon others a view of one's personal and existential unity and 'weight'.

The same is true of one's positive evaluation by others which, as has been stated earlier, is one of the constituents of the positive self-image. The resulting strategies can be of two kinds. One of them is to enhance one's value through singularity or uniqueness. On the other hand, very often social support and public approval have their price in the individual's submission to the commonly accepted rules. This is at the origin of the PIP effect.

4.4. **Limits and conflicts.** The quest by individuals to obtain from others a recognition of their singularity, stability and positivity cannot be unlimited. As was argued earlier, the establishment of a difference is often sought below the threshold where such a difference could be seen as deviance; in other words, when it does not begin to imply a negative social image and exclusion.[9]

---

[9] It can often be observed that individuals who are made excessively different through some of their characteristics, and who may often feel excluded for this reason from normal social intercourse, try hard to gain the social recognition of their similarities rather than their

Similarly, excessive coherence can be socially interpreted as rigidity, obstinacy or stubbornness; excessive stability as insipidity and monotony. The search for a positive evaluation of oneself can be seen as arrogance, immodesty and conceit when it takes the form of differentiation, and as obsequiousness and servility in its form of conformity and non-differentiation.

This leads to conflicts, some of which have already been discussed, for example in the case of conformity which, necessary as it may be, will clash with the achievement of visibility and uniqueness. The quest for social recognition of identity forces people to show two faces in public. Asserting their similarities but considering themselves different, they try to show that they are the one and the other at the same time, and in doing this they engage ceaselessly in social acrobatics in which, in order to mark their proper place, they need to get nearer and further away in turn, in a rapid succession of movements. The problems of the relationships between the self-image and its social recognition, and consequently the feeling of identity, are played out in their clearest and most dramatic form in this difficult and precarious equilibrium between activities aiming at the achievement of differentiation and of non-differentiation.

## References

Ajzen, I. 1974. Effects of information on interpersonal attraction: similarity versus affective value. *Journal of Personality and Social Psychology, 29*, 374–80.

Allport, G. W. 1937. *Personality: a psychological interpretation.* New York: Holt.

Baldwin, J. M. 1897. *Social and ethical interpretations in mental development.* New York: Macmillan.

Berkowitz, L. 1957. Liking for the group and the perceived merit of the group's behaviour. *Journal of Abnormal and Social Psychology, 54*, 353–7.

Billig, M. G. 1972. Categorization and similarity in intergroup behaviour. Unpublished Ph.D. thesis, University of Bristol.

Billig, M. G. & Tajfel, H. 1973. Social categorization and similarity in intergroup behaviour. *European Journal of Social Psychology, 3*, 27–52.

Bleda, P. R. 1972. Perception of height as a linear function of attitude similarity. *Psychonomic Science, 27*, 4.

　1974. Towards a clarification of the role of cognitive and affective processes in the similarity–attraction relationship. *Journal of Personality and Social Psychology, 29*, 368–73.

Byrne, D. 1961. Interpersonal attraction and attitude similarity. *Journal of Abnormal and Social Psychology, 62*, 713–15.

differences. For example, one of the major demands often made by the handicapped is to be treated like everyone else. But social observation shows that requests of this type are often no more than a temporary stage in the development of individual and collective identities. The history of feminism passed from a stage when claims were made for the *equality* of rights and duties with men to its present assertion of the value of the *differences* between women and men which is now being stressed by militant feminists. The social movements of blacks and Indians in the United States went through a similar development (see Tajfel 1981: chapter 15; Williams & Giles 1978, for more detailed discussions).

334     Jean-Paul Codol

1962. Response to attitude similarity–dissimilarity as a function of affiliation–need. *Journal of Personality, 30*, 164–77.

1969. Attitudes and attraction. In L. Berkowitz (ed.) *Advances in experimental social psychology*, vol. 4. New York: Academic Press.

1971. *The attraction paradigm*. New York: Academic Press.

Byrne, D. & Nelson, D. 1965. Attraction as a linear function of proportion of positive reinforcement. *Journal of Personality and Social Psychology, 1*, 659–63.

Cannavale, F. J., Scarr, H. A. & Pepitone, A. 1970. Deindividuation in the small group: further evidence. *Journal of Personality and Social Psychology, 16*, 141–7.

Clore, G. L. & Byrne, D. 1974. A reinforcement–affect model of attraction. In T. L. Huston (ed.) *Perspectives on interpersonal attraction*. New York: Academic Press.

Codol, J.-P. 1969. Représentations de soi, d'autrui et de la tâche dans une situation sociale. *Psychologie Française, 14*, 217–28.

1971. Perception des relations de bienveillance, d'individualisme et d'égalitarisme entre les membres d'un groupe fictif. *Bulletin de Psychologie, 24*, 1048–63.

1973a. Le phénomène de 'conformité supérieure de soi': expériences exploratoires. *L'Année Psychologique, 73*, 565–85.

1973b. Le phénomène de la conformité supérieure de soi dans une situation d'estimation perceptive de stimulus physiques. *Cahiers de Psychologie, 16*, 11–24.

1974a. On the system of representations in a group situation. *European Journal of Social Psychology, 4*, 343–65.

1974b. L'évolution du comportement de conformité supérieure de soi chez des adolescents de 12 à 18 ans. *Enfance, September–December*, 239–58.

1975. On the so-called 'superior conformity of the self' behaviour: twenty experimental investigations. *European Journal of Social Psychology, 5*, 457–501.

1976a. Caractéristiques de personnalité et comportement de conformité supérieure de soi. *Psychologie Française, 21*, 17–34.

1976b. Contre l'hypothèse du triangle. *Cahiers de Psychologie, 19*, 15–38.

1979. *Semblables et différents: Recherches sur la quête de la similitude et de la différenciation sociale*. Aix-en-Provence: University of Provence.

1981. Une approche cognitive du sentiment d'identité. *Social Science Information, 20*, 111–36.

1982. Differentiating and non-differentiating behaviour: a cognitive approach to the sense of identity. In J.-P. Codol & J.-P. Leyens (eds.) *Cognitive approaches to social behaviour*. The Hague: Martinus-Nijhoff.

Codol, J.-P. & Flament, C. 1971. Représentations de structures simples dans lesquelles le sujet est impliqué. *Cahiers de Psychologie, 14*, 203–8.

Cooley, C. H. 1902. *Human nature and the social order*. New York: Scribner.

De Montmollin, G. 1977. *L'influence sociale: phénomènes, facteurs et théories*. Paris: Presses Universitaires de France.

Eiser, J. R. & Taylor, S. J. 1972. Favouritism as a function of assumed similarity and anticipated interaction. *European Journal of Social Psychology, 2*, 453–4.

Exline, R. V. 1957. Group climate as a factor in the relevance and accuracy of social perception. *Journal of Abnormal and Social Psychology, 55*, 382–8.

Faucheux, C. & Moscovici, S. 1967. Le style de comportement d'une minorité et son influence sur les réponses d'une majorité. *Bulletin du CERP, 16*, 337–60.

Festinger, L. 1954. A theory of social comparison processes. *Human Relations, 7*, 117–40.

1957. *A theory of cognitive dissonance*. Evanston, Ill.: Row, Peterson.

Festinger, L., Pepitone, A. & Newcomb, T. 1952. Some consequences of deindividuation in a group. *Journal of Abnormal and Social Psychology*, 47, 382–9.

Fishbein, M. & Ajzen, I. 1972. Attitudes and opinions. *Annual Review of Psychology*, 23, 487–544.

Fromkin, H. L. 1968. Affective and valuational consequences of self-perceived uniqueness deprivation. Unpublished Ph.D. dissertation, Ohio State University.

1970. Effects of experimentally aroused feelings of undistinctiveness upon valuation of scarce and novel experiences. *Journal of Personality and Social Psychology*, 16, 521–9.

1972. Feelings of interpersonal undistinctiveness: an unpleasant affective state. *Journal of Experimental Research in Personality*, 6, 178–85.

Grush, J. E., Clore, G. L. & Costin, F. 1975. Dissimilarity and attraction: when difference makes a difference. *Journal of Personality and Social Psychology*, 32, 783–9.

Heider, F. 1946. Attitudes and cognitive organization. *Journal of Psychology*, 21, 107–12.

James, W. 1909. *Précis de psychologie*. Paris: M. Rivière.

Jamous, H. & Lemaine, G. 1962. Compétition entre groupes d'inégales ressources: une expérience dans le cadre naturel. *Psychologie Française*, 7, 216–22.

Janet, P. 1929. *L'évolution psychologique de la personnalité*. Paris: Chahine.

Jarymowicz, M. & Codol, J.-P. 1979. Self–others similarity perception: striving for diversity from other people. *Polish Psychological Bulletin*, 10, 41–8.

Jones, E. E., Bell, L. & Aronson, E. 1972. The reciprocation of attraction from similar and dissimilar others: a study in person perception and evaluation. In C. McClintock (ed.) *Experimental social psychology*. New York: Holt, Rinehart and Winston.

Lemaine, G. 1966. Inégalité, comparaison et incomparabilité: esquisse d'une théorie de l'originalité sociale. *Bulletin de Psychologie*, 20, 24–32.

1974. Social differentiation and social originality. *European Journal of Social Psychology*, 4, 17–52.

Lemaine, G. & Kastersztein, J. 1972. Recherches sur l'originalité sociale, la différenciation et l'incomparabilité. *Bulletin de Psychologie*, 25, 673–93.

Lemaine, G., Kastersztein, J. & Personnaz, B. 1978. Social differentiation. In H. Tajfel (ed.) *Differentiation between social groups: studies in the social psychology of intergroup relations*. European Monographs in Social Psychology, No. 14. London: Academic Press.

Lemaine, G., Matalon, B. & Provensal, B. 1969. La lutte pour la vie dans la cité scientifique. *Revue Française de Sociologie*, 10, 139–65.

Lerner, M. J. & Agar, E. 1972. The consequences of perceived similarity: attraction and rejection, approach and avoidance. *Journal of Experimental Research in Personality*, 6, 69–75.

McLaughlin, B. 1971. Effects of similarity and likeableness on attraction and recall. *Journal of Personality and Social Psychology*, 20, 65–9.

Marchand, B. 1970. Auswirkung einer emotional wertvollen und einer emotional neutralen Klassifikation auf die Schätzung einer Stimulus-Serie. *Zeitschrift für Sozialpsychologie*, 1, 264–74.

Maslach, C. 1974. Social and personal bases of individuation. *Journal of Personality and Social Psychology*, 29, 411–25.

Mead, G. H. 1934. *Mind, self and society*. Chicago: University of Chicago Press.

Moscovici, S. 1976. *Social influence and social change*. European Monographs in Social Psychology, No. 10. London: Academic Press.

Moscovici, S. & Faucheux, C. 1972. Social influence, conformity bias and the study of active minorities. In L. Berkowitz (ed.) *Advances in experimental social psychology*, vol. 6. New York: Academic Press.

Moscovici, S. & Nemeth, C. 1974. Social influence II: minority influence. In C. Nemeth (ed.) *Social psychology: classic and contemporary integrations*. Chicago: Rand MacNally.

Moscovici, S., Lage, E. & Naffrechoux, M. 1969. Influence of a consistent minority on the responses of a majority in a colour perception task. *Sociometry*, 32, 365–79.

Newcomb, T. M. 1953. An approach to the study of communicative acts. *Psychological Review*, 60, 393–404.

1961. *The acquaintance process*. New York: Holt, Rinehart and Winston.

Novak, D. W. & Lerner, M. J. 1968. Rejection as a consequence of perceived similarity. *Journal of Personality and Social Psychology*, 9, 147–52.

Personnaz, B., Kastersztein, T. & Lemaine, G. 1977. L'originalité sociale: étude de la différenciation sociale dans un système semi-fermé; l'expérience Schlemmer. *Bulletin de Psychologie*, 451–4.

Posavac, E. J. & McKillip, J. 1973. Effects of similarity and endorsement frequency on attraction and expected agreement. *Journal of Experimental Research in Personality*, 6, 357–62.

Posavac, E. J. & Pasko, S. J. 1974. Attraction, personality similarity and popularity of the personality of a stimulus person. *Journal of Social Psychology*, 92, 269–75.

Precker, J. A. 1952. Similarity of valuings as a factor in selection of peers and near-authority figures. *Journal of Abnormal and Social Psychology*, 47, 406–14.

Singer, J. E., Brush, C. A. & Lublin, S. C. 1965. Some aspects of deindividuation: identification and conformity. *Journal of Experimental Social Psychology*, 1, 356–78.

Singh, R. 1973. Attraction as a function of similarity in attitudes and personality characteristics. *Journal of Social Psychology*, 91, 87–95.

Snyder, C. R. & Fromkin, H. L. 1980. *Uniqueness: the human pursuit of difference*. New York: Plenum Press.

Stalling, R. B. 1970. Personality similarity and evaluative meaning as conditioners of attraction. *Journal of Personality and Social Psychology*, 14, 77–82.

Tajfel, H. 1959. Quantitative judgement in social perception. *British Journal of Psychology*, 50, 16–29.

1981. *Human groups and social categories: studies in social psychology*. Cambridge: Cambridge University Press.

1982. Social psychology of intergroup relations. In *Annual Review of Psychology*, vol. 33. Palo Alto, Calif.: Annual Reviews. Pp. 1–39.

Tajfel, H. & Wilkes, A. L. 1963. Classification and quantitative judgement. *British Journal of Psychology*, 54, 101–14.

Tajfel, H., Sheikh, A. A. & Gardner, R. C. 1964. Content of stereotypes and the inference of similarity between members of stereotyped groups. *Acta Psychologica*, 22, 191–201.

Tajfel, H., Flament, C., Billig, M. G. & Bundy, R. P. 1971. Social categorization and intergroup behaviour. *European Journal of Social Psychology*, 1, 149–78.

Taylor, S. E. & Mettee, D. R. 1971. When similarity breeds contempt. *Journal of Personality and Social Psychology*, 20, 75–81.

Tesser, A. 1969. Trait similarity and trait evaluation as correlates of attraction. *Psychonomic Science*, 15, 319–20.

Wallon, H. 1941. *L'évolution psychologique de l'enfant*. Paris: Colin.

Williams, J. & Giles, H. 1978. The changing status of women in society: an intergroup perspective. In H. Tajfel (ed.) *Differentiation between social groups: studies in the social psychology of intergroup relations.*

Ziller, R. C. 1964. Individuation and socialization. *Human Relations*, 17, 341–60.

Zimbardo, P. G. 1969. The human choice: individuation, reason and order vs. deindividuation, impulse and chaos. In W. J. Arnold & D. Levine (eds.) *Nebraska symposium on motivation*. Lincoln: University of Nebraska Press.

# 17. Social differentiation in the scientific community[1]

GÉRARD LEMAINE

## 1. Social comparison, strategies of the actors and 'comprehensive' identity

In scientific research, people who are in the best position to judge as experts, to give recognition to the work and the person doing it, are also the most threatening. This is so because they can contest what has been produced, or produce themselves the research which could confer originality upon the actor and contribute to define his or her place in the system to which they belong. In other words, the 'first circle' of researchers, their first reference group, consists of people in various groups or teams who share their competence and their interests, but who are also a source of danger because of the way in which the system of recognition and rewards functions (Hagstrom 1965; Merton 1973b; Storer 1966).

The scientific community or, more exactly, various scientific communities (which are fields of conflict as much as they are communities), constitute social systems where self-evaluation forces comparisons with, and evaluations of, others, and where social identity must be an identity which is distinctive. Social comparison, social identity and differentiation are indissolubly linked in science in the activities which aim to ensure 'one's own place'.

This assessment (in some contexts) of a person's relative ability is compatible with Festinger's (1954) theory which states that information about others who are similar to oneself is sought in order to assess one's own position, even if it is also true that at the same time one may be interested in the range of variability (Sanders 1982); but the theory of social comparison has been considerably modified and enriched since 1954. The book edited by Suls & Miller (1977) provides evidence that this is the case. The distinction between self-evaluation and self-enhancement, first made by Thornton & Arrowood (1966), is taken up again in the book; this distinction stresses the possibility

---

1 This chapter was translated from the French by Henri Tajfel.

that the search for information is linked with affective consequences for self-evaluation. When self-esteem is under threat, the comparison strategies will differ from those predicted by the original theory. To summarize very briefly, this amounts to stating that difference and dissimilarity can be used as information which is highly relevant, that someone who is dissimilar and does not present a threat will be sought after, and that people who are different can strengthen an individual's feeling of identity. Fromkin (1972, 1973) and Snyder & Fromkin (1980) have shown that similarity can be perceived as a threat to identity; and Fromkin postulated the existence of a need for uniqueness and a permanent search for distinctiveness. The subjects may seek to compare themselves with others on 'dimensions' which are not the *true* dimensions of comparison; an equilibrium is postulated here between the desire for evaluation and the desire for enhancement. The wish not to fail in the assessment of oneself may lead to a choice of reference persons who are dissimilar and less useful in providing information, and at the same time give an opportunity to draw inferences about oneself which have less validity. In other words, one does not always try to 'know'; comparisons with others who are better tend sometimes to be avoided, and sometimes comparison is avoided altogether.

There is such a profusion of studies, and the boundaries of the area are so fluid, that it is obviously impossible to summarize here the present trends and results in the domain of social comparison. Even the book by Suls & Miller has not succeeded in doing this, despite its ambition to link social comparison with attribution theory, studies of social influence, theory of self-presentation, equity theory, etc. The interesting aspect of all this work, from our point of view, is the general drift of comparison theory since 1954, and the fact that these various developments included propositions which can easily be appropriated by an ethnographer of the scientific community.

It seems to us that in order to discuss comparison, identity and differentiation, one must first describe the system inside which function the individuals and groups who are the objects of study. What are the aims of the system, what are the social agents supposed to be doing, how are hierarchies established, what are the rewards (for example, what is the nature of recognition)? But even this kind of general description is not sufficient. In each special case, it is necessary to know whether there exists locally (at the national level or in a particular discipline) an orthodoxy linked in a field to political power (e.g. leaders[2] or committees of experts); or, conversely, whether the system is potentially polycentric, in the sense that there are no sanctions against 'heterodoxy' in the distribution of posts, attribution of funds for research, etc.

2 *Patrons* in the French text which could best be translated as 'bosses'. [Translator's note]

A researcher is usually in a situation where he must show to himself and to others that he can reach a position of 'visibility', a position which is 'distinguished' or unique. To succeed is to be accorded the recognition of priority in the solution of a problem, or to work and produce on a new and original theme of research – while it is understood that there exists a constant threat of others occupying the terrain. In fact, the researcher almost always plays simultaneously against 'nature' (which always needs to be re-defined) and against his peers. Intellectual 'success' is not a guarantee of success in the competition. Even so, intellectual success can obviously be very important for a research group even if another group got there first (but timing is important here). Such a success is an indication of the quality of the work and of the choices which have been made; it is a sign for others that the group must be taken into account; and in general, it is an opportunity to become a part of the network of those who work in a specified domain.

No attempt will be made here to define 'social identity'[3]; the diversity of approaches is beyond the scope of this chapter. It is our view, however, that the notion of social identity will not become clear until much more empirical and theoretical work has been done in which hasty conclusions are avoided. For example, it does not seem reasonable to discuss social identity without reference being made to the social system in which the actors are submerged, and to which they belong. For the purposes of our argument, we shall be guided by the idea, fundamental in the present context, that social identity in the scientific community must be defined with reference to an actor's occupying a visible position while at the same time others, who are at various distances and could aspire to the same position, are made to be marginal. If one wishes to understand the special characteristics of social identity in this domain, it is also important to realize that this game of recognition serves the institutional interests of science.

As we shall see, however, there exist many modes of survival in the scientific community. It is also true that the various forms of individual behaviour observed in this context are not all strictly controlled by situational variables. The degrees of freedom which remain are such that it is possible to see a great diversity of strategies elaborated within the constraints imposed by the situation. In the perspective adopted here, scientific research can be characterized, in a first approximation, as a set of constraints (which differ according to domains and local situations to which reference was made

3 Some of the author's views about social comparison, differentiation and the search for uniqueness in open social systems have been previously discussed (see Lemaine, Kastersztein & Personnaz 1978). An important point, relevant here, seems to us the fact that social agents often reconsider and vary the importance attached to various dimensions of comparison or invent new dimensions (see below, section 3). Tajfel (1978, 1981) provided a synthesis of the work on identity, comparison and social categorization. See also Tajfel & Turner 1979.

earlier), but also in terms of all kinds of possibilities of action, of choices between a variety of options. But such a formulation is not sufficiently precise, since some constraints are not defined in advance; they also depend upon the choices made or options adopted by the social agents. At the least, this means that the choices are not only made between courses of action which are determined in advance, but also between options which are constructed by the social agents.[4]

For example, it is possible that the leader of a team is not willing to accept that his activities must be limited by the technical possibilities available at a particular moment of time. A few years ago we interviewed a researcher who was by training a chemist and who, over a number of years, had defined an unexplored field of research in another discipline because he felt that he did not have much of a chance to achieve as much success as did the best people in his original discipline. His laboratory was not equipped as well as he would have wished it to be and, according to him, there was not in the French scientific milieu (in the wide sense of the term, including funding institutions) enough political will to enable him to occupy a place in the top rank. As a result, he had at the same time changed his field of research, proceeded to construct measuring instruments (not very costly), and invented a set of techniques adapted to the problems he wished to attack and which, for a time, were attacked by virtually no one else. Conversely, the director of a biological laboratory which became out-of-date because of the invention of new techniques was not able to come to terms with the very general problem which is posed by the collaboration between researchers and the engineering technicians when the researcher cannot follow, or falls behind, the advances made in their field by the technicians. His difficulty was not just with the technicians, but also with researchers in neighbouring laboratories who were able to adapt to the new conditions of research in the domain. He could not resign himself to a change in the organization of his laboratory, or to cooperation with outside teams and researchers, because he feared that he would lose face and find himself in an inferior position while he was at the summit of the 'official' hierarchy – a set of reactions which is well known to sociologists of organizations. Waiting for the day when his pupils would be able to attack the new problems, he made 'his' researchers work on problems which were somewhat 'old-fashioned', while at the same time he stressed their high interest, challenging in this way the established hierarchy,

4 The methodological arguments which lead us to consider simultaneously the actor and the system (in the terms used by Crozier & Friedberg 1977) cannot be developed here. The agents define their aims; the system, in the case of research, is stable in some of its characteristics, e.g. priority or recognition. The system cannot be considered, as it usually is in social psychology, only in terms of a series of states of transitional equilibria, resulting exclusively from a play of interactions.

and re-defining for his laboratory a new sub-community inside which he could outclass his immediate rivals.

Thus, although it can be *accepted* that choices are dependent upon the initial scientific formation, i.e. upon an independent variable prior to the actions, this as we have seen, is not necessarily always the case. There are instances when the formation which is sometimes considered a 'stabilized' characteristic of the agents, becomes a dependent variable which is under the control of certain definite choices seen simultaneously both as constraining and as showing the way forward (see the cases of Watson, Jouvet & Guillemin, which will be discussed below). The descriptions of the two cases just given aimed to show that the agents can choose systems of reference which are highly heterogeneous (even if it remains true that it is sometimes difficult for the researchers to modify their theoretical and technical backgrounds, if only because of the need to publish, or of the fear of supercilious expertise). At one extreme, one can play the game, or games, of maximum visibility in a system which is decentralized and to whose decentralization one has contributed. At the other extreme, a protected game can be played, the 'protection' being assured by, for example, one's unchallengeable position in the hierarchy of power. In such cases, it is probable (but not always certain) that one does not talk any more to the same people or to the same groups, and that the sub-system to which one belongs is not quite the same as before.

Therefore, as can be seen, affiliations and systems of reference also depend upon actions which are undertaken; and, at the same time, social identity is affected by the games which are played, and the strategies worked out in the face of constraints, some of which remain stable over a period of time, others of which are a result of the strategies themselves. (The stable constraints consist, for example, of the state of an area of research at a certain point of time, and of research techniques which are difficult to modify – such as the apparatus employed by heavy physics, or the background training which would certainly prevent a biologist from attacking, within a 'reasonable' time limit, the problems of nuclear physics.) For a given field of work and a given period of time, the preferences that an 'abstract' sociology of science would be tempted to consider as evident (such as attempting at all costs to measure oneself against those who are better) are not evident at all. The preferences are a construction which is always in need of an explanation; social identity is also a construction, since strategies and choices may lead to affiliations and positions not assigned in advance within systems or sub-systems which were not available at the point of departure.

It follows theoretically from these preliminary remarks that social agents can use as their reference an 'empty' social space which still remains to be created; and also that they can abandon (without always proclaiming it publicly) their initial reference system. In many cases a temporary alienation is necessary for the working out of a new 'identity' (Lemaine 1974).

This could be expressed by saying that identity should be defined not only in its 'extension' but also in its 'comprehension', i.e. by taking into account its content, the characteristics which are selected for it or so constructed that they can be used in future affiliations. It seems that this distinction is inevitable if the aim is to analyse the functioning of the scientific community. As we have seen earlier, the structure of rewards and of various kinds of recognition operating in this community entails the development of certain conflicts which can either be rejected and avoided, or accepted, and even created, while still clearly remaining within the boundaries of respect for the very flexible 'rules' governing research.

The conclusion, therefore, is that the use of the notion of social identity should include a consideration of actions, political aims, strategies and creations. It is no longer just a question of group membership identity (be it a majority or a minority), of selection of other groups, or of adopting new affiliations, although social mobility remains an important concept here. One must also consider the creation and definition of empty spaces which can be filled if and when the political will to do so succeeds. Indeed, divergence or social differentiation in science – as well as in art, where the problems are of a different order – do not necessarily guarantee either success or recognition. There have been many researchers – more than one thinks, because history has not preserved, or has preserved badly, the memory of their exploits – who have created great works which were then shown to be false or devoid of meaning.

## 2. Risk and avoidance of risk in the making of choices

Our research on these themes, undertaken since the early 1970s, can be only briefly mentioned here.[5] Its concern was with the choices made by the researchers, the strategies of the research; and we also, in one of the cases,

5 (a) In 1969 (with Matalon & Provansal): in-depth interviews with fifteen researchers about their research strategies. (b) In 1972 (with Lécuyer, Gomis & Barthelemy): a study of 12 laboratories (6 in physics and 6 in biology); a detailed examination of the strategies of choices of research domains and subjects. (c) In 1977 (with Clémençon, Gomis, Pollin & Salvo): history of the studies concerned with the neurophysiology and psychophysiology of sleep. Analysis of several laboratories and reconstruction of their research strategies. Description of evidence about the phenomena of differentiation, risk taking and risk avoidance, already noted in 1972 and 1969. (d) In 1979 (with Darmon & El Nemen published 1982): a study through interviews (100) of five laboratories of fundamental research, and another study, through questionnaires (337) of twenty laboratories. An examination of the division of work in 'little' science and 'big' science. The strategies of the laboratories, mainly in 'big' science, are influenced by political decisions taken by institutions upon which the laboratories depend scientifically and financially. In the case of heavy investments, it all happens as if the planning were done in terms of scale economy.

examined problems connected with the division of work in 'little' and in 'big' science. We have always attempted to examine the behaviour involving risk taking and the avoidance of risk, which seems central to the study of differentiation in science. (Differentiation is understood here as search for originality and for a distinguished position which is visible in relation to colleagues and other agents in the agonistic field.) It should be noted that risk may refer to the choice of problems which differ in their difficulty (such as the nature of the problem, training needed for the research, technical resources), or in the existing level of competition and contest. Finally, we must mention that this work concerned researchers, laboratories and instances of judgment in France; but the work done outside France and the reports about it are compatible with the points of view adopted here.

Risk can be discussed here in terms of the interpretation made by McCloskey (1976) of the risk-taking behaviour of peasants in England before the nineteenth century.[6] Why did the peasants resist for such a long time a re-grouping of their plots of land? Why did they show a preference for having plots dispersed throughout the land surrounding the village, which was costly in transport and in time and, on the average, affected the yield? In brief, the author's argument is as follows: the peasants, who were often near starvation, were accepting a lower average yield with less hope of improvement, but their strategy had the advantage of reducing the risk of a disaster (if the yield of one plot was bad because of storms, hail, illness or insects, there was the hope that another one, which was at some distance, would do better). The average was certainly lower, but variability was reduced, and the most important issue was not to reach the threshold of shortage of food. Naturally, it was also important not to lower the average too much, in other words not to have too much dispersion; the problem was to find the optimum.

The comparison with research strategies cannot be pushed too far, as the notions of yield, disaster, etc. are far from clear in research, while McCloskey proposed a quantified model. But the notion of dispersion of risk seems interesting as it draws attention to research strategies which employ, simultaneously, measures of protection and risk taking (as will be seen, concealment is one possible way of avoiding competition).

It must also be noted that if a researcher has accumulated resources and high credit (which, as we have shown elsewhere, can be associated with inertia, cf. Lemaine *et al.* 1972), he can afford the luxury of concentrating

---

6  This model was based on data from England, but its author is of the opinion that it is applicable to other countries. In his *Les caractères originaux de l'histoire rurale française*. Marc Bloch (1931) noted that one of the reasons for a preference for fragmentation of plots was the ensuing reduction in the risk of accidents.

his efforts on a problem which he judges to be particularly important. Failure – not obtaining results which are really satisfactory on criteria adopted by the sub-community, or arriving later than others – does not really affect in a significant way his accumulated credit. This is particularly so because the term '*the* problem' is not really suitable since there usually exists a set of problems of which one or several are considered as more central than others. This being the case, it does not often happen that a 'creaming off' leaves nothing to others who are well equipped and capable. But one would need a number of studies of specific cases to find out what is the cost for a well endowed group to concentrate all of its bids in one central problem, and then not to 'succeed'. It is probable that the cost would not be the same for a 'success' preferable to all others and one which is not central to the same degree. This may well be one of the cases which is equivalent to a disaster for the peasants. We still know next to nothing about these issues. It does appear, however, that risk taking varies with the amount of credit accumulated by the researchers.

Conversely, the strategies of risk taking or of not avoiding risk can be observed in the cases of researchers who do not have accumulated credit but who find themselves in a position where an initial failure will not be counted against them in the course of their career. We shall provide three examples of this, and then describe a case in which risk taking seemed determined less by the amount of credit than by a position of marginality based on another criterion.

When Watson (cf. Watson 1968) attacked, in collaboration with Crick, the structure of DNA, he was 23 years old. If one believes his retrospective account, he had no doubt that the problem could be solved within a reasonable period of time and that this solution would bring a Nobel Prize.[7] But he had to take into account not only the Wilkins' laboratory, which was considerably in advance, but also the illustrious Pauling who, as common knowledge had it, was also interested in the problem. Watson reports in his book that he was well aware of the possibility of failure but sufficiently young for this not to affect his career. (This was not the case for Crick, who was 35 at the time and had not yet finished his doctoral thesis.)

The second example is that of the discovery of the 'spin' by Uhlenbeck and Goudsmit in 1925. They described the conditions of their discovery in articles published in 1976 (these reports, coming fifty years after the events, need

7 Watson worked on a very 'hot' problem (Merton 1973b), which many researchers wished to solve and whose solution would have a considerable impact. The problem which was attacked by Guillemin (see below) was also very hot, and his strategy, which consisted of making his rivals marginal, is worth noting.

to be critically examined, but this cannot be done here). Their first calculations were criticized fairly severely by Pauli, and Lorentz was quite sceptical. Uhlenbeck then rushed to see Ehrenfest, who was their director (cf. Uhlenbeck 1976), to ask him not to use in any way the text they had given him: they needed more time in order to re-do their calculations. But Ehrenfest had already sent the article for publication in *Naturwissenschaften*, and he knew that it would be published, unchanged, very soon; thus, it was too late. To console Uhlenbeck, Ehrenfest apparently said: 'You are both young enough to be able to afford a stupidity.' This meant, as it did for Watson, that the mistake would not be counted against scientists who were very young, while it would be serious for others whose reputation was on firmer ground.

But 'youth' is not one of our analytic categories. One could say instead that a substantial number of 'discoveries' or 'solutions' (great or small, evaluations may differ) come from researchers who are not well established and who find themselves at the margins of the system, at its periphery. To continue with the metaphor of centre and periphery, let us note that people at the centre can also afford to say foolish things, as was the case with Pauling during his work on DNA: he made a gross error in elementary chemistry. Watson and Crick were so delighted by this that they drank a toast to Pauling's mistake. As to Watson, he chose a problem (the structure of DNA) which was at the time considered as central. The value of the solution could be scientifically very high, unless the structure did not allow for a satisfactory explanation of the properties of DNA. The probability of finding the solution first was fairly low, and thus Watson took a very high risk. In addition, he made another choice relating to a scientific hypothesis (the helical structure) for which there was no alternative hypothesis. This meant that the helical hypothesis could not be falsified and that lack of success would not be illuminating. Finally, he also made a choice of method in working with a 'mechanical model' in which molecules were represented by balls connected by rods (links), while other researchers, for example Franklin, opted for an X-ray spectrographic examination. Thus, his strategy was risky in a number of ways and he knew it perfectly well (if one accepts all of his account).

If we take another case, that of Jouvet (cf. Lemaine *et al.* 1977), we find that, as a newcomer in the research on sleep and working in a laboratory devoid of traditions and background in this area, he opted very soon for a new direction of research: wet neurophysiology, i.e. the very general hypothesis of a neuro-humoral mechanism of paradoxical sleep. It is true that his discovery of inhibition of postural muscle tonus during paradoxical sleep gave Jouvet some authority in the community, which grew further as a result of his localization in the pons of the structure responsible for the paradoxical phase. But it was precisely this reputation, acquired in the beginning of the 1960s, on which he might have capitalized by persevering in classical neurophysiological studies. Instead, Jouvet adopted and developed the theory of three states (wakefulness, slow-wave sleep, paradoxical sleep) so as to differentiate himself, as he said himself, from the 'unicists', particularly Hernández-Peon. He concentrated on the paradoxical phase, studied its phylogenesis and ontogenesis, and examined the effects of anti-depressant drugs, despite his distrust as a neurophysiologist, well used to the localization of mechanisms in clearly defined structures, of the global and imprecise character of pharmacology. As he conducted his pharmacological studies, which were not conclusive, he also engaged in theoretical work about the role of biochemical mediators; but he did not altogether abandon his more traditional work on localization. It all happened as if, protected by this work, Jouvet was getting ready to be the first to appreciate fully the impact of the work done by the Swedish school of research which, using the histofluorescent technique, detected monoaminergic neurons in the brainstem.

It can thus be seen that Jouvet, a researcher who was young and relatively marginal in the field when compared with people who worked in some American laboratories (for example, Kleitman's), doubled his stakes, but did so with some caution. His strategy of risk taking, in which he had to consider the theoretical and technical difficulties of the field and the fact that he was in charge of a small team, was not the same as Watson's. It seems that Jouvet did not place all his bids on one problem and one method and that he dispersed the risk. It is also worth remembering that he was not a biochemist.

A fourth case reported by Latour in 1979 (in a sociological perspective different from ours) concerns a researcher who, like Jouvet, did not have at the starting-point the knowledge required for the strategy which he wished to implement. Although there is no doubt that Guillemin cannot be considered as having been a researcher without 'credit' during the relevant period (far from it), he was in some ways marginal, outside the 'establishment', while displaying great energy in his own niche which offered the possibility of providing him with a first-rate success.

The work Latour did on Guillemin's laboratory is mainly concerned with what he called the construction and 'deconstruction' of scientific facts. A fact in science is not really taken for granted until the conditions in which it has been established cease to be described. Conversely, these descriptions will be re-introduced when doubts are raised about a finding which a researcher or a group wish to accept as a fact. Thus, the issue is either to discard and forget or, on the other hand, to re-introduce the social and historical conditions of scientific construction or production. This makes the writing of history very difficult because a 'fact' in a published article tends to lose all of its historical referents. The actors forget the original features underlying their scientific statements and engage in reconstructing history. We must clearly distinguish between decisions concerning the truth or falsity of propositions or their compatibility with theoretical hypotheses, and the decisions about initial choices, general orientations or even working hypotheses in the framework of a theory.[8]

Latour described Guillemin's strategy over a period of about ten years, from the moment he decided to discover the nature of hypothalamic substance (TRF) which might control the secretion of the pituitary thyrotrop hormone, until the time when the laboratories of Guillemin and of Schally, an ex-student of Guillemin, demonstrated that the 'factor' was a peptide composed of a defined sequence of amino-acids. Guillemin is a physiologist, but towards the beginning of the 1960s he decided to determine the *structure* of the factor (which, in his view, was a hormone) rather than simply continuing his research showing that a substance present in the hypothalamus had physiological effects detectable in the hypophysis. Thus, to achieve his aim, he had to become a chemist in order to isolate the substance. This strategy re-defined the field of the research and placed at its periphery Guillemin's physiological colleagues who were not able to work according to the new norms, which were 'imposed' to begin with but later became accepted. Guillemin left France, where he was not offered sufficient resources, for the United States, where he was granted adequate funds to complete his undertaking: to extract

8  Concerning the issue, Mulkay & Gilbert (1981) have shown that, although scientists write in a 'Popperian' manner and tend to reason that way about the work of others, when their own work is concerned the evaluation of conformity to rules is based on an *interpretation* of what is, for example, the falsification of a hypothesis. The significance of this term depends on technical judgments of the researchers. As the situations are ambiguous, the rule is often interpreted as a function of the choices which this same rule is supposed to have guided. This is not the view of some great scientists, such as Medawar, Eccles or Monod (all Nobel Prize holders), who see in Popper one of the greatest philosophers of science and say that they have gained a great deal from his work. Monod wrote in 1973 that *The logic of scientific discovery* is '...one of the rare works of epistemology in which a scientist can recognize, or even sometimes discover, the movement of his thought, the true history, rarely written, of the progress to which he may have been able to contribute personally'.

Is it then possible that one should agree with Feyerabend (1970, 1975) that there always exist side by side a 'normal component' (cf. Kuhn 1970b) and a 'philosophical component' of the scientific activity, and that the latter consists of a critical activity, of a reflection about conceptions which are incompatible and do not cohere? Could it be that the weight of each of these components varies historically within an area or a problem? If this were so, different researchers would engage in different types of activity, the criteria for their choice of problems would not be the same, philosophical or theoretical reflection would be highly heterogeneous. it is possible that the massive growth of science has contributed to a hypertrophy of the 'normal component' and that Mulkay & Gilbert are mistaken about the validity of their observations. But it is also possible that even great scientists reconstruct, as do the others, the history of their most important achievements.

enough substance from millions of hypothalami – obtained in slaughterhouses – in order to determine the exact nature of the releasing factor. The laboratory became a factory in which chemists played the most important role. The strategy which was adopted required extremely costly apparatus for treatments and tests, and techniques from other fields, such as mass spectrometry, were imported when it became necessary to compare the structure of the natural product with the product which was synthetically produced (and was shown to be physiologically active).

In his sociological 'deconstruction' Latour showed how the 'object' had changed several times between 1962 and 1970. What is, however, of interest to us here is the description of the risks which Guillemin took at various points in the research process. For example, in 1968/69, shortly before the discovery was made, the National Institute of Health, considering that the results obtained until then had not been conclusive, threatened to cut the funds and transfer the research towards the less expensive and safer directions of classic physiology. It is true that, in view of the nature of the problem, Guillemin could not abandon physiological research altogether and, this being the case, he remained at a level of equality with other physiologists and the risks he took were not excessive. But his reputation would have undoubtedly suffered if the immense effort and funds invested in the discovery of the structure of the TRF had not produced the expected results, which were then proclaimed as unique in their validity.

According to Latour, it was not just a matter of chance that both the researchers (Guillemin and Schally) who dared to re-define the field (and also competed for the discovery and finally were awarded the Nobel Prize) were immigrants. He quotes a fragment of an interview in which Schally talked about a 'third actor':

He is the Establishment...he never had to do anything...everything was given to him...of course, he missed the boat, he never dared putting in what was required: brute force. Guillemin and I, we are immigrants, obscure little doctors, we fought our way to the top; that's what I like about Guillemin... (Latour 1979: 119)

As Latour wrote (p. 120), Guillemin and Schally:

occupied a niche which entailed a break .with existing methods and an immense amount of hard, dull, costly and repetitive work: the kind of niche from which people normally run away.

The four cases described above are compatible with the idea that daring and risk taking are often associated with a researcher's peripheral position. But, as we have said, accumulated credit also allows for daring and risk. The stories of Jouvet and Guillemin show that choices are sometimes made for the sake of differentiation, that success is seen as the end-point of options which distinguish researchers from their immediate competitors and which, at the same time, aim to re-define the field. As Bourdieu (1976) would say, the researchers engage in a battle for the definition of what is legitimate or orthodox.

This is, however, a far cry from concluding that differentiation and the search for originality result immediately in a battle of this kind. Timing is important here. 'Silent differentiation', which will be discussed below, shows that although a re-definition of orthodoxy may be the ultimate aim of a strategy, it is not always made explicit – on the contrary, it often remains carefully concealed.

It follows from the above descriptions that researchers assess their chances, compare themselves with others and evaluate the risks they take as a function of their position in the field. But these comparisons may lead to attacking problems which are considered as important, or to seeking refuge in problems which are 'minor' or considered as such by the leaders in the field. Problems of this kind can, however, be re-defined outside of the generally accepted system of ranking – for example, when they are considered small but essential contributions; they allow for a participation in a sub-community which has its own actors, colloquia and other attributes of legitimacy. The comparisons are then made in a minor key, the point of reference is displaced to an adjacent field which is less highly valued but in which it is easier to excel.

Just as it is true that the resulting comparisons yield less 'information' to those who have not abandoned the traditional points of reference, it also follows that these comparisons contribute to a shake-up of the generally accepted order. The strategies in question are not necessarily without their value or interest for the progress of knowledge; problems or areas of research which are considered as 'marginal' or 'without interest' by the dominant orthodoxy can thus become the object of sustained research effort which may result in a creation of new fields.

### 3. Choices, criteria and values: 'hypernormal' science and 'silent differentiation'

It seems that Hagstrom (1965) was correct when he insisted that competition (and, one should add, comparison with others) ensures a dispersion of researchers across the potential field of research. The strategy of dispersion which employs the 'major key' in its comparisons also aims to upset the established order; but it differs from the 'minor key' strategy previously discussed in the nature of the dimensions it introduces, in the 'value' of the problems or the field to be explored (as seen by those who believe they are laying down the law and establishing rights). The requirements of the 'major key' strategy are different – at least initially. For example, it would not be sufficient to confine oneself to an examination of the peripheral physiological correlates of sleep; instead, there would be an attempt to discover the chemical mediators responsible for the different types of states found in the cerebral structures. Dement immediately understood and recognized the interest of Jouvet's work; but it is far from certain whether a 'normal' physiologist would not have a rather different attitude if one of his colleagues drifted towards, for example, social psychology.

No matter how the problem is approached, scientific choices are at its core; the choice of a field (where the formation of the membership and reference groups, together with the pressures and the influence they exert, play a dominant role); the choice of problems, of theories, etc. We described earlier some of the choices made by Watson, Jouvet and Guillemin, and also some of those made by the researchers interviewed in the course of our studies. Very little is known about the criteria in terms of which these various research decisions are taken. Do they vary from domain to domain, and from one period to another in the history of a domain (or of '*the*' science)? Are we dealing here with factors which are invariant, or must the interpretations be as varied as the social and cognitive contexts of the research? Since the early 1960s the 'normative structure of science' proposed by Merton (1942, 1973b) has been subjected to vigorous criticisms.[9] When Merton is criticized, it must be remembered, however: (i) that his interest was less in individual motivations than in the origin and maintenance of the institution of science as a social institution; and (ii) that the ethos of science continues to play its part in research even if it were true, as some authors think, that the accepted values mainly serve to protect self-interest or as a screen behind which self-interest is hidden (Kuhn 1977). The first of these points establishes a distinction between the norms of the ethos of science and the criteria of choice as discussed here. Thus, Kuhn (1977), for example, wrote that some of the criteria (together with others which he did not enumerate) at the basis of scientific choices were: accuracy, fruitfulness, scope, consistency and simplicity.

These criteria are not all of equal importance in making decisions, and none of them is, on its own, a sufficient basis for making a choice. Even when

9 In its early version, the normative structure included: universalism, communism, disinterestedness, organized scepticism; also Storer's (1966) views about the 'social system of science' as a social reality 'internal to science but analytically distinct from the cognitive content of the scientific enterprise' (Lécuyer 1978). There exists a very large literature on the subject. A good account of the various points of view can be found in Lécuyer (1978).

several criteria are employed simultaneously, the difficulties are not eliminated, and the point is not reached when an algorithm could be used. This is, for Kuhn, a central issue. If such an algorithm (sought by the philosophers of science) existed, all conforming scientists would all take at the same time the same decisions. In the case of undemanding criteria for acceptance, they would follow points of view attractive to others; in the case of harder requirements, none of them would be inclined to develop a new theory (which would contradict another theory appearing as well-founded) until they could be sure that the criteria of fruitfulness, accuracy and scope were satisfied. As Kuhn (1977: 332) wrote: 'I doubt that science would survive the change.'

Kuhn did not claim to have solved the problem of scientific choice; in his view, studies of specific cases are needed in order to develop our knowledge in this field. The novelty he contributed is that he preferred to use the term 'values' for what had until then been referred to as 'criteria'. Criterion is, according to him, too strong a term ('criteria of choice can function as values when incomplete as rules'); there exists more latitude than is usually assumed in philosophy, but it still remains true that the 'values' of accuracy, consistency, etc. 'do specify a great deal'. Kuhn has clearly recognized that scientists have a margin of freedom, some degree of free play, in their theoretical choices; but this does not result in haphazard activities. One cannot say, as did Feyerabend (1975) – who is not quoted in Kuhn – that 'anything goes', even if there is no algorithm for the choices. After several hundred interviews and questionnaires we were not able to detect regularities which would allow predictions about the itineraries of research; in other words, there was no basis from which one could decide in which ways the freedom would be used. Kuhn has observed that his values (or criteria) must be considered as permanent attributes of science, but their application, and the weights which should be attached to them, vary a great deal with time and fields of application.

It must be admitted that we know nothing about variations in the strategies of differentiation in science which occur as a function of time or fields of research. If it is accepted that the kind of choices discussed here and those discussed by Kuhn are not independent, it is easy to envisage the amount of work which remains to be done. It is fully possible that choices which minimize the risk of failure, or the protection sought in the choice of 'out-of-date' problems (quotation marks are due here to genuine caution), are not compatible with the values of scope and fruitfulness. As we have seen, however, in the case of Jouvet – who worked for a time without competitors following close on his heels – the search for differentiation can easily be accompanied by a preoccupation with accuracy (Jouvet criticized the lack of precision in pharmacological research), scope, fruitfulness or simplicity.

No one has been able as yet to provide a systematic translation into the language of epistemology of the patterns of choices described by social psychologists. Conversely, an epistemologist like Kuhn does not seem to have recognized that the scientific choices which he attempted to understand can be influenced by the position of the actors in the field, comparisons with others, the role played by bodies which confer recognition, etc. Links have not been made between two points of view which are concerned with the same problem. For example, why is it that scientists are so very 'different' from each other? Should one consider no more than the formation, the traditions prevailing at the point of insertion, the educational role played by the people in charge, if one wishes to explain why one researcher turns out to be, in Feyerabend's (1970) terms, 'normal' rather than 'philosophical' or 'critical'? It is not likely that one can get rid of this question simply by assuming that some scientists play a game for which they have themselves laid down the rules. Power and positions of strength can play this kind of role in science only in extreme conditions (as was, for example, the case with Lysenko). As time-scales are usually quite long in the interplay of scientific activities, temporary victories of that kind are generally doomed in advance, or science is bound to deteriorate (see on this point, Polanyi 1962). This would mean, in our view, that when reflecting about this very peculiar activity which is science, one must not bury with premature haste the notions of ethos developed by Merton which were mentioned earlier, nor should one discard too quickly the ideas about criteria or values influencing scientific choices.

In the case of the distinction between researchers who are 'normal' and those who are 'critical', it is possible to see a meeting point between the perspectives of epistemology and social psychology. It is not very important at this point whether normal science and critical science are conceived as permanent components of the activity or seen as distinct phases succeeding one another with some regularity in the various disciplines. The earlier discussion about choices without risk and conservative strategies leads to the assumption that institutional or organizational factors operate in normal science or the normal component of science. It is possible, as Kuhn (1970b) wrote in his polemic with Popper, that if all members of the scientific community made untypical choices, the scientific enterprise itself would be endangered. Popper's answer to this (1970) was that 'normal' science is a reality of our times, but that it also constitutes a danger for science (and civilization). It would be more fruitful, it seems, to find out which factors lead researchers to be, as Popper said, 'not too critical' and, conversely, which are those that strengthen Feyerabend's 'philosophical component'. It is probably difficult to find in science an equivalent of a 'disaster' in the sense of the term used by McCloskey (see above), but there seems to be no doubt that scientists tend to protect themselves from failure or, more precisely, from what they define as failure in the scientific context of their aspirations, the competition, etc. This fear of failure leads to 'hypernormal' choices which imply little risk and are well signposted by practice and tradition; but it can also result in a drift towards fields, problems and techniques which could contribute to the progress of knowledge.

At the same time, there are interventions from those who are responsible for the passing of judgments, the defences put up by the laboratories and their leaders which aim to prevent evaluation (defences which are often not conducive to the taking of risks), the weight of temporal constraints often linked to the density of the population in a research area, the symbolic and material sanctions, etc. All this is also related to the position – central or peripheral – in the field, the background formation and personal factors. *The field of choices constituted in this way* never becomes entirely closed; it is always on the move, and it is extraordinarily complex in research. All we know about it consists of descriptions and qualitative models which are easily disturbed when new factors need to be taken into consideration.

There is another factor which we have been able to identify as responsible for 'normal' or 'hypernormal' choices. This has been referred to as the weight of technology (Lemaine 1980). It channels the research activity (since apparatus contains a good deal of reified theory); it causes the people in charge to wish to maximize the yield of high investments (when there is a maximal use of apparatus and a maximal production of 'results', the reasoning begins to be made in terms of scale economy); and it also leads those who are responsible to exercise caution, when the risk of failure does not apply only to people who take the decisions but also involves entire groups of researchers. It can thus be seen that the activity of research and invention can be inhibited in a milieu and a type of organization which, in principle, are supposed to be receptive to many forms of boldness. The result of it all is like an aggregation (Boudon 1977) of the strategies of the agents of research, be they individual or collective. But it would not be very useful for a social psychologist to confine his discussion to individual aspects; the processes of influences and of power exerted inside groups must also be considered. As has been shown earlier, there are several factors which influence the field of choices in a conservative direction; for the researchers' task is not simply to 'choose' – they must also elaborate.

The tendency of the individual actors to protect themselves from risk may lead to avoiding what they might consider a 'disaster'; but at the same time, they would be acting, in a sense, contrary to the expectations of the 'politicians' of science, and also to some of the ideals of the community which they themselves share as a matter of principle.

But too much stress on these inhibitions would produce a distorted view of the functioning of the scientific community. There are locations and laboratories where 'hot', 'interesting' and 'beautiful' problems are attacked, problems which are perceived as central and important for the progress of the discipline. These 'hot' domains attract, as Merton (1973b) wrote, talented scientists 'concerned to work on highly consequential problems rather than ones of less import. Hot fields also have a high rate of immigration and a low rate of migration, again until they show signs of cooling off' (p. 331).

It is possible, of course, that 'hot fields' are those in which investments are made and, consequently, it is easy to find work in them for people who are 'talented'. Observations we have been able to make in heavy physics are compatible with Merton's view. This area, which has attracted a great deal of funding, has shown and is still showing a trend of emigration towards molecular biology and neurobiology, which are considered by some as 'hotter' than their original discipline. A similar instance can be found in the migration in the behavioural sciences towards ethology and the genetics of behaviour. This is not due just to a fear of failure. Hopes of success also play a powerful role, but it is very difficult to discover which are the institutional or organizational features and the characteristics of individuals which favour the one or the other.

In an early study (Lemaine *et al.* 1972), an attempt was made to determine what kind of politics of a laboratory (and of instances of judgments) would tend to lead to choices favouring 'the advancing front of research'. The discovery in England in the early 1950s of the structure of DNA and the work on the functioning of the phage group by Mullins (1972) and by Thuillier (1972) give some idea about the kind of places where 'hot' problems or 'domains' are attacked. Merton (1973a) examined the consequences of the so-called 'Matthew effect' ('For unto everyone that hath shall be given, and he shall have abundance; but from him that hath not shall be taken away even that which he hath.') for the attribution of merit, for recognition and communication, and also for the strategies of choice. Thus, young researchers who have lived in a 'creative milieu' (in the sense that they belonged, or still belong in some way, to a first-rate productive centre) would aim 'very high', and would be interested in the 'great', the 'capital' or the 'beautiful' problems rather than in the 'minor problems' of normal science. The high aspirations and risk taking of these young researchers are imitative of the practices adopted by the eminent people with whom they have worked, practices which serve as a model and also as a source of what becomes a 'style' or a 'school'. Reputation and eminence are maintained in betting on some options and choosing some problems, since the accumulated credit, the lag of judgments and the overestimation linked with positions already held, offer a protection from the feeling and fear of failure (Merton's text is interpreted here in the sense of our argument).[10]

We agree with Merton that the influence of a model is important, but one should also insist on the effects of the political aims of the decision makers (the *patrons*) which are often imposed on those who work with them without too much worry about 'democracy'. The main theme of this chapter, social differentiation, must also be taken into account. As was stressed earlier, this leads to a displacement towards different areas of research or, as Holton (1962) put it, towards new areas of ignorance, which may be more or less 'hot' in their cognitive level, their impact or fecundity.

The 'temperature' of a problem in science tends, however, to change quickly as a result of new activities. It is perhaps because of awareness of this rapid transformation that a number of scientists (more than is generally thought) are inclined to conceal their drifting or displacement towards new problems. An example will be helpful here. A biologist, director of a research team, regretted (as do many scientists) the fact that the number of publications remains the criterion of production on which evaluations are based. There was nothing for it, as he put it, but to choose an 'easy' subject which, one *knew*, would guarantee a good return. As he had other aspirations, he spent more than half his time in doing 'classic' and 'honest' research which provided steady protection and continuing advancement for members of his group; but he reserved the remainder of his time and energy for more 'ambitious' research which presented much less certainty and which was also, according to him, much more central for the development of his field and the success of his group. This type of strategy can be observed when it is possible to conceal a part of one's activity, an option which can mainly be used in 'light' research.

These strategies of 'silent differentiation' may or may not imply a high cognitive risk; they do manage, however, to minimize institutional risk. They are also relatively less dangerous for a 'comprehensively' defined social identity, since the agents are safeguarding a second identity. The game is protected, and the very fact that some people feel the need for such protection reveals a good deal about the stakes which are involved in doing science.

This concealment from others often signifies a long march towards differentiation in the course of which – if success follows – the old problems around which competition is raging are abandoned. A field is articulated with

10 Feuer (1974) reminds us of Einstein's view that young scientists should be freed from the constraints of reaching definite conclusions as quickly as possible. This is a judicious observation about the role of evaluation which, as we have seen, often incites to 'hyper-normal' science.

its new problems, sometimes not too distant from the original field and problems, in which the agent can achieve an uncontested position. This creation of new fields, which always goes on in science, can often be referred back – as has already been said – to the operation of certain social comparisons presenting a threat to an identity which, in science, is linked to a position of visibility rather than to simple 'affiliations'.

These exceedingly discreet games played at the margins of the field can sometimes become ostentatious if they manage to reach the centre. It is for this reason that the metaphorical notions of a stable 'centre' and 'periphery', advanced earlier in this chapter, must be treated with some caution, particularly so in certain disciplines. It is not only the problems or the 'objects' of research which can become displaced, but also the actors themselves, the researchers and their teams. This incessant drifting is capable of challenging stability and orthodoxy on condition that the range of games which are considered as acceptable is not strictly circumscribed in advance by political and scientific authority. It is then that one can observe dispersion towards problems which are neglected or 'of little interest', and the abandoning of models not yet fully exhausted for the sake of others which are more promising from the point of view of production and visibility.

It is when issues of this kind are considered that it becomes necessary for the study of choices in science to take into account the nature of the *social system* inside which the competition operates. For example, what are the relevant organizational or institutional characteristics which vary from one period to another within 'the same' discipline, or for the same period from one discipline to another? Why is it that some periods are richer in scientific 'revolutions' than others in which the critical or philosophical components become more prominent?

It appears that a certain type of organization, and the irrationality that goes with it, result in a strengthening of the 'normal' component of science. Conversely, in a system which is decentralized, strategies of differentiation are capable of displacing the *loci* of thinking, of producing, of the constant reconstruction of social identity. The capacity never to remain standing still is the major characteristic of this peculiar system which is science.[11]

---

11 This chapter was already written and translated when I came across the text by the physicist John Ziman (1980) on 'What are the options? Social determinants of personal research plans', now to be published in *Minerva*. His analysis of risk taking, of the social factors involved in scientific conservatism, of the role of technology in the working out of choices, is so close to the argument presented here that one could almost assume that the work on these particular points has been done in common. (He also discusses other aspects of choices.) Ziman's text is highly encouraging for a researcher whose interest in these problems began over ten years ago.

## References

Bloch, M. 1931. *Les caractères originaux de l'histoire rurale française*. Paris: Colin.

Boudon, R. 1977. *Effets pervers et ordre social*. Paris: Presses Universitaires de France.

Bourdieu, P. 1976. Le champ scientifique. *Actes de la Recherche en Sciences Sociales*, 2–3, 88–104.

Crozier, M. & Friedberg, E. 1977. *L'acteur et le système*. Paris: Éditions du Seuil.

Festinger, L. 1954. A theory of social comparison processes. *Human Relations*, 7, 117–40.

Feuer, L. 1974. *Einstein and the generations of science*. New York: Basic Books.

Feyerabend, P. 1970. Consolations for the specialist. In I. Lakatos & A. Musgrave (eds.) *Criticism and the growth of knowledge*. Cambridge: Cambridge University Press.

1975. *Against method*. London: New Left Books.

Fromkin, H. L. 1972. Feelings of interpersonal undistinctiveness: an unpleasant affective state. *Journal of Experimental Research in Personality*, 6, 178–85.

1973. *The psychology of uniqueness: avoidance of similarity and seeking of differentness*. Paper No. 438, Institute for Research in the Behavioral, Economic and Management Sciences. West Lafayette, Indiana: Purdue University.

Goudsmit, S. 1976. It might as well be spin. *Physics Today*, June, 40–3.

Hagstrom, W. 1965. *The scientific community*. New York: Basic Books.

Holton, G. 1962. Models for understanding the growth and excellence of scientific research. In S. R. Graubard & G. Holton (eds.) *Excellence and leadership in a democracy*. New York: Columbia University Press.

Kuhn, T. S. 1970a. *The structure of scientific revolutions*, 2nd edn. Chicago: University of Chicago Press.

1970b. Logic of discovery or psychology of research? and Reflections on my critics. In I. Lakatos & A. Musgrave (eds.) *Criticism and the growth of knowledge*.

1977. *The essential tension: selected studies in scientific tradition and change*. Chicago: University of Chicago Press.

Latour, B. 1979. *Laboratory life: the social construction of scientific facts*. Beverly Hills, Calif.: Sage.

Lécuyer, B.-P. 1978. Bilan et perspectives de la sociologie de la science dans les pays occidentaux. *Archives Européennes de Sociologie*, 19, 257–336.

Lemaine, G. 1974. Social differentiation and social originality. *European Journal of Social Psychology*, 4, 17–52.

1980. Science normale et science hypernormale: les stratégies de différenciation et les stratégies conservatrices dans la science. *Revue Française de Sociologie*, 21, 499–527.

Lemaine, G., Darmon, G. & El Nemer, S. 1982. *Noopolis. Les laboratoires de recherche fondamentale: de l'atelier à l'usine*. Paris: Editions du Centre National de la Recherche Scientifique.

Lemaine, G., Kastersztein, J. & Personnaz, B. 1978. Social differentiation. In H. Tajfel (ed.) *Differentiation between social groups: Studies in the social psychology of intergroup relations*. European Monographs in Social Psychology, No. 14. London: Academic Press.

Lemaine, G., Matalon, B. & Provansal, B. 1969. La lutte pour la vie dans la cité scientifique. *Revue Française de Sociologie*, 10, 139–65.

Lemaine, G., Clémençon, M., Gomis, A., Pollin, B. & Salvo, B. 1977. *Stratégies et choix dans la recherche: à propos des travaux sur le sommeil*. Paris/The Hague: Mouton.

Lemaine, G., Lécuyer, B.-P., Gomis, A. & Barthelemy, C. 1972. *Les voies du succès*. Paris: Groupe d'Études et de Recherches sur la Science. Mimeo, 343 pp.

McCloskey, D. N. 1976. English open fields as behavior toward risk. In P. Uselding (ed.) *Research in economic history: an annual compilation of research*. Greenwich, Conn.: JAI Press.

Merton, R. K. 1942. The normative structure of science. In R. K. Merton (1973b).

    1973a. The Matthew effect in science. In R. K. Merton (1973b).

    1973b. *The sociology of science: Theoretical and empirical investigations*. Chicago: University of Chicago Press.

Monod, J. 1973. Préface. In K. R. Popper 1973.

Mulkay, M. & Gilbert, N. 1981. Putting philosophy to work: Karl Popper's influence on scientific practice. *Philosophy of the Social Sciences, 11*, 389–407.

Mullins, N. C. 1972. The development of a scientific speciality: the phage group and the origins of molecular biology. *Minerva, 10*, 51–82.

Polanyi, M. 1962. The republic of science: its political and economic theory. *Minerva, 1*, 54–73.

Popper, K. R. 1970. Normal science and its dangers. In I. Lakatos & A. Musgrave (eds.) *Criticism and the growth of knowledge*.

    1973. *La logique de la découverte scientifique*. Paris: Payot.

Sanders, G. S. 1982. The effect of social comparison on ability evaluations. *European Journal of Social Psychology, 12*, 63–74.

Snyder, C. R. & Fromkin, H. L. 1980. *Uniqueness: the human pursuit of difference*. New York: Plenum Press.

Storer, N. W. 1966. *The social system of science*. New York: Holt, Rinehart and Winston.

Suls, J. M. & Miller, R. L. (eds.) 1977. *Social comparison processes: theoretical and empirical perspectives*. Washington, DC: Hemisphere/Halstead.

Tajfel, H. 1978. Social categorization, social identity and social comparison. In H. Tajfel (ed.) *Differentiation between social groups: studies in the social psychology of intergroup relations*.

    1981. *Human groups and social categories: studies in social psychology*. Cambridge: Cambridge University Press.

Tajfel, H. & Turner, J. C. 1979. An integrative theory of intergroup conflict. In W. G. Austin & S. Worchel (eds.) *The social psychology of intergroup relations*. Monterey, Calif.: Brooks Cole.

Thornton, D. A. & Arrowood, A. J. 1966. Self-evaluation, self-enhancement and the locus of social comparison. *Journal of Experimental Social Psychology*, Supplement 1, 40–8.

Thuillier, P. 1972. Comment est née la biologie moléculaire? In P. Thuillier (ed.) *Jeux et enjeux de la science*. Paris: Laffont.

Uhlenbeck, G. E. 1976. Personal reminiscences. *Physics Today*, June, 43–8.

Watson, J. D. 1968. *The double helix*. New York: Atheneum.

Ziman, J. 1981. What are the options? Social determinants of personal research plans. *Minerva, 19*, 1–42.

# Subject index

# Author index